THE GOOD NEIGHBOR

THE GOOD NEIGHBOR

THE LIFE AND WORK OF

Fred Rogers

MAXWELL KING

ABRAMS PRESS, NEW YORK

Library of Congress Control Number: 2017956802

ISBN: 978-1-4197-2772-6
eISBN: 978-1-68335-349-2

Printed and bound in the United States
10 9 8 7 6 5 4 3 2 1

Abrams books are available at special discounts when purchased in quantity
for premiums and promotions as well as fundraising or educational use.
Special editions can also be created to specification. For details, contact
specialsales@abramsbooks.com or the address below.

Abrams Press® is a registered trademark of Harry N. Abrams, Inc.

ABRAMS The Art of Books
195 Broadway, New York, NY 10007
abramsbooks.com

PHOTO CREDITS

Insert 1: pages 1–3: reproduced with permission of the McFeeley-Rogers Foundation, with the exception of page 3, top right: reproduced with permission of the McFeeley-Rogers Foundation and Joanne Rogers; 4–8: reproduced with permission of the Fred Rogers Company, with the exception of page 8, bottom: © Lynn Johnson. Reproduced with permission of the Fred Rogers Company and Ohio University.

Insert 2: page 1: © Lynn Johnson. Reproduced with permission of the Fred Rogers Company and Ohio University; 2: top, © Jim Judkis, bottom, © Walt Seng. Reproduced with permission of the Fred Rogers Company; 3: top, reproduced with permission of the Fred Rogers Company, bottom, © Walt Seng. Reproduced with permission of the Fred Rogers Company; 4: top, © Jim Judkis, bottom, reproduced with permission of the Fred Rogers Company; 5: © Lynn Johnson; 6–7: reproduced with permission of the Fred Rogers Company; 8: top, © Lynn Johnson, bottom, reproduced with permission of the Fred Rogers Company.

For Margaret Ann King
My Polestar

There are three ways to ultimate success:
The first way is to be kind.
The second way is to be kind.
The third way is to be kind.

—FRED ROGERS

CONTENTS

PART IV

PART V

PROLOGUE: A BEAUTIFUL DAY

FRED ROGERS had given some very specific instructions to David Newell, who handled public relations for the PBS children's show *Mister Rogers' Neighborhood*. Rogers said he wanted no children—absolutely none—to be present when he appeared on *The Oprah Winfrey Show* in Chicago. No children? How could that be? By the mid-1980s, Rogers was an icon of children's television, known for communicating with his young viewers in the most fundamental and profound way. Why would he want to exclude them from a program showcasing his views on how they should be understood and taught?

But Fred Rogers knew himself far better than even friends like Newell, who had worked with him for decades. He knew that if there were children in the studio audience, he wouldn't focus on Winfrey's questions, he wouldn't pay heed to her legion of viewers, and he wouldn't convey the great importance of his work. The children and their needs would come first. He couldn't help it, never could help it. Decades before, Rogers had programmed himself to focus on the needs of little children, and by now he had reached a point at which he could not fail to respond to a child who asked something of him—anything at all.

He asked David Newell (who also played Mr. McFeely, a central character on Rogers's program) to be clear with Winfrey's staff: If there are children in the audience, Fred knows he'll do a poor job of helping Oprah to make the interview a success. But the message wasn't received. When Rogers came before Winfrey's studio audience on a brisk December day in 1985, he found the audience composed almost entirely of families, mainly very young children with their mothers.

Winfrey's staff had decided that after she interviewed Rogers, it would be fun to have him take questions from the audience, and maybe provide some guidance to mothers. And he certainly tried, telling them that to understand children, "I think the best that we can do is to think about what it was like for us." But the plan didn't succeed. As soon as the children started to ask him questions directly, he seemed to get lost in their world, slowing his responses to their pace, and even hunching in his chair as if to insinuate himself down to their level.

This wasn't good television—at least, good adult television. Everything was going into a kind of slow motion as Fred Rogers became Mister Rogers, connecting powerfully with the smallest children present. He seemed to forget the camera as he focused on them one by one. Winfrey began to look a little worried. Although she was still about a year away from the national syndication that would make her a superstar, her program was already a big hit. And here she was losing control of it to a bunch of kids, and what looked like a slightly befuddled grandfather.

Then it got worse. In the audience, Winfrey leaned down with her microphone to ask a little blond girl if she had a question for Mister Rogers. Instead of answering, the child broke away from her mother, pushed past Winfrey, and ran down to the stage to hug him. As the only adult present not stunned by this, apparently, Fred Rogers knelt to accept her embrace.

Minutes later, he was kneeling again, this time to allay a small boy's concerns about a miniature trolley installed on Winfrey's stage to recall the famous one from his own show, the trolley that traveled to the Neighborhood of Make-Believe. The boy was worried about the tracks, which seemed to be canted precariously at the edge of the stage. As the two conferred quietly, Winfrey stood in the audience looking more than a little lost. Seeing that the show was slipping away from her, she signaled her crew to break to an ad.

For Fred Rogers, it was always this way when he was with children, in person or on his hugely influential program. Every weekday, this soft-spoken man talked directly into the camera to address his television "neighbors" in the audience as he changed from his street clothes into his iconic cardigan and sneakers. Children responded so powerfully, so completely, to Rogers that everything else in their world seemed to fall away as he sang, "It's a beautiful day in the neighborhood." Then his preschool-age fans knew that he was fully engaged as Mister Rogers, their adult friend who valued his viewers "just the way you are."

It was an offer of unconditional love—and millions took it. *Mister Rogers' Neighborhood* often reached 10 percent of American households, five to ten million children each day who wanted to spend time with this quiet, slightly stooped, middle-aged man with a manner so gentle as to seem a little feminine.

Over time, as new generations of parents—some of whom had grown up with the *Neighborhood* themselves—swelled the ranks of his admirers, Fred Rogers achieved something almost unheard of in television: He reached a huge nationwide audience with an educational program, a reach he sustained for almost four decades. Rogers became a national advocate for early education just at the time that psychologists, child-development experts, and researchers worldwide were finding that learning that takes place in the earliest years—social and emotional, as well as cognitive—is a crucial building block for successful and happy lives.

Mister Rogers's appeal was evident from the beginning of his career, as the managers of WGBH in Boston discovered one day in April 1967. At that point, his program aired on the Eastern Educational Network (a PBS precursor) and was called *Misterogers' Neighborhood*. It had been shown regionally for only a year. Recognizing its popularity, the managers organized a meet-the-host event and broadcast an invitation for Rogers's young viewers to come to the station with their parents. The staff was prepared for a crowd of five hundred people.

Five thousand showed up. The line stretched down the street toward Soldiers Field, where the Harvard football team played, and created traffic slowdowns reminiscent of game days. The station quickly ran out of snacks for the children. As the line wound into the studio, Rogers insisted on kneeling to talk with each child, just as he would on Oprah Winfrey's show nearly two decades later. The queue got longer and longer until it stretched past the stadium.

To Fred Rogers, every child required special attention, because every child needed assurance that he or she was someone who mattered. This was far more than the informed opinion of an expert educator; it was a profound conviction, one that had motivated Rogers from his own childhood. When Mister Rogers sang, "Would you be mine . . . won't you be my neighbor," at the start of every episode of his show, he really meant it.

Kindness and empathetic outreach had motivated Rogers since he was a sickly, chubby boy himself, whose classmates in industrial Latrobe, Pennsylvania, outside of Pittsburgh, called him "Fat Freddy" and chased him home from school. The lonely only child often spent school lunch breaks in his puppet theater in the attic of his parents' mansion, entertaining a friendlier classmate who'd come home with him in a chauffeur-driven car. As Fred Rogers acknowledged later, the isolation of his childhood, though painful, was a key source of artistic invention that showed up in the sets, scripts, and songs on a program where he created an idealized version of his hometown.

Back in the 1930s, when Fred Rogers was growing up, living in a neighborhood meant safety, security, comfort, and help. Despite his problems, in Latrobe young Rogers had a piece of geography, a piece of the town, that was his own. He had neighbors and relatives who understood him, who helped him when his parents didn't understand, who took him into the library to find books he would care about, who rescued him when he was bullied on the street. Eventually, living in the neighborhood meant friends and classmates who valued him and wanted to share their experiences.

It meant familiar and comforting sights and sounds: the clang of the trolley coming up the hill, the sound of trucks making deliveries to the shops, the smoke belching from industrial chimneys that said *there are jobs here*, his parents' house and the big backyard behind it, his grandparents' house, the school building where he went to learn each day. The fabric of that neighborhood gave the young boy in the 1930s a sense of place that was profoundly reassuring at a time when he felt acutely his own shyness and the pangs of loneliness. And it was this kind of "neighborhood" that he recreated for young viewers.

Fred McFeely Rogers's life, and the way it was incorporated into his hugely popular television show, is more complex than it may appear on the surface—as was the man himself. Those who aren't aware of Rogers's real work may see only the stereotype: the kindly, graying figure who was so understanding and helpful to children, but also peculiar in ways easy to satirize.

But Fred Rogers was much more than his gentle, avuncular persona in the *Neighborhood*. He was the genius behind the most powerful, beneficial programming ever created for very young children; he was a technological innovator and entrepreneur decades before such work was popularly recognized; he was a relentless crusader for higher standards in broadcasting; he was an artist whose deep creative impulse was expressed in the music of his show; and he was a Presbyterian minister, bearing witness to the values he saw as essential in a world that often seemed to lack any ethical compass. He was a husband and father, and a loyal friend. He was also, in many ways, a driven man.

Fred Rogers can seem too good to be true. Readers of his life story might ask, "Who's behind the man in the sweater: Was he a real man or a saintly character? Is there something we don't know? What's the story?"

There is indeed a story: a difficult childhood; a quest to escape feelings of isolation engendered by his parents' protectiveness, and by their great wealth; a struggle to remake himself in a mold of his own choosing; and after he found his vocation, a lifelong drive to meet the highest standards he could discover. Mister Rogers wasn't a saint; he had a temper, he made bad decisions, and on occasion he was accused of bad faith. He had difficult times with his own sons when they were young. Despite his deep empathy with the tiniest children, he could, at times, be tone-deaf in relating to adults. The man who conveyed a Zen-like calm on television saw a psychiatrist for decades.

But his powerful connection to America's parents and children has persisted, even years after he stopped making television. In 2012, almost ten years after his death, hundreds of thousands of Americans turned to Fred Rogers for comfort in the wake of the elementary-school massacre in Newtown, Connecticut. Four months after Newtown, when deadly bombers struck the Boston Marathon, once again Americans across the nation looked for solace in the words of Fred Rogers.

Sadly, they did so yet again after the May 22, 2017, bombing at an Ariana Grande concert in Manchester, England, in which twenty-two people lost their lives, including young children.

After each unspeakable tragedy, Rogers's words, sought out on the internet, were forwarded everywhere: "When I was a boy and I would see scary things in the news," Rogers had told his young viewers, "my mother would say to me, 'Look for the helpers. You will always find people who are helping.' To this day, especially in times of disaster, I remember my mother's words, and I am always comforted by realizing that there are still so many helpers—so many caring people in this world."

Few indeed are the TV personalities whose capacity to console survives them in this way.

Along with his skills as an educator, Rogers possessed a unique and powerful ability to give reassurance and comfort to others, including many whose childhoods were far in the past. He helped generations of young children understand their evolving world, and their own potential in it. Through his program, his many television interviews and family-special productions, and his dozens of books and articles, he helped parents grasp the critical importance of early childhood learning, and to understand their own role in making their children's lives more joyful and rewarding.

He also influenced subsequent generations of producers of children's television. Rogers's work is still distributed by PBS and the Fred Rogers Company, though it is no longer broadcast regularly. Its impact resonates in ongoing programs, such as *Blue's Clues* and *Daniel Tiger's Neighborhood*, that speak to small children gently and understandingly, as Mister Rogers did.

As journalist Mary Elizabeth Williams put it on *Salon.com* in 2012, on what would have been Fred Rogers's eighty-fourth birthday: "One of the most radical figures of contemporary history never ran a country or led a battle. . . . He became a legend by wearing a cardigan and taking off his shoes. . . . Rogers was a genius of empathy . . . fearless enough to be kind."

Rogers's former colleague Elizabeth Seamans adds: "Fred was quite daring. People think of him as conservative, in the little fifties house with the cardigan sweater, but he was completely fearless in his use of the medium and as a teacher . . . I think he was brilliant—a genius."

Musician, bandleader, educator, and guest on *Mister Rogers' Neighborhood* Wynton Marsalis observes: "Fred Rogers was one of a kind—an American original, like Louis Armstrong, Duke Ellington, Johnny Cash. There was no one like him.

"Every original and innovator doesn't have to have psychedelic hair. There's a cliché version of who's an original. It's always somebody making a lot of noise, and being disruptive of some status quo. His originality spoke for itself. He was so creative. He spoke very clearly, and he showed a lot of respect [for his audience]. And he also integrated a lot of material."

Marsalis adds: "Fred Rogers tackled difficult issues, like disabilities. He expanded kids' horizons of understanding and aspiration. He raised the bar."

THERE IS NO BETTER illustration of Fred Rogers's true daring in the medium of television than the seminal 1981 episode featuring Jeff Erlanger, a quadriplegic, highly intelligent nine-year-old who'd been in a wheelchair since age four. The camera zooms in on Mister Rogers asking Jeff about the mechanics of his wheelchair in a tone no different from one he might have used when asking the young man about his favorite flavor of ice cream.

"This is how I became handicapped," says the sweet-faced boy with a self-awareness that would put most adults to shame. As Jeff details his medical condition in a calm, measured way, Mister Rogers listens intently and praises Jeff's ability to discuss it in a way that might help other people: "Your parents must be very proud of you."

Together Jeff and Mister Rogers sing "It's You I Like": "It's not the things you wear / It's not the way you do your hair / But it's you I like / The way you are right now / The way down deep inside you / Not the things that hide you."

Fred Rogers dealt with difficult topics in a style that calmed and nurtured children. When his pet goldfish died, Mister Rogers didn't replace the fish. Instead he told his viewers—his "television neighbors"—what happened, and used the occasion to talk about loss and sadness and death.

KEY TO THE SUCCESS of *Mister Rogers' Neighborhood* was Rogers's iron insistence upon meeting the highest standards without qualification. So painstaking was Fred Rogers's approach that some of his friends and coworkers came to refer to "Fred-time": Whenever one sat down to talk with him, urgency seemed to dissipate, discussion proceeded at a measured, almost otherworldly pace, and the deepest feelings and thoughts were given patient attention. Occasionally Rogers brought production of the *Neighborhood* to a halt, leaving a full crew idling on the set while he rushed to the University of Pittsburgh to consult with Dr. Margaret McFarland or other child-development experts on the show's direction. If he was not sure an episode's content was optimal, he wouldn't let production proceed.

Fred Rogers's rigid personal standards that wouldn't allow him to ignore any individual child sometimes came off as a stubbornness that brooked no argument. Former producer Margy Whitmer observes: "Our show wasn't a director's dream. Fred had a lot of rules about showing the whole body, not just hands. When actors or puppets were reading something, Fred wanted the kids to see the words, even if viewers couldn't literally read them. The camera moves left to right, because you read left to right. All those little tiny details were really important to Fred."

For all his firm standards, Fred Rogers was willing to show his own vulnerability on the air. In a segment with a folk singer named Ella

Jenkins, Mister Rogers and cast member Chuck Aber sang a song that goes, "Head and shoulders, baby / one, two, three / knees and ankles." Mister Rogers got all mixed up and, laughing hysterically, touched head and shoulders while the others were on knees and toes.

Margy Whitmer figured she'd be asked to cut the scene. But Fred Rogers said, "No, we're going to keep it. I want children to know that it's hard to learn something new, and that grown-ups make mistakes."

Fred Rogers never—ever—let the urgency of work or life impede his focus on what he saw as basic human values: integrity, respect, responsibility, fairness and compassion, and of course his signature value, kindness. In many ways, he was ahead of his time. In the 1970s, he became a vegetarian, famously saying he couldn't eat anything that had a mother, and in the mid-1980s he became co-owner of *Vegetarian Times*, a popular magazine filled with recipes and features. He also signed his name to a statement protesting the wearing of animal furs.

On the show, he often invited actors of diverse backgrounds, such as François Clemmons, an African American singer and actor who played a police officer; Maggie Stewart, the African American "mayor" of Westwood, adjoining the Neighborhood of Make-Believe; and Tony Chiroldes, the owner of a shop that sold toys, books, and computers in the Neighborhood, and who sometimes taught Mister Rogers words in Spanish.

Humility and kindness to all people originated not only through Rogers's Christianity, but also his careful study of other religions and cultures. Rogers was a student of Catholic mysticism, Buddhism, Judaism, and other faiths, and many of his admirers came to see an almost Zen-like quality in the pace of his work and his life. As time went on, this characteristic became more telling in distinguishing Rogers and the *Neighborhood*. While communication technology proliferated, becoming ever faster and more complex, Fred Rogers used it in ways that were slow, thoughtful, and nuanced. Among the values he represented to viewers was the unusual one of patience. He was that unique television star with a real spiritual life. He worried about the lack of silence in a noisy world and pondered how those in the field of television could encourage reflection. Today these ideas may seem quaint, yet they can also seem radical and more pressing than ever.

Mister Rogers recognized the way children live in the moment: "When Fred fed the fish on the show, he would tap a little food into the fish tank, then Bobby Vaughn, the cameraman, would pan down and zoom in. Children across the nation would watch in total silence as flakes of fish food slowly moved through the water," Elizabeth Seamans observes.

"Fred could take that risk with the pressure of the clock. In television, every second counts. He allowed himself to be oblivious appropriately because he also knew when to move on. His timing was incredible. I think that was linked to his life as a musician, because that beat and rhythm, that dance-like relationship with the unseen viewer, is a sixth sense."

Finally, there was another aspect of Rogers's life and work that's in sharp counterpoint to mainstream American culture: his relationship with money. He never seemed to care much about it. When asked how he coped with increasing fame, he observed, "You don't set out to be rich and famous; you set out to be helpful."

Of course, given his family's wealth, Fred Rogers never had to worry about money the way most Americans do. Indeed, he was handed great gifts: a concert grand piano when he was about ten, a new car after his marriage to Joanne Byrd, a vacation cottage on Nantucket just as they were having children. Still, Rogers never focused on making money in his long television career.

When he set up a company in 1971 to produce *Mister Rogers' Neighborhood*, he established it as a nonprofit. Eventually tax attorneys had to pressure the company to pay Rogers a higher salary; his compensation had been set at a level too low to be credible under the tax laws. As he grew older, Rogers and his wife lived more and more modestly.

They sold their house in Pittsburgh's East End and lived in a large apartment. Rogers drove a Chevrolet, and then an old Honda. He dressed modestly and eschewed luxuries. He and Joanne never fixed up their small cottage at the western end of Nantucket, a simple, rustic structure with small, modestly furnished rooms and no central heating, much like the fisherman's shack it had been originally. All around it, more elaborate homes showcased their owners' wealth.

Most significantly, Rogers turned down offers from the major networks to take his show from PBS to commercial television, where he could have earned millions as scriptwriter, songwriter, and star.

Nor would he ever allow the artifacts of the *Neighborhood*—the puppets, the trolley—to be turned into toys marketed directly to children. His nonprofit company did contract the production of these items for sale to parents, but because Rogers would not tolerate any advertising directed at children themselves, the toys never delivered the massive profits that could have lined his pockets.

In addition to giving up significant income from more aggressive commercialization of the *Neighborhood* and the puppets, Fred Rogers gave up something else, something he would have valued highly: a legacy as strong and lasting as that of *Sesame Street* and the Muppets. The pointed commercialization of *Sesame*, including marketing directly to children, gained millions for the Children's Television Workshop and Jim Henson, but it also created an international base for the show. Today *Sesame* is seen around the world and still appreciated by scores of millions of children, parents, and teachers.

By contrast, *Mister Rogers' Neighborhood* is sometimes available on broadcast television, and as of this writing, can be purchased from PBS, iTunes, or Amazon. Certainly, children see it, but nowhere near the numbers who still experience *Sesame*. Fortunately, the Fred Rogers Company has produced successful new programming like *Daniel Tiger's Neighborhood* that captures the spirit of Rogers and advances his legacy. But clearly, Fred Rogers's highly ethical choices cost him something more than money.

In this and in most other ways, Fred Rogers's life offers an interesting contrast to a twentieth-century world consumed by rapid change and inexorable growth. In everything he wrote, in all the programming he produced, in the life of caring, kindness, and modesty that he led, he set a very clear example. His legacy lives in the concept of a caring neighborhood where people watch out for one another, no matter where they come from or what they look like. Far from being old-fashioned, his vision is in fact more pertinent than ever in a fractured cultural and political landscape.

Fred Rogers's work still resonates not only because he recognized the critical importance of learning during the earliest years. He provided, and continues to provide, exemplary leadership for all of us, at all ages, at a time when the human values Rogers championed seem to be a thing of the past. Today, the kindness he embodied and championed could not be more relevant.

In our era, the geographical concept of the neighborhood in the United States is vastly diminished. Many young people coming into the workforce today are moving away from where they grew up, to live and take jobs in other parts of the country. More than half of marriages today end in divorce. Gentrification of urban neighborhoods has displaced millions of people from the places they considered home.

These and other factors have evolved into a much harsher landscape that, most often, offers little of the neighborhood solace and succor that supported young Fred Rogers. The grocer down the street doesn't know the young boy walking by on the way to school, and the matrix of helpful cousins, aunts, uncles, and close friends has scattered across the country.

So where do we find the strength of neighborhood today, in a world of dramatic globalization, an environment of rapid technological change, a planet increasingly consumed with fear of the other? So many people are overwhelmed today with the relentless pace of change, and a sense of their being left behind, that anger, resentment, misogyny, and blame are driving the public discourse.

In his work, Fred Rogers himself pointed the way back to the neighborhood. He used the cutting-edge technology of his day, television, to convey the most profound values—respect, understanding, tolerance, inclusion, consideration—to children. He gave them a reassuring and inviting neighborhood based on a skillful blend of the most old-fashioned values, derived from his Christianity, in a new medium.

Millions of his viewers grew up to be adults who hold on to those values and maintain a loyalty to Fred and his work.

He exemplified a life lived by the Golden Rule: "Do unto others as you would have them do unto you," found in some form in almost every religion and philosophy through history. His lesson is as simple and direct as Fred was: Human kindness will always make life better.

PART I

———

It always helps to have people we love beside us
when we have to do difficult things in life.

—FRED ROGERS

I.

—

FREDDY

NANCY MCFEELY ROGERS had come back to her parents' house in Latrobe, Pennsylvania, forty miles southeast of Pittsburgh, just before Fred Rogers was born. She wanted to be sure that she would have as much help and support as possible for what might be a hard delivery. Nancy's first baby was coming two and a half years after her marriage to James Hillis Rogers, a handsome, dark-haired young man who had finished his engineering studies at Pennsylvania State University and the University of Pittsburgh.[1] Jim Rogers and his young bride, also dark-haired and attractive, made a striking couple in this small but growing industrial city in western Pennsylvania in the mid-1920s.

Fred McFeely Rogers was born on March 20, 1928, in Latrobe in the McFeely house, a handsome, old brick home at 705 Main Street.[2] Her doctor had warned Nancy Rogers that the baby's birth could be hard for such a small woman. The labor was a long and arduous ordeal. During much of it, Ronnie, the family's Pomeranian dog, was huddled under the birth bed, adding its voice to that of Nancy as she struggled. By the time Nancy's son—named after his maternal grandfather, Fred McFeely—was born, she was exhausted. The family doctor advised her not to think about having another child, which might be not only difficult, but devastating—even fatal.[3] It was advice that Nancy and Jim would follow.

Young Fred was to become a great favorite of his maternal grandparents, Fred and Nancy Kennedy McFeely. Nancy Rogers was immediately protective of her new baby, smothering him with maternal love and guarding him against the outside world. In one of the photographs from that time, she is seen hugging the young boy close to her, one arm wrapped around his frame and the other protectively holding his arm. She is slight, with an angular beauty; he is a bit chubby, with a quizzical look on his face.

Sixty-five years later, Fred Rogers would say in a television interview: "Nothing can replace the influence of unconditional love in the life of a child. . . . Children love to belong, they long to belong."[4]

More than anyone else in Fred's life, his mother gave him that unconditional love. Certainly, her overprotective mothering contributed to the little boy's shy and withdrawn nature, but what is even more clear is that her absolute devotion, along with her extraordinary generosity, contributed essential ingredients to Fred Rogers's developing character and gave him the resilience to overcome an introverted, sometimes sickly (with severe asthma), and sheltered childhood. His mother was renowned throughout the family and the city of Latrobe for her giving nature and her boundless kindness.

Nancy Rogers came from a wealthy Pittsburgh family that moved to Latrobe, which is bisected by the Main Line of the Pennsylvania Railroad. Her father, Fred B. McFeely, built the family business, McFeely Brick, makers of silica and fire clay bricks for furnaces, into an important Latrobe manufacturing firm. Westmoreland County had abundant coal and other natural resources, and the proximity to Pittsburgh, a major river-shipping center, gave the city additional commercial advantages.

Nancy Rogers spent her life giving to the people of Latrobe. During World War I, the fourteen-year-old girl knitted sweaters for American soldiers from western Pennsylvania who were fighting in Europe (knitting was one of the great passions of her life; she continued knitting sweaters for family and friends—including a new cardigan each year for Fred—for over six decades).[5] The next year Nancy lied about her age to get a driver's license so she could help local hospitals and doctors' offices during the terrible flu epidemic of 1918.[6]

Her father needed to sign off on paperwork to allow her to drive. To discourage her, he informed her that first she'd have to learn to rebuild an engine in case the truck broke down on the road. With the help of local mechanics, the determined young woman learned quickly and was soon on the road. Though she spent months hauling away used bandages and other medical waste, she managed to escape falling victim to the flu herself.

By the time her first child was born, she was regularly volunteering at the Latrobe Hospital, and Fred was often left with a caretaker while Nancy pursued her work. She'd once dreamed of becoming a doctor, but that was an impractical ambition for a young woman in western Pennsylvania in that era. She contented herself with a lifetime of volunteer work at the hospital.

A longtime friend of Nancy Rogers, Latrobe Hospital nurse Pat Smith, later recalled, "She would come into the nursery and just work. If a baby were crying, she wouldn't hesitate to assist with the feedings or tenderly rock them in her arms in the nursery rocking chairs. She wouldn't leave until she was certain that all was secure, and that included making sure the staff had time for dinner, usually at her expense."[7]

The Rogers's home, a three-story brick mansion at 737 Weldon Street, was in the affluent area of Latrobe known as "The Hill." Fred Rogers grew up with a cook to make his meals and a chauffeur to drive him to school. He was a cherished only child until his sister, Nancy Elaine Rogers Crozier, called Laney, was adopted by Nancy and Jim Rogers when Fred was eleven. Given the age gap between them, Laney recalled in an interview that she always saw him as "a very grown-up playmate."

Years later, Fred Rogers told Francis Chapman of the Canadian Broadcasting Company that "his parents adopted his sister, Laney, as a present for him. . . . I don't know whether Fred had requested a sibling or not, but Fred thought that his parents thought that it would be nice for him to have one."[8]

Given his family's wealth and stature in the community, Fred Rogers's formative years were spent in an environment in which his family had an extraordinary influence over his friends and neighbors, and almost everyone in Latrobe. By the time Fred Rogers was born, the city's population was around ten thousand. And Latrobe is still recognizable today as the very attractive cityscape of brick and stone houses and commercial buildings that Fred captured in his *Mister Rogers' Neighborhood* trolley-track town. With its tidy homes and many parks and playgrounds, it looks like quintessential small-town America.

To put the wealth of Fred Rogers's family into perspective, it helps to examine not just the industrial heritage of the McFeely family, but also that of Nancy McFeely Rogers's maternal ancestors. They included William J. A. Kennedy of Pittsburgh (a salesman) and his wife, Martha Morgan Kennedy, who worked as a housekeeper for a leading banker, Thomas Hartley Given, in an era in which the Mellon banking fortune was built in Pittsburgh. Martha divorced Kennedy and married Given, who provided, through his investment genius, a huge family fortune that carried down through subsequent generations. Records at the McFeely-Rogers Foundation indicate that when the estate of Thomas H. Given settled on June 30, 1922, his fortune was valued at roughly 5,509,000 dollars, or about 70 million dollars today.[9]

One of the most fascinating aspects of the Martha Kennedy–Thomas Given romance is that Given built most of his considerable estate as a very early investor in Radio Corporation of America. And RCA, of course, made huge profits for its investors, including Given's heirs (about half his fortune at the end of his life was in RCA stock), through the development of television, where Fred eventually made his career.

Fred Rogers grew up keenly aware of the influence of his family, derived from the exceptional largesse and charitable works of his parents, and from the fact that Jim Rogers played a leading role in many of the large businesses in Latrobe.

A childhood friend of Fred's, Ed "Yogi" Showalter, remembered that even in grade school Fred Rogers seemed to be adopting his parents' penchant for good deeds. "I think he inherited that from his family." Showalter explained that Fred reported to his parents that kids in his class were discussing the fact that a young classmate's parents couldn't even afford shoes for him. Within days, the boy showed up at school in brand new high-top shoes.[10]

Showalter also remembered that all the children in class at Latrobe Elementary got out of school early on Fred's birthday so that they could go downtown to the movies, courtesy of Nancy Rogers. Another classmate, Anita Lavin Manoli, recalls that the Rogers family would travel to Florida each year, often for a long winter vacation. When Nancy Rogers got back to Latrobe, she had presents in hand for Fred's fellow students and teachers.[11]

The Rogers family philanthropy and the religious basis for it became two of the most important strands in young Fred Rogers's life. For Nancy, the centerpiece of her giving was the Latrobe Presbyterian Church: the Scots-Irish Rogers and McFeely clans were staunch members of the church, located on Main Street in the center of town. Her whole family attended.

In her role as a community watchdog, Nancy Rogers could find out which families needed help. As often as not, the solution to a problem involved Jim and Nancy Rogers writing a check, which they did on an almost weekly basis. Nancy Rogers also organized a consortium of several Latrobe churches—including the Presbyterian, Lutheran, Methodist, and Episcopal—into a network of ministers and volunteers called "Fish," according to the Reverend Clark Kerr of the Latrobe Presbyterian Church, whose father was one of the ministers with whom Nancy worked.[12]

The name "Fish" was picked because of its Christian symbolism: The symbol of the fish was used as a secret sign by early Christians; Jesus referred to fish and fishing throughout his teachings; and several of Jesus's twelve apostles were fishermen. Nancy Rogers gathered intelligence from the ministers of the churches, from other volunteers, from her husband's workplace connections, and even from her own children and their experiences at school. When she learned of a family in need, she would bring this information to "Fish" and the group would make plans to help. If money was needed, Nancy could be counted on to dip into her own funds to buy clothing, food, or medical care.

In Jim Rogers's role as key manager of several of the Rogers-owned companies—including Latrobe Die Casting and the McFeely Brick Company—he could watch out for the families of employees and step in with a loan or a gift when needed. Jim Okonak, secretary of the family holding company, Rogers Enterprises, Inc., and executive director of the family philanthropy, the McFeely-Rogers Foundation, remembered that scores of employees from several Rogers companies would come on pay-day to the pay window outside Jim Rogers's office to pick up their cash wages. Often, some of them would be back the following day to take out loans from Jim Rogers because part of their wages had disappeared in the many taverns and bars that lined the streets between the steel mills and other manufacturing plants. These loans were all chronicled in a great ledger book; when Jim Rogers died, the book recorded thousands of "loans" that were never collected.[13]

Okonak also recalls Jim Rogers's habit of chewing tobacco, which he only indulged when he walked the floors of Latrobe Die Casting, McFeely Brick Company, or other Rogers-led firms. He would put a chew in his cheek, loosen his tie, and walk through the rows of manufacturing machines, addressing each employee by name, inquiring about their work and about their welfare.[14] Back home, Rogers would report family problems to his wife, who would organize community aid efforts. The young Fred Rogers went to school with the children of these families and carried a constant awareness of how special his family was in this small, tight-knit city. He was proud of his mother's good works, and at the earliest age he shared the family devotion to the Presbyterian Church, but he was also increasingly self-conscious and shy.

In the early twentieth century, this kind of "enlightened capital-ism" was not confined to the Rogers family. George F. Johnson of the Endicott Johnson Corporation in upstate New York initiated what he called a "Square Deal" for his workers that provided everything from parades to churches and libraries to "uplift" workers, encouraging loyalty, and at the same time, discouraging unionization. The company had a chess-and-checkers club and funded health and recreational facilities.

The family trust also supported the construction of local pools, theaters, and even food markets.

Ironically, the very generosity that made Fred Rogers's parents so popular with adults sometimes made Fred a target of other children. Because he was so easily identified as the rich kid in town, and because of his sensitive nature, he spent part of his earliest years as an outlier in Latrobe. And he suffered from childhood asthma—increasingly common in the badly polluted air of industrial western Pennsylvania. During some of the summer months, Fred was cooped up in a bedroom with one of the region's first window air-conditioning units, purchased by his mother to help alleviate his breathing problems.[15]

ALL THE WAY BACK to the eighteenth century, before the French and Indian War helped accelerate the dispersal of the indigenous Indian population—mostly Lenni Lenape, or Delawares, as the whites called them—the area around Fort Ligonier and what would become Latrobe was mostly wilderness. Only the hardiest scouts, explorers, and trappers ventured into the new territories well west of Philadelphia and north of Virginia.

That part of western Pennsylvania had been one of the earliest and longest-sustained areas of human habitation in North America. A little more than fifty miles west of present-day Latrobe is Meadowcroft Rockshelter, believed to be one of the oldest sites, perhaps the oldest site, of human habitation recorded on the continent. The massive rock overhang was used for shelter as long as sixteen thousand to nineteen thousand years ago, by primitive peoples, some of whom were the ancestors of the American Indians who later dominated this territory before the coming of the British and the French.

At the end of the French and Indian War in 1763, a torrent of new settlers poured into the area. In fact, few regions in the world saw such rapid expansion, extraction of natural resources, and industrial development as the territory now known as western Pennsylvania.

In the first half of the nineteenth century, settlers arrived from Germany, Ireland, Scotland, England, and parts of the eastern United States. Among them was a group of German Benedictine monks who founded Saint Vincent Archabbey and Monastery in 1846 in Latrobe under the guidance of Father Boniface Wimmer. It is the oldest Benedictine monastery in the US. About the same time, the monks founded Saint Vincent College, which later bestowed honorary degrees on both James Hillis Rogers and his son, Fred, and has educated thousands of Pennsylvania's native sons and daughters.

One of the largest contingents of settlers from the Old World was composed of Scots-Irish Presbyterians—an ethnic group with roots back to Scotland and Northern Ireland—who were discouraged by misfortune in Ireland: a series of droughts, increasing land rents from their English landlords, and disagreements with the Protestant hierarchy in Ulster. Some of the Rogers, McFeely, Kennedy, and Given families were represented.

By the mid-nineteenth century, Latrobe flourished very quickly once a new rail line through the site connected Harrisburg and Pittsburgh. One of the very first businesses in town was the new Pennsylvania Car Works, which manufactured rail cars for the Pennsylvania Railroad. More, diverse business followed quickly: the Loyalhanna Paper Company, Latrobe Tannery, Whitman & Denman Tannery, the Oursler Foundry, and other iron works and foundries, as well as numerous coke works, brick works, and agricultural businesses. The founder of the Pennsylvania Car Works, which also repaired railroad cars, was Oliver Barnes, who got rich buying land around and ahead of the route he laid out for the railroad's expansion into western Pennsylvania.[16]

Located just north of the best coal and coke fields in western Pennsylvania, blessed with an abundance of rich and beautiful farmland all around, only forty miles from the confluence of the Monongahela, Allegheny, and Ohio Rivers in Pittsburgh, and built around rail yards on the main line linking eastern Pennsylvania and the Atlantic Seaboard to Pittsburgh's new "gateway to the West," Latrobe simply couldn't miss as an industrial and commercial center.

At the end of World War I there was an abundance of strong manufacturing firms in Latrobe, including the Saxman Family's Latrobe Steel Company (still a world leader in specialty metals products), the Burns Crucible Steel and Metallic Company, the Besto Glass Works, Peters Paper Company, and West Latrobe Foundry and Machine Company.[17]

Later there were many others: Vanadium-Alloys Steel Company, the McFeely Brick Company, Kennametal (another international leader in specialty metals products), Latrobe Die Casting, and Stupakoff Ceramic and Manufacturing Company. At one time or another, James Hillis Rogers, Fred's father, served on the boards of many of these companies. Latrobe Die Casting, a small and struggling firm in the late 1930s, was bought by a savvy James Rogers, who built it into a much larger tool and die manufactory with hundreds of employees before it was sold after his death.

And McFeely Brick, founded by the family of Fred's grandfather Fred B. McFeely, was also built into an important Latrobe manufacturing firm before the family sold it years after McFeely's death. As an adult, Fred Rogers served on the boards of both the McFeely Brick Company and Latrobe Die Casting, and played an unwilling and unhappy role in a major labor strike at Latrobe Die Casting in 1980.

Many of Fred's ancestors, on both sides of his family, were farmers and merchants. Besides the McFeely clan's focus on mill work and manufacturing, one of Fred's forebears, John McFeely, went out to California to try his hand in the 1849 gold rush before coming back to the Pittsburgh region as a manufacturer of blankets for Union troops during the Civil War and, finally, founding Steubenville Furnace and Iron Co. in Ohio in 1872.[18]

FRED'S CHILDHOOD FRIEND Anita Lavin Manoli, when asked about the wealth of Fred's family in relation to most of his peers' families, says, "I think he was always sort of in denial of that." She speculated that part of Fred's lifelong embrace of simplicity was in reaction to it.[19]

But Manoli also credits the modesty and humility of the Rogers family for the humility that evolved in Fred Rogers's character. "His mother and father were millionaires who were not pretentious at all. Of course, they lived in a beautiful home. Of course, they had servants. Of course, they went to Atlantic City in the summer. Of course, they ultimately went to New England and had a home on Nantucket. But they were not pretentious people. They were very simple, down to earth."[20]

She also gives credit to Fred's parents for the development of his work ethic: "I think that's what drove him. He didn't have to work. He could have just played golf and learned to play polo or something. But he didn't; he worked."

Fred's sister, Laney, remembered her father's fierce work ethic—which he had learned working summers on his grandparents' farm; the ten dollars he got for a whole summer's work was immediately turned over to his parents. Jim Rogers drilled that ethic into his son.[21]

Still, for all the positive influence of his parents' faith, hard work, and philanthropy, over time their protectiveness of Fred seemed to have contributed to an insecurity and insularity that made his earliest years painful. Another childhood friend, Rudy Prohaska (whose mother, Anna Prohaska, worked for years for the Rogers family and sometimes cared for Fred when his mother was out on volunteer work), remembers other children bullying Fred, calling him names, and chasing him. "There were a lot of people in school who irritated me by the way they treated him. I couldn't take the name-calling and all that. My personal opinion is, Fred was just too sheltered."[22]

Prohaska and other friends all talked about how Nancy Rogers contributed to Fred's tentative and uncertain character. To a large extent, the careful sheltering of the only Rogers son was a natural outgrowth of the times for such a wealthy family. Although the Rogers estate survived the stock market crash of 1929 and the ensuing Great Depression largely unscathed, millions of people around the nation were living in abject poverty, sometimes lacking even food.

Prohaska came from the other end of town. "We came through the Depression, but it was rough. We had food, we had clothes on our back, maybe not the best. But when you went to their place [the Rogers home], it was overwhelming, the fine furniture and all. But they never put on the dog."[23]

Despite the deep appreciation most of the local people expressed for the Rogerses' philanthropy and for their unpretentiousness, Nancy and Jim Rogers worried that Fred could be a target of resentment or even a criminal act. When the twenty-month-old son of Charles Lindbergh and Anne Morrow Lindbergh was kidnapped from their estate near Hopewell, New Jersey, in 1932, it contributed to an atmosphere of near-panic among some wealthy American families with young children. The Rogers family listened to the news with horror when, two months after the kidnapping, the little boy's body was found, his skull shattered.

The ensuing trial of Bruno Richard Hauptmann so dominated the news that newspaper columnist H. L. Mencken called it "the biggest story since the Resurrection."[24] The whole nation seemed riveted to news of the case, and public fears led to legislation that made kidnapping a federal offense. The Federal Kidnapping Act, or the Lindbergh Law, enabled federal law enforcement officials to pursue suspects across state lines. For Jim and Nancy Rogers, whose small son was only a couple of years older than the only child of the famous aviator and his writer wife, the Lindbergh story and the prospect of someone kidnapping Fred was deeply affecting.

Nancy had their chauffeur, Grant Ross, drive her little son to school every day, pick him up for lunch and bring him home, and then take him back to school. At the end of every school day, Ross would wait to take Fred home, carefully guarding the young boy's every moment out in the community.[25] Naturally this must have contributed to Fred's feeling of being apart from his schoolmates and his neighbors.

Later in life, Fred Rogers reported that although he loved the small-town atmosphere of Latrobe, he struggled to fit in with his peers. He turned to reading, listening to music, and playing by himself with his toys and puppets. Fred took solace in his nascent artistry, evolving his own puppet theater in the attic of the family home, sometimes performing before family and friends, and beginning what would be a lifelong love of the piano.

Nancy Rogers's earnest, sometimes controlling, management of young Fred Rogers's life extended to arranging playmates for him. For almost a full year in elementary school, Peggy Moberg McFeaters was chauffeured with Fred back and forth to school at lunchtime by Rogers's family driver Grant Ross.[26] Fred and Peggy would share a lunch prepared by the family cook and then go up to the third-floor attic, where one of the large rooms had been organized as a playroom, complete with a small stage for Fred's puppet theater, developed even before he'd started school.

Years later, Peggy recalled: "Fred entertained me with his puppets and marionettes. I sometimes think I was watching the beginning of *Mister Rogers' Neighborhood*."[27]

In her account, Fred carefully studied her to see what she reacted to with enthusiasm. Fred Rogers, who years later would seem almost preternaturally young and childlike as an adult, was preternaturally mature and sophisticated as a purveyor of puppet entertainment for his young classmate.

Young Fred also found himself growing up in a family, and a house, that was increasingly a social center of this more-and-more prosperous community. His parents loved to throw parties, inviting the families of other wealthy business owners from Latrobe. Three-quarters of a century before Fred's birth, Latrobe hardly existed. And by the end of his life, it had retreated economically, losing population and vibrancy and influence as a center of business. But when he was a child, the town's prosperity and social scene were at their height.

Through their good deeds, business acumen, and love of the community and the society of their peers, Fred Rogers's parents became the first couple of Latrobe. Their home was a constant center of dinner parties, informal gatherings of friends, and even large bashes thrown open to the whole community.[28] Their annual Christmas party was famous for a bountiful table and an open-door policy that brought together everyone, from tool-and-die workers, to neighbors down the street, to members of the exclusive Rolling Rock Club in nearby

Ligonier—bastion of the famed Mellon banking family, led by Jim Rogers's friend General R. K. Mellon. Everyone enjoyed the food, drink, and song through the evening.

Fred's sister, Laney, remembers that each Christmas her parents would buy a big turkey for the family of each person who worked for one of the Rogers's enterprises, and that all year long they would send food baskets to families they'd heard were short of food.[29]

Rudy Prohaska tells of visits from the Rogers family chauffeur, Grant Ross, an African American man, who brought a basket of presents from the Rogers family the day before the Prohaska family was to go over to the Rogers's house for the big Christmas party: "The first time I knew I had a Santa Claus, he was black. Grant would come down on Christmas Eve with the yellow convertible—a Packard—and my dad and him would unload presents from the Rogers family."

After Anna Prohaska stopped working for Jim and Nancy Rogers, she still got a Christmas card with a check in it every year until she died, her son recalls, tears filling his eyes.[30]

Though Fred Rogers would later refer to is parents' generosity with pride, he also remembered retreating upstairs during his parents' parties to his own room, to his puppets and music. Meanwhile, downstairs, songs of that era—"Over the Rainbow" by Judy Garland, "One O'Clock Jump" by the Count Basie Orchestra, "Stormy Weather" by Ethel Waters—would waft up the stairs from the phonograph. Listening, Fred would memorize the melodies and later play them on the piano. His little sister, Laney, would later recall that Fred had a "photographic memory" for music and could hear a tune at his parents' house or at the movies and be able almost instantly to play it by ear.[31]

Fred's parents took him and his sister with them on frequent trips to New York, where young Fred attended the opera and musicals with his parents and their friends. Nancy Rogers loved to shop in the New York department stores, and Jim would drive her there in a big black Cadillac limousine, with Fred riding beside him in the front of the car, listening to jazz on the car radio—talking on the way there and the way back about the musical performances they got to see in the big city. The Rogers family was partial to Cadillacs; Fred's mother even had a baby-blue Cadillac convertible.

Sometimes Jim stayed home to manage the businesses that comprised Rogers Enterprises, Inc., so Nancy Rogers would drive there with her mother, Nancy McFeely. Very frequently, Fred would accompany his various family members. Nancy Rogers often traveled to New York to do some of her Christmas shopping, which was an epic enterprise. She bought dozens of presents for every member of her family, and for friends, neighbors, Jim's business associates, members of her church group, all the people who worked for the Rogers family, and many of the less fortunate families in Latrobe with whom she came in contact. She shopped for Fred's school teachers and sometimes for the teachers of his friends. One year, she bought presents—scarfs, handkerchiefs, gloves—for every one of Laney's teachers at the Oldfields School in northern Maryland, where she had recently been enrolled. She bought about fifteen hundred Christmas presents each year, sometimes more.

The wealthy families that managed Latrobe's big industrial companies created a year-round social whirl that revolved around festive parties at the Latrobe Country Club, as well as at the Rogers house and the homes of other families. According to Fred's aunt Alberta Vance Rogers, "We'd all get together and end up at the country club. One time, my husband [Fred's uncle Pete] got sorry for the horses and brought them into the clubroom. It was lots of fun for those who were drunk."[32]

The course superintendent and golf pro at the country club then was Milfred (Deacon) Palmer, the father of legendary golfer Arnold Palmer, who was just a year behind Fred Rogers in school. Arnold Palmer recalled that his father wasn't a club member, and so he wasn't allowed into the club for social functions. Palmer later bought the club, played golf there regularly, and often held court over lunch in the main dining room.[33]

Fred Rogers was not a sports enthusiast. Once, Arnold Palmer and his father were in Florida and visited the Rogers family at their hotel. The elder Palmer gave Fred a golf lesson, which Arnold (Arnie) later described—smiling indulgently as he did so—as a bit of a struggle to find the athleticism in Fred.

Palmer also remembered the very central and important role of the Rogers family in the community. He and his parents turned out each year to celebrate the holidays at the Rogerses' big Christmas party. But he remembered Fred as "very individual . . . a loner."[34]

"He was a very meticulous student. He didn't run with the guys like I did, and he didn't drink beer. I did. We all did. . . . His interests were music and religion and history and that sort of thing. But a nice guy. We liked each other."

One of the most traumatic events for this young "loner" came one day in his early years at Latrobe Elementary School. For some reason, classes were dismissed early that day. When school let out, Grant Ross was not there to pick up Fred, so the young man set out to walk the approximately ten blocks to his house by himself. "It wasn't long before I sensed I was being followed—by a whole group of boys," Fred recalled years later. It was a story he told publicly only decades after the incident.[35]

"As I walked faster, I looked around. They called my name and came closer and closer and got louder and louder." Soon they were chasing him, shouting, "Freddy, hey fat Freddy. We're going to get you, Freddy."

It was terrifying, but Fred managed to run to the house of a family friend, who let him in and called the Rogers residence to have someone come and pick him up. It was a stark example of the vulnerability of this very sensitive child. His elders advised him to meet bullying with indifference: "The advice I got from the grown-ups was, 'Just let on you don't care, then nobody will bother you.' "[36]

But he did care; more than anything in the world, Fred Rogers cared. It was caring that defined the character of his mother, and it was caring that increasingly influenced the evolving character of this shy but resolute young boy. Fred never accepted the advice that pretending not to care would alleviate his loneliness and pain.

As he grew older, Rogers struggled to work out a set of responses to the challenges of life that could turn his caring, his belief in love, and his great sensitivity into a life course based not on fragility, but on a quiet strength. He found a way to be true to himself that enabled him to build a uniquely thoughtful set of defenses that relied on empathy and sympathy. Ultimately, he developed a powerful authenticity that propelled him to popularity in Latrobe. The solitary boy playing in his puppet theater found a way to become one of the most famous and respected residents of a hometown that hadn't always embraced him.

Peggy Moberg McFeaters, who conceded in an interview that many of Fred's schoolmates once thought of him as "a bit of a sissy," said she and others all eventually learned, "He was really a great guy, not too different from the rest of us."[37] Young "Freddy" became a focused young man, and then an adult who drew on the very sensitivity that had once seemed a weakness.

2.

BREATHING ROOM

FROM HIS VERY ARRIVAL in the world, and well into his childhood, Fred Rogers worried his mother, Nancy.

Fred's birth was so difficult that Nancy and her husband, Jim, decided not to have another child, until they adopted Fred's sister, Laney, eleven years later. Though young Fred had to adjust to sharing his place in the family, Laney's main memories of her older brother are that "he was so kind and so sweet. He would carry me around. He would walk with me, hand in hand. He would follow me around the yard, so I didn't trip and fall. But I'm sure that there were times when he just wished this little thing hadn't come to live in the house with him."

Laney recalls her mother telling her, much later, that Fred had suffered terribly from colic as a baby, and Nancy had struggled to find ways to help him find relief. She felt the pain of her little baby as if it was her own.[1]

Jim Rogers was overjoyed to have a son, despite young Fred's difficult arrival. Later, when Fred outgrew his colic, he developed serious childhood asthma. It all contributed to making Nancy and Jim Rogers very protective parents. They took great pains to safeguard their sickly little boy, sometimes keeping him home from school for protracted periods of time.

Sometimes Fred's parents also kept him at home during the long, hot days of summer when the western Pennsylvania air pollution was at its worst, and they tried numerous other strategies to help him. At one point, Fred's mother and a family friend, Alcy Clemons (she was his babysitter; years later, he played the piano at her wedding), even took young Fred to Banff, Canada, and Sault Ste. Marie, Michigan, hoping the cleaner air there would help the boy's breathing.[2]

The trip did help, but then mother and child had to come back home to the heavily industrialized Pittsburgh region. Like most cities in western Pennsylvania in the first half of the twentieth century, Latrobe had some of the most polluted air in America, with soot and particulate matter that exacerbate asthma. It was a particularly difficult place for an asthmatic to grow up. Ironically, some of the Rogers/McFeely family businesses in the Latrobe area were among the polluters that contributed to the bad air that afflicted Fred and other young children.

When he was about ten years old, Fred's asthma was particularly bad. Nancy Rogers had an innovative idea. She had learned of another young boy in Latrobe who was also suffering badly from asthma that summer. She thought that if the Rogers family could buy a window air conditioner—a brand new phenomenon in western Pennsylvania back in the 1930s—and put it in this older boy's bedroom, Fred and the boy could both get relief and could keep each other company during the hot summer months.[3]

According to Jeanne Marie Laskas, a western-Pennsylvania-based writer and columnist for the *Washington Post* who frequently interviewed and wrote about Fred, Nancy worked with the other little boy's family and the Rogers family physician to arrange for Fred to be cloistered in an air-conditioned room in the summer of 1938.

Laskas quotes Fred telling the story of spending the whole summer, through long days and nights, in his new friend Paul's room. His parents wanted to give Fred some company during this cloistered period: "Paul and I were cooped up with the air conditioner, the first one in Latrobe. The family doctor and my parents went together and bought it, put it in Paul's room, and then I went to live there all summer. They thought that's what you do with kids who have asthma. Put them in there and just get them through. Paul was probably sixteen. I was probably ten.

"Now that I think about it, I think how he must have hated that. He was an only child, I was an only child, and here's this kid invading his space. When we'd go to an ice-cream parlor, he would order something and then I would order the same thing, of course; being that much older, he was a real hero. And then he would whisper to the person who was making the things to change the order—so that when his came, mine would be different, and I would be disappointed. But I see now that I was the sibling that he never had to take things out on before. We rarely left that room. We had our meals there. After that, we got an air conditioner at our house."[4]

Typically, Nancy Rogers was both wonderfully thoughtful about Fred and somehow insensitive to the effects of such a radical seclusion. She spared no expense. After the Rogers family air-conditioned Paul's room, they bought conditioners for their summer retreat on the slope of Chestnut Ridge just outside Latrobe. They also paid to air-condition the entire enormous brick house on Weldon Street.[5] Though this certainly contributed to everyone's comfort, Nancy undertook the project first and foremost to protect her little boy.

This pattern in the relationship of Nancy Rogers and her young son was repeated frequently as he grew up: Fred struggling with sickliness (which he outgrew eventually), shyness, and loneliness, and his mother trying desperately hard to ride to his rescue. Though deeply appreciative of his mother's love and her caring nature, Fred had to work hard to find ways to establish his independence as a youngster and a teenager.

This was less true with his father, who could be very serious and sometimes a bit aloof from young Fred. But their relationship was still very important.

Fred's sister, Laney, remembers her father as having an engaging sense of humor, but she also remembers him as something of a tough guy. The Rogers household was run on a strict schedule. Laney recalls that the family sat down to dinner together every night, in assigned seats, at exactly 6:30 P.M. for a meal prepared by the family cook. Laney and Fred were both chubby as children. Laney observes: "Mother was very geared to food. Later in life, when our friends were leaving—you know, if they had been to the house for dinner, [she would say], 'Oh, take leftovers with you. Eat! Eat!' She just always wanted to feed people."

Conversation at the Rogerses' dinner table was never overly serious. Jim Rogers presided over the table, more relaxed than in his role as corporate chieftain. Laney notes that "Dad was two different people. If you saw him out on the street, he was called Mr. Latrobe. He was always in a three-piece suit, and a hat. And he was always polite, and always friendly, shook hands, and had a chat with anybody.

"He was serious. But just at home, he could relax and enjoy his family. And I think that in the family that close little group of relatives knew a different Jim Rogers than people saw."

She also recalls some raucous times in the family dynamic: "Dad had a cupboard that had a lot of musical instruments in it. We had cymbals; we had an old violin; we had recorders. And Dad was a kind of a frustrated musician, and he would have liked to have been able to play. . . . From time to time, we'd get these things out, and we would have a parade throughout the house. We went up and down the stairs, just everybody banging away and having a grand time."

Jim Rogers was also able to relax on family vacations in New England and in Florida, where he and Fred often played tennis together.

Though he loved and admired his father, Fred never wanted to develop into the young businessman that Jim Rogers hoped for. Later, his wife, Joanne Rogers, reported that Fred often felt he got quite conflicting signals from his mother—who was open and caring to the point of being emotional—and his father, whom Joanne described as more reserved, even to the point of reflecting Victorian-era values in his background and upbringing. Fred told Joanne that he never felt he could satisfy the conflicting demands of his mother and his father, who was usually serious and sometimes distant, always hoping Fred would toughen up and become his father's business partner.[6]

The family money gave Fred freedom and resources but also left him feeling constrained and even trapped. Laney remembers that when her parents gave Fred a car in high school—an exceptional luxury for a teenager in western Pennsylvania in the 1940s—he would drive it to school, but he wanted to hide it from his friends so they wouldn't know he had been given such a privilege. Fred would park the car a couple of blocks down the street from the high school, get out, and walk the rest of the way to his classes.[7]

In pictures from the 1930s, when Fred was a very young child, he often appears guarded, withdrawn, and unsure of himself. But by the time he got to high school, Fred Rogers looks like a strong, confident, smiling young man as he gazes directly into the camera and shows signs of the exceptional intelligence, sensitivity, and focus that made him so successful as an adult.

Remarkably, by the time Fred Rogers was a teenager, he was very different from the ten-year-old who had spent the summer in Paul's air-conditioned bedroom. In his high school years, Rogers became extraordinarily effective.

Before he graduated and headed off to an Ivy League college, he had developed into the star of the Latrobe school system: student council president, editor of the *Latrobean*, finalist in the Rotary Oratorical Contest, actor in high school theatrical productions. He was a serious, accomplished scholar who was inducted into the National Honor Society.[8]

And he was showing signs of the mental toughness that were hallmarks of his character as an adult. He wanted to concentrate on his studies and his school activities, and he was growing tired of the annual interruptions of his education posed by his family's long trips to Florida in the winter. Finally, in his last few years of high school, he balked and insisted on staying home by himself so he wouldn't miss school.

When Jim and Nancy and Laney headed south for their six-week sojourn at the Belleview Biltmore Hotel in Belleair, Fred stayed home alone, dedicating himself to schoolwork and the piano. And by then his parents knew Fred could take care of himself (with a little help from relatives in Latrobe). He had a car to drive himself to school and was totally focused on his academic achievements.[9]

HOW DID YOUNG FRED Rogers transform himself from a shy, sickly kid into a confident high schooler, and then adult? Looking back over

Fred's long life through the lenses provided by his friends and associ-ates, his family and his own writings, it's clear that the support of his parents and grandparents was concentrated in three key areas that came together to help Fred find himself and develop his extraordinary artistic and creative persona: faith, independence, and music.

The first important element was the pervasive influence of the church. Some of his earliest memories were of the comfort he drew from attending the Latrobe Presbyterian Church on Main Street with his mother and father and his mother's parents, Fred and Nancy McFeely. As a very little boy, Fred would attend Sunday school at the church. But when he was still quite young—around five years old—his mother invited him to sit up with her in a pew during the regular church ser-vice. Fred always had a lot of questions, even during the sermon, but his mother never shushed him up. She would always answer, quietly and respectfully, treating the little boy's concerns as seriously as those of an adult.

Although the Church could often be a severe place, particularly in families that subscribed to its most conservative and austere vari-ants, this wasn't the case in Fred's childhood. His mother was deeply religious, but her life was more joyous. More than anything else, she communicated to her son the rewards of service to others, to the com-munity, and to the church. She took care of the needs of so many poor families in Latrobe that eventually the school nurse at Latrobe Elemen-tary School would just order shoes, coats, eyeglasses, and even furniture and have the bills sent directly to Nancy Rogers.[10]

Many other children of Presbyterian families in western Pennsyl-vania had stricter and harsher childhoods than Fred. The actor Jimmy Stewart, for example, who grew up near Latrobe in Indiana, Pennsylva-nia, had a tough, demanding father who put great pressure on his son well into his adult life. Alexander Stewart's sense of Presbyterian pro-priety led him to relentlessly pressure Jimmy to leave the profession of acting, which he did not consider a proper, Christian calling, to return to Indiana to run the family hardware business.[11]

By contrast, Fred was almost never pushed by his father, even though Jim Rogers didn't particularly value television, and like Alexander Stewart, he very much wanted his son to come home to join him in managing the family enterprises. Although he was a strong figure in the family, Jim Rogers was tolerant and always very careful not to bully Fred. He treated his son with respect and support, no matter their differences.

Nancy Rogers almost never communicated the harsher side of Presbyterianism to her son. In her son, she imbued the delights of Christian service. Fred took great pleasure in everyday acts of thoughtfulness and kindliness; throughout his life, when he met a stranger who needed help or friendship, he would drop everything to offer his time and attention.

A typical story about Fred's giving nature comes from a woman who once worked as an intern on *Mister Rogers' Neighborhood*. She recalled that when she accompanied Fred on a trip to Boston, they were scheduled to have dinner at the home of an influential executive at WGBH, the public television station in Boston. A limousine had been hired to take them to the executive's home. When they got there, the limo driver asked Fred when he should pick them up after dinner. Instead, Fred invited him in, to the bewilderment of the hostess. After dinner, he sat up front in the limo with the driver, a man named Billy, to get to know him.

Before the evening was over, Fred and the intern went back to Billy's house in West Roxbury to meet his parents. Fred came in and played the piano as people streamed in from around the neighborhood to listen. A few years later, when Fred learned that Billy was in the hospital dying, he called to talk with him and to say good-bye.[12]

THE SECOND ELEMENT in Fred's young life that enabled his independent growth as a young man was the love and support he got from the McFeelys, Nancy Rogers's parents. A constant presence in Fred's life, they provided some of the warm encouragement Fred sometimes missed from his father. Most critically, they acted as a gentle, artful counterweight to the protectiveness of Fred's parents, helping Fred move toward independence while never undermining his relationship with his mother and father.

His maternal grandparents lived in and around Latrobe during most of Fred's youth. Their love and support were truly transformative for him. Their importance came from their generosity of spirit, but it also came from their very close relationship with Fred's mother.

The namesake of his grandson, Fred McFeely took his role as mentor and grandfather very seriously. He welcomed Fred's visits, listened carefully to his concerns, and stood up for the boy's interests in the family. When he felt that Fred's parents were being too restrictive, he urged more freedom for the young man, gently persuading them to loosen the reins. Nancy Rogers was a very smart and sophisticated young mother, particularly for small-town western Pennsylvania at that time, and she managed to relax the maternal bonds enough to give Fred the right signals about his independence.

For his part, Fred McFeely always made sure his grandson knew, directly and sincerely, how much he enjoyed his company. "Freddy, you make my day very special," McFeely frequently told the shy little boy, reminding him of his importance to the adults in his life.

Fred's sister, Laney, remembers that when she and Fred were children they would go with their parents to visit their grandfather every Sunday at McFeely's farm not too far from Latrobe. The farm was called Buttermilk Falls for the big waterfall along the stream that ran through the middle of the property. It had cows and pigs and other animals, and both children loved to visit and play there. They called McFeely "Ding Dong" because, early on, he had taught them the words to the nursery rhyme, "Ding Dong Dell."[13]

Young Fred often played outside with his grandfather. One Sunday, Fred went off by himself and climbed up on some old stone walls and part of the stone foundation to an old building. Immediately, his mother intervened, calling out a warning to Fred that he could hurt himself playing on the stones and that he should get down right away.

But his grandfather came to the rescue: "Let the kid climb on the wall. He has to learn to do things for himself," Fred McFeely told his daughter.[14] And McFeely explained—not for the first time—the importance of experimentation for a young child and the power of learning through experience, even when risks were involved.

Fred Rogers was deeply grateful to his grandfather, and he never forgot that moment on the stone wall. "I loved my grandfather for giving me that," he said later. "He seemed to know when to let go," added Rogers. It was from Fred McFeely that young Fred felt he got the freedom to grow and develop his interests.[15]

Fred's grandmother, Nancy McFeely, also contributed to his growing independence in ways that were skillfully supportive of her daughter. Together, Nancy McFeely and Nancy Rogers noted Fred's intense interest in music as a three- and four-year-old boy, and they made sure he could use the modest family piano, giving him the chance to play and to learn. Fred started playing the piano before he was five, and his family purchased a small pump organ for about twenty-five dollars to help him develop his musical talent.

He could soon pick up tunes he'd heard, impressing his family with his ability to play by ear. This almost instinctive ability to connect with music, and to express his feelings through the piano and the organ, were seminal to the development of Fred's talents. As a little boy so often shy and reticent, Fred Rogers found a place to express himself, banging out tunes that reflected his emotions.

The pivotal moment in the evolution of Fred's love of music occurred when he was almost ten years old. Fred had formed a strong attachment with his maternal grandmother, and he turned to her for support almost as often as he did to his grandfather. He confided to his grandmother how very much he wanted to own his own piano. "Nana" McFeely listened carefully to Fred, and they discussed why he wanted a piano and what it would mean to him. As a little boy, Fred was not very acquisitive or focused on what money could buy, a trait that stayed with him for the rest of his life. But this was clearly important to him, and he convinced Nana that the acquisition of a piano was not just a whim, but an important building block in his young life.

Finally, thinking that a little piano for a little child couldn't be that expensive, Nana McFeely offered to buy one for her grandson. When Fred was next visiting his grandmother at her residence in the Squirrel Hill neighborhood of Pittsburgh (Nancy and Fred McFeely kept residences in both Latrobe and in Pittsburgh), he told her he was going downtown to look at pianos. His grandmother said that could be a good idea, and she made sure Fred knew where to go and how to get there on his own.

He took a trolley the four miles from Squirrel Hill to the Steinway & Sons store on Liberty Avenue (since moved to Penn Avenue) in downtown Pittsburgh.[16] According to the staff there, Fred spent several hours playing every piano in the store, and then told the salesmen that he had picked his favorite: a secondhand 1920 Steinway Concert Grand Model D Ebonized piano that had been shipped recently to New York for a full "heirloom" restoration to restore the sixteen-year-old piano to perfect condition.[17]

It was nine feet long, weighed about a thousand pounds, and, as a secondhand piano, was worth a little less than 3,000 dollars in 1936. It was, and still is, the gold standard when it comes to concert grand performance pianos. The same model piano, brand new, now sells for nearly 130,000 dollars, according to Steinway staff. The salesmen chuckled among themselves as the little boy headed to the trolley to ride back to Squirrel Hill to see his grandmother.

They were stunned a little while later when Fred returned with a check—nearly 50,000 dollars in today's currency—for the full price of the piano.[18]

Nana McFeely had made a promise, and she was going to keep it. She kept her commitment to let Fred pick out his own piano, and it utterly changed his life.

Although it might seem like an extraordinary extravagance for such a young child, it was a bold and principled move by Nancy McFeely. She knew she could afford it, and she was convinced by Fred himself that it would make an exceptional difference for him at a critical juncture in his life.

Fred Rogers took the piano with him everywhere for the rest of his life—to New York, back to Pittsburgh, to Toronto, and back to Pittsburgh again—and composed most of his famous music on his concert grand. The music that he conceived and composed was the force that propelled his work, his career, and his artistic growth. Just as importantly, it gave him confidence in his abilities and his character and gave him a lifetime of solace and comfort. And it was this music that helped give Fred Rogers a place as one of the great innovators in the evolving fields of television and education.

Nana McFeely's investment paid off handsomely.

As young Fred developed as a pianist, he would play show tunes and even opera arias on his piano, all from memory, after family trips to New York City. He could hear a tune once and give a rendition of it. His sister Laney recalls that the family would stay at the Seymour Hotel on Forty-Fifth Street near Times Square, Broadway, and the New York Theater District, going to musical-theater productions and Radio City Music Hall, immersing Fred in a rich musical environment. "Broadway musicals were very much in fashion in those days," says Laney. "He [Fred] would have just memorized it, sitting there watching it. . . . And his friends would come. . . . He'd come in the door with three or four people trailing along after him. . . . Everything he ever heard, he could play."[19]

THERE WERE TWO OTHER pivotal moments in Fred Rogers's young life—one delivered by fate, and the other artfully managed by his always vigilant mother. Each of them helped Fred move toward independence. Fred was about fourteen years old, a couple of years before he asserted his independence by insisting on staying home to attend school while the rest of his family went off for their annual winter vacation in Florida. He had developed an infection in his groin, and the family doctor decided the young boy needed an operation.[20]

His parents, realizing that their son still didn't fit in as comfortably at school as he wished, thought Fred would be embarrassed to have to talk about such an operation with other children his age. They made up a cover story that he and they could use to explain his absence, and that would enable him to hide the fact that he had the operation.

At first Fred was grateful. But a little while later he began to feel some resentment that a story had to be concocted. It almost seemed to Fred that his parents were ashamed of him, and that their protective gesture was somehow a negative commentary on him as a person. It deepened his commitment to going his own way and developing his own life.

Years later, when Fred was putting together notes for a memoir (he never did write one), he emphasized the importance of this operation—and the impact it had on his maturing sensibility—as a further step in the evolution of the new, independent Fred Rogers.[21]

Clearly, Jim and Nancy Rogers were simply trying to be helpful, and to be sensitive to the feelings of their young son. For Fred's part, his resentment probably reflected, more than anything else, that he was already moving away from his family in ways that were completely natural.

The other pivotal moment in Fred's high school life was the opportunity that presented itself when Fred's mother learned that a star athlete at Latrobe High School, Jim Stumbaugh, was hospitalized. Stumbaugh was also a very dedicated student, and he was anxious to keep up with his schoolwork. Stumbaugh's mother, a widowed teacher who lost her husband when her son was only eight, was friends with the Rogers family.[22]

Family accounts report that Nancy Rogers saw a chance for Fred to connect with one of the most popular boys in the school. Although Fred was doing well in school at this point, both as a student and with his extracurricular activities, he was still somewhat shy and withdrawn from classmates. And his mother—always eager to improve young Fred's life—saw an artful way to help him make a connection that could help him socially.

Stumbaugh was a campus hero in multiple sports, including football, basketball, and track. He had injured a kidney playing football and had to spend several days in the hospital for treatment. Nancy suggested to Fred that he could pick up some of Jim's books at home and his assignments at school and take them over to the hospital, and perhaps even help Jim catch up on his schoolwork.

Nancy's idea worked brilliantly well, and Fred established a friendship with Stumbaugh that would last the rest of their lives.

Fred is remembered by his classmate Anita Lavin Manoli as "head and shoulders above everybody else in terms of the fine arts, poetry, reading." But, she says, he was never involved in athletics—it was the only thing at which he did not excel. And she remembers Fred in high school as someone who was "prominent, not because of who his family was, but because of his accomplishments."[23]

Another classmate, Richard "Puffy" Jim, recalls that when Fred started high school, he was viewed as a little bit nerdy and even sickly, but when he finished, Fred was accepted and thought of as a "regular guy." Jim cites Fred's relationship with Stumbaugh as transformative for the young Rogers.[24] By the end of high school, Fred had a girlfriend, Doris Stewart, with whom he went to the prom. By some accounts, they even double-dated with Stumbaugh and his girlfriend.

During this time, Jim recalls, he saw an example of Fred's emerging social confidence and toughness. He first met Fred in their freshman year in high school when Jim stopped into the school auditorium to listen to students practicing for an oratorical contest. He recalls that Fred's voice was still a bit high and squeaky. While Fred was speaking, other children in the audience began giggling and even laughing out loud. But Fred stayed focused, undistracted, and moved forward to the end of his speech without hesitating. He just "plowed right through it," according to Jim, who was impressed.[25]

Fred Rogers's own impression of his high school years is that they started out painful and frightening, and that his newfound relationship with Jim Stumbaugh helped him make a transition to social integration with his peers. In his oral history for The Television Academy

Foundation's Interviews, Fred said: "I was very, very shy when I was in grade school. And when I got to high school, I was scared to death to go to school. Every day, I was afraid I was going to fail.

"When Jim was injured I went to the hospital—and years later he told me 'I couldn't imagine why Fred Rogers was bringing me my homework.'

"At any rate, we started to talk. And I could see what substance there was in this, uh, jock. And, evidently, he could see what substance there was in this shy kid.

"So when he got out of the hospital and went back to the school, he said to people, 'You know, that Rogers kid's okay.' That made all the difference in the world for me.

"It was after that that I started writing for the newspaper, got to be president of the student council. What a difference one person can make in the life of another. It's almost as if he had said, 'I like you just the way you are.' "[26]

Jim Stumbaugh and Fred Rogers stayed in touch for the rest of their lives, even though Stumbaugh moved away from the region to North Carolina. Decades later, when Stumbaugh was sick with cancer, Rogers flew down to see him and talk, even though Rogers had injured his ankle and was on crutches at the time.

And when Stumbaugh died, Rogers was there to speak at the funeral. "He was tenacious about those friendships," said Maggie Kimmel, a University of Pittsburgh professor who worked with and wrote about Fred Rogers.[27]

Fred Rogers finished high school almost as much of a star as Jim Stumbaugh: He was the recipient of many awards and honors and an accomplished scholar headed for Dartmouth, an Ivy League college. It was, of course, the love he received from his parents and grandparents that made the critical difference.

It's also likely that swimming helped the young Rogers evolve into a more confident young man in high school. Fred Rogers had learned to swim as a boy during his family's many winter trips to Florida.

But nothing made more difference than the thoughtfulness of his always attentive mother. Nancy Rogers devoted her life to her two children and to community service. In return, Fred and Laney adored their mother and remained devoted to her memory after she died. Though Nancy may have hoped for a career as a doctor—and she certainly had the intelligence, the focus, the social skills, and talents for a highly successful career—she found important work shaping the trajectories of her children's lives and strengthening her community.

Graduating from high school in 1946, just after the end of World War II, Fred felt a great sense of excitement about all the possibilities that lay ahead of him. And he had the strength of someone who had come through adversity. It was well that he did: He faced a challenge at Dartmouth, the college he had picked, as great as the one he'd faced in high school.

3.

COLLEGE DAYS

ALMOST NO ONE in Fred Rogers's family can remember exactly why he picked Dartmouth College. Fred's ambitions were ordered around his idealism, not any hopes for success in the sort of business world that might have prized an Ivy League degree. Fred himself said little about Dartmouth, except that he was miserable there, and that his attraction to Romance languages may have piqued his interest in the school, which had, and still has, a fine language program.[1] He did tell some of his relatives that he thought developing his language skills might help prepare him for a career in the diplomatic corps, if he chose to go in that direction.

A little bit of research might have tipped off the reserved, very serious, and very idealistic young Fred Rogers that Dartmouth, famous throughout the Ivy League in those days as a beer-soaked, jockstrap party school, might be a poor fit.

So why did he pick Dartmouth? Fred's statement about the college's prowess in the language field isn't terribly convincing, since Fred expressed what seemed like an even greater level of interest in religion, music, and children. He told his parents and his sister, Laney, that he intended to become a Presbyterian minister after he graduated from college, and that he was already focused on the nearby and very highly regarded Western Theological Seminary in the East End of Pittsburgh (later called Pittsburgh Theological Seminary). And music was the singular passion of Fred's young life, though he had doubts that he could turn his love of music into a career, or even a principal field of study.

Fred's father still harbored hopes that his son would get some business training, as Jim Rogers had done, and come back to Latrobe. It is hard to find the thread that led to Dartmouth; there seems to be no legacy of Dartmouth grads in the family. Jim Rogers went to Penn State and got business training at the University of Pittsburgh. His parents were not college educated.[2]

On Fred's mother's side, there also seems to be no indication of a connection to Dartmouth, all the way back to Fred's great-grandparents and great-great-grandparents. His mother, Nancy, went to the Ogontz School for Young Ladies in Philadelphia, and her mother attended Women's College of Baltimore (now Goucher College).[3]

It seems likely that Fred Rogers was simply unsure of himself in his first year at Dartmouth, and unsure of the best direction to secure the right kind of education to launch a career. And clearly, he was conflicted about which career to select. Though he was passionate about music and children and education, he may have thought that a more traditional approach to education and career—something like the diplomatic corps or teaching French in high school or college—would be a safer bet on the future. Many a young man has been led by such insecurities away from his passions toward something seemingly more secure. And Dartmouth, with its strong reputation, must have seemed like a safe course of action: something that would please his upper-class, and fairly traditional, parents.

But it was a disaster. Fred's sister, Laney, remembers that his roommates were "footballers," that there were frat parties all the time, and that the completely unathletic and teetotaling Fred Rogers was very uncomfortable there. This was predictable, given Dartmouth's reputation as a sports-oriented and very macho school (it was still all male, and didn't go coed until more than twenty years after Fred left) and Fred Rogers's more sensitive and thoughtful nature.[4]

Almost from the time he arrived in Hanover, New Hampshire, the gangly, somewhat nerdy, and idealistic young Fred Rogers felt out of place. By the time the bitter New Hampshire winter set in—lots of mornings below zero—he was miserable.

Fred and Dartmouth were a mismatch from the first. Despite its very real academic excellence, the college's reputation in popular culture—movies, television, and books—has frequently revolved around Dartmouth's penchant for wild parties and out-of-control drinking.

Chris Miller, who graduated from Dartmouth about a dozen years after Fred Rogers was there, wrote the script for the famed movie *Animal House*. Miller is said to have based the movie on his own Dartmouth fraternity, Alpha Delta Phi.[5]

Fred soon moved out of his dorm room and moved in with his French teacher, who gave him a more civilized living environment and helped him develop his considerable skills with language. At the same time, his passion for music began to reassert itself. Nevertheless, by all accounts, Fred was lonely and a bit homesick.

ENSCONCED IN THE DEEP FREEZE of a New Hampshire winter, not exactly friendless but still somewhat lonely and feeling out of place, Fred thought of home, and of music. And he did what he had done in high school: He found a way to turn adversity to a focus on what he wanted to study and where he wanted his life to go in the future.

This was a pivotal theme of Rogers's life: From his earliest years, he took his fears, his loneliness and isolation, and his insecurities and turned them to his advantage. Somehow, he was almost always able to take his feelings into a place of deep introspection and emerge with a fresh, and often brilliant, new direction. He did this as a child, as a high school student, and throughout his life as a writer, an educator, and a television producer.

Rogers's favorite quotation, which he often cited and which he kept framed near his desk in his office, came from *The Little Prince*, by the French author, airplane pilot, and war hero Antoine de Saint-Exupéry: "*L'essentiel est invisible pour les yeux.*" In English translation, the full passage reads: "And now here is my secret, a very simple secret: It is only with the heart that one can see rightly; what is essential is invisible to the eye."[6]

Fred Rogers took profound stock of his feelings to find meaning, often spiritual meaning, that he could turn into understanding, and eventually into the sort of serious focus that could yield power. It was based on a profound conviction that what's on the surface—the everyday pain and frustration and small joys of life—is not what is essential. The essential is to be found in depth and introspection, in searching for meaning, and then finding the truth that comes from that meaning. For Fred Rogers and for Saint-Exupéry, truth always came from the heart, not from an overintellectualization of life.

Saint-Exupéry died on a flight from North Africa over the Mediterranean Sea near the end of World War II, just as Rogers was excelling in high school back in western Pennsylvania. Saint-Exupéry inspired Fred Rogers to think, to seek, to understand, and to accept. As a seeker who could go deep below the surface and help children—and their grown-ups, for that matter—find the essential, Fred Rogers imparted what he'd gone through himself as he shaped his life, not in spite of his fears and insecurities, but because he could turn them into an education.

At Dartmouth, he didn't cry and complain, or drop out of college and wander around the country trying to find himself. He went back to the essential in his life—to music. In it, he found the answer that helped him move ahead.

And Fred Rogers had some good luck: The teacher to whom he went for guidance, the cellist Arnold Kvam, turned out to be a great friend.[7] Professor Kvam, who served for many years as the director of the Handel Society at Dartmouth, had recently transferred from Rollins College in Winter Park, Florida. Part of his mission in New Hampshire was to build a strong music program for Dartmouth. But that was going to take years. Kvam told Rogers he couldn't offer a music major at Dartmouth until he had evolved a strong enough department to support one.

After judging Fred Rogers's musical skills and his dedication, Professor Kvam promptly directed him south to Rollins: "Fred, we won't have this department ready for you in the four years that you'll be here. Why don't you look at the place that I just came from?"[8]

Later, Fred Rogers recalled that through his conversations with Kvam, he moved toward switching his major from Romance languages to music, and he was willing to leave Dartmouth if needed. At Kvam's suggestion, Rogers considered a trip down to Florida to look at Rollins, with its strong program in music that he could major in right away.

Fred took part of his Easter break to fly down to northern Florida.[9] He knew Rollins would be a bit of a comedown academically from Dartmouth; although Rollins today enjoys a reputation as one of the best colleges in the United States, it was not operating at that level back in 1948. Fred's parents probably suffered a pang when he told them he was thinking of leaving the vaunted Ivy League for a smaller school in the South.

Professor Kvam had told a group of students in the Conservatory of Music at Rollins College about the young man from Dartmouth with real talent as a pianist. On the spur of the moment, they decided to jump in a car and drive out to the airport to meet him.[10]

One of the young music majors in the car was Joanne Byrd from Jacksonville, Florida, a highly talented pianist who was among the leaders in the music department and one of the most popular girls in school. Pictures of Joanne from around that time show a bright, smiling, broad-faced girl, very pretty, with a turned-up nose and a mischievous look on her face. Joanne was a very accomplished student, but she was also a great lover of fun, with a puckish sense of humor and a powerful exuberance. Joanne was one of the instigators of the spontaneous group trip to the airport.

With no other plan than to ride out to the airport to meet the young musician from Dartmouth and take stock of him—would they welcome him aboard, or decide he wasn't the right fit?—Joanne and her chums sang songs, gossiped, and traded speculations about Fred as they cruised through the warm Florida sunshine to meet his plane.

Years later, Joanne remembered: "We piled into the antique Franklin that had lots of room. We were hanging out the windows of the car when he came out. We grabbed him, and took him right with us, and made him one of us.

"He blended in so well. We took him first to the music department, and to the practice rooms. He sat right down and started playing some pop stuff. And we were so impressed, because none of us could do that. We couldn't just sit down and play jazz. And he could. He could do it all."[11]

Joanne added that the twenty or so music majors, many of whom came to greet Fred, were all part of a "very tight" group of friends who shared the same interests and almost always socialized together. But just as nothing had clicked into place for Fred up north at Dartmouth, everything seemed to click at Rollins, and the school accepted his transfer application immediately.[12]

"Rollins was just the opposite of Dartmouth, I felt," said Fred later. "Dartmouth was very cold, and Rollins was very warm. I just felt so much at home there. And so the next year I went to Rollins. I had had two years at Dartmouth, and I got a one-year credit (for his Dartmouth studies) at Rollins. And there, [I] declared a music major, in composition."[13]

Fred had made a transition to a new world: relaxed, warm and friendly and open, defined by good humor and a sense of fun, as opposed to macho intensity. And it was a world completely characterized by a love of music, at least at the Conservatory. It was perfect, and it was to be a very happy time for Fred.

One of his new friends there, the pianist Jeannine Morrison (who later became a performance partner with Joanne, playing and recording piano duets) recalls, "He was all smiles and happy to be there. He said, 'Oh, this is like . . . heaven after Dartmouth.' "[14]

4.

LOVE AND MUSIC

JOANNE BYRD grew up in Jacksonville, Florida, in the 1930s, before ubiquitous air-conditioning made the deep South's heat and humidity more bearable. But the heat didn't bother the energetic and cheerful little girl, who spent most of her days biking around the neighborhood and playing outside with other children. When she came inside to play the piano, Joanne would sometimes have to wipe the damp keys with a cloth or a handkerchief.[1]

Like her future husband, Fred Rogers, Joanne grew up as an only child, doted on by a mother and father who each tried to convey the best of their own lives to their bright and promising daughter. Her father gave her a lifelong appreciation of books, reading, and language, and her mother bequeathed a passion for music.

Wyatt Adolphus Byrd, known to all his friends as "Admiral" (a joking reference to the famed polar explorer and aviator Admiral Richard E. Byrd), was a literary man who always had a book underway, read to his daughter, gently corrected her grammar, and took her on frequent visits to the local library.[2] He grew up in Alabama, dreaming of becoming a school teacher. And he was, for a while.

"I think he taught in a little, one-room schoolhouse in Alabama," says Joanne. "He loved it. But he didn't get paid anything much. Because of the Depression, he went into sales, selling coffee. He was traveling a lot when he met my mother, and it was her brother-in-law who introduced her to him. The brother-in-law had hired him to do the coffee selling."[3]

Byrd became a traveling salesman, working his way across the South selling wholesale to retailers from Texas to Florida. The highlight of that part of his career was the time he slept soundly through the night in a hotel room in Key West and woke up the next morning to discover that half the hotel had been removed by a hurricane.[4]

For Byrd, work as a salesman lost its appeal during the Depression. He finally managed to nail down a better-paying, secure job with the US Postal Service in Jacksonville. It was there that he spent so much time nurturing his young daughter's appetite for books and learning, in effect, keeping his teaching career going.

Wyatt Byrd sometimes rode on trains in the mail car, dropping off mail bags of letters in small towns in the South. And he would often take his little daughter to see the mail car when the Byrd family traveled.

"He was on the train a lot, sorting the mail," recalls Joanne. "He threw it out to the cow catcher or whatever they called it."[5] In fact, only the most adroit Postal Service employees worked the mail cars; they had to be able to kick a full mail bag out the door of a speeding train into a "catcher arm" at local stations where the trains didn't stop. Joanne was beamingly proud of her father's skills.

Joanne's intrepid nature as a little girl stayed with her for the rest of her life and helped advance her successful career as a performing musician. But one time the little girl became truly terrified.

"A teenage neighbor who taught Sunday school classes at church told us about the lesson of the second coming of Christ. She said, 'He's going—he will come again, and we will never know when, or where it will happen. Why . . . it could happen tomorrow.' All of a sudden, I could feel my whole body flush. I absolutely panicked.

"I must have been around six or seven. I ran out of the [neighbor's] house over to my mother, crying as if my heart would break. She said to me, 'What is the matter? Are you hurt?'

"And I said, 'No, no, no . . . but Mary Maud said that Jesus is coming tomorrow, and I don't want him to come.'

"I still feel that way. I'm not ready. But Fred was. Fred was ready for him to come."[6]

The family of Joanne's mother, Ebra Edwards Byrd, was much more religious and devoted to churchgoing in the Southern Baptist tradition than Wyatt Byrd's family. Ebra Byrd's father owned a large tenant-farming operation in the southern part of the state of Georgia. But Joanne never became as dedicated a churchgoer as Fred Rogers. Though Joanne remained a Christian her whole life, she had a more skeptical nature that caused her to question everything she learned and heard, including religion.

According to Joanne's recollections, "My father was a very spiritual person, but not interested in organized religion. My mother had grown up in a very religious atmosphere as a Southern Baptist. In fact, every summer, there was a family reunion held at the little church out in the country. My grandparents' church service always involved foot washing as part of the ceremony. I believe it was more important to them than Communion."[7]

But Joanne's mother's most important contribution to her daughter's life wasn't the church; it was music. Ebra loved the piano, the radio, and the phonograph. Over time, she learned how to play some of her favorite tunes, mostly ragtime, by ear. She talked to Joanne about the music she loved and gave her a feeling for melody and rhythm at the earliest age.

While Wyatt would sit reading his books, Ebra and Joanne would listen to music on the radio and try to pick out tunes on the piano. Sometimes when Joanne was at the piano, just learning a few of the keys, her mother would sit nearby thumbing through a magazine and listening to the notes from her daughter's playing, nodding approvingly.

"She didn't read music," recalls Joanne. "As I learned to read music, she learned a little bit about reading music. And she would sit with me at the piano—because I started when I was five—and she would sit with me at the piano for all my practice time, and it was wonderful, because I wasn't alone. I can't say enough about that for young children and music, that if their parents can invest that time with them, it makes it a less solitary thing."[8]

Like Fred Rogers, Joanne enjoyed a rich and fully engaging childhood because of the direct involvement of parents who played with her, talked with her, and shared the most important things in their lives.

Joanne's music education took a powerful turn when she was just five years old. Her best friend, Myra Lee—sister to the teenage girl who so frightened Joanne with stories of the second coming of Christ—lived right across the street from the second-floor apartment the Byrds rented from an owner who lived on the first floor. Joanne would play in the street with Myra, and go over to the Lees' house to play in the yard.

Occasionally, Joanne would go into the neighbor's house and play their piano. The teenage sister, Mary Maud, walked back to Joanne's house with her after one such session and told Joanne's parents, "I think she's very talented, and I'd love her to meet my piano teacher."[9] Joanne's mother was impressed that a teenager would make the effort to help a five-year-old; and when Mary Maud offered to go with Ebra and Joanne to meet the music teacher, Louise Norton, the three of them made the trip together.[10]

That changed everything. Louise Norton didn't take students so young as Joanne—preferring to wait until they were about seven—but she, too, was impressed with the little girl's musical talent, and her upbeat, dedicated nature. She agreed to take Joanne on as a student if Ebra would help teach her the musical scales. Joanne Rogers's music career was launched.

Louise Norton stuck with Joanne Rogers for thirteen years of instruction, teaching her most of what she learned about music and playing the piano, instilling in her a great love for the power and beauty of music, and, eventually, pushing Joanne to pursue her studies further in college.[11] With Norton's encouragement, Joanne entered music competitions and won a National Guild of Piano Teachers scholarship that took her to Rollins College.[12]

Were it not for the care and dedication of Louise Norton—and of course the thoughtfulness of Mary Maud Lee—Joanne's life with music and with Fred Rogers might have turned out quite differently.

Joanne got to Rollins a couple of years ahead of Fred, who was on his detour to Dartmouth the year Joanne entered the Conservatory of Music at Rollins College, which had a very strong reputation for the training of performance musicians. Joanne, who aspired to make a career as a pianist performing classical music, threw herself with dedication into her studies.

She aspired to a "music performance degree," a bachelor of music degree that establishes the credentials of the degree holder. Joanne's social life revolved around the other students in the conservatory. Though she and her friends were lighthearted, constantly cracking jokes, their dedication to their studies precluded an expansive social life. The work of a student at the conservatory included the usual classwork and homework that students in all disciplines faced, plus endless sessions of practicing their instruments. It was grueling, and though Rollins enjoyed a reputation at that time as a college with a strong student social life, Joanne hardly had even a date or a night out until Fred Rogers showed up.

When he did, the two of them fell immediately into a strong friendship that put them together much of the time, and eventually led to their being defined as a "couple" on campus. Though formal dates were rare, Fred and Joanne hung out together all the time. They were both shy, from religious backgrounds, and most of the time just holding hands was as physical as their connection became.

"I really liked him a lot," recalls Joanne. "But . . . we didn't date singly very much, except for dances. And I would always invite him to the sorority dance . . . the two years I was there with him."[13]

Although Joanne was impressed with Fred's musical abilities, she also thought he might wind up running an orphanage. He talked about children and their education all the time, and he often went to visit nursery school classes and children's centers to observe the children and their teachers, and to develop his own thoughts on education. She remembers that she had never encountered quite such a focused young man, and that his focus seemed to center around children as well as music.

A big part of their burgeoning relationship was based on humor: Each had a strong, sometimes arch, sense of humor. Their sense of fun matched up; they had a very similar, jocular view of life, and they always enjoyed the same jokes.

Fred was aware of his family's wealth, and he was sensitive to people seeing him in the context of that wealth. Joanne, who came from a very different background, made a constant joke of the one luxury item she owned, a small diamond ring she got from her mother, and what she portrayed as Fred's attraction to it: "It was a little-finger ring that had diamonds all around it, and inside. It was nothing but diamonds, kind of a triangular shape, very, very charming. So I said, 'I know you like me for my diamonds.'"[14]

She teased him relentlessly: "You know, there are lots of people here at Rollins who have money—a lot," she told him. "And a lot who have a lot more than you do."

While visiting a classmate from the nearby town of Sanford, Florida, Joanne and Fred had an encounter that sparked their mutual sense of humor. "His father owned an upholstery company," says Joanne of their friend, "a car upholstery company. . . . [And] the, sort of, village character drove the cab in that town. A woman . . . very kind of boisterous. And so she came to [our friend's father] and said, 'Larry, my cab is a mess and I need new seats. Look—here—the springs are coming through.'"

When the cab driver came back later to pick up her taxi with its new upholstery, she was delighted with the comfort of the new seats and thanked the upholsterer profusely.

"Larry, this makes my sweet ass smile," she said with feeling.[15]

Fred and Joanne loved the story. For the rest of their lives, when they were traveling anywhere and were tired and finally got to sit down and rest, one would turn to the other with a mischievous grin and say, "Oh, this makes my sweet ass smile."

Joanne always felt that their shared sense of humor, as well as her pragmatic nature, were keys to the success of their relationship: "I think, throughout our life, maybe I brought a little more of the light side of life to him. I think I'm a practical person. And I guess I was less frightening to him than some of the other girls might have been. I think he liked it that I was not extravagant. And I liked it that I was not extravagant."[16]

Their jokes, and their shared sense of life as an adventure that is made more exciting if you don't take yourself too seriously all forged the bonds of their relationship. Fred and Joanne shared the same traits with the tight-knit group of students in the Conservatory that formed their almost exclusive social network at Rollins.

One of those friends, Jeannine Morrison, remembers Fred as something of a "cutup," a class clown who loved pranks. One of the things Morrison recalls is that Fred altered the language of a plaque on campus to make it a joke: "Outside of our sorority house was a lovely marble plaque, etched, that said, 'Life Is for Service.' Fred was always covering up the 'ser' so that it read, 'Life Is for vice.' I have photographs of that, where he blanked it out one time. So, just a lot of laughs. That's how he and Joanne, I think, really got to know one another a little better. . . . He just always thought she was so amusing and so funny and so upbeat; which she is, of course."[17]

Jeannine Morrison also remembers that as soon as Fred learned that her father had insured her hands to protect the value of a future career as a pianist, he would pretend to try to close her hands in the car door to collect the insurance.

But Fred could have a deadly serious side as well, and at one point, he even became something of a campus activist. When the revered and beloved leader of Rollins College, Hamilton Holt, retired after twenty-four years as president, a new president was brought in from the University of Chicago and almost immediately became controversial within the faculty and the student body.

According to Joanne's recollections, the new president set out to make changes quickly at the college and often did so without consulting others: "He didn't make himself popular right away. . . . We were used to having a president who got the whole college together and said, 'Now, we're thinking about doing this or that or the other thing. And we want the Rollins family to know about it, and what do you think?' "[18]

Before long, there was an active movement on the campus to have the new president removed, and somewhat uncharacteristically, Fred Rogers became a leader. A strong collaboration between students and faculty finally led to the replacement of the new president with one who took the more traditional Rollins approach of collaboration.

One of the interesting aspects of Fred's role on campus in this period—Joanne called him a "rabble-rouser"—is that he never repeated it later in life. Fred eschewed politics, and even much public discussion of political issues, for most of his career. A registered Republican, his family knew him as a holder of very progressive and inclusive views on social issues; but for the most part he kept these views in the family and avoided engagement in almost any kind of politics, local, national, or organizational. The only exception was his support for his good friend H. John Heinz III when Heinz ran for the US House and, later, the Senate from Pennsylvania—but even that endorsement was staged in the background rather than in a highly public way.

Unlike high school and Dartmouth, where Fred was a bit of a loner, he had a lot of friends at Rollins; as Joanne recalls, he was one of the most popular students on campus.

Fred was deeply wounded when one of those friends decided that it offended his sense of ethics to socialize with people who came from a background of privilege and wealth. He dropped Fred, which, to Joanne's annoyance, further worried Fred about his family's money.

"Of course, that all passed over," says Joanne. "But it hurt Fred so badly, because he really, really liked this young man. But he had another friend, who was a roommate that he liked very much. And they remained friends over the years. So, he had a lot of good friends in college."[19]

One of Fred and Joanne's best friends at Rollins was the singer John Reardon, who went to New York after graduation. Reardon became famous as one of the leading baritones of his time, singing with the New York Metropolitan Opera from 1965 to 1977 and making many appearances on television, including on *Mister Rogers' Neighborhood.*

Another lasting friendship Fred forged at Rollins was with his French teacher, Baroness von Boecop, known colloquially at the college as "The Baroness." She had come to the United States as a refugee during World War II and taken a teaching position at Rollins, and she was also the director of a French center on campus, La Maison Provençale. Fred minored in French, and he and the Baroness would hold all their conversations in French.

According to Joanne, "She had been married to a Dutch baron.

She was a wonderful French teacher, because she wanted things exactly right. Fred was a wonderful student, and he did all sorts of things for her because she admired him."[20]

Most importantly, Baroness von Boecop pushed Fred in other ways than his language studies. She encouraged Rogers to pursue excellence, to set high standards for himself. And she urged Fred to get into the theater and gain experience as a performer.

"She encouraged me to do stuff on the stage," recalled Fred years later in an interview. "I had never done anything on the stage. But she forced me in . . . in these little French productions. . . . I don't think I ever wanted to be on the stage. . . . [I'd] much rather [be] doing things in the background."[21]

As Joanne got to know von Boecop better, she developed a more jaundiced opinion of "The Baroness" and viewed her as something of a social climber. Joanne suggested that von Boecop may have found the Rogers family's wealth attractive: "She was one of the most snobbish people that I have ever known. . . . I never felt that she liked me, and I didn't care for her much." She particularly liked Fred's company, Joanne said, "Because Fred came from an upper-middle-class, more elite family, so he appealed to the snobbish side."[22]

That appeal eventually led to a long trip to Europe that Fred made with The Baroness to hone his skills as a speaker and writer of French.

According to Joanne's recollection, von Boecop said, "I want to take you to Europe, and we're not going to speak any English."[23] Joanne remembers it was the summer after Fred's first year at Rollins that he and von Boecop took their trip together: "They visited friends of hers in Paris, in Brussels, and in Amsterdam, I believe—all over Europe.[24]

"He had to listen to her friends, to speak to them and socialize," says Joanne. "During that time, he really did become very fluent, and she was a taskmaster: The mouth must be a certain way and the sounds must be exact, to the point where he was very, very good. I give her credit for that; she was a wonderful teacher."[25]

One of the most unusual aspects of the trip to Europe was Fred's "adoption" of a young French orphan. Von Boecop arranged a visit to a Catholic orphanage run by French priests. There Fred met Gilbert Bonin, a young boy who showed great intellectual promise, according to his teachers.[26]

Fred and his family informally "adopted" Bonin, paying for and guiding his education. At one point, Fred's mother wanted to bring Bonin to the United States, but von Boecop resisted, arguing that the boy would be better off remaining in his native land. The proof of this came years later, when Bonin forged a highly successful business career as one of the top executives at the French cheese company La Vache Qui Rit (The Laughing Cow). Fred stayed in touch with Bonin for the rest of his life, writing letters and visiting occasionally in Paris.

Baroness von Boecop not only started Fred on the stage, she also gave him one of his earliest experiences shaping the education and development of a young child. Fred Rogers always held on to his friends and kept them close, and he stayed in touch with The Baroness until her death in 1983. Fred learned about her passing in a letter from Gilbert Bonin. When he heard of von Boecop's death, he told his friend Jeannine Morrison that he was so glad he'd had a five-day visit with her in France just a year earlier.[27]

Rogers was an outstanding student at Rollins, performing particularly well in his music and French classes, but he worried constantly about his grades and drove his friends crazy with anxious complaints about how poorly he was faring in his studies.

Joanne recalls that Fred "was always fearful he was going to fail. And he would always say, 'Oh, I know I flunked that. I just know it.'

"And we'd all get so upset about it for him. And he always came out with an A. We finally said to him, 'We're not worrying about you anymore!' Here we were all with bad—not bad grades, but worse than he had. [And] he had the most difficult teacher in the music department."[28]

Professor John Carter challenged Fred because he saw such great talent in his pupil. They also became great friends and stayed in touch after Fred and Joanne left college.

Fred Rogers did so well in his studies that he graduated magna cum laude from Rollins in 1951, with a bachelor of music degree.

One of the distractions Fred had to cope with at Rollins was the regular arrival of his whole family during the winter months. It had been the habit of the Rogers family—Jim, Nancy, their young daughter Laney, and often a coterie of friends—to travel each winter down to the Belleview Biltmore Hotel in Belleair, Florida, for a couple of months' vacation away from the cold of western Pennsylvania. But once Fred enrolled in Rollins, the family changed their plans and came to Winter Park, the home of Rollins College, to be near Fred.

Although Fred appreciated his parents' company, he was also a bit leery of what seemed to him to be their somewhat ostentatious living circumstances in Winter Park. The Rogers family would rent a large villa and arrive with cars and friends and servants. Fred did take Joanne and some of his other friends over to visit with his parents, but he worried anew about seeming too wealthy to the other Rollins students.

According to the recollections of Jeannine Morrison, "I remember that one of the automobiles that they drove was a convertible, and Laney at the time was, I think, eleven years old, and she was taking swimming lessons at Rollins. She would leave, wrapped in a towel in her bathing suit, [and] sit in the back of this convertible while Grant, the chauffeur, drove her back to the house. She would sit propped up like Madame [de] Pompadour, and Fred would say, 'Oh my goodness, look at Laney. Isn't that disgusting.'"[29]

Fred may have felt defensive about his family's wealth, but for the most part, he adored Laney, who thought of him as an ideal older brother. He included her in activities with his friends, teaching her about music and books and many other things, and never got angry with her. They remained close friends all their adult lives.

As to riding with the chauffeur, Grant Ross, Laney thought of Ross as a friend, not as a servant: "I always said Grant was my best friend," said Laney years later in an interview. "Grant was a chauffeur, he was a butler, he served at the dinner table, he did everything; he worked in the garden, he just did everything. But Grant was my best friend."[30]

When Ross was in the hospital in Maryland near the Oldfields School, a girls' boarding school north of Baltimore where the young

Laney was enrolled, she rushed over to meet her parents at the hospital. When she threw her arms around his neck, another patient in the ward upbraided Nancy Rogers for letting her young daughter hug a black man.

"She doesn't know the difference," said Nancy, explaining that Laney, like Fred, had been brought up to believe there's no difference between people of different races.[31]

Fred sometimes joined his parents' social life during their visits to Winter Park. He would bring a few of his college friends over to spend the weekend at his family's rented house, assigning rooms by writing up individual name cards and tacking them to bedroom doors, along with a saying on each card that reflected Fred's appreciation of each person.

"He did celebrate his twenty-first birthday while his parents were there," recalls Morrison, "and they had a big celebration at the house that they had rented . . . the back of the house fronted on Lake Maitland. He had an inboard motor boat, his father did, and he used it, of course, and water skis, and we would go there and just have a grand time."[32]

But Fred was always careful to manage his own time in the most thoughtful and deliberate way, and he honed his unique ability to focus on what was important to him, undistracted by his family or his friends. He kept that focus on music, the original purpose that had brought him to Winter Park, Florida, in the first place.

In effect, he began his career as a composer at Rollins, a career that would include the composition of about two hundred songs and fourteen operas. Fred Rogers was still a student at Rollins when he wrote the satirical lyrics to "Row, Row, Row Your Boat" that King Friday would regularly sing on the *Neighborhood*. And it was there that he began his first opera, *Josephine the Short-Neck Giraffe*. Morrison remembers that in the original version, written in French, Josephine gets a long neck by the end of the opera. But Fred changed it when the opera was performed on his program on PBS. With help from her friends, Josephine accepts who she is and is at peace with a short neck.

At Rollins, Fred Rogers also composed a more formal piece of music entitled "Three-Voice Fugue, for cello, viola and violin." And he wrote a libretto, entitled "Lyric Poems (by James Joyce)," and a piece composed for performance by Jeannine Morrison, "Variations on a Theme of Chopin." Morrison kept her copy of the "Variations" and played it in concert several times, including once with the Pittsburgh Symphony Orchestra. When a musician friend of hers heard it performed, he wanted to take it to his publisher, but Fred demurred.[33]

"He said, 'No, those were written at Rollins College, and they were written for Jeannine, and I don't want them played by anyone else.' I thought that was very moving," says Morrison. She elaborates: "Aside from that, he probably said to himself, 'They're not good enough to publish.' Because that was always his thing, 'not good enough' or 'not quite up to par' or some such expression."[34]

During Fred's last year at Rollins, Joanne—who was a year ahead of Fred because of the year he lost transferring from Dartmouth—had already gone on to graduate studies at Florida State University in Tallahassee, about 250 miles away. She and Fred corresponded, but she didn't hear as much from him as she had expected. She did hear from some of her friends there that Fred was occasionally dating other girls. She still cared a great deal for Fred and wasn't quite sure how she might fit into his future.

Now Fred needed to figure out exactly what he would do after his own graduation. His father was still hoping Fred might join him in business back in Latrobe, but Fred told Jim Rogers he had been accepted at the Western Theological Seminary, and that he was thinking of pursuing a career as a Presbyterian minister.

But then Fred took a trip home from college during Easter break of his senior year and ran smack into the new thing that was going to change the world, and the life of Fred Rogers.

IN 1951, VERY FEW American households even had television sets. A TV was a luxury and, in many quarters, a curiosity. Few could have predicted the drastic way it would transform popular and national culture.

The Rogers family had one of the first televisions in Latrobe, a small, ten-inch set on four spindly legs in the "music room," or parlor, of their house. Fred Rogers first encountered the television during Easter Break, and he chose to tune into children's programs because of his strong interest in young children and education.

Fred Rogers thought what he saw was awful.

"I went home my senior year for a vacation in Latrobe, and I saw this new thing called television," said Fred years later. "And I saw people dressed in some kind of costumes, literally throwing pies in each other's faces. I was astounded at that."[35]

Television appalled and attracted him at the same time. Fred instinctively understood the extraordinary power of the medium, even as others saw it merely as a diversion or a minor entertainment. And he also understood its potential for education, perhaps more fully than anyone else at the time.

But even though Fred Rogers had the foresight to see the potential of the new medium, he was also sickened by the crass, low-grade humor of the television he saw.

"And I thought: This could be a wonderful tool for education, why is it being used this way? And so I said to my parents, 'You know, I don't think I'll go to seminary right away; I think maybe I'll go into television. . . . Let's see what we can do with this.'"[36]

Jeannine Morrison reports that when Fred got back to college after the Easter break, he confided to friends that he'd like to do something for children, something educational but "lighthearted": "He just thought it was so sad that children didn't have anything of substance to relate to. He was very much engrossed in the idea that it should be constant, that the person doing the show should always be the same. He started thinking seriously that he would like to do something really worthwhile for children."[37]

Given Fred's changing plans, there were some tense moments between him and his father—who had accepted the seminary but now was disappointed yet again by Fred's new idea. His mother, who had been pleased at the idea of Fred as a Presbyterian minister, now had to conceive of her son in television. But they accommodated Fred's new direction with their characteristic grace.

"The way our family was, I didn't hear a lot about it," Laney said later. "I know that that summer there was tension and I think disappointment, but Fred went off to New York.

"I don't think there was any idea of, 'Well, you go out on your own if you're going to do that.' Mother and Dad were not like that at all. They were, in fact, very supportive of whatever we wanted to do. They just wanted the best for everybody. They actually sent his piano to New York City. Took it up, took the window out, and shipped this thing through the window."[38]

Although Fred's decision might seem like a spur-of-the-moment reaction on the part of a college senior trying to figure out what to do with his life, in fact it was something much more deliberate. Fred Rogers was interested in lots of things: in religion, in becoming a minister, in music composition, in playing the piano, in children and education—and, now, in television production. Because of his well-developed ability to focus and to think his way over the hurdles he encountered in life, he could envision what television might offer to children and to himself.

He understood that the right kind of programming, grounded in a good knowledge of child development, could become a highly inventive and creative way to help young viewers. And he understood that television could give him a unique opportunity to marry his skills in music and entertainment with his interest in children's education. Fred saw that there could be a career opportunity that would blend his aspirations in the more structured field of education with his powerful, more free-form creative instincts. He saw the chance to be both an educator and an artist, and he knew right away that he wanted it.

In a July 22, 2000, interview, just a few years before his death, Rogers articulated this early vision. Right away, he could see what he'd like to offer on a television program: "I'd love to have guests and present a whole smorgasbord of ways for the children to choose. Some child might choose painting, some child might choose playing the cello.

There are so many ways of saying who we are, and how we feel. Ways that don't hurt anybody. And it seems to me that this is a great gift."[39]

It was a perfect solution for this complex young man—so sensitive and yet so very deliberate in understanding and advancing his own life.

JOANNE CAME BACK to Rollins in 1951 for Fred's graduation. A lot of her other friends were graduating in Fred's class, too, but she especially wanted to see Fred and be present for the awarding of his bachelor's degree.

"I did not get back to hear his senior recital," recalls Joanne, "but I did come back for his graduation. . . . I knew it would be important. . . . And I thought he would be pleased if I did so."[40]

Joanne found that she and Fred could pick up their close relationship almost without a pause: "Well, it was just like, take up again where we had been. And there wasn't any awkwardness, or—although, I was probably a little more cautious, because I knew that he had dated other girls that year."[41]

Joanne could sense Fred's excitement about his bold, new idea of going into television production, and she knew he was making a very big, strategic decision for his future. Intuitively, she understood the importance of something that could bring together music, creativity, children, education, and theater, all in one career for Fred Rogers.

But she also understood that if Fred went to New York in the coming year while she was finishing her second year at Florida State, they would not be just 250 miles apart, as they had been during the past year—they would be 1,000 miles apart. What would happen to their relationship?

PART II

———

The real issue in life is not how many blessings
we have, but what we do with our blessings.
Some people have many blessings and hoard them.
Some have few and give everything away.

—FRED ROGERS

5.

BASIC TRAINING

WHILE JOANNE BYRD was still working on her master's degree in music at Florida State University in Tallahassee, Fred Rogers was ready to move to New York. Given the many excursions he'd made to the city growing up, he knew just where the best neighborhoods were. Fred got a one-bedroom apartment on the Upper East Side, at 9 East Seventy-Fifth Street, one of the loveliest and safest areas of Manhattan.[1]

With a little help from his father, Fred got a job as an apprentice at the National Broadcasting Company (NBC), a division of the Radio Corporation of America (RCA), in which the Rogers family was a major stock holder.[2] He started work on October 1, 1951, a few months after his graduation from Rollins. To advance his musical skills while he began work in television, Fred had his Steinway piano—the concert grand his grandmother had bought him fifteen years earlier—delivered to his new apartment.

Down in Florida, in her second and last full year in graduate school, Joanne rented a room in the home of her piano professor, Ernst von Dohnányi, the Hungarian composer and conductor who had come to Florida State in 1949, after World War II. For the rest of her career, Joanne felt that her skills as a pianist had received remarkable development during the time at Florida State and she continued her studies with Dohnányi, on and off, until his death in 1960.

And, during her time in Tallahassee, Joanne got the opportunity to meet her teacher's grandson, Christoph von Dohnányi, who came from his home in Germany to study with his grandfather. Christoph felt insecure with the English language when he first arrived, so Joanne and her friends enjoyed adding to his vocabulary.[3]

Joanne and Christoph became friends, a friendship that later included Fred. The three stayed in touch throughout their lives, and both Fred and Joanne took pleasure in the scope of Christoph's successful career as a conductor, highlighted by nearly twenty years as music director of the Cleveland Symphony Orchestra, one of the finest symphony orchestras in the world.

During her first year at Florida State, when Fred was still at Rollins College, Joanne had heard little from him, which surprised her. Now that Fred was in New York, once again Joanne had little correspondence with him. From friends, she heard that he was very busy with his new life. For the second time in as many years, Joanne was puzzled and unsure where their relationship might lead in the future.

She got a letter from her good friend Jeannine Morrison, who was in New York studying music. Jeannine was seeing a lot of Fred, and as they had their last year at Rollins, they were dating in a casual and occasional fashion. Fred gave Jeannine a key to his apartment so she could practice on the Steinway. Jeannine and Fred later said that theirs was a friendship, not a romantic relationship.[4]

In fact, both Fred and Joanne were a bit confused about where their relationship might be heading. They talked only once in while on the phone, exchanged a few letters, and each casually dated other people. But they knew they still cared a great deal about each other; more than anything else, it was the distance between them that was making it difficult to move forward with a romantic relationship.

Then Joanne and Christophe von Dohnányi went together to attend a music conference in St. Petersburg, Florida. Joanne remembered Fred's parents very fondly, and she remembered that now that Fred was gone from Winter Park, they were back to vacationing at the Belleview Biltmore Hotel in Belleair, on the Gulf of Mexico coast just north of St. Petersburg. Joanne still felt as if she was a good friend of Jim and Nancy Rogers, and she thought it would be nice for them to meet Christophe.

When they stopped in at the large house that Jim and Nancy were renting on the grounds of the hotel, Joanne noticed that Fred's parents were closely observing them, and that they took note of the fact that Joanne and Christophe were traveling together.[5]

Joanne never found out whether Fred's parents got in touch with him to mention that they had seen Joanne Byrd traveling with another young man, but she thinks they probably gave him a call. And she was amazed that, just a couple of weeks later, she got a letter from Fred proposing marriage. She hesitated just long enough to think over her choice, and then quickly decided. She went to a phone booth and called Fred's number in New York.

She was a little nervous while she waited for Fred to answer; as Joanne looked around, some graffiti on the inside wall of the booth caught her attention. When Fred picked up the line, Joanne said hello and then nervously blurted out, "Shit," extemporaneously citing the graffiti.

But Fred was not rattled; he laughed, took it all in good-natured stride, and the conversation soon came back to his proposal. The next word Joanne blurted out was, "Yes," and Fred and Joanne were engaged to be married.

Before Fred's letter came, Joanne had been wondering whether Fred and Jeannine might be the ones to tie the knot; and Fred had been worrying that Joanne might marry Christophe.[6] Now Joanne Byrd was to become Joanne Rogers. The more she thought about Fred Rogers—so funny and so serious at the same time—she knew they would be the right match. Fred also felt absolutely sure, and he wanted a wedding as soon as possible. To cement the relationship, he soon flew down for Joanne's graduation from Florida State with an engagement ring tucked safely into his pocket.

In Tallahassee, Fred asked Joanne to take him to the Episcopal church very near the Florida State campus where she went to church, so he could visualize her there.[7] Joanne and Fred sat together in a pew and looked up to where Joanne sang with the choir.

Fred pulled the engagement ring out of his pocket, placed it on Joanne's ring finger, and then sealed the engagement with what Joanne recalls as a "very romantic" kiss. Joanne remembers: "I had always called him Roge. I called him Roge from early times, because his grandmother called him that."[8]

Now they needed to make some wedding plans. After consulting with their respective parents, Fred and Joanne decided they would get married in early July 1952. Fred's parents and his grandmother Nancy McFeely were reluctant to tackle the Florida heat and humidity in the summer. Both the Rogers and Byrd families agreed on New York, where Fred was living and where Joanne would join him.

The wedding was not held in the New York Presbyterian Church that Fred usually attended; Joanne remembered later that the minister there had probably been out of town. They settled on the High Episcopal Church of the Resurrection on East Seventy-Fourth Street. The service was followed by a very elegant reception at the Carlyle, located at the corner of Seventy-Sixth Street and Madison Avenue, near Fred's Upper East Side apartment.[9] Designed in Art Deco style and named after the Scottish essayist Thomas Carlyle, the hotel has a long history as one of the most fashionable establishments in the city. Not long after the Rogerses' wedding, John F. Kennedy leased a thirty-fourth-floor apartment there, which he kept during his presidency.

Fred and Joanne went to Montreal on their way to Europe for their honeymoon. They traveled there by train and took a river cruise out along the Saint Lawrence River and back. Fred enjoyed the opportunity to polish his great skills with the French language; Joanne recalls that their taxi driver just assumed that Fred was French: "He said to me, 'How is it that you, an American, are married to a Frenchman?'"[10]

Then they headed right back to New York City, where Joanne moved into his one-bedroom apartment and Fred hurried back to his work at NBC. Fred later said that it was his music degree from Rollins that got him a job at NBC. No doubt, it helped: NBC's programming then included a lot of shows that emphasized or featured music. But there was another factor: Fred's loyal and considerate father, always on the alert for a chance to help a family member or a friend.

Or even an acquaintance, for that matter: Jim Rogers once wrote a large check to a waitress at a restaurant after she told him she was putting all her tips toward her college tuition, and he set aside a large contribution from his own stocks and bonds to create what he called the "sinking fund" to meet the unanticipated needs of the Latrobe Presbyterian Church.[11]

When Fred convinced his parents that he really wanted to go to New York to get into television, Jim Rogers went into action. Kirk Browning, who was directing the NBC Opera Theatre at that time, later recalled: "One day, Chotzi Chotzinoff, my producer, came to me and said, 'Kirk, we're obliged to do a favor for an executive of RCA. There's a man named John Royal, who is vice president of RCA, and he has come to me and explained that a friend of his has a son with a musical background who is graduating and would like to come in and get familiar with TV in some way, as an apprentice.' In those days, there was no union for production personnel.

"I said, 'Well, Chotzi, I don't need an assistant because the staff we presently have are all I need.' He said, 'I can't say no to John Royal. I have to take this young man. Find something for him to do.'

"I remember a very soft-spoken, sort of deferential, very appealing young man with a wry sense of humor. I do remember that he was a much better pianist at this point than I was. I was always asking him to play some of the music that he studied. There was one Rachmaninoff prelude that I particularly enjoy. That was the piece of music I asked for over and over, because he played it beautifully."[12]

Fred Rogers could have had no greater good fortune than to be put under the tutelage of Kirk Browning, one of the most talented and accomplished television directors of the era. Browning was an exceptional producer and director for NBC during the 1950s, and he went on to produce and direct major programs for PBS stations, including *Live from the Met* and *Great Performances*. He directed Frank Sinatra's first television special for NBC, as well as many *Hallmark Hall of Fame* programs.

He also did the television adaptations of a number of plays, like *Damn Yankees*, *The Taming of the Shrew*, and *Death of a Salesman*. Perhaps his most famous accomplishment was the opera *Amahl and the*

Night Visitors, written expressly for NBC by the Italian composer and librettist Gian Carlo Menotti and directed by Browning.[13] All together Browning won four Emmy Awards and a Peabody Award for excellence in television.

During the two brief years that they worked together, from 1951 to 1953, Fred Rogers and Kirk Browning became friends, and they sustained the relationship for the rest of their lives. It was logical that they would find each other compatible: Browning also came from a wealthy family. Like Fred, Kirk dropped out of an Ivy League school, Cornell, and focused for a time on developing his skills as a writer. Browning loved music and had studied it in school, just as Fred had.

When World War II came, Browning chose to serve in the American Field Service, driving an ambulance that carried injured British soldiers from the battlefields of North Africa, writing poetry between enemy bombardments. After the war, he struggled to make a living farming part of his family's Connecticut farm. As chance would have it, he sold eggs to a neighbor, Samuel "Chotzi" Chotzinoff, a close friend of RCA CEO David Sarnoff. After a career as a music editor and critic at the *New York World*, Chotzinoff became director of the music department at NBC.[14]

Chotzinoff chatted frequently with Browning when Chotzinoff stopped by to pick up eggs, and he was impressed with the young man and his knowledge of music. When Chotzinoff invited Browning to come to work at NBC, Kirk protested that he knew absolutely nothing about TV.

"Nobody knows anything about television," replied Chotzinoff, "and you have a musical background, and NBC is interested in going into musical programming." It was a response that could have applied equally to Fred Rogers as to Kirk Browning. Much of early television involved music, because it was essentially radio programming, with pictures added.[15]

Joanne Rogers became friends with Browning as well; she and Fred formed a lifelong friendship with Kirk and Barbara Browning and later shared vacations with them on Nantucket, off the coast of Massachusetts.

During those first months in New York, when she wasn't out exploring the neighborhood and the city, Joanne spent much of her day practicing on the piano—Fred's concert grand, which occupied a good portion of their one-bedroom apartment—so that she could continue her growth as a musician: "I would practice, and then sometimes go out into that big city, surrounded by so many things, I didn't know where to start. And I would just go back home again and practice some more. I tried to make New York a small town, I think, by being in my neighborhood a lot of the time."[16]

Joanne Rogers often dropped in to see Fred at NBC as part of her exploration of her new city: "It was exciting, and fun. We'd watch Fred at a rehearsal."

She also concentrated on getting to know and understand Fred better, and to get a grasp on their quickly evolving relationship: "You know the person, but you don't know them that well. And while we were on the go and busy a lot of the time, there's a lot of learning to do about getting along, thinking of the other person and what he might like to be doing. For the first few years, it's very difficult just to learn to live together."[17]

Given that they'd both been raised more or less as only children, she figured out quickly that each needed space: "I never had even had a roommate in college. We had suite mates, you know—but a little cubicle, at least, with your own room. So to share a room with somebody—that's the least of it, though.

"We waited until we were married about seven years before our kids came along. And I've always been glad of that, because we knew that the marriage was going to be okay."[18]

As the young couple settled in, Fred Rogers was getting a world-class education in television. The timing was crucial: In the 1950s, NBC was uniquely committed to creativity and quality, partly because everything about television was new and being invented on the spot by the people Fred was working with.

Fred was lucky enough to have been dropped right into the middle of the tenure of the head of NBC, Sylvester "Pat" Weaver, who created an almost magical period in the early evolution of television. The whole NBC crew, led by Weaver, believed they were on a mission to create a magnificent new era of American high culture, all through the new medium of broadcast television. Many critics then viewed television as an exciting new art form, and they focused on Pat Weaver's work as evidence of its cultural potential. Weaver himself wrote, "Television is a miracle . . . [that] must be used to upgrade humanity across a broad base."[19]

The new technology was the culmination of an extraordinary period of invention that had started in the previous century and had dramatically improved living conditions and the overall health and wealth of society, but it also led to a faster-paced and intense level of complexity. Dramatic population growth, transformative environmental degradation, and scientific advances fueled the Industrial Revolution, the petrochemical revolution, and set the stage for the telecommunications revolution that is still in midcourse.

THESE TECHNOLOGICAL ADVANCEMENTS shaped the wealth of the Rogers family as well as the thinking and work of Fred Rogers. His interest in using technology for education, and his embrace of a deep and simple life committed to universal human values, flowed directly from the world-changing developments of the nineteenth century. They set the stage for the tech-driven world we live in today—an environment that Fred Rogers reacted to in a very powerful way.

The Industrial Revolution shaped the western Pennsylvania environment in which the Rogers, McFeely, Kennedy, and Given families (Fred Rogers's clans) lived and worked. Western Pennsylvania was a focal point of the Industrial Revolution, and Rogers's forebears were among the early investors in manufacturing and in the technology that enabled radio and television. It can be said that Fred Rogers lived out the conundrum of modern life: embracing technology and using it in imaginative ways to benefit children, while rejecting the dehumanizing aspects of complex technological advancement.

The evolution of electrical engineering—the practical uses of electricity to power devices—enabled all these things, including early experimentation that would lead to commercial television. A cadre of inventors struggled for decades to evolve television—the ultimate long-distance communications device, carrying sight, sound, movement, the human voice, and all the action of a faster-paced world. Numerous English, Scotch, German, and Russian scientists labored for years over the puzzling question of how to use electricity and technology to carry a live picture over the airwaves. Their experiments focused into two camps: those who were trying to evolve a mechanical solution to transmitting a live picture and those who focused essentially on an electronic solution.

At the very beginning of the twentieth century, the Russian innovator Boris Rosing made a significant advance by taking the mechanical system of rotating discs developed by Paul Nipkow, a German, and coupling that system with a cathode ray receiving tube that had been in development under the German engineer Karl Braun.[20]

This was one of the key breakthroughs in transmitting a live moving picture. Ultimately, the electronic side of television development triumphed, and the cathode ray tube (CRT) became a standard piece of equipment for years in television sets and, later, computers.

Working with Rosing in his lab in St. Petersburg, Russia, was the young scientist Vladimir Zworykin, who would immigrate to America and evolve the CRT technology, ultimately under the leadership of David Sarnoff at RCA.[21] Zworykin and Sarnoff and their American team developed a commercial television system that used the cathode ray tube for both transmission and reception, brought commercial television to the US, and then dominated broadcasting for years. (There are many who feel that Zworykin and Sarnoff stole some of their technology from another leading television pioneer of the time, Philo Farnsworth; in fact, RCA later agreed to the payment of some royalties to Farnsworth.)

Interestingly, Zworykin got his PhD from the University of Pittsburgh a year before Fred Rogers was born in nearby Latrobe, and he left the Pittsburgh-based Westinghouse Corporation in frustration with management's lack of interest in his experiments in television technology.[22] Had the Pittsburgh managers of Westinghouse seen the same potential in television that Sarnoff and his staff at RCA saw from where they sat in New York, the history could have been quite different. As it was, Zworykin's work (and, indirectly, Rosing's work back in St. Petersburg) went to the savvy Sarnoff in New York—and some of the money went back to the heirs of the banker Thomas Given, including Fred Rogers.

ALL THIS ENTREPRENEURIAL ACTIVITY set the stage for Sarnoff to hire Pat Weaver not long after World War II. NBC had been started back in the 1920s as radio, and it wasn't until the late 1940s that the stage was set for the rapid commercial development of television. Sarnoff encouraged Weaver to develop the best and most exciting television programming possible, to enable RCA to dominate commercial television just as it had dominated the technological evolution of the medium between the two world wars. And Weaver took this as a mission to set the highest possible standards for television programming—which, of course, created just the right environment for the highly idealistic young Fred Rogers.

Pat Weaver was tall, at six feet, four inches; handsome, with short, curly red hair and bright blue eyes; and charming. Like Browning and Rogers, Weaver came from a wealthy family. Unlike Rogers and Browning, Weaver stayed right through his Ivy League college years to graduate from Dartmouth.[23] He recruited other idealistic Ivy League graduates to help fashion NBC into what he hoped would be a cultural powerhouse and the leader in television programming.

He was forty-one in 1949 when he joined NBC after years in advertising, and his tenure as the leader of the network would last only seven years. But during that time, he proved himself brilliant at conceiving new shows, pulling together the advertising support to make them possible, and fashioning the creative and production teams to imbue them with excellence.[24] At one point under his direction, NBC hosted eight of the top ten programs on TV.

Weaver fostered such pioneering television efforts as *Your Show of Shows with Sid Caesar and Imogene Coca,* the *Today* show, *Tonight Starring Steve Allen, Home* (with Arlene Francis), *Wide Wide World* (hosted by Dave Garroway), and the children's show *Kukla, Fran and Ollie.* His programs carried interviews with intellectuals such as anthropologist Margaret Mead, poet Robert Frost, and architect Frank Lloyd Wright. Weaver fashioned many of the protocols and practices that made network television so successful, like the practice of assigning the task of creating a show to the network's internal staff and selling different segments of the show to different advertisers.

As Pat Weaver's fame grew, Sarnoff grew jealous of the attention paid to him. Finally, when *The New Yorker* magazine chose to profile Weaver instead of Sarnoff, David Sarnoff pushed him out and replaced Weaver with Robert Sarnoff, his son.[25] Weaver was gone from the network by 1956. The important thing for Fred Rogers, though, was that Weaver's genius was given full rein at NBC during Fred's two years there, and Weaver's support of creative freedom and the setting of high standards of excellence for programming helped foster those very qualities in Rogers himself.

Nothing better exemplified these standards than the 1951 production of *Amahl and the Night Visitors.* Fred's work on *Amahl* took him out of his usual role of assistant to the producer ("That meant going and getting coffee and Cokes," said Rogers) and gave him the chance to work as the floor manager for the program's director, Kirk Browning.[26]

As floor manager, Fred had the responsibility of communicating the directions and the vision of Browning to the crew on the studio floor, and then communicating back from the floor to the director, who was usually in the control room. *Amahl* was a high point in NBC's creative period, and it was the most exciting project Fred Rogers worked on at the network.

In keeping with Pat Weaver's ambitious cultural agenda for NBC

Television in the 1950s, the network had given renowned Italian composer Gian Carlo Menotti a commission to create an opera specifically
for TV—a first. Weaver, who viewed *Amahl* as an opportunity to kick
off his new anthology series, *Hallmark Hall of Fame*, and to try to bring
opera to a mass TV audience, said, "I appealed to our creative people at
NBC to conceive of programs that would use entertainment to enrich,
inspire, and enlighten viewers."[27]

Menotti said that he was inspired to create *Amahl* as he wan-
dered the galleries of the Metropolitan Museum of Art in New York
City. When he stood in front of the painting *The Adoration of the Magi* by
Hieronymus Bosch, he was transported back to his childhood in Italy,
where children receive gifts from the Three Kings, not Santa Claus.
Amahl, a disabled boy living in Bethlehem, walks only with the aid of
a crutch. But by the end of the opera, he has received an unimaginable
gift from the three royal visitors.

Amahl and the Night Visitors premiered live on Christmas Eve
in 1951 from Studio H in Rockefeller Center, current home of *Saturday Night Live*, and has since been performed over twenty-five hundred
times. Kirk Browning and his young assistant Fred Rogers were thrilled
with the reception accorded the opera, which got a positive write-up on
the front page of the *New York Times* and attracted five million viewers,
a record for an opera telecast.[28] It appeared every Christmas until 1961,
with the first two presentations in black and white and the subsequent
ones in color.

Rogers later remembered that the conductor Arturo Toscanini
(music director of the Metropolitan Opera in New York, the New York
Philharmonic Orchestra, and the NBC Symphony Orchestra) conducted the NBC orchestra in its performance of *Amahl*: "After the dress
rehearsal," said Rogers, "Toscanini said to Menotti, in Italian, 'This is
the best you've ever done.'"

The only downside for Fred was that for the first time in his life,
he missed Christmas at home with his family. His sister, Laney, remembers that the whole family was disappointed when Fred had to work right
through the Christmas holidays to help produce the television opera.[29]

But working on *Amahl* enabled Fred to help Browning shape an ambitious American cultural moment, just the sort of thing Fred had dreamed of when he was at Rollins. In a later interview, Rogers explained his excitement at getting to work on NBC Opera Theatre productions: "Radio began as a vehicle to broadcast classical music. Television, in the early days, was doing the same thing. Until television became such a tool for selling, it was a fabulous medium for education. That's what I had always hoped it would be."[30]

According to Browning, "*Amahl* was rather an important moment in television history. It's interesting to me that that was the first opera that Fred was on, because here we have this crippled boy [Amahl] who is visited by the Magi [the Three Kings of Biblical tradition] on the way to the birth of Jesus. That's something that resonates in Fred's later work.

"I had known a little bit about Fred's background and his childhood. I extrapolated from the conversations that we had that he had a somewhat—not a difficult childhood, but there had been difficult moments in his childhood, moments when he needed a sort of comfort level."[31] In fact, as Browning recalled, the production of *Amahl and the Night Visitors* provided a seminal television experience for Rogers, an experience that brought together his interests in childhood, music and religion.

By Kirk Browning's lights, Fred Rogers rose to the occasion: "All I remember is that I never had any fault to find with anything he did. He ran the floor beautifully . . . it was a very useful period for him to learn the mechanism of live TV, in real time. He learned lots of very useful things by being a floor manager, as I did."[32]

It proved to be marvelous basic training. Rogers had to be calm and cool under pressure, had to be able to anticipate problems and opportunities, and always needed to ensure that everyone on the crew understood the flow of the program.

Later when he visited the set of *Mister Rogers' Neighborhood*, Kirk Browning was impressed with how well Fred had taken his NBC learning and applied it to the challenges of making children's television for PBS: "When he . . . started his show in Pittsburgh, he called me and asked me if I'd come out and help him set up the style of direction for the program.

"I said, of course, I'd be glad to come out. When I went there, he and the director had done the job for Fred that I did for NBC. They had evolved a technique that was so good for what Fred was doing that I said, 'Fred, I have nothing to say at all. . . . You have the most perfect ways.'

"I said, 'There's nothing I could possibly say that would improve what he's doing.' He has found the perfect language, visual language, to talk to the viewer."[33]

Fred Rogers's other experiences at NBC, though not as profound as working on *Amahl*, provided a broad-based education in television production and in working with performers and studio crews. One of the programs he spent the most time on was *The Kate Smith Evening Hour*, a variety show that aired from 1951 to 1952 on Wednesdays at 8:00 P.M., featuring everything from animal acts to comedy routines, along with ample opportunities for Smith to demonstrate her formidable singing chops. Musical guests included country music greats Maybelle and June Carter and Hank Williams.

Kate Smith's stirring version of "God Bless America" was a standard rendition at sports events for years. Her popular radio program (1937–1945) featured comic talent like Henny Youngman and Abbott and Costello.

Rogers enjoyed working with the larger-than-life singer: "She was a very imposing person," he recalled. "And her mother and her dog were with her all the time. She had some of the first contact lenses I'd ever seen. They looked like fish bowls. And she wore a huge corset. It was almost like an iron lung that she would get in. She was an enormous woman with one of the most beautiful natural voices—just a glorious instrument.

"One funny day—didn't seem funny then—she was standing in front of this painted set of a farmhouse, singing a farm song. I thought it was over, so I gave a cue to the stagehand to raise the scenery so that we could get on to the next scene. Well, the song wasn't over—there was just a little bit left. The set started to go up, and on camera it looked as if

Miss Smith was going down into the ground. But it was live, you know, and people were very forgiving with live television."[34]

In addition to the valuable experience Fred gained managing *The Kate Smith Evening Hour,* he learned almost as much from being an assistant on *The Gabby Hayes Show,* which ran from 1950 to 1954 on NBC. Hayes's offering was a Western entertainment program that was one of the first cowboy shows for children ever broadcast on television. It featured George "Gabby" Hayes, a vaudevillian from upstate New York who turned himself into a cowboy for movies and television.

Rogers asked the wily Hayes how he managed to connect so well with his audience, and Gabby replied that the only way to manage a television role in which one is asked to speak directly to a disembodied, distant audience is to convince oneself that one is speaking only to one little child. "Just one little buckaroo," Hayes told Rogers; just think of talking only and directly to "one little buckaroo."[35]

Rogers admired Gabby's skills as a performer, but he also came to appreciate Hayes as an individual and a character: "Gabby Hayes would come in his Western clothes and show old Western films. He would introduce them, and at the end say, 'See you, buckaroos,' or something. What fascinated me was that he had a Western accent, but when the program was over, he'd go to the dressing room, and on nights he had his Metropolitan Opera tickets, he'd get into his formal clothes and go to the opera. He had a box there; he loved the opera. Often you don't know the depth of someone that you see only on television."[36]

One of the most awkward moments for Rogers came when NBC started to experiment with color television for a commercial audience in 1954. There were only three sets in all the RCA/NBC universe that could broadcast in color: one in the office of RCA CEO David Sarnoff, another with NBC Chairman Niles Trammell, and the third in the office of NBC President Pat Weaver. Fred Rogers, who was red-green color-blind, got the assignment to move colored objects around the set so that these three biggest bosses in his world could assess the quality of a color broadcast.

"All we did in the studio," said Fred later, "was to move things from one place to another so that the camera could take pictures of them. My first day on the job, somebody said, 'Move the green parrot to the left.' I said, 'Which one is the green one?' "[37]

Having a color-blind floor manager seemed almost impossible to some of those working on the crew with Fred. But it was early television—a time when the rules got made up as everyone went along—and the crew made it possible for Fred, color blindness and all, to fit in. Interestingly, it never became an important issue later in his career.

At one point, desperate to solve a problem that threatened to ruin one of the broadcasts he was working on, Fred Rogers turned to his wife, Joanne, for help. Because she was already accustomed to public performance as a pianist, Fred went to her when the lead singer for one of the NBC music shows balked at going onstage: "Something happened at the dress rehearsal. The lead said, 'I'm not going to do it.'

"It was scheduled to be broadcast that night, live. My wife took the lead to our apartment and gave her a cup of tea and talked. Joanne is a wonderful person. Somehow, magically, she brought her back to the studio and they went on with the program. Maybe the lead singer just wanted attention. . . . That might be one of the best things to remember: that the best things of life are way offstage."[38]

During the 1950s, the Rogerses and the Brownings vacationed together on Nantucket, and in 1959 Kirk Browning found a wonderful, quaint old house way out on the western end of the island that rented for just 300 dollars for the whole summer. "An old farmhouse called the Coffin Farm had eight hundred feet of beachfront on the bay and then the ocean on the other side," remembered Browning years later. "It was the most romantic, beautiful spot in the world."

When the Brownings were there, they invited Fred and Joanne to join them. At the end of the summer, Browning learned that the house was for sale. It was a bargain price, but still beyond Kirk's means, since his family's fortune had been diminished by the Great Depression.[39]

Browning knew Fred's family's wealth had not suffered a similar fate, and he suggested to Fred that he look at the house as a possible purchase. Browning also remembered that Fred's parents had visited Nantucket, and he wondered if Jim and Nancy Rogers might not buy the house for Fred and Joanne.

"At some point, I told Fred, 'The house is now on the market for nine thousand dollars. I don't have the money, but I know you love this house.'

"Fred went to his family, who helped him buy the house. I think he paid eleven thousand dollars. I can't tell you what the house is worth today. Then over the years, he bought all the land around the house, and it became part of a larger complex of the family."[40]

Fred and Joanne got "The Crooked House" (which earned its name from the fact that the whole place leaned over slightly but comfortably with age) in 1959 and spent many happy summers on the water in the little village of Madaket.

The adjacent land became the site for the homes of Fred's sister, Laney (and her husband, Dan Crozier), and the Okonak family, Fred's cousins on his father's side. The Crooked House is still in the Rogers family.

6.

THE CHILDREN'S CORNER

FRED ROGERS MIGHT HAVE STAYED at NBC his whole career. Many of his friends at the station told him that his skills would inevitably lead to great success as a producer and director of commercial television. Or he might have gone on, as Browning did, to a career in public television in New York. But once again his father intervened. Always on the lookout for ways to help Fred, especially ways to help bring his son back to his roots in western Pennsylvania, Jim Rogers contacted Fred in 1953 to let him know that there was an interesting new television opportunity developing in Pittsburgh.[1]

Jim Rogers conveyed the news that a group in Pittsburgh was working to start the first community-based public television station in the United States. And an old friend of the Rogers family, Leland Hazard of the Pittsburgh Plate Glass Company, a global supplier of paints, fiberglass, chemicals, and other specialty materials, was leading the effort. Hazard had been talking to Jim Rogers about the potential of public television, and the two had speculated about the possible intersection of Fred's fledgling career in television and the new Pittsburgh station, WQED, which eventually became part of the Eastern Educational Network, a group of regional public television stations that exchanged programming. The plan was for the station to go on the air in 1954.

Educational television originated in Boston, where the New England textile baron John Lowell Jr. provided a series of free lectures for people in the city in an 1836 bequest. This early public improvement project later produced the Lowell Institute, which included the Cooperative Broadcasting Council, made up of local cultural institutions and universities. WGBH got its license in 1951 and went on the air not as a stand-alone entity, but as part of the Council, with a concert by the Boston Symphony Orchestra. The first person to show up for work was the crafty innovator Hartford N. Gunn Jr., who filled the new schedule with more music, science, and other educational programming.

Now Pittsburgh was ready to join the experiment in public edification in this new medium. Leland Hazard and Jim Rogers wondered whether Fred might not have an interest in being in on the ground floor. Fred quickly did his own research. He even flew out to the University of Iowa to see what educational programming might look like (the school had been experimenting with it since the 1930s).

And he decided that it just might be the right thing for him: "When I heard that educational television—which is now called public television—was going to be starting in Pittsburgh, only forty miles from where I grew up, I told some of my friends at NBC that I thought I'd put my name in and apply for the station. They said, 'You are nuts, that place isn't even on the air yet, and you're in line to be a producer or a director or anything you want to be here.' And I said, 'No, I have the feeling that educational television might be, at least for me, the way of the future.' "[2]

When Fred Rogers moved back to Pittsburgh in 1953 to help start WQED, there were lots of positive aspects for his family. His parents were thrilled to have him close to Latrobe. Jim Rogers kept hoping that Fred would eventually play a role in some of the family businesses.

Married to Fred just a little more than a year, Joanne Rogers saw family-oriented Pittsburgh as a place to raise children when she and Fred were ready to start a family. Fred and Joanne went shopping for houses, and they eventually bought a 1920s two-story, red-brick house on Northumberland Street in Pittsburgh's East End, near the Pittsburgh Golf Club, with its outstanding recreational facilities that might appeal to children.

But none of these factors were at the core of Fred's decision to move back to the Pittsburgh area. His careful calculation was that WQED—brand-new, unformed, and chaotic—would give him the creative freedom to involve himself in writing and performing and directing, as well as managing the station. Though his mentor Kirk Browning had warned Fred that by leaving New York he might be sacrificing the chance for a brilliant network-television career, Fred Rogers understood that life as an executive would disappoint him.

In ways that no one else, except possibly his wife, Joanne, understood, Fred Rogers was driven by the need to find outlets for his powerful creativity. NBC was already a large, bureaucratic institution. Not even David Sarnoff or Pat Weaver got the chance to express their creativity, except through the work of others.

Rogers felt strongly that eventually he would find the network atmosphere stultifying. And he recognized, almost instinctively and very astutely, that the ad hoc, madcap chaos of WQED might be just the right stew for him. As one of the first employees at the new public television station, he could experiment in an environment where the staff was desperately trying to cook up some local programming: music from a local university music department, poetry discussions with "Miss Emily," a local woman with a passion for reading and writing poetry.

"I was just at the right place at the very right time," Rogers later recalled. "I knew that the decision to leave New York and to come to Pittsburgh and launch in this place nobody had ever heard of was the correct one for me. It gave me a chance to use all the talents that I had ever been given. You know, I loved children, I loved drama, I loved music, I loved whimsy, I loved puppetry."[3]

Fred Rogers joined WQED in 1954 as program manager, under the leadership of general manager Dorothy Daniel. He and Daniel and a handful of others worked furiously in the fall of 1953 and the spring of 1954 to get ready to go live with *The Children's Corner*, a new show in black and white. The éminence grise of the station, the mastermind working in the background, was Leland Hazard, the Pittsburgh Plate Glass Company executive and friend of Jim Rogers.

Hazard was a big believer in Fred Rogers's potential. According to Sam Silberman, an early director at WQED, Hazard put his considerable influence behind Fred at key moments in the early years of the station: "Leland Hazard was a very strong, powerful man who would speak very softly and communicate strength just in his behavior. He and Fred were very close. . . . Leland and his wife, Mary, never had children, so I think to a great degree they adopted Fred as their child and supported him in all of his efforts."⁴

Hazard was a leading businessman in the city, but he was also a veteran civic leader, with a passion for educational television. Once WQED was set up, he became its president while continuing his work at Pittsburgh Plate Glass. As a longtime friend of the Rogers family, he knew enough about Fred to know that he was passionate about the potential for educational television to help children. And Hazard shared Rogers's commitment to gentle, thoughtful programming for young children at a time when a lot of television programming was wild, slapstick, thoughtless, and inappropriate for children.

Leland Hazard also shared Rogers's abhorrence of commercials that interrupted children's television. As Hazard wrote in the *Atlantic* magazine in 1955, "After three years of thought and action I am ready to set down a few certainties about educational television. To some it means surcease from the insistent voice of the advertiser. To some, usually parents, it means the hope of children's programs in which no hoofs clatter, no pistols crack, and no one gets killed."⁵

With WQED about to go on the air in the spring of 1954, there were still few plans or resources for local programming. The station faced the prospect of starting up as nothing more than a transmitter of content from other stations and other sources. Station manager Dorothy Daniel decided that the highest priority should go to developing a program for local children. When she told Leland Hazard that two staff members had responded to the request for thoughts on a live children's program on WQED, program manager Fred Rogers and secretary Josephine Vicari, he was pleased and excited.

As Fred Rogers recalled years later: "When Daniel asked who wants to do a children's program, Josie and I said, 'We'll do it for an hour a day.'

"Can you imagine producing an hour a day? I combed the country for free films we could put in. All we had planned to do was have

Josie sing some songs. I would play the organ for her to sing, and then she would introduce these films. We had things like how to grow grass in New Hampshire. No one had any idea how hard it would be to fill an hour of programming a day."[6]

Only later did Rogers and his crew marvel at how they had somehow managed to produce five one-hour, live television programs each week with hardly any budget. And much of the time Fred had to sandwich the duties of program manager into the rest of his day.

Rogers later estimated that they had about 150 dollars a week for their show, but that amount was taken up by their salaries. In effect, they had virtually no money to buy or develop programming. All they had was their own imaginations.

Josephine Vicari (she changed her name to Josie Carey at the suggestion of Dorothy Daniel) was shorter than Fred, with close-cropped, dark hair and a round face that always seemed to be creased with a broad smile. Most importantly, she had boundless energy, the sort of spontaneous creativity that enabled her to respond to the chaos of improvisation with the same kind of willing good humor that Fred employed to make all things seem possible.

Josie Carey was born in Pittsburgh, just two years after Fred's birth in Latrobe. She grew up in Butler, Pennsylvania, just north of Pittsburgh, working in the kitchens of a series of Italian restaurants her grandparents and parents owned and operated. She was happy with the chaos of the restaurants and talking with large numbers of customers, which helped make her sociable and spontaneous and comfortable with strangers.

And she was a great reader. In her oral history for The Television Academy Foundation's Interviews, Josie said: "In my childhood, my favorite place in the world was the library. I made up my own games and stories. I entertained myself, which provided me with a background that served me well later."[7]

Perhaps even more importantly, Josie was addicted to listening to the radio as a child, which began her lifelong infatuation with educating and entertaining young people. She loved soap operas and listened to so many that she could tell by voice inflections who was a villain and who was a heroine.

Carey had harbored some hopes of studying theater at Pittsburgh's Carnegie Tech (now Carnegie Mellon University), which then and now has enjoyed a strong theater-arts program. But family resources were limited, and she had to make do with learning secretarial skills at Duff's Business Institute in downtown Pittsburgh: "I figured I could always be a secretary until things worked out to end up where I was supposed to be."[8]

She got a job with an ad agency that created a weekly woman's program on a local commercial television station. There she became an assistant producer, which meant doing anything and everything to get the show on the air. The program attracted the attention of Dorothy Daniel, who invited Carey to come to WQED. A large woman with a round face and big round glasses, her hair pulled back into a bun, Daniel told Carey she could imagine her getting to perform at WQED if she joined the effort.

Captured by Daniel's enthusiasm, Josie Carey came to the new station in the fall of 1953, at about the same time as Fred Rogers. For several months, she had been pitching in around the office, doing everything from secretarial work to going door-to-door raising money.

"She had this incredible energy," said WQED producer Rick Sebak. "I think it would be too easy to put her in the category of standard TV hostesses of that era. She was beyond that. It was just the energy and the curiosity and the sense of fun that comes across on those old TV shows."[9]

As soon as Josie arrived, she and Fred hit it off, and they began talking about their ideas for children's programs. They discovered an exciting consistency in their thinking that helped them develop ideas together confidently.

Fred had been planning his own program, to be called *It's a Small World*, starring Fred's puppets (including a ventriloquist's dummy called Hisher Boop Truck, first called "Elmer" and then renamed by a little girl) and animated furniture that moved around and talked. Although he was excited about bringing his ideas to Dorothy Daniel, talking with Josie Carey convinced him that it would be easier to produce and sustain a one-hour children's show, day after day, with a collaborator.

Another early coworker remembered Carey's easygoing, natural affinity for improvisational television with the talented Rogers: "She loved the camera and the camera loved her. She was very creative. In those days, no one had done it before, so you came up with your own ideas, and Josie was very capable of doing that. She created everything that she did, and that is a very special talent because you were never copying someone else."[10]

As Josie Carey later recalled: "We went to Mrs. Daniel and said, 'We're thinking alike and can help each other.'

"She said, 'Oh, yes.' Mrs. Daniel let you do almost anything. She was wonderful. We had a staff meeting once a week on Mondays and the janitor was invited."[11]

Josie and Fred began to craft rough scripts for the program that they could take to Daniel to get her approval. For the most part, they knew they would just be making it all up each day as they went along.

The night before the station was scheduled to go on the air on April Fool's Day, 1954, Dorothy Daniel gave a dinner party for the staff, board members, and supporters. At each place at the table, there was a small gift for each staff member to express Daniel's gratitude for their hard work. Although Daniel hadn't seen Fred performing with his puppets, and didn't know how much Josie and Fred would use puppets on The Children's Corner, she knew Fred had an interest in puppetry. On a whim, she had purchased a small tiger puppet to put at Fred's place.[12]

Rogers took this gift as encouragement, and he and Josie incorporated the hand puppet into their first show. They had a model of an old grandfather clock that was to be a central part of the set, and the two of them had planned to find a stuffed bird that they would somehow engineer to pop out of the clock and speak to the children watching.

But they hadn't found a bird. Instead, the next day Fred put the tiger puppet Dorothy Daniel had given him on his hand, got behind the clock, and had the puppet pop out of the clock and say, "Its 5:02, and Columbus discovered America in 1492." Daniel Striped Tiger, named by Josie and Fred in honor of Dorothy Daniel, was born. From then on, Daniel would pop out of the clock each day, say the time and share a historical fact with the children in the TV audience. The role of puppets in shaping *The Children's Corner*, and Fred Rogers's career, was beginning.[13]

At first, Josie and Fred just planned to use the puppets occasionally, to fill in when they ran out of other things. They used a lot of free film from libraries and other stations. And, Josie explained, they invented activities: "We eventually had somebody from the Pittsburgh Symphony come once a week with his instrument, to talk about it and play it. We had a magician come in and teach the children magic. We had a man teach Morse code. We had a tap dancer. We had aerobics before aerobics was big. We showed them how to make pizza before anybody had ever heard of pizza."[14]

But invariably gaps occurred. A lot of the film Fred got on loan for the program was very old, and the WQED equipment was second-hand. With annoying frequency, the film would snap, and Josie and Fred would have to quickly ad-lib while someone—most likely assistant Margot Woodwell—fixed the film. At other times, a scheduled guest or performer didn't show up.

When an actress known as "Miss Pat," who did occasional interviews for the *Corner*, once failed to appear to interview two local bakers she'd recruited, Woodwell had to jump in to do the interview: "It was two men who were cake decorators, who wore white bakers' suits with short sleeves. One had tattoos up both his arms. These guys were absolutely monosyllabic. There was this dead silence as they decorated a cake.

"I said, 'Could you tell me how you do this?'

"They said, 'Ya' learn.' "

Margot Woodwell had to turn quickly to Fred and Josie to bring some action back to the program.[15]

As often as not, when such an interruption broke the flow of the show, Fred would grab Daniel Striped Tiger or one of his other hand puppets, get behind a small puppet stage created for the show, and talk with Josie. And a kind of magic would take place.

Once when Josie came rushing over to WQED from another station where she had been doing some freelance work, she was visibly upset by something that had disrupted her work. As Fred Rogers remembered it: "She came in and just said to Daniel, 'I am so upset.'

"She bared her soul to Daniel the puppet. I wonder if she even knew that we were on the air and the camera was on. She probably did. But she trusted Daniel's ears so, and she trusted her audience, so that she could be her whole self."[16]

As the chemistry built between Fred and Josie and their audience of small children, Fred gained the confidence to bring out more of his puppets, including King Friday XIII. They perched behind the puppet stage and talked with Josie Carey. Once when they were shooting on location at South Park just outside Pittsburgh, Fred surprised Josie with a new puppet, X the Owl, who suddenly appeared, crying out that he had "x-caped"—thus, the name X.

As usual, Josie instantly related to the new puppet; soon they were singing together. As the relationship between Josie and the puppets developed, the whole tenor of the show changed. The essence of the program became these conversations, and the dialogue between Fred as puppeteer and Josie Carey as hostess emerged as both the charm of the show and the opportunity for educating children.

For years, Fred Rogers had been shy and somewhat guarded about his love of puppets. Even Joanne Rogers said later that she had never seen him playing with the puppets in the early years of their marriage.[17]

Since he'd been a child in elementary school, Rogers had invested thousands of hours of creativity into his puppets, but he wasn't sure if their character and charm would resonate with anyone but him. But now as he brought out the puppets, his role as creator, performer, and, most importantly, listener, emerged. He found his way as an artist. Josie, guileless and trusting, fell in love with the puppets and talked to them as if they were living.

Sometimes after a long conversation with one of the puppets, when the show ended, Josie would rush over to tell her friend Fred Rogers what she and the puppets had been talking about. "I would get so engrossed in the conversation, especially with Daniel, that after it was over I would go around the back of the set and tell Fred what Daniel had said to me, totally forgetting that Fred was Daniel." The puppet characters were as real to her as they were to Fred.[18]

But it wasn't just Josie who loved Daniel and the other puppets. Dorothy Daniel, Leland Hazard, Margot Woodwell, the cameramen, the soundmen—everyone at WQED—found the conversations between Rogers's puppets and Josie Carey to be charming and engaging.[19] The crew loved Fred, who treated them with respect and patience. And everyone was caught up in the serendipity of the show as it evolved more and more into puppetry.

Then the letters poured in from parents, who appreciated how much Josie and the puppets meant to their children. They didn't know very much about Fred, because he had no regular performance role on the show other than with the puppets. But he did appear on a couple of occasions, once as "Prince Charming" instructing Josie in ballroom dancing, and once as a minister performing a fictional wedding.

Josie remembers only one really negative letter from a parent out of all the mail they got: "It hurt for days. . . . She was mad because her children hadn't gotten something they had sent for. It turns out that our crew had gotten so overwhelmed with the mail that they burned some of it. They were volunteers, they were kids, and that's why she never got an answer."

Of course, Fred Rogers called the complainant to apologize and explain.[20]

The devotion of the kids in the audience for *The Children's Corner* almost led to an early disaster. Josie and Fred had set up a Children's Corner Club for their viewers, who could earn club stripes for simple achievements. The fourth stripe came for learning the club song, and Fred and Josie decided that they would invite all the children who got all four stripes to come to a special birthday party for Daniel Striped

Tiger, which the station held about three months after *The Children's Corner* first went on the air.

Josie said later: "We expected a handful of kids—four stripes, you know. We looked out the window about an hour before we went on the air and there were children lining the whole block. We couldn't fit them in the studio. They were in the studio, they were in the gallery, and in the backyard.

"We had gotten little cakes and a little piece of ice cream and a cold drink for each child. We had to cut the cakes in four, the ice cream in four, and if you got one, you couldn't get the other, or if you got a drink, you couldn't have cake or ice cream, because we had to stretch it out for everybody. Every child knew that song. There wasn't anybody who came to that party under false pretenses. They sang as one voice . . . I still get goose bumps when I remember it. It was probably the most exciting moment in my career."[21]

Because WQED was brand new, and the *Corner* was its signature program, one of the local newspapers covered the club party, and the popularity of the show became the talk of the town.

There were some mistakes, of course. The program was still largely unscripted; Fred and Josie just wrote up a rough plan for each show on a yellow legal pad, often just one sheet long, and then improvised from it. The story line and the dialogue were not worked out. Fred, as the voice of the puppets, and Josie, as the host of the show, would create the content as they went along. This made for some delightful spontaneity, and the occasional problem.

One of the characters on the show once said to Josie, "Oh, you smell good this morning." She explains her reply: "I didn't want to say 'perfume,' and I said, 'Oh, toilet water.'" A parent of one of the viewers wrote in to say, "My three-year-old came out of the bathroom drenched . . . and she said, 'I'm wearing toilet water, just like Josie.'"

Another time, Josie told the children they could get the weather by dialing a weather station in Denver. Fred and Josie and their assistant Margot Woodwell got phone calls from bemused parents who reported that their children were racking up long-distance phone charges to Colorado.[22]

Fred had to run back and forth between the organ, which he played when Josie sang, and the puppet stage, where he crouched down with his hand raised to one of the holes in the facade of the stage to present one of the hand puppets. And he discovered that if he had left any coins in his pocket, they would jangle loudly as he ran. So often he would run just out of range of the camera, leaning over so he could clutch his pocket tightly with one hand to keep the change still.

Then he discovered that his shoes squeaked on the wood floors of the old stone mansion in the university section of Pittsburgh that the new station was using for studios and offices. Fred bought a pair of rubber-soled sneakers to make the mad dash from organ to stage without disrupting the show with squeaking. Later this rather pragmatic decision became a signature element of Fred's.[23]

Then there was the time that Josie was playing the part of "Emily Brontosaurus," whose job it was to tell the children about other animals: "As Emily, I was supposed to bring in a friend from the zoo every time I was on. So we had a lion cub, and it got spooked by the lights or the noise and went for me. Unfortunately, I had a big tail [on her costume]. It clawed into the tail, and Fred jumped in front of the lion and distracted it. But then it went for Fred's sweater. They had to stop the show until the man from the zoo came to get the lion cub."[24]

DESPITE THE SPONTANEITY and chaos of the show, there were standards about what could be said and what might be shown to the children who were watching. The standards were not articulated but came instead from the thoughtful care that Fred Rogers put into the dialogue between the puppets and Josie.

Even that early in his career, Fred was clear about the importance of appropriate child development, which he was reading about and discussing with friends and associates. Josie and the rest of the crew picked up on Fred's interest. They had the support of Dorothy Daniel and Leland Hazard in trying to set good standards.

Rogers recalled: "We had an idea where we might like to go with the story line, but most of it was unrehearsed. There was a whole array of puppets. At first, children seemed so much safer having the puppet say what the child was feeling, rather than the child himself."

Much later, academics at the University of Pittsburgh with whom Rogers studied child development explained to him that his own instincts, as someone who had stayed in close touch with the feelings of his own childhood, helped guide him to just the right dialogue for children.[25]

Josie Carey took particular pride in being told by parents how much they trusted her, and The Children's Corner, to properly care for their children: "We had a big book called the Scrapograph and we put the children's pictures on it, or the things that they drew. They were part of our program. . . . And the mothers that I meet now say that I was such a good babysitter. They could trust their children to watch Children's Corner. They knew [their children] were not going to learn anything they weren't supposed to know."

All the care and effort that Fred and Josie put into the show paid off in 1955, when The Children's Corner won a Sylvania Award for the best locally produced children's programming in the country.

Carey was thrilled about going to New York to get the award, but Fred wasn't interested: "Fred would not go with me to collect that award. I had to get a friend of mine to go by train with me to . . . New York to collect it."[26]

At the time, there was a handful of other children's programs on television, some of them very good, like Kukla, Fran and Ollie and Ding Dong School, and almost all of them, like The Children's Corner, produced in a fairly ad hoc fashion. One of the earliest was DuMont Television's Small Fry Club, which featured host Bob Emery playing the ukulele and introducing film clips. It went on the air in the spring of 1947. A year later, NBC debuted Kukla, Fran and Ollie, which built a fiercely loyal audience of young children with its puppets and host Fran Allison.[27]

Both shows were successful in attracting an audience of children and parents at a time when the post–World War II baby boom was just beginning. The birth rate in the US spiked at the end of the war and stayed unusually high until the 1960s, providing a new market for television. But most of the programs, like DuMont's *Captain Video and His Video Rangers* or CBS's *Winky Dink and You*, didn't have the sort of connection for little children that Fran Allison of *Kukla* or Josie Carey of the *Corner* offered. The combination of a personal, engaging host and puppets clearly had some special magic.

Kukla was created by an eccentric puppeteer named Burr Tillstrom, who, like Fred Rogers, combined his passion for puppets with strong feelings about the importance of quality programming for very young children. Also like Rogers, Tillstrom grew up playing with puppets and developed his creations into a very unscripted and spontaneous television show that charmed children and parents. Although the original *Kukla* series went off the air in 1957, more than a decade before *Mister Rogers' Neighborhood* went into national production, Tillstrom and Rogers are often compared to each other because of how deeply they each respected the needs and sensibilities of young children.

Tillstrom grew up on the North Side of Chicago in the 1920s, putting on puppet shows for his parents, using his toy teddy bears as props. He attended the University of Chicago, but dropped out to concentrate on his puppet theater. He struggled to find a paying audience, but finally found employment in the mid-1930s in a Chicago Park District puppet program that was sponsored by Franklin D. Roosevelt's Works Progress Administration. It was on that Chicago program that he created the hand puppet Kukla, whose name derived from a Russian term of endearment for a doll.

Burr Tillstrom was lucky enough to perform his puppet art at NBC during the 1950s, when Pat Weaver was president of the network. Tillstrom—like NBC intern Fred Rogers—benefited enormously from Weaver's leadership in that "golden era" of television. Weaver was pushed out of NBC by David Sarnoff, president of NBC's parent, Radio Corporation of America, in 1956. A year later, Tillstrom's run at NBC was over.

The other early television program that is credited with adhering to high standards of quality was *Ding Dong School*, hosted by educator Frances Horwich and shown on NBC in the 1950s. Clearly, Fred Rogers was aware of it, and of Frances Horwich's approach, which involved a style like that later adopted by Mister Rogers: speaking to the child in the audience as if he or she was right across the room from the host.

Horwich, who won a George Foster Peabody Award for excellence in television programming in 1953, was cited by *New York Times* television critic Jack Gould for her work: "She imbues in the youngsters a sense of friendliness, confidence and faith that is truly magical television. She is a teacher, yes, but she is also a very genuine friend of the tots who sit entranced before the receivers." Later, though, when she began promoting the products of sponsors of her show—not just in the form of commercials, but embedded in the program itself—Gould and Fred Rogers were both disappointed and critical of this intrusion. Jack Gould now called it "a reversion to hucksterism at its most callous level," deploring Horwich's "blatant coercion of unsuspecting small children."

He concluded with a line that could have been written by Fred Rogers: "Even in this age of television with all its materialistic outlook, little boys and girls between the ages of two and five still are something very special—and precious."[28]

Rogers felt let down by Horwich, who had a doctorate in education from Northwestern University and had been a critic of advertising aimed at children. The experience hardened Fred Rogers's increasingly adamant opposition to commercials for children.

As comfortable as the collaboration was between Fred Rogers and Josie Carey, there were some differences between his careful nature and her easygoing improvisational style, and as time went along, these differences loomed larger. Once, when they were having great fun creating the show, Josie was so enthusiastic she told the children she didn't want to leave them as the show was ending: "We were having such a good time, and I kept saying, 'No, I don't want to go. I don't want to go. I want to do more. I want to stay here.' But they took us off the air, of course, and the switchboard lit up with little kids: 'Let her come back on; that wasn't nice!'"

Josie was amused, but Fred was worried that the children would be upset and frightened. With increasing frequency, he would chide her for saying anything that he thought might be misconstrued by kids in the audience.

Josie did some freelance work for the local commercial television station, KDKA. During the taping of one of these freelance efforts, one of the writers, Sterling Yates, wrote a gag about someone losing their baby.

"Oh," said Josie on the show, "where was the last place you saw it?"

Yates, who played opposite Josie in this bit, said, "I think it's in the glove compartment of a car that was headed to Cleveland."

Fred heard about this from Josie, who thought it was quite funny. But Rogers was appalled, and he lectured Josie on the dangers of small children misunderstanding the joke. The same KDKA programming had included a small hand puppet, which looked like a baby. The "baby" wound up on the floor, followed by a joke in which Yates accused one of the show's guests of "dropping" his baby.[29]

Again, Fred, who almost never lost his temper, was furious with Josie for countenancing material he saw as harmful. Fred could not understand how such a good-hearted person as Josie, who clearly understood and liked children, could put such potentially frightening material on children's television. It was the beginning of a rift that would prove fatal to *The Children's Corner*.

Josie was an entertainer. She was thrilled to be on television, to be part of show business, and she loved the easygoing, zany, anything-goes quality of the entertainment field. She wanted, more than anything else, for her show-business career to flourish. She very much liked working with the writers at KDKA, particularly with comedian and jazz musician Sterling Yates, whom she described as "the total opposite of Fred. He would do anything for a laugh, and he didn't care what the message was."

In fairness, on KDKA, Carey and Yates thought of themselves as entertainers, not educators, and they were aiming at an older audience than the preschool kids Rogers was targeting at WQED.

Joe Negri, a highly accomplished jazz guitarist who played at clubs and on local radio and television all around Pittsburgh (later he appeared as Handyman Negri on the *Neighborhood*), was a friend of Josie's.

He observes: "She was a very talented girl. I had written songs with Josie, too; she was a wonderful lyricist. Maybe . . . Josie was more of a musical theater sort of writer, whereas Fred was more interested in writing about lessons for the children, in songs like 'You've Got to Do It,' about how you just have to keep doing it if you want to learn to ride a bike."

Rogers was headed in another direction from Josie. More and more, he thought of himself as an educator, as a champion of the needs of children. And he was building a burning passion for setting the highest standards of excellence in children's television. Increasingly, that meant Fred and Josie were at odds.

"It got so that Fred started to worry about wording," recalled Josie. "You never fight with Fred. But once we had a twenty-minute discussion about whether to use the word *would*, *should*, or *could*."

And they kept talking about the glove-compartment joke that infuriated Fred: " 'Do you realize,' said Fred, 'that it's one of the worst things you can tell a child? A child is so afraid of being left or lost, and it's such an enclosed place, the glove compartment. That child is going to feel that he's being put into a small place—that he's lost his parents.' "

Josie lost her patience with all this anxiety over words: "I said, 'Hey, it's a joke. It's a silly program. The kids know it's silly.' Fred thought it was just horrible."[30]

Even as *The Children's Corner* enjoyed great success, and Fred struggled with his working relationship with Josie, WQED got a new general manager. Dorothy Daniel went onto the board of directors, and

William Wood joined the station as the new, demanding manager of a station now past start-up and beginning to grow. An experienced professional, Wood's goal was to create a more orderly management structure out of the WQED chaos.

In one of the oddest moments in television history, William Wood decided that one of his first moves to professionalize the station would be to fire Fred Rogers. It seemed that he decided that Rogers lacked the appropriate production credentials to run a show like *The Children's Corner*.

As Josie later recalled, one of Wood's objectives was to save money for the station:

"They were going to fire everybody, especially Fred, because they figured he was just a producer, and, you know, they could get somebody else for half the money. I don't know what Fred was making. The whole place was staffed mostly with volunteers. There were only four or five people who actually got paid. I think he [Wood] actually did fire everybody on a Friday, and rehired us the next Monday."[31]

Over the weekend, Wood got the message—from Daniel, Hazard, and the board—that he, not Rogers, would be out of work if he did not relent. Perhaps Wood felt threatened by Fred Rogers, who was playing so many different roles—producer, writer, performer, director, program manager—that it seemed he was everywhere at once. But Leland Hazard and Dorothy Daniel put things back on course, and reestablished the successful team behind *The Children's Corner*. In the end, Wood was even prevailed upon to write Fred a letter thanking him for his excellent work. The two coexisted at WQED for several years, wary of each other, but able to work together.

But Josie was finding it more and more difficult to make a connection with Fred. She said she really didn't think he liked entertainment, and he hardly ever watched commercial television or listened to the radio: "Sometimes Fred didn't want to have any connection with the outside world. Most people have a radio in their cars; Fred had his taken out.

"He'd only watch television once a week, *The Alfred Hitchcock*

Hour [*Alfred Hitchcock Presents*, in the 1950s, was succeeded by *The Alfred Hitchcock Hour* from 1962 to 1965], because he liked to see Alfred Hitchcock come in and say hello. And then he'd turn it off."[32]

As much as Josie was embracing the world of entertainment, Fred seemed to be moving away from it, toward a dedication to early childhood education. "He started to get quieter, and he started to get more interested in a child's reaction," said Josie.

Nothing irritated Carey quite like the popcorn incident; it convinced her that Fred was so particular in his standards that they were just not going to be a good fit for the long haul: "I was on, and he was popping popcorn. He put too much popcorn in the popper, and the lid came up and started dancing around and the popcorn started falling over. We finished the program. Then he said, 'Now we have to do that again.'

"I said, 'Why? That was fun! The kids will love it.'"

But Fred was concerned that particularly for little children, the uncontrolled popping and spilling could be frightening. Luckily the popcorn erupted during a taping session, not live on air.

"We had to do that whole section all over again, because too much popcorn came out of the popper," said Carey with a combination of frustration and amazement.

Later Josie Carey said she wished she had fought that decision by Rogers. To her, the popcorn spilling out all over the place was just plain good old television programming. It was entertaining.[33]

For Fred, though, it was the sort of thing that was fundamentally important: If Sterling Yates stood for a good laugh no matter what, Fred Rogers would stand for the right thing for children, no matter what. He had gotten into television to make it better, to make it more appropriate and educational for young children. The slapstick, pie-in-the-face quality of early television was just what he wanted to change. Later in his career, he let his sense of humor come out more on air, especially when he wanted to show children that adults make mistakes, too.

One of the things that highlighted the significant differences between Rogers and Carey was the opportunity to work in New York.

Rogers's former employer, NBC, sent a producer to Pittsburgh to look at another WQED program, *Parents and Dr. Spock*, featuring the renowned pediatrician Dr. Benjamin Spock. Dr. Spock had published *The Common Sense Book of Baby and Child Care*, one of the most successful bestsellers of all time, and he was still teaching at the University of Pittsburgh.

NBC executives figured there might be great potential in his local television program for parents. But when the producer got to Pittsburgh and reviewed Spock's program, she was disappointed. According to Fred Rogers's recollection, she was sitting in the lobby of the WQED building watching *Parents and Dr. Spock* when she happened to catch part of *The Children's Corner*. When she got back to New York, she recommended that NBC try to acquire the *Corner* and hire Fred Rogers and Josie Carey.[34] Josie, of course, was very excited. Predictably, Fred was full of reservations.

Josie remembered that though she and Fred agreed to go to New York one day a week to shoot a once-a-week version of the *Corner* for national distribution, they didn't want to abandon WQED, in part because the *Corner* was so important to the fortunes of the Pittsburgh station. "We made a lot of money for WQED," said Josie. "They wouldn't be on the air if it weren't for [*The*] *Children's Corner*. That first year, we were the ones that kept that station going, and that's when NBC found us. We said, 'We can't leave; they need us here.'"[35]

Josie was somewhat wistful and sad about missing the opportunity for full-time employment at a New York network station. But Fred never really wanted it, and he threw up roadblock after roadblock to the executives at NBC. First, he said he would only fly in on Saturday mornings to shoot the NBC program, and that he had to fly right back out again Saturday evening. Although NBC wanted Fred to stay around to promote the show, Rogers explained that he had to be back in Pittsburgh for his Sunday morning church service at his Presbyterian church.

And Rogers let NBC know that though they could present ads aimed at parents, they could not advertise anything, even the show itself, in commercials aimed at children. The NBC executives reluctantly agreed, and they placed the show in their public-service department rather than the commercial division. They figured that when Fred eventually appreciated how much money he could make, he would come around and agree to aim ads at children. They explained to Fred that they made their money from ads, and he could, too. And they explained the potential of commercializing his puppets. They might just as well have tried to explain the benefits of atheism to the Pope.

The network executives tried to get Josie and Fred to adopt silly costumes that would amuse the children. Fred explained that each of them was a real friend to the children, and they wanted the children to see them for the real people that they were. When Fred and Josie sang their very charming but overtly religious song, "Goodnight, God," NBC objected.

"They called us in," recalled Fred, "and said, 'We think it's better that you not . . . uh . . . mention God on the program.'

"And I said, 'Well, then, I don't think we'll come back.' They had a lot of viewers for our program, so they rescinded that. You can be an agent of what's good and not be terribly direct about it."[36]

Fred, of course, understood the need to subordinate overt religiosity on network television; throughout his career, he skillfully focused on strong humanistic values without dwelling on religion. But he was not inclined to give the NBC executives a break.

The Children's Corner was very popular on NBC. Carey recalled that they immediately broke the record for fan mail for a children's program on any station. The *Corner* started out as a program that replaced the ventriloquist Paul Winchell and his dummy Jerry Mahoney, and it quickly became so successful that NBC gave it a regular, weekly slot. But Rogers was not really interested in going back to commercial television, and eventually NBC executives grew weary of his opposition to advertising to children. *The Children's Corner* on NBC was canceled after thirty-nine weeks.

Fred Rogers had been given fair warning by Frances Horwich of *Ding Dong School*, who was about to be replaced by a new game show called *The Price Is Right*. Programming for younger kids was being pushed aside in network schedules for shows like *Davy Crockett* that appealed to older children, and for shows for adults.

For his part, Rogers was relieved that he didn't have to travel weekly to New York anymore. But Josie worried that her chance at stardom might be slipping away: "Had we stayed in New York, and insisted that NBC promote us and do the things that people do to become stars, well, you know, things would have taken a different turn."

She went on to host *Josie's Storyland* and *Funsville*, two KDKA commercial children's programs, and later had a successful children's program in South Carolina in the 1970s. But she never became a national star.

When she and Fred ended their working relationship, wrapping up *The Children's Corner* in Pittsburgh after seven years, she was working regularly on KDKA and willingly signed over to Fred the rights to the puppets and the songs that had been developed on the *Corner.*

Later Josie came to regret that decision, but she also became rather philosophical about the fact that Fred did become a national figure and she did not: "We had a wonderful time. He had a great sense of humor and he's very caring, very interested. . . . He didn't really want to go to New York. He wanted to stay at WQED, and I think in the early days before he decided to become a minister, he was starting to feel a call of some kind. He was my best friend in those days. We were really very, very close."[37]

7.

ON-AIR MINISTRY

AFTER FOUR YEARS of working in television, and just as his career was taking off, Fred Rogers remained committed to the idea of the ministry. He couldn't quite give up the idea of service through the church he'd found attractive as a young boy sitting in the pews with his mother. Nancy and Jim attended the Latrobe Presbyterian Church every Sunday; Fred Rogers came with them.

The Latrobe Presbyterian Church had always been a cornerstone of the family's life. Nancy and her husband, Jim, set up two charitable foundations, The Latrobe Foundation and the McFeely-Rogers Foundation, which stewarded millions of dollars for the Latrobe community, funding dozens of amenities like parkland and community recreational facilities. But for Nancy, the centerpiece of her giving was the Latrobe Presbyterian Church, where she was grounded by her deep religious faith.

The noblesse oblige that Fred Rogers adopted, putting his commitment to children and their education ahead of any personal gain, might never have been possible without the family wealth that gave him, and his mother, such freedom. If Rogers had been born poor, his attitudes would quite likely have been different.

As his future colleague Eliot Daley observes: "Look at the choices that Fred had to make. . . . He was born into a lot of money, a lot of privilege, a lot of this and that, and he could have done anything. He could have been a playboy; he could have done all kinds of stuff. And I think it was a quiet series of probing choices . . . that had proved to be diversionary, but all against the backdrop of—you know, we were dropped in here for some reason."[1]

In 1955, feeling a conflict between his work on *The Children's Corner* and the call of the ministry, Fred Rogers split the difference: He continued to work as the creator, scriptwriter, songwriter, and producer of the show, as well as the program manager for WQED, while also enrolling part-time at the Pittsburgh Theological Seminary.[2] Rogers still wasn't sure television was serious work. He knew the ministry would be serious, but he also realized that he would badly miss the excitement of television if he left it.

Josie Carey, his partner at *The Children's Corner*, remembered that Fred would try to come into the station early in the morning to get his work started, then rush over to the seminary (almost thirty blocks away, across the busy streets of Pittsburgh's East End) to take a course or two, and then drive quickly back to WQED. He would drop his text books and jump into preparations with Josie for that afternoon's one-hour live broadcast of the *Corner*.[3]

Josie had been a Catholic-school student as a child, and she later said she was almost as religious as Fred. Together they sometimes created an easygoing blend of religion and television: "We had two songs that we did once a week. One was 'Goodnight, God,' and one was 'Good Morning, God,' and there are people who still sing 'Goodnight, God.' Some ladies have taught it to their children, and it's still a part of their nighttime routine. It was a beautiful song, but we can't do things like that anymore. You're not allowed to do anything religious, anything with religious overtones on the children's programs."[4]

She remembered Fred as an odd blend of the very serious and the spontaneously funny. He could be silly and unconstrained on the set. Away from work, he had no interest in socializing, going to parties, or participating in the various benefit productions in Pittsburgh that often called for local television talent. He watched very little television himself, and other than reading books and spending time with his family, he put all his time into work and his religious studies.

Fred and Joanne's son James, called Jim, was born in 1959, the seventh year of the Rogerses' marriage. As Joanne explains it: "Things were moving smoothly at the time." Joanne was teaching piano as well as performing concerts in the Pittsburgh area. When Jim was born on September 4, 1959, she recalls: "Fred and I enjoyed the complete care of him, and my piano was put on the back burner."[5]

She didn't go back to her instrument until 1970, when the Rogerses found a housekeeper to aid them. By then, they were a family of four, with the arrival of John Rogers on June 18, 1961 (Father's Day). As Joanne describes it: "It was our adventure of early parenting, with all the joys and anxieties that attend it."

Balancing his new role as a father with his studies, as well as his role at The Children's Corner, Fred Rogers managed to earn top honors and a leading prize for homiletics, the art of preaching, at the seminary.[6] The president of the seminary, Dr. Clifford E. Barbour, gave Fred a copy of his seminal work, Sin and the New Psychology, with the inscription: "My favorite and most brilliant student."[7]

When Rogers graduated in 1963 with a master of divinity, after eight years of study, he got his degree magna cum laude, as he had from Rollins College.

Fred's tenure at the seminary was during a time of deep dissension and controversy both for the Presbyterian Church in America and for the seminary itself. There were hard divisions between the very conservative United Presbyterian Church and the more liberal and progressive practitioners of the faith, and their battles were so hard-fought that they finally caused the seminary to appoint a special commission to release a set of recommendations to heal the divisions within the faculty and the institution.[8]

Rogers was always on the liberal side of this equation, and he later became a parishioner and sometime preacher at Pittsburgh's Sixth Presbyterian Church, a famous bastion of the progressive. The Sixth Church emphasized inclusion, and it was known in part for welcoming gay and lesbian parishioners, a position that was wholeheartedly supported by Joanne and Fred Rogers: "Fred was very happy in our [Sixth]

Presbyterian Church because there are no exclusions," recalls Joanne. "There's no exclusivity. If there had been a church called 'Reconciliation,' I think he would have joined it."

Joanne emphasizes Fred's belief that religious faith should bring all sorts of people together, not pull them apart.

She recalls that Fred kept trying to arrange a date with a woman for one of the male friends they met at the Sixth Church, before their new friend finally told Fred and Joanne he really wasn't interested: "Finally he said to Fred—about the third time they were together—he said, 'You know, Fred, I'm gay.' And Fred had no idea. It didn't matter one way or the other."[9]

Fred's social leanings were strongly progressive, but he learned from both his seminary experience and his television role to be circumspect about his views. Fred's nature was the opposite of quarrelsome, and he eschewed the endless left-right debates of the seminary. Some of his friends in Pittsburgh were disappointed that Fred didn't speak out publicly on behalf of the disadvantaged or vocally champion tolerance and inclusion, the values in which he so fervently believed. But Rogers worried that such public posturing would cause confusion with the parents and children he reached on television. And he always felt that actions—kindness, understanding, and openness in relationships—were more important than words.

According to Dr. Andrew Purves, professor of reformed theology at the seminary, Fred's political reticence stayed with him forever: "I don't remember him ever speaking on the floor of the Pittsburgh Presbytery. . . . I have seen him at meetings of the Presbytery, just sitting quietly by himself."[10]

And though he was at times quite frustrated with the Pittsburgh Presbytery and the Presbyterian Church itself, he stuck with it in large part because of the strong western-Pennsylvania, Scots-Irish, Presbyterian culture that had nurtured his family for decades. It was a culture that was bred to the bone in Fred Rogers, as it was to so many of the boys and girls growing up in western Pennsylvania in the middle of the last century.

The Pittsburgh essayist and poet Annie Dillard remembered that her childhood was defined, in part, by church, Bible camp, and the very serious and sometimes dour example of the Presbyterian elders who populated her East End neighborhood.

Even the architecture reinforced the notion of a severe and sober world: "The church building, where the old Scots-Irish families assembled weekly, was a Romanesque chunk of rough, carved stone and panes of dark slate. Covered in creeper, long since encrusted into its quietly splendid site, it looked like a Scottish rock in the rain. Everywhere outside and inside the church and parish hall, sharp carved things rose from the many dim tons of stone. . . . If your bare hand or arm brushed against one of the stone walls carelessly, the stone would draw blood."[11]

The Presbyterian values—hard work, responsibility and caring for others, parsimony, duty to family, ethical clarity, a strong sense of mission, and a relentless sense of service to God—drove every moment of Fred Rogers's life. Though an artist at heart—writing scripts, operas, musical scores, creating puppets and tales of fantasy—he could never escape a life of duty. The miracle is that he so wonderfully, so successfully, put the two together.

David McCullough, the Pittsburgh-raised historian and author who knew and appreciated Fred Rogers, emphasized the importance of Rogers's ability to bring his creativity down to the practical level of producing extraordinary television: "I've always liked writing about people who made something," said McCullough. "He made something."

McCullough, who grew up in the same time, region, and culture as Fred, adds that a key to understanding Rogers is the western Pennsylvania work ethic: "The Pittsburgh work ethic is not a Puritan work ethic. In Pittsburgh, if you were a good worker, you were respected, you were welcome."[12] The Puritan ethic could be a bit abstemious and pinched; while the Scots-Irish, Pittsburgh ethic is more inclusive, expansive, and appreciative of a strong commitment to work.

One of the most influential people in Fred's spiritual life was Dr. William Orr, the chain-smoking seminary professor who focused on the New Testament, loved more than anything to debate theology with his students, particularly Fred Rogers, and came as close to anyone Fred had known to being a living saint. When Rogers first arrived at the seminary, he asked the staff in the admissions office: "If you were starting your theological education right here and now, and you had time to take only one course, what would that course be?" He knew that his commitment to WQED would mitigate any greater course load.

As Rogers explained, "They didn't even hesitate, 'Oh, Bill Orr's Systematic Theology,' they said unanimously.

"Thus began a lifelong friendship. For the next eight years, three or four days a week, I would leave the frantic life of television production and drive to the seminary to study with a person who not only taught Christian theology—he lived it. Oh, we learned about epistemology and Christology, and eschatology, sanctification, and justification, and existentialism, but most of all, we witnessed the unfolding of the life of one of God's saints."[13]

More than once, Rogers saw Dr. Orr leave for lunch on a winter's day and come back without his overcoat, having given it to someone he encountered living on the street. Orr told Rogers not to worry: He had other coats back home. With everyone at the seminary, students and faculty alike, Orr was willing to give freely of his time, his books, his money, or anything that was needed.

Rogers found Orr, with his emphasis on kindness and caring and his deep belief in forgiveness, to be an example of how to live, and Fred decided to work hard to emulate his professor. When Rogers asked Orr what was the most important word in his theology, Orr replied that the word *forgiveness* was paramount because it alone could defeat the Devil.

"One little word shall fell him," Bill Orr told his student, who adopted the idea of forgiveness as the essence of human kindness. Rogers was strongly influenced by Orr to try to lead a life dedicated to human kindness, and he also found inspiration in Orr's principle of "guided drift."[14]

As explained by the Reverend William Barker, a friend and seminary mate of Rogers, Dr. Orr's philosophy was that one needed to live a life that was open to change and serendipity, that embraced the possibilities of life rather than the confines of a rigid set of rules.

"Once Bill Orr was talking about the Christian life, one in which you're kind of going along on a stream," said Bill Barker, nearly half a century later in an interview. "You can put out some poles from time to time to keep from bumping into the logs or hitting the banks, but primarily you guide yourself along. Still, it's with a sense that you're being carried along in ways you're perhaps unaware of."[15]

This notion of "guided drift," that we're guided by our principles but are also free to embrace the flow of life, was one Fred Rogers made his own and shared with friends for the rest of his life. It strongly influenced his willingness to experiment and take chances in his career.

Rogers remembered Dr. Orr as so focused on his teaching that he was forgetful of virtually everything else around him: "Talk about absentminded, as far as outside things were concerned. I mean, he'd come into the room—he was a smoker—and he would flick his ash in the wastebasket. One time it caught fire. He was lecturing, and he just took his foot and put the fire out. He didn't skip one syllable—just kept on talking."[16]

Fred got such pleasure from listening to Orr, and watching him perform, that he used to come back to the seminary years after graduation to attend his old teacher's lectures.[17] Rogers offered a simple explanation: "You know how, when you find somebody who you know is in touch with the truth . . . you want to be in the presence of that person."[18]

Andrew Purves remembered that after retirement, Bill Orr became confined to a nursing home, suffering the ill effects of his years of smoking. Fred Rogers visited him at least once a week for several years. Dr. Purves, who referred to Fred's visits to Orr as examples of the "covenantal faithfulness that Fred Rogers represented," marveled at how thoroughly the student had become the teacher.

Certainly, Orr's appeal to Fred Rogers derived from his intellect and his ability to explain theology and scripture to the younger man. But it was the example of Orr—someone living a Christian life Rogers could emulate—that was the real draw.

Fred Rogers, age 2, with his mother, Nancy McFeely Rogers (c. 1929 or 1930)

Fred Rogers as a baby, c. 1928

Fred Rogers as a boy, around age 4

Fred Rogers with his grandfather Fred Brooks McFeely, 1935

Fred Rogers, age 5, playing his first piano, 1933

Fred Rogers, age 11, holding his adopted sister, Elaine, 1939

Fred Rogers with his grandmother Nancy
McFeely, 1947

Joanne Byrd Rogers, 1950

Left to right: Fred's mother, Nancy Rogers; his grandmother Nancy McFeely;
Fred Rogers; Fred's sister, Elaine Rogers; and his father, James Rogers, c. 1948

Filming on the set of *The Children's Corner* at WQED, 1955

Josie Carey and Fred Rogers filming an Attic segment of
The Children's Corner, 1954

Fred Rogers with his sons, John (left) and James (right),
on the set of CBC's *Misterogers*, c. 1963

A WGBH Open House that drew more than five thousand people, 1967

Margaret Hamilton (left), aka the Wicked Witch of the West, as Princess Margaret H. Lizard, 1975

Maggie Stewart as Mayor Maggie of Westwood, which adjoins the Neighborhood of Make-Believe, 1975

Fred Rogers at the Senate hearings supporting public television, 1969

Neighborhood cast photograph. Clockwise from left: Chuck Aber, Joe Negri, David Newell, Don Brockett, Bob Trow, Betty Aberlin, Maggie Stewart, Fred Rogers, and Audrey Roth, 1990s

Fred Rogers with child development specialist Dr. Margaret McFarland, 1970s

Cameraman Bob Vaughn films Fred Rogers at the WQED studios in Pittsburgh

Fred Rogers with producer Margy Whitmer, 1992

Another Rogers friend, the Reverend George Wirth of the First Presbyterian Church of Atlanta, explains: "For Fred, Dr. Orr was one of the great mentors of his life, because Dr. Orr, a world-renowned Biblical scholar, one of the top theologians and professors in the seminary, was one of the most humble, approachable, loving people you could find. Fred's life was like Will Orr's life: great things, but never self-centered or self-aggrandizing, or self-anything. Father to son, in one sense; but brother to brother—older brother to younger brother—in another."[19]

Inevitably there were those at the seminary who compared Bill Orr to Christ—and others, later, who made the same comparison of Orr's student, Fred Rogers. Both men were dismayed at such suggestions, but the comparisons were persistent.

Dr. William Hirsch, a friend of Fred and Joanne from the Sixth Presbyterian Church who also knew Orr, chose to focus on the distinction Dr. Orr made between the Old Testament and the New Testament: "Well, if you met Christ, what would he be like? If you really think about that, he wouldn't be like your grandmother that was always just cooking you cookies, and patting you on the head. I think Fred had the qualities of Christ—the mother nature and the father nature.

"You know, that's why I think Jesus is really what God is, not the father God that is so scary. Dr. Orr used to say that the God of the Old Testament was more like the Devil than God, this creature that brought down fire and picked and chose who he was going to love and not love. But Fred had that feminine quality of mother love and acceptance, and no matter what you did, he loved you.

"So what would Christ be like? He would be like Fred. He would encourage you to do things that were right and would help other people."[20]

The Reverend Burr Wishart, who worked with Fred Rogers during the years that Wishart ran The Pittsburgh Foundation, which provided some of the funding for the *Neighborhood*, shared Hirsch's feeling: "I would lay him down against most of the prophets I know about from the Bible. I think he stands right up with the best of them. Fred preached. He was so talented at addressing the issues of morality and truth and caring and love and forgiveness, all the values that moral assumptions cover. He did it every day on the tube in various extraordinary ways. I loved not only his direct talk about some issue important to kids like bed-wetting; there was always a truth coming out. That's delicious.

"He would take offense at it, but he was the most Christlike human being I have ever encountered."[21]

Lisa Dormire, who worked on *Mister Rogers' Neighborhood* and later served as a vice president of the Pittsburgh Theological Seminary, saw the comparison of Rogers and Jesus in terms of authenticity: "I think he had very Christlike qualities, and that is part of what drew children. Children know a fraud more than anyone. . . . I truly believe he was one of the most authentic and Christlike people that I have ever known in my life. Just his manner. His ability to listen. . . . Everyone you talk to that had any encounter with him: It was a real moment in their lives."[22]

Interestingly, Rogers himself saw Jesus's strength more in terms of Jesus's authenticity as a real person than his mythological power as the son of God. In his occasional sermons, Fred Rogers would marvel at how genuine Jesus's childhood was: "And like so many other teenagers absorbed in their own pressing, growing needs, Jesus got scolded and went home with his parents.

"All this is to say that Jesus, the Christ, the Son of the Living God, was not only born a baby, he grew through all the stages of becoming an adult human being that each one of us grows through. He felt the pains of separations, the shames of being scolded, the joys of knowing that he was worthwhile, the frustrations of trying to convince people of the truth, as well as the angers that everyone knows.

"You see, I believe that Jesus gave us an eternal truth about the universality of feelings. Jesus was truthful about his feelings: Jesus wept; he got sad; Jesus got discouraged; he got scared; and he reveled in the things that pleased him. For Jesus, the greatest sin was hypocrisy. He always seemed to hold out much greater hope for a person who really knew the truth about himself or herself even though that person was a prostitute or a crooked tax collector. Jesus had much greater hope for someone like that than for someone who always pretended to be something he wasn't."[23]

Fred Rogers felt that part of the authenticity, the realness, that Jesus achieved came from his skillful use of storytelling. During his life, Jesus turned more and more often to the use of parables. At one point, he literally did all his teaching through them, taking everyday problems and situations and transforming them into short, vivid, compelling moral lessons. The most famous is that of "The Prodigal Son." Jesus understood, as did Fred Rogers, that a message delivered in story form is much more powerful than a sermon or an admonition.

In a speech in the early 1990s to a group of educators who worked with very young children, Fred Rogers employed storytelling to make the point that it is almost always a mistake to stifle the joyfulness of a child, even in the most serious setting. Fred told a story from his own life: "Last month I went to Cleveland for my Aunt Alberta Rogers's funeral. Aunt Bert was a very old lady who had lived a wonderfully full life. People of all ages felt comfortable with her because she was always herself. At any rate, after the service, all the family and friends gathered in the social hall of the church; and, as everyone was looking at pictures and reminiscing about the times we had had with Aunt Bert, one of her great-grandchildren—four-year-old Helen—started to do cartwheels across the floor of the social hall. And she did them very well.

"I learned that she had been going to gymnastics class ever since she was two years old—ever since a very wise doctor had suggested that class (rather than Ritalin) for this super-active girl. It was obvious that she had caught her gymnastics enthusiasm for the sport and she was well on her way to using it to express who she was and how she was feeling. I thought how pleased Aunt Alberta would be to see her little Helen doing that—especially right then! Doing cartwheels in the church! Dealing with her loss as she celebrated the life of her very special great-grandmother."[24]

In a way, it was serendipity that led Fred Rogers to Dr. Margaret McFarland, another great storyteller whose teaching methods employed narratives prominently. When the staff at the Pittsburgh Theological

Seminary asked Fred, about halfway through his studies there, what sort of ministry he envisioned for himself, they were surprised to learn that Rogers hoped to find a way to make his television work a ministry to children. Nothing like that had ever been fashioned from Presbyterian fabric, and Fred's teachers were somewhat at a loss to know how to guide him.

But one of them came up with the idea that if Fred was to find a way to work with children, he needed to study child development as well as religion. It was suggested that Fred could benefit from working with Dr. McFarland at her Arsenal Family & Children's Center, which she had established in the 1950s in the Lawrenceville section of Pittsburgh. Fred Rogers's studies under Dr. McFarland's tutelage led to a lifelong collaboration between the two that changed the trajectory of Fred's work and had a profound impact on the future *Mister Rogers' Neighborhood*.

As much as anything, it was Margaret McFarland's example that inspired Fred Rogers's embrace of storytelling as a central device for teaching. Associates of Dr. McFarland at the University of Pittsburgh School of Medicine sometimes marveled at the sheer number of stories that McFarland came up with to transmit her instruction. Sometimes it seemed as if she really couldn't just come out and tell you something; it had to be embedded in a tale.[25]

When Rogers finally graduated from the seminary with a master of divinity degree in 1963, he had also completed several years of study under McFarland and other Arsenal Center experts. Fred Rogers felt that he was ready to take his new ministry back to television to serve children.

But he got a surprise: the elders of the Pittsburgh Presbytery didn't agree. Despite the course of Fred's studies, and the case he made for working with children, the elders felt he should follow a traditional path: He should go to a church and become an assistant pastor and then work his way up to the top post and deliver sermons on Sundays. The local Presbytery had the authority to rule on any such assignment, and Fred was stuck.

But he was determined not to give in. He didn't want to take over a church, and he particularly didn't want to give sermons. He was very comfortable on television, but he got nervous and decidedly uncomfortable in the pulpit. Jeanne Barker, wife of the Reverend Bill Barker and, like her husband, a lifelong friend of Fred and Joanne Rogers, remembered that Fred always resisted giving sermons: "I remember once they [the teachers at the seminary] sent him out to preach at church. He was so shy about having to stand up and preach. He got really tense, having to stand in a pulpit."[26]

When Bill Barker was about to be installed as the minister of a new church, he asked his good friend Fred Rogers to come and give the installation sermon, a lesson that would set the tone for Barker's tenure as pastor. But Fred was so nervous in the pulpit, Bill and Jeanne remembered, that the tone he set was more about tension than anything else.

According to Bill Barker, the leaders of the Pittsburgh Presbytery were very conservative and lacked the imagination to see the potential of Fred Rogers's idea. Barker, who had attended the seminary at the beginning of Fred's time there and was now teaching part-time at the seminary, got frustrated: He decided he would go to bat for his friend and directly challenge the elders of the church. "I had to convince the Pittsburgh Presbytery eventually. They had the traditional idea that if you are going to be ordained as a Presbyterian minister, you are going to be in a pulpit, you are going to wear a black robe, and you are going to stand up there at eleven on Sunday morning, you know, the whole routine."

In speaking out this way, Barker was risking his own position in the church, as well as the possibility of creating more animosity among the elders toward Fred.

Bill Barker invited himself into one of the meetings of the Presbytery and made an impassioned plea for Rogers's ministry to children: "Look, here's an individual who has his pulpit proudly in front of a TV camera. His congregation are little people from the ages of about two or three on up to about seven or eight. And this is a whole congregation of hundreds of thousands if not millions of kids, and this is a man who has been authentically called by the Lord as much as any of you guys sitting out there."[27]

It worked. The elders relented, and somewhat reluctantly approved Fred's plan to try to build his own Presbyterian ministry through television. At the time, it was the most unusual plan for a young minister to come out of any local Presbytery in the United States. When Fred was ordained, he turned again to his friend Bill Barker to give the charge at his ordination ceremony.

As Rogers recalled years later, Barker laid it on thick, partly for the benefit of the church elders, about the fact that now Fred's "pulpit will not be so much the traditional piece of oak wood up in front of a group of pews there, but in front of a camera, a TV camera, that red eye that you see in the studio on those two or three cameras that are being moved around. . . . I was telling him, and trying to tell the church, too, that this was Fred's very unique form of serving God."[28]

On a subsequent trip to Scotland, Bill Barker bought two Presbyterian-clergy tartan ties, a traditional pattern that signified an ordained minister of the church, and gave one to Fred. Ever thankful to his brother minister, Fred Rogers wore the tie for years to come, including during some of his television tapings. Later, at the end of his life, Fred chose to be buried in the tie. But as successful as Barker had been in standing up for his friend, the leaders of the Pittsburgh Presbytery were unmoved on another front. Not long after Fred was ordained, he applied for funds to advance his television ministry. No dice: The elders ruled that they were not going to devote any of the Presbytery's resources to television. Neither Fred nor Bill Barker could change the elders' minds.

Once again, Fred Rogers was stuck. He had ended his work on *The Children's Corner* at WQED during the last year of his studies at the seminary, mostly so he could finish those studies and get his degree. Now he was without a program or any sort of base from which to advance his work with children. Josie Carey had moved on to full-time work at KDKA. Fred began to spend some time volunteering at early childhood education centers recommended by Dr. McFarland, testing some of his creative work with puppets and music to see how children in the centers responded to his own performances, without Josie and the trappings of the *Corner*. He was encouraged, and he enjoyed working with the children and their teachers. But it wasn't television; it wasn't his calling.

When Fred ended the *Corner*, Josie was upset and unhappy, but she accepted his explanation that he needed to focus on his studies. Margaret McFarland had inspired him. He believed in the work he could do for children with her help. And he believed that all the pieces he had been fashioning into a new professional life—television, education, the ministry, the puppets, the theater, music—could come together in a way that might make the most important work he had ever imagined. He just needed a television program.

8.

DR. MARGARET MCFARLAND

FRED ROGERS'S KEY ADVISOR and collaborator—you might even call her his childhood-education guru—sits in her home outside Pittsburgh for a videotaped interview. It's 1988; Dr. Margaret McFarland and Fred Rogers have worked together for thirty years. Her input on almost all the scripts and songs of *Mister Rogers' Neighborhood* was the defining element of her career in child development. It was a field she chose as a young girl, and she never wavered from her determination to help children and families.

Eighty-three years old, in a white blouse and a dusty-rose-colored jacket, Dr. McFarland looks small, thin, and frail, with a toothy smile framed by a prominent chin and nose: a little bit of Margaret Hamilton as the Wicked Witch of the West in *The Wizard of Oz*, but kinder. In a wavering voice, she speaks slowly and deliberately. The deep chair that frames her makes her appear even more diminutive and childlike.

The interview is an attempt by Rogers and PBS station WQED to get some of her thinking on tape for posterity. Over the course of an hour and a half, Dr. McFarland's deep intelligence and her authoritative explanations give an ever-increasing weight to her presence. The effect, which builds throughout, is to assert her power as an intellect and as a teacher. She is suffering from an abdominal ailment and seems slightly uncomfortable throughout. In just a few months, Dr. Margaret McFarland will be dead; but her legacy lives on, with millions of children who grew up on *Mister Rogers' Neighborhood*.

Though Margaret McFarland was a slight figure with a soft voice, she was also an exceptionally forceful woman who knew exactly what she wanted to accomplish. She was uncommonly successful at reaching her goals, which always revolved around young children and their needs. She spent years researching and teaching about child development, and she worked with the most influential people in her field: Dr. Benjamin Spock at the University of Pittsburgh and the Arsenal Center (before Spock moved to Cleveland to teach at Western Reserve University, now Case Western Reserve University); T. Berry Brazelton, another famed pediatrician who taught at Pitt and Harvard; and Erik Erikson, the psychologist who did so much to shape thinking about childhood and taught at Harvard and Berkeley.

All these giants in the field of human development revered McFarland. Erikson once said, "Margaret McFarland knew more than anyone in this world about families with young children."[1]

When she answers a question in the videotaped interview, she smiles broadly. The camera never strays far from her face as she tells a story about the connections Fred Rogers made with children at her University of Pittsburgh research and teaching facility, the Arsenal Family & Children's Center: "There was a little girl at the Arsenal whose bird died. And when Fred came with his puppets, and she told Fred about the death of the bird—when he got the puppets out of his satchel, she found it urgent to tell each of the puppets about the death of the canary.

"The children confided to Fred and to his puppets many important things," she says, and then describes what gave Fred Rogers such rapport with little children: "Fred can recall—and can afford to recall—his own childhood."[2]

She focuses on how comfortable Rogers was making a direct connection back to his earliest years—the very thing that first impressed McFarland, who was sustained by the same powerful connection to her own childhood.

During the second half of the interview, McFarland observes how Fred Rogers's cultural sophistication lent weight to his programming for preschoolers: "You see, Fred Rogers has had . . . experience far beyond most of us. He's traveled. He's studied French with rich people. He reads Greek for pleasure."

She notes how daunted children can be to encounter Fred Rogers out in the real world: "One day, a young mother was coming down the street . . . and her two-and-a-half [-year-old] was hip-hopping ahead of her . . . when he saw Fred.

"The little boy stopped dead in his tracks, turned around and fled, hiding behind his mother's skirts. He knew Mister Rogers from television, and didn't know what to make of seeing the man on the street near his own home. When Fred walked ahead, the boy followed him all the way to Rogers's house, into which Mister Rogers disappeared."

Rogers saw that the little boy was still standing outside, conflicted, but hoping to see more of the host of *Mister Rogers' Neighborhood*. Fred Rogers reemerged from his house, talked to the little boy, and then walked all the way back down the street toward the boy's house, quietly conversing with him. "I think children perceived him as sometimes childlike, but often as though he were a parent," explains Dr. McFarland.[3]

Dr. Margaret McFarland grew up in Oakdale, Pennsylvania, in the suburbs outside Pittsburgh, in the early part of the twentieth century, part of a large population of Scots-Irish and German immigrants who'd come to the rivers and mountains of western Pennsylvania to work in the mills and the mines in the second half of the nineteenth century. Margaret adored and admired her father, a Scotsman with a thick brogue. Later she told friends that as a little girl, she'd always wanted to be introduced as the daughter of Mr. McFarland, and never to be introduced by her own given name. But that hope was short-lived: Her father was an invalid who died when Margaret was just five years old.[4]

Years later, talking with Fred Rogers in her office at the University of Pittsburgh, McFarland marveled at how critically important each parent can be to a child. Each parent, she explained, sounds different, feels different, even smells different to the child, who needs all the distinct qualities of the mother and the father to feel whole. One can sense, in McFarland's conversation with Rogers, the terrible desperation the little girl felt when she lost her father. Margaret McFarland turned to her mother, full of fear that she could just as suddenly and unexpectedly lose her, too.

Margaret's mother tried to make up for the loss by spending more time with the little girl, talking with her all the time, and giving her the love and attention she feared she was missing from her father. In this, Margaret's childhood was similar to Fred Rogers's, given his close relationship with his own mother. McFarland later remembered, with deep appreciation, that her mother had successfully remade Margaret's childhood from one of sadness to one of "pleasure" in her mother's company.[5]

But soon things took another dark turn: Not long after Margaret's father died, she contracted rheumatic fever. It was a frightening time for the little girl, kept at home by her illness. Her mother worked hard to help young Margaret, but her daughter's childhood was populated with the darkest fears: Would she lose her life, too? Would her mother get sick, become an invalid, and die? Would Margaret ever be able to fully recover from the effects of rheumatic fever and have a normal life?

What turned the tide for McFarland in these early, frightening years was the same thing that later helped the young Fred Rogers emerge from his own childhood fears to become a capable and confident young man: the attention of a caring adult who focused on the child, listened, talked about fear and about life itself, and gave the child a direct connection to the adult world.[6] The family doctor noticed young Margaret's loneliness, and he helped her move ahead. In those days, doctors routinely made house calls, and he came back again and again to check up on her. When her recovery had progressed far enough that the doctor felt confident about letting Margaret go back outside, he invited her to come with him in his car as he made the rounds of house calls to his other patients.

Day after day, the doctor would pick up Margaret at home and let her ride with him in his car, talking with her the whole time about her life, and about the details of the cases of his other patients, many of whom were infants and children. Margaret would wait in the car while the doctor visited each house and then talk with him about the other children when he came back to drive to the next stop.[7]

Young Margaret McFarland got the benefit of the company of this thoughtful and caring man, and she got an education in what it meant for him to work with little children. "I loved him dearly," said the grown-up Margaret years later, remarking that the doctor became a "surrogate father" to her.[8]

Her experiences with the family doctor helped Margaret overcome her fears about losing both of her parents. With his help, she came out of her shell to become a far more engaged child. Most importantly, her rides with him kindled the interest that would later become her life's work: child development. Her long conversations with the kindly doctor, who explained what each of his child patients was experiencing, became the stuff of young Margaret McFarland's imagination.

By the time Margaret was a teenager, she had decided to study child development (not medicine, interestingly) and to become a specialist in the workings of families with young children. She studied at Goucher College near Baltimore, Maryland, where she received her undergraduate degree, then went on to Columbia University in New York to get her doctorate. After graduation, Dr. McFarland spent four years in Australia, teaching young teachers how to manage kindergarten classes. But she tired of being so far away from home, and came back to join the faculty at Mount Holyoke College in western Massachusetts.[9]

Meanwhile, back in Margaret's hometown, Dr. Benjamin Spock was trying to interest the leaders of the University of Pittsburgh in starting a program for very young children that could serve the community and provide a base for the sort of research into children and families that he wanted to conduct. Spock—who was teaching at the Pitt School of Medicine as well as writing and practicing medicine—was already, arguably, the most famous pediatrician in the United States. His book about raising and caring for children, *The Common Sense Book of Baby and Child Care*, had been published a few years earlier and had made Dr. Spock a household name in America, and eventually, much of the rest of the world. Spock's baby book became the second-bestselling book in history (after the Bible) and a trusted reference for millions of parents. Over the years, Benjamin Spock also courted controversy: Some leaders in the media and popular culture faulted him for being far too lenient with young children, a criticism that later appended to one of his followers, Fred Rogers. Dr. Spock, like Rogers later, encouraged young parents to realize that they themselves had all the tools to help their children, and that engaging with children deeply was more important than incessantly correcting them. A champion rower (he won an Olympic gold medal with the Yale crew in 1924), Spock also became controversial for his opposition to the Vietnam War in the 1960s.

Even in the early 1950s, Spock was influential enough to get the university to commit funds to starting his research and education center. When he got the approval, Spock located the center in a couple of houses in the Arsenal section of the city, whose name derived from the nineteenth-century arsenal that manufactured much of the munitions supply for the Union Army during the Civil War. Located in the Lawrenceville section of Pittsburgh, it was about a twenty-minute drive from the university.

Spock needed someone to run the center for him; he was too busy teaching, writing, and practicing medicine. An associate at Pitt gave him the name of Margaret McFarland, who was already establishing a reputation for depth and thoughtfulness as a scholar of early childhood education. It was just the chance McFarland needed, and she returned to Pittsburgh to become the director of the center, which took the name Arsenal Family & Children's Center. It opened in 1953 and provided early education for Pittsburgh children for decades. It also served as the site for some of the most important research into child development in the twentieth century.

Spock intended that the Arsenal Center would provide a site for pediatric students at Pitt to study the behavior of children and their families in a very stable Eastern European ethnic community. He hoped the center would go on for decades, providing the basis for long-term longitudinal studies of child development. In fact, the center still exists, though it separated from its research base at Pitt and became a stand-alone nonprofit in 1980.

By the time Fred Rogers came to study at the Arsenal Center, it was a teeming petri dish of the most progressive thinking in the rapidly developing field of child development. Just at this point, when Rogers was evolving from the off-the-cuff zaniness of *The Children's Corner* to making serious educational television, he could not have found a richer intellectual environment in which to learn about child development and to establish rigorous standards for his own work.

Like Fred Rogers later, Ben Spock tried to influence parents to treat their young children as individuals and to have the confidence to be flexible and responsive with them. Under the leadership of Spock and McFarland, the Arsenal Center attracted other cutting-edge thinkers who agreed with some of their approaches, like Erik Erikson, who came there in the 1950s to spend time working with Spock and McFarland on their research.

When he was approached by Spock, Erikson was based at the Austen Riggs Center, a private psychiatric treatment center in Stockbridge, Massachusetts. He'd also been on the faculty at the Pitt medical school during the 1950s, and he taught at Harvard and the University of California, Berkeley. The 1950 publication of his book *Childhood and Society* established his reputation as one of the leading thinkers in the world on the topic.

Erik Erikson had studied with Anna Freud, the daughter of Sigmund Freud, and became one of the first psychoanalysts to work with children. He focused much of his thinking on the question of ego identity, and he is credited with being the originator of the term "identity crisis." (Interestingly, Erikson himself struggled with identity as a young man; he was from a Jewish family but turned out to have had a Danish father who had been the lover of his Jewish mother; Erikson was teased at school both for being Jewish and for looking Nordic.)

According to Erikson's philosophy, it was essential for a child to grow up in a healthy environment if he or she was to go through the various stages of psychological development in a normal way. Like Spock and Rogers, Erikson felt that parents, and their interaction with their children, were critical. He won both a Pulitzer Prize and a National

Book Award for his book *Gandhi's Truth*, and he was selected to deliver a Jefferson Lecture, one of the highest honors in the humanities.

As if it weren't enough for this new center to have Spock and McFarland and Erikson, the Arsenal was also able to attract Dr. T. Berry Brazelton, another noted pediatrician and author acclaimed for his research, who wrote twenty-four books as well as a syndicated newspaper column. He is probably best known today as the author of a book and a cable television show from the 1980s that shared the same title: *What Every Baby Knows.*

Perhaps Brazelton's primary impact on the field of pediatrics was his ability to get other doctors to pay more attention to the behavioral and emotional expressions of their patients. Just as Rogers later focused his television production as much on the social and emotional development of young children as he did on their cognitive growth, Dr. Brazelton paid attention to the feelings, activities, and behaviors of his patients as well as to their physical conditions. An early study led by Brazelton focused on mothers and babies managing breastfeeding together; he saw their actions as a very early form of communication that was in effect a precursor to spoken language.

IN VICTORIAN TIMES, children were viewed as rather annoying miniature adults, and the infant and toddler years were thought of as a difficult period that parent and child alike should get through as quickly as possible. Research in the nineteenth and twentieth centuries revealed that young children are voracious learners, and that early childhood is a critical period in terms of the development of outlook, capacity, function, and even the physiology of the brain. The great thinkers at the Arsenal Center were focused on just how parents and teachers could best understand and approach this most-important period in a child's life.

To some extent, Spock and the other academics at the Arsenal Center were reacting to decades of Victorian and post-Victorian child-rearing practices that emphasized keeping children in their place. It was a time memorialized by the saying: "Children are best seen, not heard." The Arsenal Center experts knew that such thinking could lead parents to miss great opportunities to engage their young children and help them learn.

Toward the end of the twentieth century, after some parents had taken this lesson a bit far in terms of permissiveness, there was a negative reaction to Spock and his lessons in some parts of popular culture. But the strongest criticism of Spock's methods misses the point that he was redressing an imbalance in how children were viewed and raised. As Fred Rogers himself often noted, what works best is a fine balance between flexibility, creativity, structure, and discipline. And the best discipline is not punishment, but teaching a child the art of self-discipline.

When Fred Rogers's teachers at the Pittsburgh Theological Seminary had the good sense to send him over to Margaret McFarland, he found the perfect environment in which to marry his creative work with high academic standards. Rogers took the teachings of McFarland, Spock, Erikson, and Brazelton and gave them a practical role in the real world of early childhood education. He gave their research immediacy and currency by thrusting it into the new world of television and popular culture.

Eventually, it was Fred Rogers who taught multiple generations of American parents how very critical the first few years of human life could be, and how social and emotional learning is more important at that age than cognitive learning. More than any other popular voice in American culture, Fred Rogers taught this powerful lesson to parents, teachers, and to children themselves through his gentle, slow-paced but richly textured programming.

MCFARLAND'S APPROACH TO TEACHING graduate students from the medical school and other programs at Pitt was completely distinctive. Although she certainly cited leading thinkers in the field—like

Jean Piaget, Lev Vygotsky, and Anna Freud—and assigned their texts to be read by her students, her lectures were not lectures at all. Instead, they took two unusual forms for a university professor: stories or parables that conveyed her meaning through narrative, and discussions with parents and children about learning, which were held in the presence of McFarland's students.

Nancy Curry, who studied with Fred Rogers under McFarland and later became a professor at Pitt and a consultant to *Mister Rogers' Neighborhood*, remembers the power of the McFarland method: "The field of child development . . . was relatively new. The literature, Margaret knew very, very well . . . and so that's what we learned in our courses. That's what Fred was learning, too.

"Every week we would have a case conference up in the attic, where Fred would come, too, and we would discuss one child. Then psychologists would test the child, the teacher would report on the child, and then the consultant . . . would discuss what we had presented.

"Nurses came, and doctors—I think they were first-year residents—came for a term. . . . Margaret would bring families into her classes and have us observe them and discuss them. And the families knew we were research people and they were neighborhood people, which is what Spock wanted . . . he wanted the neighborhood kids in the room."[10]

When McFarland brought families into the center, into the midst of a discussion among teachers, researchers, and students, she would always spend time in small talk with the parents to make sure they were relaxed and comfortable in the setting, and didn't feel like guinea pigs.

Once, she took the entire time allotted for the class in small talk about cooking with a young mother who seemed wary. Hedda Sharapan, one of the key staff members at Fred Rogers's Family Communications, Inc. remembers: "But the story with Margaret is that she was doing a case study and had the physicians—medical students—lined up in her office to watch her discussion with a parent. There was a problem with the child. The woman came into the session late—the mother—and she said, 'I am so sorry. I've been baking, and I forgot the time.'

"So Margaret started talking to her about what she was baking—and this was a family recipe—and on and on and on, and only in the last few minutes did they actually talk about the little boy. And the medical students, afterward, said to Margaret, 'You wasted all that time, talking about the cookies, the recipe.' She said, 'How could I ask them to trust my competency until I showed her that I trusted hers.' "[11]

McFarland and Rogers shared this sensitivity to the feelings of other people. And they shared a great sensitivity to the impact of specific language, particularly with impressionable young children.

Nancy Curry remembers how carefully and thoughtfully Dr. McFarland dealt with each detail of her studies with children: "She taught us to be careful observers, to use our empathy and our own experiences as children to understand the child we were observing, to relate these observations to psychodynamic theory, and then respond with clinical insights to children in our care. This method of teaching made working with and learning about children enriching and exciting."[12]

DR. MCFARLAND was a notoriously impetuous driver. Nancy Curry recalls an instructive instance: "One of my fondest memories was of Fred accompanying our class on a field trip to a wooded area that was beloved by Margaret from her own childhood. Fred arrived in his yachting whites [as a young man still under the influence of his parents, Rogers could be a much more dapper dresser than in later years] and agreed to drive half the children in his car while Margaret drove the others. Once on the parkway, we were amazed to be in the wake of a transformed Margaret who drove at such a speed and took such risks that Fred and I were both breathless and not a little terrified. Our relief at arriving became tempered by the daunting task of scaling an almost perpendicular hill in search of the waterfall where Margaret promised the children a surprise."

One of the children was particularly fearful. It was the 1950s, in the middle of the Cold War between the United States and the Soviet

Union, and the child's fears fixed on what he had heard from adults about the possibility of a nuclear bomb.

"How can we see the mushroom-shaped cloud through all these trees if we are bombed?" he wailed.

When Curry and Rogers finally got back to Fred's car and began the harrowing job of following McFarland back to the Arsenal Center, "the little boy now was lying on the back seat, sucking his thumb . . . and clutching his penis," recalled Curry. "Fred, exhausted and rumpled, muttered, 'Leave him alone. It's probably the happiest he's been all day.' "[13]

Curry and Rogers did appreciate McFarland's serious nature as a scholar. But they and other students sometimes wearied of that serious side, particularly when Dr. McFarland would cite a seemingly endless stream of famous scholars to support her teaching. Eventually, Nancy Curry and Fred Rogers made up their own fictional early childhood expert to fill in when they couldn't remember all their teacher's citations.

"It was hard to keep all the experts and their theories straight," said Curry later, "so we invented an imaginary expert, 'Orvetta Wells,' a universal child theoretician to whom we could turn when we forgot to attribute some bit of wisdom: 'As Orvetta Wells would say . . . ' we would mutter when a teacher would drop one too many names."[14]

According to David Newell, a.k.a. Mr. McFeely, one of the earliest cast members on Mister Rogers' Neighborhood, McFarland's very gentle, unassuming, and sweet manner was deceptive: "Margaret reminded me of a person who would work in a Fanny Farmer candy store! Little did people know that she held her own with Ben Spock and Erik Erikson.

"She was no shrinking violet. She, like Fred, had [a] backbone of steel. For both of them, outward appearances were deceptive. . . . I think sometimes people interpreted them outwardly only."[15]

Nancy Curry agrees that Margaret McFarland only seemed soft: "Well, at first I thought she was like a saint. Nobody in my life had ever made me feel as good as she did. She had a very controlling side, quietly controlling. The guys at the Western Psych [a psychiatric hospital affiliated with the Arsenal Center] would say that she was 'the iron fist in a velvet glove.' "[16]

Eliot Daley, former head of the early Rogers for-profit company Small World Enterprises, notes that Rogers and McFarland shared similar childhood experiences and developed much the same nature as adults. These similarities of background and character are the secret to how well they collaborated over the years. Daley thinks of Rogers and McFarland as studies in contrasts: sweet and innocent, but focused and sharply determined; each somewhat masculine and somewhat feminine (or "androgynous," to use Daley's term); caring and thoughtful about other people, but with a steely resolve about their own goals.

"And, you know, he may have . . . actually absorbed some of that [character] from Margaret McFarland," Daley said in an interview several decades after his work with Small World: "There's a harmony there; there's a resonance between. Fred spent so many hours with her."[17]

It was, in a way, an almost perfect partnership. Rogers brought an intense creativity and a worldly connection to the fields of television and entertainment. McFarland brought an academic rigor and authority that Rogers desperately wanted as the underpinning for his programming. Their work together was so intense that Rogers, uncharacteristically, ordered the doors locked and no interruptions from anyone else when they were closeted in one of their offices.[18] And they sustained a great love and respect for each other throughout their decades together.

Pittsburgh-born historian and writer David McCullough best described McFarland's special skills as an instructor: "There was a wonderful professor of child psychology at the University of Pittsburgh named Margaret McFarland who was so wise that I wish her teachings and her ideas and her themes were much better known. She said that attitudes aren't taught, they're caught. If the teacher has an attitude of enthusiasm for the subject, the student catches that whether the student is in second grade or is in graduate school. She said that if you show them what you love, they'll get it and they'll want to get it."[19]

Fred Rogers remembered that when McFarland wanted to expose the little children at the Arsenal Center to the work of a sculptor, she gave these instructions to the artist she invited to visit her classes: " 'I don't want you to teach sculpting. All I want you to do is to love clay in front of the children.' And that's what he did. He came once a week for a whole term, sat with the four- and five-year-olds as they played, and he 'loved' his clay in front of them. The children caught his enthusiasm for it, and that's what mattered. Like most good things, teaching has to do with honesty."[20]

9.

TORONTO AND THE CBC

FRANCIS CHAPMAN studied English literature and philosophy at university in Canada, where he grew up, and he thought he might translate that into an academic career when he graduated. His father was an architect, his mother a concert pianist, and he was raised in a big house in Toronto full of people and talk and intellectual ferment. "There were six children, and it was a very full house. It was a very large house—my father, mother, grandmother, six kids, dogs and cats, and various hangers on who would come to stay," he recalled years later.[1]

The intellectual intensity of academia might well have suited him. But when it came time to go to work, Chapman balked at the formality of an academic life, and he plunged into something wholly new and different—television. It was the early 1950s, the Canadian Broadcasting Corporation (CBC) was just getting started, and Chapman was intrigued.

"The first year of television for Canada came around," said Chapman, "and I heard that there were openings on the stage crew. So I joined the stage crew ahead of considering an academic career because I thought this sounded like an interesting opportunity."

It paid off right away. Soon he was working as an assistant director. Then he got an opportunity to make what he called an "expedition" to Africa to use his directing skills to document stories there. "We produced a film and a recording of Pygmy music, later released by Folkways," he said. "We drove . . . through France, and shipped across the Mediterranean to North Africa, to Ghana. . . . That was a very interesting time, because there were political upheavals in Ghana.

We interviewed Kwame Nkrumah, who was about to be president of the new republic. And then we drove on to the Belgian Congo."[2]

All this was very heady stuff for the young Chapman, and he—quite accurately, as it turned out—envisioned an exciting future as a director of television and film.

But suddenly one of the CBC bosses threw a curveball into this fledgling career. Chapman was back in Toronto, and Fred Rainsberry, a top CBC executive in charge of children's programming, asked him to take on a rather odd role: in Chapman's words, he was asked to "look after" a young television creator and performer from Pittsburgh, Pennsylvania. Rainsberry told Chapman that Fred Rogers was "a treasure that ought to be taken care of."

Although Chapman was somewhat nonplussed by this unusual assignment, he took an immediate liking to Rogers: "I spoke to Fred on the telephone—that was the first time we met—and we very soon hit it off. He had a very nice sense of humor, but I was aware that he was very, very serious—extremely serious, about his work and that this was an important step in his work."[3]

In fact, it was this very intensity of purpose that led Fred Rogers to Canada and a newly minted career at the CBC. Toward the end of his studies at Pittsburgh Theological Seminary, Fred Rogers had ended his work on WQED's *The Children's Corner* to devote all his time to his school work, hoping to quickly finish at the seminary and become an ordained Presbyterian minister. At least, that was the story at the time.

Years later, his wife, Joanne, would recall that he was becoming frustrated with *The Children's Corner* and felt that he could fashion a much better program for young children based on his own experience and his studies in early education under Dr. Margaret McFarland. And he knew that his work with Josie Carey, as popular and successful as it had been, wasn't the right road to his future.[4]

According to Rogers's later recollection, Rainsberry told him he had seen *The Children's Corner*—and he had seen Fred speaking directly with children at a public appearance Rainsberry had attended. He was hoping to convince Rogers to come to the CBC to produce a daily fifteen-minute program for children. It seemed a godsend: Rogers would have the ample resources of the CBC to focus on high quality, and he would have the freedom to shape his own show.

In a letter composed on May 12, 1958, Fred Rogers told Rainsberry of his excitement about his opera for children, *Josephine the Short-Neck Giraffe*, begun in Rogers's student days at Rollins: "The script is nearly complete. It's an ambitious work, but I believe it could be a spectacular work for the whole family."

Fred Rogers offers to swing by Toronto while on a summer road trip with Joanne if Rainsberry "might be interested in using this musical fantasy. One of the record companies in New York wants to record it, but I feel it should be produced as a live television drama or a fully animated cartoon before it's put on disc."[5]

The two Freds hit it off, though clearly *Josephine* was not ideal for a fifteen-minute format. As we know now, Rogers's student opera didn't make it onto the air until 1989, when it was shown on the *Neighborhood* in a thirty-minute program. But in proposing this to Rainsberry, Fred Rogers presented himself as a self-confident musician and composer, articulating his ideas for ambitious future children's programming as he wound down his role on *The Children's Corner*.

In 1960, Rogers's whimsy kicks in as he writes to Rainsberry as "Doctor Painsteary": "Joanne and I are expecting a little playmate for Jamie in June. We'd always hoped to have at least two children. Jamie's such a dear; we just hope that his sister/brother will be just as good."

In a later letter to Rainsberry in 1961, Fred Rogers details his new courses at the seminary, including psychology and counseling (in a Freudian framework), as well as Old Testament theology. Clearly his studies, combined with the joys but also the anxieties of being a new parent, contributed to some unease.

He tells Fred Rainsberry: "You'll never know what your phone call did for my spirits the other night! It had been a long day of plannings and doings, and I had come home to wonder if man wasn't really meant to just sit by his own fire, and develop a craft which could easily be carried out at home. Whittling was very tempting at the moment (but I don't know the first thing about whittling)."[6]

Whittling aside, in 1962, Fred Rogers went ahead by himself to Toronto to see how a new show would work out before he moved Joanne and the two young boys to Canada. When *Misterogers* debuted in 1963, Jim was four. His younger brother, John, was two.

The family didn't make the move north until the show was well into production. Once Fred was comfortable with the CBC and the development of *Misterogers*, Joanne and the boys moved up to a rented house in Rosedale, an affluent section of Toronto directly north of downtown, not far from the CBC studios. Both Joanne and Fred later remembered Toronto as a wonderful place to live, and they fit into their new neighborhood, where there were plenty of parks for young boys to play.

Fred Rogers saw a great deal of Francis Chapman's large family in the year before his own family arrived, and he became friends with all of them. One of the reasons Rogers fit so well into the family was music, as Chapman later recalled: "In a very primitive way, I played a little bit of violin. One of my brothers played the cello; my sister played viola and piano and violin. There was always music in the house."[7]

Rogers played the piano with Chapman's mother, who had trained as a concert pianist in England where she had grown up, and with the rest of this extended family. And Chapman threw himself into his assignment of helping Fred Rogers and Fred Rainsberry achieve their goals for children's television. That job, Chapman later remembered, was "to help Fred realize his own dream of a very serious series addressing the needs of young children, and of addressing their fears and providing on the television screen a kind of comfort and a home."[8]

But this program was going to be different, because Fred Rainsberry had a surprise for Fred Rogers: He wanted Rogers to come out from behind the puppet stage and appear in person on television. Except for a couple of very brief appearances on the *Corner*, Rogers had rarely appeared on camera, and he didn't want to. He was naturally unassuming, even somewhat shy, and he was most comfortable behind the scenes and behind his puppets. Asked years later whether Rainsberry easily persuaded him to appear, Rogers said firmly, "No."

Fred Rogers continued: "When I got to Canada, Fred Rainsberry said, 'I want you to be on camera; I've seen you talk with kids.' And I said, 'Oh, I thought you wanted me to come and do puppets and music, which is what I've always done.'

"He said, 'No, you can do that, too. But I want you to look into the lens, and just pretend that's a child, and we'll just call it *Misterogers*. Let's just do that.' "9

Fred Rogers was attracted to the fact that while Rainsberry was a professor of philosophy at the University of Toronto, he also was head of children's programming for the CBC.

In turn, Fred Rainsberry was sure that Fred Rogers's authenticity as a person would come through on camera, and he was adamant about Rogers giving it a try. Like Rogers himself, Rainsberry had become convinced through his academic work that television had the potential to be an important educational tool, if properly conceived and managed to the highest standards.

According to his son-in-law, "Fred Rainsberry was a fierce foe of schlock, and a guardian against children being seen as another market segment of consumers. Canadian children's television in the 1950s and 1960s was kinder, gentler—and usually a lot more fun and emotionally connected—than its American counterparts because Fred Rainsberry was committed to that philosophy."10

So here was a well-connected television executive who shared Rogers's antipathy to the exploitation of children, who had the resources to enable Rogers to pursue his vision, and who had sought out Fred in Pittsburgh.

What's more, Rainsberry had become something of a student of the nascent early childhood education movement. He shared with Fred Rogers one of the books on child development he had been reading, and finally he convinced Rogers to appear on camera to see if that could become one of the important ways in which, together, they could advance educational television.11

The new showcase for Fred Rogers's talent was an instant success. *Misterogers*, a fifteen-minute, daily show taped in black and white, debuted on the CBC in 1963 and ran until 1967. It was a miniature version of what would later become the half-hour *Neighborhood*. Many of the elements that would distinguish *Mister Rogers' Neighborhood* in Pittsburgh—the trolley, the cardigan sweater, the puppets, the music, the Neighborhood of Make-Believe, the gentle, reassuring tone of Fred Rogers—were part of the show, distributed nationally in Canada.

Francis Chapman recalls extensive discussions with Rogers about the separation between elements of the program: "Well, he didn't want the children to confuse make-believe with reality. Therefore, he wanted a definite transition saying, 'We're going from this to that. This is one world, that is another, but it's a play world.'"[12]

Chapman later felt that the very depth of Rogers's own involvement in creating *Misterogers*—writing the scripts, performing the puppets, writing and performing the music, directing and producing the show—insulated him from his fears about performing. That is, Fred Rogers was so intent on shaping a good program that he didn't even think about portraying a character—he was just Fred being Fred.

"Well, it was really very, very simple," recalls Chapman, "because Fred was so totally honest, a naturally honest person—I don't mean that acting is not honest. He just couldn't be anything but himself. He managed that very, very comfortably and easily, once he found that what he did was accepted by the people around him. The studio people found it difficult at first—Fred seemed almost too good to be true—but they very quickly discovered that he was as true as he seemed. He was so focused on doing the right thing by his audience that he wasn't anxious."[13]

The other strong element of the show that later appeared in Pittsburgh was Rogers's emphasis on the fears and insecurities of young children. He frequently talked to Rainsberry about his work with Dr. McFarland, emphasizing their strong belief that good programming for children must address social and emotional needs, not just cognitive learning.

According to Chapman, "He . . . would tell me what theme or

the fundamental message was that he wanted to get across—or the fear, the childhood fear, that he wanted to address. It . . . was all Fred's. I would be a sounding board, but it was Fred's instincts that ultimately decided everything.

"Ultimately, it all sprang from his own childhood recollections and, I suppose, his sufferings as a child, even though he had good parents. He was extremely sensitive, and now it was his turn to help other children come through."[14]

Rainsberry, Chapman, and the CBC gave Rogers his first real opportunity to take the concepts from the Arsenal Center and put them to work on TV. What's more, Rogers suddenly had access to the sort of resources he could only have dreamed of at WQED.

In fact, the trolley and castle were created for the Canadian program by CBC designers and in collaboration with producer Bruce Attridge. Francis Chapman explains, "We had very good facilities: magnificent carpentry shops and special-effects shops at the CBC. That was one thing that Fred was luxuriating in; he had a much better budget and materials to work with than he had had previously in Pittsburgh. . . . Owl had his house and King Friday had his castle, and the castle wall."[15]

Another thing that predominated in this new environment—and that would also become a hallmark of Rogers's later work—was Fred's extraordinary focus and intensity. "We would do fifteen minutes in the morning, and fifteen minutes in the afternoon," says Chapman, explaining the taping sessions for the quarter-hour slots. "It was tight, and it was only possible because Fred was so disciplined. He had his schedule and knew exactly when he had to have a script ready. He worked from home when he was writing, and he was very disciplined about his work. He would get up at a certain hour and go through the scripts."

With the help of Rainsberry and Chapman, Rogers could control every aspect of the show, including the selection of the cast. "We sometimes used the casting department of CBC," says Chapman, "but of course we auditioned them ourselves. I had had a lot of dealings with the drama department, so I knew quite a few actors, and I would suggest certain people."[16] But Rogers could also demonstrate unexpected flexibility. When the show's keyboard operator suddenly died, Fred accepted a substitute who was quite macho and aggressive and seemed incompatible with Mister Rogers. The reason: he was a very skilled musician, and Rogers respected that.

Fred Rogers and Francis Chapman worked so closely together that even after collaborating all day, they would often talk on the phone after work. Once when Chapman got a ride home with Rogers, Fred brought his two young sons, Jim and John, along for the drive.

As Chapman was getting out of the car, he and Rogers continued discussing several aspects of the show. Finally, growing impatient with this ceaseless talk about work, five-year-old Jim asked, "Uncle Francis, does it always take this long to say good-bye?"[17]

As was so often the case with Fred Rogers and the people with whom he worked, Chapman and Rogers became fast friends; Chapman later visited Fred and Joanne Rogers in Pittsburgh and at their vacation house on Nantucket.

Already, the intensity of his devotion to work was taking a toll on Fred Rogers. Chapman remembers that early on, Rogers was seeing a psychiatrist for advice: "He underwent psychoanalysis, but I don't remember what he learned from the psychoanalysis. I think he told me once that his analyst had found him so interesting that he took him on for free—which wasn't necessary for Fred, but it was nice."

At the core of Rogers's issues was a tension between his dutiful side and his creativity. He consulted the psychiatrist Dr. Albert V. Corrado for much of his adult life, and recommended him to close friends.[18] One of the things Chapman recalls about Fred's treatment was that Rogers said his sessions with the psychiatrist sometimes focused on the concept of the Oedipus complex, a fixation on a parent of the opposite sex.

And Rogers had shared with his wife, Joanne, how much he had struggled as a boy navigating between the very different expectations of his gentle mother and his businessman father. He felt he benefited from a chance to step back in his sessions with Dr. Corrado and gain perspective on the day-to-day elements of his intensely focused and deliberate life. Later, Fred Rogers also consulted Dr. Corrado with some regularity on scripts for *Mister Rogers' Neighborhood*.[19]

Joanne and Fred Rogers loved Toronto overall, but their time there was difficult in terms of parenting, mostly because of a series of mishaps that plagued the life of young John Rogers. In Rosedale Park, where Joanne loved to play with her two young sons, John fell off a set of climbing bars for children and broke his jaw.

As older brother Jim remembers it: "He had to wear a jacket to sleep in, basically, that had one sleeve that—all the way around the sleeve, there were wooden slats that ran from shoulder to wrist, and the reason was so that he couldn't bend his arm to suck his thumb, which would have messed with the broken jaw. I just remember feeling so bad for him."[20]

No sooner had John's jaw healed than he pulled over a pot of boiling coffee and badly burned his leg. When Joanne got the boys to Nantucket, she had to try to keep John from swimming in the ocean, which the whole family loved, to keep the bandage on his leg dry.[21]

Then when they got back to Canada, John needed surgery to repair hernias in his abdomen and in his groin, which proved to be a great trial to him and to his father. Although the surgery, which took place in a hospital in Toronto, was successful, it had a disastrously traumatic effect on young John, and on Fred as well. The operation was long and difficult for such a young child. John was very frightened, and that fright intensified when the staff chose not to give him any sedation before they started procedures. Joanne later recalled that when nurses pricked John's finger to take blood, Fred was with him.

"They needed a blood test," said Joanne, "and Fred said he was just terrified, and he held him and talked to him soothingly while they did that. So, he was just settled down back with us again when they came and said it was time to go, and they just grabbed him and took him. He was screaming and crying."[22]

The hospital staff, some of whom seemed to Fred and his young son to be laughing and joking while this went on, would not let Fred go with his son. It took them forty-five minutes in the operating room to anesthetize the traumatized little boy. The vision of his young child, panicked and screaming for his father as he was taken down the hall, haunted the hypersensitive Fred Rogers for the rest of his life.

Fred's older son, Jim Rogers, later recalled that his father felt guilty for years that he had not been able to help John. That same sort of guilt had shown itself earlier when Rogers's older son was barely a year old, in Florida with the family on vacation.

As the story was relayed to him later: "Mom . . . had taken me down by the water's edge and was holding me, and a big wave came in and pulled me out of her arms and out into the surf. Dad frantically ran out and managed somehow to grab a hold of my foot and drag me out of the water. It must have been a terrifying thing for him.

"He would often say to me, 'Oh, you swim so well, and I'm surprised that you would even go near the water after what happened to you.' And I just remember thinking, 'Well, you know, it was scary for you. I don't remember it, so it doesn't really bother me.' "[23]

The trauma younger son John suffered in the hospital in Toronto led to several years of his being quite accident-prone and fearful, according to psychiatrists who saw the boy after he returned to Pittsburgh.

As Joanne Rogers remembers it: "John went to nursery school over at the Arsenal. And he just showed a lot of anxiety. So we asked if the psychiatrist there, who was training psychiatrists in work with children . . . if he would watch John. Margaret (McFarland) suggested it." Joanne adds that John acted out the entire surgery for the doctor.

Fred Rogers never really got over feeling terrible about John's surgery. John himself recalls not his surgery, but an accident-prone aftermath, at ages "five, six, seven, maybe eight years old": "One thing I remember . . . that was quite troubling, was slamming my hand with the car door a few times in a row, and it got to the point where my parents wouldn't allow me to close the car door. There must have been something in my unconscious that affected me."[24]

Through the years of producing *Mister Rogers' Neighborhood*, Fred took every opportunity to create programming—some of it regular episodes and some of it special material—that would constructively deal with the fears of young children, so that parents and teachers and hospital staff, and the young children themselves, might get as much helpful information as possible. Some of his teaching videos about going to the hospital are still used at prominent hospitals, like Bellevue in New York City.

In 1966, Fred and Joanne Rogers decided to move back to Pittsburgh. As their visas were about to expire, they faced a decision about becoming Canadian citizens. Quickly they agreed that they wanted to raise their sons as US citizens, and that Pittsburgh would be a great, family-oriented city in which to do so. And the whole family was a little homesick for western Pennsylvania.

Certainly, John and Fred's experience in the hospital in Toronto factored into this decision. Once he returned to Pittsburgh, Fred went out of his way to work with hospital staff at Children's Hospital of Pittsburgh to ensure that young children were treated with the utmost sensitivity.

Fred Rogers would return to the US with invaluable experience as a writer, puppeteer, host, and producer of just the sort of show he had hoped to make. It became the template for the public television program in the United States that would make Fred famous as an educator of young children. But he also went back to the US with one of the worst memories of his life.

Fred Rogers seldom got angry. But his associates at Family Communications, Inc., later reported more than one incident in which he became absolutely furious if he thought he observed hospital staff being thoughtless and insensitive with young children. "To think that one morning in a hospital can cripple two-year-olds emotionally," said Rogers years later in a speech to a family court association. "What I've come to appreciate more and more, the older I get, is the long-lasting effects of things that happen to us in childhood."[25]

But there was a problem with Fred's plan to move back to Pittsburgh: He had no job there, and no prospect of one. Fred would be giving up a promising career at the CBC and going back to a very uncertain future in Pennsylvania. But once again the Rogers family fortune gave

Fred the freedom to pursue life and work where he wanted. He and his family bought a huge house in the fashionable East End of Pittsburgh on Beechwood Boulevard—a mansion by Pittsburgh standards at that time, at eleven thousand square feet—and hoped for the best.

They sent the two boys off to private school in the city. Joanne was very happy to be back and to have her boys in school in an American city. For his part, Fred was somewhat at loose ends, hoping that WQED would find the funds to produce a children's program that would provide a vehicle for his ideas, his music, and his puppets. To stay busy, and stay involved in early education, Fred worked as a volunteer with children at preschool classes in the Bellefield Presbyterian Church in Pittsburgh's Oakland section, where he used his puppets to teach children. He observed their reactions to his work carefully to see what connected with real children in a live setting.

The University of Pittsburgh and WQED were located nearby, and he could stay in touch with Dr. Margaret McFarland at the Arsenal Center and his associates at the television station. But nothing encouraging was developing at WQED, and in the fall of 1966, Fred Rogers was beginning to worry about his future in broadcasting.

PART III

All our lives, we rework the things from our childhood,
like feeling good about ourselves, managing our angry feelings,
being able to say good-bye to people we love.

—FRED ROGERS

IO.

THE BIRTH OF *MISTER ROGERS' NEIGHBORHOOD*

WHEN FRED ROGERS GOT BACK to western Pennsylvania in the fall of 1966, he wasn't at all sure where his career was going, or how he could bring it back to life in Pittsburgh. He was confused about where he could find support for the kind of children's television he wanted to make: Would WQED or the Eastern Educational Network (EEN) help with funding? The EEN, incorporated in 1961, was a regional coopera- tive that exchanged shows like *The French Chef* (with Julia Child) among its member stations. Eventually it morphed into NET (National Educa- tional Television, sponsored by the Ford Foundation, and later partially owned by the Corporation for Public Broadcasting). In 1970, it became PBS (the Public Broadcasting Service).

Were there foundations willing to bankroll Rogers's ideas based on his experience so far in children's television? All he knew for sure was that he and Joanne wanted to raise their two boys in Pittsburgh, near Latrobe, where he grew up and where his family still lived. Still, with nothing encouraging developing at WQED, he couldn't help but feel that his promising television career was stalling out.

In the 1960s, most children's television was light and breezy, devoted largely to fun. Shows like *Howdy Doody, Captain Kangaroo,* and *Lunch with Soupy Sales* all focused on entertaining the young members of the audience and keeping them in their seats, as well as selling lots of branded products to kids in the TV audience.

With the advantage of family wealth, Fred Rogers could bide his time to make his mark in children's television. And he had one other great advantage: He knew exactly what he wanted to do. Based on his experiences in New York, Pittsburgh, and Toronto, Fred had developed a crystal-clear vision of the sort of program he wanted: one where he could take his work with music, puppeteering, scriptwriting, and storytelling and marry it to the strong principles of child development he had learned from McFarland, Dr. Benjamin Spock, and others at the Arsenal Center.

A precise picture of what would become *Mister Rogers' Neighborhood* was lodged in Fred Rogers's head, and the intensity of this picture was matched by his own rock-hard determination to get it done. Outwardly, Fred might seem to be underemployed and adrift, and his parents—particularly his father—were worried about him. Inwardly, he had never been more sure of his course.

But he was going to have to figure out how to garner the support necessary to do it. Then he got a call from a local advertising executive, George Hill, the chief of his own eponymous agency.[1] Among his clients was the Joseph Horne Department Store in Pittsburgh (a local business where Andy Warhol had worked in the display department in the summer of 1947).

Joseph Horne wanted to have a program on the air between Thanksgiving and Christmas that could attract families and children and bring them into Horne's rather than their chief competitor, the somewhat better-known Kaufmann's Department Store. (The Kaufmanns famously contracted with Frank Lloyd Wright to design Fallingwater, their country retreat.)

Someone in Hill's agency mentioned Fred Rogers and his work in Toronto. "I said, 'Well, I don't know Fred Rogers, but I'll call him,'" recalled Hill.[2]

Hill and Rogers had lunch in Horne's dining room; Rogers recounted his work history in Canada and his vivid ideas for children's television. Soon they were on the cusp of a deal. But then Fred told Hill there was a nonnegotiable condition: no commercials. This was a novel concept for the chief of an advertising agency, whose client wanted to attract customers. But Rogers was intractable: He believed it was immoral to present ads to little children, who were not capable of distinguishing between a program and the commercial that was selling them something. Rogers did not object to marketing to adults, only to children.

Remarkably enough, the leaders of the department store agreed that the program would have no advertising for Horne's, just a line telling viewers that Horne's was the sponsor of this children's program at the beginning and end of each show. And equally unexpectedly, it worked: "Horne's got all kinds of rave reviews as a result," said Hill, who explained that the positive publicity for Horne's did as much or more for the store than advertising could have done.[3]

Fred had gotten the chance to try out his new ideas during his time at the CBC—and with a push from Fred Rainsberry, to begin shaping his role as "Mister Rogers" in front of a camera. But the Canadian program, though successful, could not fulfill Rogers's ambition. Fred was working for Rainsberry and the CBC, not for himself. He wanted to use his connection to the Arsenal Center to advance his high-minded ideas, and he wanted to do it on his own turf, working closely with Dr. Margaret McFarland. Fred Rogers wanted to run his own show.

The program with Horne's turned into a run of thirteen fifteen-minute episodes, with the full sponsorship of the store. They were taped at Pittsburgh's ABC affiliate, WTAE, and aired on Sunday mornings.

At the time, guitarist and composer Joe Negri (later Handyman Negri on the *Neighborhood*) was providing music on other children's shows at the station: "In the afternoon, we had cartoon shows, like *Popeye and Friends*. I'd sit and talk with the cub scouts and the girl scouts who were the audience.

"My second year at WTAE, he [Fred] came over to do a . . . program I thought was the prototype of the Neighborhood of Make-Believe, which was to come later. I was put on the show to be his musical director. I would help supply the music for the backgrounds.

"Then a few shows in, he said, 'How would you like to walk through the Neighborhood and just talk to some of the puppets?' So, I started doing that with X the Owl, King Friday, Henrietta Pussycat."⁴

As Rogers assembled the elements for the new show, with George Hill's guidance and support, he would get his shot. For the first time, Fred Rogers could create just the program he envisioned. Of course, the educational material and the emotional messages in the program, initially called *Misterogers' Neighborhood* (carrying over the title of the CBC show), came from Fred's work with Margaret McFarland.⁵

The rest of the program flowed straight out of Rogers's life: from his childhood, his family, and the small town of Latrobe. It flowed out of the attic of his parents' house on Weldon Street, where a small, shy elementary-school child amused a handful of playmates with his puppets; and from the streets of Latrobe, where the young Fred Rogers listened for the clang of the trolley before crossing the street. He took inspiration from neighbors, merchants, and the local librarian who first introduced him to books.

Fred Rogers loved his home town, even though at times he had been unhappy there. In the *Neighborhood*, he used his memories of Latrobe to create an idealized version of the town, where children could feel understood and valued.

The new program incorporated most of the highly imaginative elements that later became famous on the *Neighborhood*: the puppets, the sneakers, the sweater, the trolley, the slow pace and quiet manner that invited children into the world of this gentle man, who looked right into their eyes and talked their language. At the start of every show, Fred Rogers sang, "It's a beautiful day in the neighborhood . . ." The *Mister Rogers'* "anthem," composed by Rogers, like all the other songs on the program, signaled to millions of kids watching that Fred Rogers valued them "just the way you are." The song was not just reassuring; it was catchy.

The new *Misterogers* program was a lightly staffed operation. Elaine Lynch had been working for Fred Rogers as a secretary since she'd met him as a receptionist at George Hill's ad agency. While still employed by Hill: "I was typing the scripts . . . On the left side of the page it would say, 'King Friday' colon, and then you would go over to the right side of the page, and he would say something like, 'We shall meet in the castle at five and a quarter.' And then perhaps the next line would be 'Henrietta Pussycat' colon, and to the right it would say, 'Meow, meow, why?'

"And occasionally Fred would call and say, 'I need a stuffed toy. Can you get it from Horne's?' Our offices were right across the street, so I would run over and get a couple of things for him to choose from. He particularly liked the Steiff stuffed animals, or he would get airplanes, rugs, that kind of thing. And so besides just doing scripts and stuff, while I wasn't considered a prop person, I was getting props from the store."[6]

The program was essentially local in its reach, but it was very successful for WTAE. It got good viewership in the Pittsburgh region, created a strong community, and generated fan mail from many viewers. After Elaine Lynch typed up Rogers's handwritten responses to mail, he would sign them.

Fred still believed in educational television, and he wanted to produce on WQED, not on a commercial station like WTAE. But the money problem remained. Horne's show on WTAE, like the CBC program, was only fifteen minutes long, and Horne's wasn't in a position to fund a longer, daily program. WQED was interested, but didn't have the resources. It was up to Fred to raise the money. Once again, George Hill was a key to the future.

Hill had become Fred's de facto agent and business manager: "I never had a contract with Fred; I just showed up, you know, with the Horne's thing, and then I continued to work."[7]

Fred made clear to Hill that he thought it was time for him to move back to public television; and Hill, who was well-connected locally, managed to tap some local funders for support. In addition, Rogers had connections, through Leland Hazard and his father, to corporate funders, and through his friend H. John Heinz III (later the US senator from Pennsylvania) to the Heinz philanthropies and other foundations.

With bits and pieces of funding from a variety of places, Fred rejoined WQED in 1966, confident that with some additional support, he could start a longer, regularly scheduled program to fulfill his goals.

Hedda Sharapan, who first met Fred when she was a graduate student at the small school in the basement of the Bellefield Presbyterian Church, soon joined him at WQED. At that point, *Mister Rogers' Neighborhood*, a black-and-white, half-hour show, was produced on WQED and shown in several other American cities besides Pittsburgh—including New York, Boston, Chicago, and Philadelphia—on the Eastern Educational Network, a precursor to PBS and the system of National Educational Television (NET).[8]

Although NET also contributed funding to keep Rogers on the air, the schedule was impermanent, and the future uncertain. Sharapan remembers that the question of funding for Fred's future work was pervasive; when he finished shooting a sequence of programs in the spring of 1967, he told all the children goodbye because he had no idea whether he might be able to continue.

"I remember sitting with a little boy who actually broke down in tears," said Sharapan later. She watched Fred reacting to the child's tears, trying to reassure the child while he himself was so uncertain about the future. And Sharapan was wondering in her own way what miracle might keep things going.[9]

Another key player on the early iteration of the *Neighborhood* was David Newell, a Pittsburgh native who went to work for Fred in 1967 for 7,000 dollars a year. Newell had had a lifelong interest in the theater and became unusually close to Rogers as the show developed. Initially Newell had been hired as a production assistant on the *Neighborhood* after volunteering a few days a week at WQED. He knew Fred Rogers's work from watching *The Children's Corner*: "I sensed an intelligence there, and respect for what they [Rogers and partner Josie Carey] were doing."[10]

His role on the *Neighborhood* expanded when Rogers wrote a role for a speedy deliveryman who could help bring some of the props onstage. His character's first delivery was of an armadillo, for a show on armor and protection. His easy rapport with Fred Rogers led to a collaborative effort to make his character a little more well-rounded, so that Mister Rogers might ask the speedy deliveryman to slow down and sit with him for a while.

Newell was also plunged almost immediately into the search for money. As word got around to other East Coast cities in the EEN that the *Neighborhood* could be canceled, there were spontaneous demonstrations protesting the threat to the program. The educational stations in those cities were stunned at the intensity of the demonstrations; nothing in their programming histories had ever drawn such strong public reaction.

As luck would have it, the Sears-Roebuck Foundation was run then by a high-minded businessman named William F. McCurdy, who was very interested in television and the opportunity to fund programming that might reflect well on the Sears image. McCurdy was to become key to Fred's future. Fred Rogers himself later remembered that the producers at NET "ran out of money and weren't able to produce any more [children's] programs. There was a group of women, mothers in Boston, who heard that we might be going off the air. They marched door-to-door to get people to make contributions to the Children's Programming Fund. They said that it was essential to keep this program on the air."[11]

Fred and his savvy PR man, David Newell, made trips to cities where the *Neighborhood* was on view and hosted local families at their educational television stations. The results were electric. Thousands of children and their parents showed up for events in Boston, Los Angeles, and elsewhere, impressing the television staffs and the media in these NET cities (Los Angeles and Miami had been added) and cementing strong relationships with families.

Station managers in these cities—often overwhelmed with crowds five or ten times the size they expected—shared their stories with WQED and the national NET executives. Word of the marches and the fund-raising spread to other cities, including New York, Los Angeles, and Chicago.

For "Mister Rogers Day" at KCET in Los Angeles, the staff planned for a crowd of several hundred—only to be stunned when ten thousand people, mostly excited, screaming kids, lined up outside the station to see their hero. To manage the huge crowd, KCET staff tried to organize the eager fans into smaller groups to see Mister Rogers, but the whole day teetered on disorder.

McCurdy and others at Sears, based in Chicago and New York, read the papers and were intrigued by the show of passion, including that of the parents trying to save children's programming. "It came to the attention of Bill McCurdy," said Rogers. "He had been talking with NET about underwriting something, never thinking that they might be interested in children's programming. So he got with Paul Taff [director of children's programs for NET], and he said, 'What's this *Neighborhood* program about? I understand it needs funding.'

"Paul said yes. And Bill McCurdy said, 'Why don't we try that if we're going to launch into public broadcasting? How much do you need?' Paul Taff told him and he went to the Sears Foundation and they said sure. That was the beginning of our network programming in this country."[12]

At first, Taff tried to convince Rogers to minimize costs—and the fund-raising burden—by limiting the program to fifteen minutes, as it had been in Canada and in the shows sponsored by Horne. Fred stuck to his guns; he wanted thirty minutes for each show, as they were currently presented, and he wanted exactly the program he had envisioned. Taff relented.

"Again, I did not create Fred Rogers," said Taff years later. "I just knew what he was doing was right. I had that responsibility at NET to bring the best children's programming I could. And he was the epitome of that."[13]

At one point in their collaboration, Paul Taff flew to Nantucket to review scripts with Fred. When Taff and his wife were leaving the island, Nantucket fogged in, as it often does. Fred had already brought the Taffs to the airport; instead of leaving them to wait for the fog to lift, Rogers stayed with them for hours until their plane was cleared.

"And that, in a sense, could sum up the relationship," said Taff later. "Typical Fred. He was not going to leave us on Nantucket alone."[14]

What Rogers had conceived for his program—what made him so very adamant about getting just the terms he needed from Taff and McCurdy and others—was the exact blend of reality and fantasy that he believed children needed and that later became his acclaimed signature programming mix.

"I really feel that [in] the opening reality of the program," Fred explained in an interview, "we deal with the stuff that dreams are made of. And then in the Neighborhood of Make-Believe, we deal with it as if it were a dream. And then when it comes back to me (at the end), we deal with a simple interpretation of the dream. . . . Anything can happen in make-believe, and we can talk about anything in reality. Margaret used to say, 'Whatever is mentionable is manageable.' "[15]

Rogers had learned at the Arsenal Center—and in the basement of the Bellefield Presbyterian Church—that children learn through this mix of fantasy and reality, of playful creativity and measuring their growing sense of reality against the adults with whom they deal. His genius was to bring it to life on the screen.

On the fund-raising front, it was George Hill who once again provided the critical support for Fred. As he often did for friends and associates, Fred Rogers had offered a few weeks' vacation in his Nantucket cottage to Hill, who was enjoying the beach in front of Fred and Joanne's Madaket home when he got an urgent call from Rogers summoning him to a spur-of-the-moment meeting at the Sears, Roebuck and Co. offices in New York.[16]

In a later interview, Hill recalled that he told Fred Rogers: " 'If there's a plane, I'll be there.' I met him, and we went to Sears' offices. I can't remember the exact conversation, but it went something like this: 'We at the Sears Foundation are looking for a project for children. We've seen your program. We like what you do. And we would like to underwrite you nationally.'

"It was that simple," added Hill. "And then I think he [Bill McCurdy] said something like, we have some people who will take care of the details. . . . It was amazing. It really put us over the edge and made everything work."[17]

That funding relationship, borne out of Hill's perseverance, Rogers's talent, and McCurdy's abiding interest in aligning Sears with the highest-quality television, lasted for twenty-four years, rivaling the funding of *Masterpiece Theatre* by ExxonMobil. It enabled Fred Rogers and WQED to take risks and to establish themselves as leaders in the field of children's television.

For Fred Rogers and David Newell, the memory of the big-city demonstrations on behalf of the *Neighborhood* always remained very poignant. It was powerfully important to Rogers that it was parents who turned out to save the *Neighborhood* for their children.

The only complication arose when one of the earliest *Neighborhood* scripts created a character named "Mr. McCurdy," a genial mailman who was to be part of the regular show. The real Mr. McCurdy worried that this could look like a favor that might appear to be a quid pro quo for the Sears funding.

"Mr. McCurdy was my name in the first script," recalled David Newell. "But minutes before the first taping, Sears called, pleased with everything except the name. McCurdy was maybe too self-serving. Fred said, with twenty minutes to go before the first taping, we have to get you a name. Seconds later, he blurted out McFeely."[18]

Because of McCurdy's scruples, Fred borrowed his own middle name, the last name of his beloved grandfather. David Newell became Mr. McFeely, the "Speedy Delivery" mailman who graced the show for over three decades.

The extraordinary importance of the Sears support was that it gave Fred Rogers freedom from commercial pressures, and the freedom to focus only on the highest academic standards—his own and those of Dr. Margaret McFarland. The result was television that quickly won the trust and affection of children and their parents.

Fred's dream was realized: He was given a full weekly schedule— half an hour each day, five days a week— and national syndication across the country. The new show, still in black and white, debuted on February 19, 1968. Season One was composed of an astonishing 180 episodes. Soon, with support from Sears, other charitable funders, and National Educational Television itself, Rogers and his production company, a for-profit called Small World Enterprises, were producing sixty-five programs in color each year.

FRED ROGERS WAS FIRST and foremost an accomplished musician whose passion for the art form equaled his spiritual convictions. The combination both gave him a unique "platform" from which to reach children and their parents and allowed him to grow as a creative artist. A notable highlight of the new *Neighborhood* was music that guided kids from one segment on the stage set into the Neighborhood of Make-Believe.

Mister Rogers' Neighborhood was taped live in the studio, and Fred Rogers encouraged musical director and jazz musician Johnny Costa, leading an excellent trio, to improvise. When Fred Rogers opens the door to Mister Rogers's television "house," his viewers listen to the trilling notes of the celeste, or celesta, a French keyboard instrument with a sound as delicate and endearing as Mister Rogers himself.

When Johnny Costa was first approached in 1968 about the job of music director of the *Neighborhood*, he was reluctant to accept the position, not wanting to play "kiddie" music, but Fred encouraged him to play arrangements as musically complex as those Costa would do for adults.

Indeed, as Costa once noted: "What we do isn't simple. Fred doesn't write simple tunes, and the jazz arrangements I do are very sophisticated, too. Fred always says if it's for the children, it has to be the best we can give."[19]

Joe Negri, the *Neighborhood* "handyman" who is also a jazz-guitar virtuoso, adds: "In those days, a job was a job, and it was a good job. And we all needed work. I never considered working on the *Neighborhood* as something that was beneath me."[20]

When young trumpet sensation Wynton Marsalis appeared on the show later, in 1986, he had no trepidation about doing so, because of the musicians Fred Rogers worked with: "Of course, I didn't know about how much he [Fred Rogers] knew about music, and how much he was a musician. I always knew they had the hippest music on TV. If you were a musician, you knew Joe Negri and Johnny Costa. My daddy [Ellis Marsalis] had played with Johnny Costa, and knew Johnny Costa's character. Johnny Costa was known as an Art Tatum type figure by piano players. And the band [on the *Neighborhood*] was out of sight."[21]

Negri and Costa, friends since their days as composition students at Carnegie Mellon, both worked at the local commercial stations, too, as musical consultants, and continued to perform on the local club circuit, sometimes together, or separately with their bands.

Fred Rogers also used music to help fund the television show. Initially he'd incorporated Small World Enterprises in 1955 to sell and distribute *The Children's Corner* materials, primarily songbooks and records.

At first, Small World consisted of Elaine Lynch and Fred Rogers, working out of a set of back-to-back apartments in the Cathedral Mansions apartment building on Ellsworth Avenue in Pittsburgh's Shadyside neighborhood, not far from WQED. While Lynch worked in one apartment, Rogers had the other to himself for writing, away from phones or other distractions.

Small World had licenses for an array of products through Golden Books and Hallmark. But the main business was in children's music. Elaine Lynch recalls: "Fred and [band leader] Johnny Costa and George Hill, while they were doing . . . *Mister Rogers' Neighborhood* . . . were also making LPs of Fred's music, and we were selling them through Columbia House, the children's arm of CBS Records."[22]

Then record stores across the country started allocating more space to rock and roll. Even venturing into the music business had been a tough sell to Fred Rogers until he decided that if the records were targeted to parents, it might be a way for bringing families together.

Though the profits brought in by Small World products were in effect helping to underwrite the TV shows, "When we went to color and realized how much more it was going to cost to do that, we found that the corporations and the foundations were not willing to contribute funds to something that was profit making," recalls Elaine Lynch.[23]

One day in the early 1970s, Fred Rogers woke up and saw his picture on the milk carton as he prepared breakfast. It hit him that as an employee of WQED, his own image was not his to control: The station had brought in a little extra revenue by selling his picture.

Fred Rogers decided to transform Small World into a nonprofit, Family Communications, Inc. As he once related, "I didn't know anything about it. I was advertising something, or promoting something, that this station just didn't bother to ask me about. So much of the money that was coming to make the *Neighborhood* was being used for administration (by WQED). But I felt that we could be better stewards with that money if it came directly to us. In 1970 we formed Family Communications, Inc. From then on, we rented our offices and the studios and all the other facilities that we needed at WQED."[24]

The other motivating factor for Fred was his deep frustration with the controlling way WQED doled out the funds he himself had raised. Paul Taff of NET remembered that he was sometimes called in by WQED managers who reported having difficulty dealing with Rogers's requests. According to Taff, Fred was almost always right; WQED was being cheap.

One example: Though Rogers was producing his show in color, WQED denied him a color monitor for use on the set. He didn't need it, they said, because he was color-blind—which he was. Taff came into Pittsburgh and quickly concluded that Rogers's on-set staff did need the monitor. And they got it. Taff remained an essential supporter of Rogers in those early years.[25]

Leland Hazard and John Heinz collaborated on the legal and business planning that put Family Communications together for Fred and afforded him the corporate freedom to manage his own production. Together, all these things gave Rogers the ability to set his own standards. He became an even more fierce defender of quality in his program.

Bill Isler, former head of Family Communications, observes:

"Fred had great business instincts. . . . He understood business from the feet of his father and grandfather in ways people never gave him credit for."[26]

Fred Rogers was no pushover. Eliot Daley recalls a comment made by Leland Hazard as they left a contentious meeting with Fred Rogers: "I wonder at what age is it that Fred no longer likes you just the way you are?"[27]

II.

THE PASTORE HEARING

VERY QUICKLY, the program Fred Rogers had first formulated in Toronto, and then refined with the support of Horne's Department Store, became the fully formed *Mister Rogers' Neighborhood*—the children's program that defined his contribution to television, to early childhood education, and to American culture.

Only a year after the 1968 debut of *Mister Rogers' Neighborhood* on NET, Fred Rogers had achieved such credibility that he was selected to testify before Congress on behalf of educational television. The age-old fiscal tussle between the White House and Congress was playing out once again.

Searching for ways to defray the rising cost of the Vietnam War, President Richard Nixon needed some budget savings. He wanted Senator John Pastore of Rhode Island to assist him by chopping the funds for public television. Because public TV was still relatively new in 1969, Nixon was betting that it lacked the array of powerful stakeholders to defend its funding that some of his other potential targets would have.

On the table was a special appropriation to establish the Corporation for Public Broadcasting. President Lyndon B. Johnson, Nixon's predecessor, was an advocate of public television and had proposed the 20 million dollars to kick-start its national adoption. Nixon was in his first year of office; he had never been much of a fan of public media (or any media, for that matter), and he was certainly no fan of programs pushed by Johnson, a Democrat considered a liberal spendthrift by Nixon and other Republicans. The president wanted Pastore's Subcommittee on Communications to cut at least 10 million dollars from the appropriation.

Nixon had reason to hope that Pastore—an Italian American "tough guy"—might join him in viewing public television as something of a government frill. Although a Democrat, Pastore was known as a blunt, no-nonsense social conservative who shared the Republican interest in keeping federal spending in line.[1]

Public television had been evolving city by city for some years, with the initial stations located at colleges and universities. The first community-based public station with broad support was WQED in Pittsburgh, whose primary champion, the corporate lawyer Leland Hazard, had helped bring Fred Rogers aboard.[2] Hazard and other Pittsburgh civic leaders saw benefit in creating a station that was entirely devoted to the interests of their community, rather than to an academic institution.[3]

Over the next fifteen years many others followed their example, and by the time of Pastore's hearing in 1968, there were scores of community and university stations around the country, loosely affiliated with organizations such as the National Educational Television network and the Eastern Educational Network.

The champion of this group, then and always, was WGBH in Boston, which had gone on the air in 1955, a year after WQED. From the beginning, WGBH was the most ambitious and successful creator of new programming in the public television world, and it commanded a fervently loyal base of supporters in New England. In coming decades WQED and WGBH would be considered rivals in strong programming, with WQED building a record of fine documentary films, and WGBH offering such educational and entertainment triumphs as *NOVA, Masterpiece Theatre, The French Chef* (with Julia Child), *Frontline*, and *Where in the World Is Carmen Sandiego* (made in partnership with WQED). The television pioneer who brought Boston's station on air was Hartford N. Gunn Jr., who was still its general manager in 1969 (and would go on to become the first president of PBS).[4]

Earlier that year, when executives of public television were strategizing about the prospective Pastore hearings, Gunn had taken the lead. A graduate of Harvard Business School who was known as a cunning strategist, Gunn had a risky, intuitive, and crafty idea. He wanted to bring on the host of his station's most popular program, the forty-one-year-old Fred Rogers.[5]

The risk was clear. Rogers wasn't then nationally known; he was simply the host of a children's show, lacking the title-filled résumé and public-affairs gravitas US senators might expect to see. But from his own experience and from his observation of WGBH viewers, Gunn knew that Fred Rogers had a powerful ability to make quick, strong connections with people.

Now Gunn was betting that Rogers's direct, disarming manner could win more support for public television than the traditional businesslike style of most of the executives who ran the stations. Most importantly, Rogers could make strong connections on two fronts: in person and through the camera. That mattered because the hearings would play to both the senators gathered at the Capitol and television viewers who would later see film clips of testimony. Gunn knew that he and his allies had to win both audiences, not only to get the 20-million-dollar appropriation, but also to secure reliable, annual funding for public television.

Gunn invited Rogers to Washington to testify before Congress. Rogers agreed, and he brought along friends with *Neighborhood* connections: the advertising executive George Hill, who had helped Rogers in the program's early years and could provide informed moral support,[6] and Pittsburgh optometrist Bernard "Pepper" Mallinger, who had appeared as a guest on the *Neighborhood*, examining Rogers's eyes in programs designed to explain medical procedures to children.

Hill simply wanted to be there to hear Rogers speak and to offer his public-relations expertise should Rogers need it. Mallinger, who had a gentle and thoughtful manner, had been very effective at helping to disarm children's fears. But in Washington he would have a different role: Rogers and Gunn wanted him to explain to the senators how children process information coming to them from television and other electronic media. Through his studies, Fred Rogers knew that information delivered this way could be tricky for very young children, and he hoped Mallinger's testimony could help Pastore and the other senators understand the complexities being addressed through the *Neighborhood* approach.[7]

Hartford Gunn was betting that a mix of dry testimony, consisting of his own talk about the administration of public television, and Pepper Mallinger's report on children's visual and intellectual processing of electronic information would be suddenly enlivened and brought home emotionally by the persuasive powers of Fred Rogers. It was a pretty big gamble in view of what was at stake for the future of public television.

In what is still considered one of the most powerful pieces of testimony ever offered before Congress, and one of the most powerful pieces of video persuasion ever filmed, the mild-mannered Fred Rogers employed his gentle demeanor and soft voice to dominate the proceedings, silence a roomful of politicians, and nearly bring the gruff committee chairman to tears. It has been studied ever since by both academics and marketers.

The Pastore hearing signaled the birth of a new champion: Fred Rogers as a national advocate not only for public television but also for the great vision that had inspired him since the early 1950s: that television has the power to be uplifting and educational, not just for children, but for everyone. Over the coming decades, Rogers would be the most consistently visible campaigner for this idealistic notion.

In Senator John Pastore, Fred Rogers wasn't really confronting an enemy. It was true that Pastore was no great friend of free and open communications. A social conservative, he used his subcommittee position to saber rattle at television he felt pushed the bounds, including everything from crime shows to the comedy series *Laugh-In* to Noxema shaving-cream ads with a sexy theme ("Take it off. Take it all off."). And he became the bête noire of *The Smothers Brothers Comedy Hour*, a

1960s program delivering social satire and political commentary. Pastore tried to have a government panel preview the comedy of Tom and Dick Smothers, biting critics of the Vietnam War and Lyndon Johnson. But the show's network, CBS, fended him off.[8]

Despite all this, Pastore was sympathetic to the idea of public television. After all, Lyndon Johnson, one of his great friends and mentors, was its principal backer. Pastore had given the keynote address during the 1964 Democratic Convention at which Johnson was nominated to run for re-election to the presidency.[9] Pastore was familiar with Johnson's hopes for public television. He would have to be convinced at the hearing, but he was predisposed to listen.

The hearing took place on May 1, 1969. More than four decades later, the exchange between Pastore and Rogers still can be seen online. The chairman of the Senate Subcommittee on Communications curtly commands his witness to begin: "Okay, Rogers, you've got the floor."

In his disarming, guileless way, Rogers immediately alters the tone of the proceeding. With his first words, delivered in the same measured cadence he uses in the *Neighborhood*, he slows listeners to his own very deliberate pace. He starts by telling Pastore that he won't read his prepared remarks, as they would take about ten minutes.

Pastore draws laughter with a condescending riposte: "Would it make you happy if you read it?"

But in his soft, slightly nasal, western-Pennsylvania twang, Fred Rogers replies that he'll be glad to just talk about the work. (Perhaps the only person unhappy with his decision was Elaine Lynch, his secretary back in Pittsburgh, who had been asked to type up Rogers's remarks from a longhand version on a yellow legal pad. She had dutifully created manuscripts for Rogers to read and share with those at the hearing. "I worked so hard in typing that speech," she recalled later, "and then he didn't read it. I was so disappointed."[10] Rogers did intend to read the text, but his extraordinary situational sense told him it would be better to be direct and personal with the brusque Pastore.)

Continuing to speak slowly and quietly, Rogers becomes

passionate as he describes his work: "One of the first things that a child learns in a healthy family is trust, and I trust what you have said that you will read this. It's very important to me. I care deeply about children.

"My first children's program was on WQED fifteen years ago, and its budget was thirty dollars. Now, with the help of the Sears-Roebuck Foundation and National Educational Television, as well as all the affiliated stations—each station pays to show our program, it's a unique kind of funding in educational television—with this help, now our program has a budget of six thousand dollars. It may sound like quite a difference, but six thousand dollars pays for less than two minutes of cartoons. Two minutes of animated, what I sometimes say, bombardment. I'm very much concerned, as I know you are, about what's being delivered to our children in this country. And I've worked in the field of child development for six years now, trying to understand the inner needs of children. We deal with such things as—as the inner drama of childhood. We don't have to bop somebody over the head to . . . make drama on the screen. We deal with such things as getting a haircut, or the feelings about brothers and sisters, and the kind of anger that arises in simple family situations. And we speak to it constructively."

Listening intently, Pastore asks Rogers about the program's length. A moment later, he asks his staff, "Could we get a copy of this, so we can see it? Maybe not today, but I'd like to see the program."

Fred Rogers goes on, becoming more intense as he describes the hundreds of programs he made for the EEN, or Eastern Educational Network: "And then when the money ran out, people in Boston and Pittsburgh and Chicago all came to the fore and said we've got to have more of this neighborhood expression of care. And this is what—this is what I give. I give an expression of care every day to each child, to help him realize that he is unique. I end the program by saying, 'You've made this day a special day, by just your being you. There's no person in the whole world like you, and I like you, just the way you are.'

"And I feel that if we in public television can only make it clear that feelings are mentionable and manageable, we will have done a great service for mental health. I think that it's much more dramatic that two men could be working out their feelings of anger—much more dramatic than showing something of gunfire. I'm constantly concerned about what our children are seeing, and for fifteen years I've tried in this country, and Canada, to present what I feel is a meaningful expression of care."

Senator Pastore famously responds: "Well, I'm supposed to be a pretty tough guy, and this is the first time I've had goose bumps for the last two days."

Rogers thanks Pastore for his reaction, and for his interest in the work. He explains that he is the host, the composer of all the music, and the writer of the scripts for *Mister Rogers' Neighborhood*. Then he asks to quote the lyrics of a *Neighborhood* song.

For the next sixty seconds, before a silent hearing room, Fred Rogers recites the words of a children's song, one that he considers very important, one that "has to do with that good feeling of control which I feel that children need to know is there. And it starts out, 'What do you do with the mad that you feel?' And that first line came straight from a child. I work with children doing puppets in—in very personal communication with small groups—

" 'What do you do with the mad that you feel / When you feel so mad you could bite / When the whole wide world seems oh so wrong, and nothing you do seems very right / What do you do / Do you punch a bag / Do you pound some clay or some dough / Do you round up friends for a game of tag or see how fast you can go / It's great to be able to stop when you've planned the thing that's wrong / And be able to do something else instead—and think this song—

" 'I can stop when I want to / Can stop when I wish / Can stop, stop, stop anytime / And what a good feeling to feel like this / And know that the feeling is really mine / Know that there's something deep inside that helps us become what we can / For a girl can be someday a lady, and a boy can be someday a man.' "

Senator Pastore's dramatic and very famous closing line: "I think it's wonderful. I think it's wonderful. Looks like you just earned the twenty million dollars."

With the widely viewed testimony, public television's start-up funds were secured, and Fred Rogers was lauded nationally as an advocate for it, as well as for better children's programming. In fact, the following year President Nixon asked Rogers to chair the 1970 White House Conference on Children and Youth, an event with over a thousand attendees from all over the country that had been held once a decade since being established during the Theodore Roosevelt administration.

As Gunn had foreseen, Fred Rogers achieved this impact by simply demonstrating who he was—Mister Rogers, the earnest, authentic, consciously moral person he had set out to be decades earlier. In place of the formal stuffiness typical of congressional testimony, he was personal, informal, and direct, talking about human feelings and relationships without using the language of sociology or psychology.

In the videotape of Rogers's testimony, seen by millions of television and web viewers in the forty-plus years since the event, he is so even-mannered and deliberate as to seem unconcerned about the prospect of testifying before Congress and the national press. In fact, as Pepper Mallinger recalled years later in an interview, he and Rogers were both nervous because "it was a little overwhelming."[11]

Pastore was intimidating, Mallinger added: "He didn't seem to be a warm and friendly person. He was a guy who [was] all business—at least in that situation."

But Rogers, though he hated being called a "performer" in his role as Mister Rogers, was a consummate performer who knew how to read his audience. He could see Pastore responding to his comments about young children and education, and he focused intently on the senator as he delivered his testimony. Afterward, Fred Rogers was somewhat spent. Pepper Mallinger remembered that he, Rogers, and George Hill shared relief as they drove back to the airport in Washington that day.[12]

Pastore himself became a friend to Rogers, and they corresponded for several years after the hearing, discussing children and grandchildren, television and values.[13] In 1970, when Rogers conducted hearings in his role as chair of the White House Conference on Children, he turned the tables and asked Pastore to appear as a witness.[14]

In the years after the Pastore hearing, for Fred Rogers, there was some irony—even a hint of tragedy—in his newfound prominence as a champion of better television. Although he soldiered on for decades, trying to produce optimal children's programming and making scores of speeches about the potential of television, the medium itself happily took the low road, pursuing high ratings and low taste as its leaders sought to extract as much money as possible from the American public. Exceptions were quality and thought-provoking programs from talents like Norman Lear.

Public television continued to produce a great deal of quality programming in addition to the Neighborhood. Still, later in life, Fred Rogers began to wonder aloud about how useful an advocate he had really been. In talking with his wife, Joanne, he deplored the meanness and venality of popular culture and its mirror, commercial television.[15]

For a while Joanne worried that Fred was becoming depressed; but then he bounced back. Through hours of daily prayer, he came to feel that his work had been acceptable: that he had done the very best he could with his array of gifts to help public television and the children and adults it served.

If Fred Rogers had lived, he might have felt vindicated by the widespread re-airing of his testimony in early 2017, when funds for public television were once again on the congressional chopping block in the wake of the 2016 election. Once again, he was the champion his audience remembered, and that a nation counted on.

12.

LANGUAGE AND MEANING

WITH HIS FAMILY RESETTLED happily in Pittsburgh, where the boys enrolled in St. Edmund's Academy, near their home, now Fred could focus on ways to refine the *Neighborhood*. His new program, already a success for WQED despite its short tenure on the air, was helping shape the lives of millions of young children.

Mister Rogers' Neighborhood was then in color and had been nationally shown on educational television for about two years. Given his famous appearance defending public television in the Pastore hearings before the United States Senate and his chairmanship of the White House Conference on Children, Fred Rogers was a public figure now—known throughout the country, idolized by millions of children and many of their parents, already getting some pointed satirical treatment on other television programs for his ever-so-gentle manner.

Mister Rogers' Neighborhood was bringing the importance of early childhood into the mainstream of popular culture. Fred Rogers's instinct to use television, the most powerful popular culture tool of his time, to advance such a high-minded educational agenda was a stroke of pure genius. It provided a direct line to the rise of the early education movement in America and much of the rest of the world.

It wasn't until the twentieth century that research into child development flourished and a new, deeper understanding of childhood emerged. The researchers came to understand that childhood was utterly distinctive and powerfully important, and the learning that could take place in those first few years, if grown-ups would pay attention, was the most crucial earning of all. An extraordinarily important part of the capacity of each person would develop in these early years, including language, creativity, and even the physical development of the brain.

This is what Fred Rogers got, what he apprehended, what he learned and internalized and made his very own passion. This is what he wanted to give to children and to convey to adults through *Mister Rogers' Neighborhood*.

Rogers took intense care in shaping each episode of his program. Every word, whether spoken by a person or a puppet, had to be scrutinized closely, because he knew that children hear things literally. As his former associate Arthur Greenwald put it: "There were no accidents on *Mister Rogers' Neighborhood*."[1]

If something wasn't quite right, Fred Rogers might worry enough to stop performing the puppet dialogue that was an essential part of every episode of *Mister Rogers' Neighborhood* and come out from behind the set.

Despite all the care that had been taken to prepare the script, one day something still felt wrong. Fred had written it longhand on a yellow legal pad and given it to his secretary Elaine Lynch to type out. He had reviewed it carefully and also shared it with a couple of other producers to get their comments.

After this first pass, Fred—or Elizabeth Seamans or Eliot Daley or one of the other staff members of Family Communications, Inc. (FCI) who sometimes helped Fred write scripts for the *Neighborhood*—would usually walk down Fifth Avenue from the WQED studios to the University of Pittsburgh to review the material with Dr. Margaret McFarland, sometimes for several hours. This script had gone through that whole rigorous process to ensure excellence, and still Fred was worried that something wasn't perfect.

So Rogers committed a cardinal sin in the highly expensive world of television production: He stopped work, left a high-paid crew in the studio cooling their heels, and went back to Pitt to consult Margaret McFarland again. Many of the crew were union members, and the clock was still running while Fred headed down Fifth Avenue to find McFarland. This was costing FCI a pretty penny (which would bother Fred; he was known to be a parsimonious manager), but it had become a second religion to Rogers that in matters having to do with television for children, excellence was the only acceptable standard. He was back in about an hour, McFarland correction in hand, and the show went on.

This adherence to the highest standards had become even more of a concern to Rogers over the years, from the earliest, slapstick days of *The Children's Corner*, through his studies with McFarland when he was a student at the seminary, to his leadership of FCI, the nonprofit production company he had founded to make *Mister Rogers' Neighborhood*.

As television (and later the internet) infiltrated almost every home in America, it offered marketers and commercial enterprises an extraordinary opportunity to exploit young children, and Fred became the icon of protecting them. He did this through the example of his own program and its high standards, but he also did it by championing the importance of childhood itself. From his own struggles as a child, he had formed a powerful sensitivity to the feelings of young children.

Later, as a public figure, Rogers's shyness and modesty would take him to extremes to avoid adults who sought him out because of his notoriety (once, when he was receiving an award from a local Pittsburgh church, he had the seminary official who was escorting him take him down to the catacombs and passages under the old church to help him escape the crowd that awaited him at the front entrance).[2] But whenever he encountered a child, in any circumstances, he felt it a sacred duty to respond and protect.

Nancy Gruner, who worked in the early years at WQED as Fred's "girl Friday," remembers a time when she and Joanne and Fred went to dinner at the Hotel Saxonburg, north of Pittsburgh, one of Fred's favorite spots because he could count on an undisturbed evening. In the middle of the meal, a little boy appeared at the table, his head just below the tabletop at Fred's side. Fred looked down.

"My dog died," said the boy, simply, and in an instant Rogers was kneeling on the floor with the boy talking about pets and death and a little child's struggle to understand.[3]

EARLY ON, ELIOT DALEY helped with scripts for the *Neighborhood* as well as overseeing business matters at Small World Enterprises: "Rogers didn't want other people to get writing credits. His stated objection was that he was uncomfortable with having a viewing child think that somebody was putting words in his mouth—which I understood."[4]

Key to the scriptwriting process was consultation with Margaret McFarland, sessions that might run up to three hours. In advance of his appointment, Daley would tell Dr. McFarland which theme he wanted to explore, such as children's fear of the dark. He observes: "Margaret was a very kind of a wispy, bird-like woman; very, very slender, very frail looking—tough, but very frail looking. And had a kind of a squeaky voice.

"Margaret would just start talking . . . I couldn't figure out what the heck she was talking about; she was just sort of all over the place, and meandering about, you know, this visit that she had with her cousin in Kansas. . . . It was totally disconnected stuff . . . and I'd think, Oh god, is she losing it?

"For an hour, I would just be marinating in this miasma of inchoate, disconnected thought. And then it would be sort of like if you could imagine that you were standing point blank in front of a pointillist painting, and then somebody drew it away from you. . . .

"She would lift you back away from it, and you would suddenly see that every darn thing she'd been talking about was woven together as a thread in this tapestry . . . that just revealed to you everything about a child in darkness. . . . She was just incredible."[5]

Then Rogers would vet the script. His secretary Elaine Lynch remembered how careful he was with each word. When one script referred to putting a pet "to sleep," Rogers excised it for fear that children would be worried about going to sleep themselves.[6]

Dr. Daniel R. Anderson of the University of Massachusetts, who worked with Fred, remembered a speaking trip to Germany at which some members of an academic audience raised questions about Rogers's direct approach on television: They were concerned that it could lead to false expectations from children of personal support from a televised figure. Anderson was impressed with the depth of Rogers's reaction, and with the fact that he went back to production carefully screening scripts for any hint of language that could confuse children in that way.[7]

According to David Newell, Fred would constantly go back to review the lyrics of his songs to make sure nothing might mislead children. Among other changes, he provided new lyrics for the "Tomorrow" song that ended each show to ensure that children watching on Friday wouldn't look for a show on Saturday that wasn't there.[8]

Hedda Sharapan recalls that Fred halted taping of a show when a cast member told the puppet Henrietta Pussycat not to cry. Rogers came out from behind the puppet set to make clear that his show would never suggest to children that they not cry.[9]

The eye doctor Fred Rogers recruited to help him show children what happens when they have their eyes examined, Dr. Bernard "Pepper" Mallinger, reports that Rogers had an almost uncanny ability to think what little children were thinking and to formulate their questions when making *Mister Rogers' Neighborhood.*[10] As Rogers and Dr. Mallinger taped an exam of Fred's eyes—part of a series of programs to help children understand what medical care is all about—Fred surprised Mallinger with a question as the doctor peered into his eyes with his ophthalmoscope.

"He said, 'Can you see what I'm thinking?' " recalled Mallinger. "It would have never, absolutely never, entered my mind. But he realized what children thought about. And of course, I explained that I can only see the inside of the eye, and cannot see any of his thoughts . . . or fears, or concerns."[11] Rogers knew how to conceive of, and anticipate, the concerns of his young viewers.

Rogers was so exacting about language that he even inspired his own on-air "language." In 1977, while on a break, Arthur Greenwald and fellow writer Barry Head cracked open a bottle of Scotch, and to blow off steam, coined the term "Freddish" to describe the grammatical rules in writing for Fred Rogers. Head and Greenwald, also a talented cartoonist, even created an illustrated manual called "Let's Talk About Freddish," a loving parody of the demanding process of getting all the words just right for Rogers.[12]

They'd been working long hours on a projected three-part video series to prepare children for the experience of going to the hospital, a subject near and dear to Fred Rogers's heart. Both were accustomed to Rogers's multipart process: "I spent hours talking with Fred and taking notes," says Arthur Greenwald, "then hours talking with Margaret McFarland before I went off and wrote the scripts. Then Fred made them better."

"Speaking in 'Freddish,'" said Greenwald in an interview, was about anticipating "how the young audience might misunderstand, and preventing that misunderstanding by providing the right piece of information. What Fred understood and was very direct and articulate about was that the inner life of children was deadly serious to them."[13]

There were nine steps to Freddish translation:

First, "State the idea you wish to express as clearly as possible, and in terms preschoolers can understand." Example: "It is dangerous to play in the street."

Second, "Rephrase in a positive manner," as in "It is good to play where it is safe."

Third, "Rephrase the idea, bearing in mind that preschoolers cannot yet make subtle distinctions and need to be redirected to authorities they trust." As in, "Ask your parents where it is safe to play."

Fourth, "Rephrase your idea to eliminate all elements that could be considered prescriptive, directive, or instructive." (i.e., ask): "Your parents will tell you where it is safe to play."

Fifth, "Rephrase any element that suggests certainty." (i.e., will): "Your parents CAN tell you where it is safe to play."

Sixth, "Rephrase your idea to eliminate any element that may not apply to All children (as in, having PARENTS): "Your favorite GROWN-UPS can tell you where it is safe to play."

Seventh, "Add a simple motivational idea that gives preschoolers a reason to follow your advice": "Your favorite GROWN-UPS can tell you where it is SAFE to play. It is good to listen to them."

Eighth, "Rephrase your new statement, repeating Step One (i.e., GOOD as a personal value judgment): "Your favorite GROWN-UPS can tell you where it is SAFE to play. It is important to try to listen to them."

Ninth, "Rephrase your idea a final time, relating it to some phase of development a preschooler can understand (i.e., growing): "Your favorite GROWN-UPS can tell you where it is SAFE to play. It is important to try to listen to them. And listening is an important part of growing."[14]

Arthur Greenwald adds another subtle example of Freddish from his video work: "Fred saw a rough cut of one of the film sections we did for a hospital video that included a scene where the nurse was inflating the blood pressure cuff and said, 'I'm going to blow this up.'

"Fred made us redub the line, saying, 'I'm going to puff this up with some air,' because 'blow it up' might sound like there's an explosion, and he didn't want the kids to cover their ears and miss what would happen next. Sure enough, he was right.

"The trick is to provide the context in the explanation," Greenwald continued. "Preschoolers don't have any context. Kids are afraid of going down the drain because all they see is stuff being sucked down the drain." Fred Rogers even wrote a song called "You Can Never Go Down the Drain."[15]

As simple as *Mister Rogers' Neighborhood* may look onscreen, the process of putting the shows together was as painstaking as the above example suggests.

ELIZABETH SEAMANS JOINED the staff of the *Neighborhood* in 1970. After graduating from Harvard College, she took a job as reporter for the *Boston Herald Traveler*, but she quit when she was asked to interview the mother of a murdered three-year-old. She headed to Pittsburgh to visit her sister and look for a job. Shortly after arriving, she was offered an unpaid internship on *Mister Rogers' Neighborhood*. Soon she became a paid staff member, writing scripts and playing the onscreen wife of Mr. McFeely, though she claimed never to be completely comfortable with performing.[16]

Once Seamans learned Rogers's system for keeping the content of the program true to his standards, she was given the latitude to write scripts and review them with Dr. Margaret McFarland. Elizabeth Seamans describes one seminal episode: "Daniel has been forgotten by a certain motherly figure and he feels abandoned, so we get to talk about all those feelings about children whose mothers forgot to pick them up at daycare, or came home late."

Seamans strove to meet Fred Rogers' exacting standards; she understood how serious and necessary they were: "The Neighborhood of Make-Believe . . . was scripted out like a drama, word for word for every puppet character and every real character."[17]

From 1972 until 1976, she wrote approximately fifteen scripts a year in a sixty-five-script season, in five blocks of three each. Fred Rogers would do the remaining ones in ten blocks of five —a truly daunting workload.

In contrast to the scripted parts of the *Neighborhood*, the "real-life" segments with actors and special guests like Van Cliburn and Tony Bennett were more free-form. Seamans explains: "Fred liked to be on with people he trusted, because so much was ad-libbed in the unscripted segments. That's pretty much how he vetted people."[18]

When Elizabeth Seamans was composing scripts, she'd present

Fred Rogers with three possible story lines; he would pick one. Themes were often suggested by staff members with small children, or even taken from viewer mail. For his entire career, the connections Fred Rogers made with his television "neighbors" resulted in a torrent of fan mail. And he always answered, even if he needed help to handle the volume; he never wanted to miss a single chance to help a child learn.

Producer Margy Whitmer recalls that she'd sit down with Hedda Sharapan to go through the piles of mail: "Some of the ideas from viewers were wonderful. The staff would get together to narrow down the themes: 'We really need to do something about daycare, or the environment.' Then we'd go over them with Fred, and he would pick what he wanted to develop."[19]

When Mister Rogers sang, "Won't you be my neighbor?" at the start of every show, he was inviting the kids watching to share their thoughts and feelings about topics that mattered to them. Nothing was more important to him than making children in the extended "neighborhood" feel not only secure, but also "heard," especially on topics parents might have a hard time grappling with, like the death of the family dog or sibling rivalry.

For Rogers, the very act of asking questions, and trying to answer them honestly, was the key to growing and learning: "We can't always know what's behind a child's question. But if we let a child know we respect the question, we're letting that child know that we respect him or her. What a powerful way to say, 'I care about you!' "[20]

Once Rogers and Elizabeth Seamans had selected a theme for a script, they'd sit in his office and go over it at great length. He'd give her subtle directions on how to articulate the theme of the episode even as they were selecting it. She described it as "Let's tease it up together. There was lengthy conversation, maybe for an hour and a half."[21]

Next up, a trip to see Margaret McFarland, in which Seamans would review developmental aspects of the script.

After these sessions, a follow-up would focus on specific language after the overall theme had been articulated. In between, Seamans got additional detail from Fred Rogers and developed the script further. And though she was entrusted to write the core script for the Neighborhood of Make-Believe segments, Rogers himself always wrote the openings and closings. As Seamans put it: "Word for word, the crafting of those was hugely important to him."[22]

She cites one example of Margaret McFarland's advice that affected a script Seamans wrote that involved a child's fear of bees: "She [Dr. McFarland] said, 'Do you know what bees mean to young children?'"

Danger, yes, but also "penetration, body integrity, what's me and what's not me inside and outside, not just ouchy bee stuff, it was way past that."[23]

Arthur Greenwald notes that the process of writing for the *Neighborhood* could try a staffer's patience: "It could be exasperating. I remember Elizabeth Seamans being driven crazy by Fred. . . . She'd written a script where a telephone repairman comes to fix something in the Neighborhood, or in the TV house with Fred. She wanted to put in a bit to explain where Fred's tools go in his belt.

"Fred made a comment, 'Well, we know, Betsy, why you're concerned about that.' It was some sort of psychoanalytic reference to women's concerns."[24]

When Seamans had Greenwald over for dinner, she was so mad that she flicked spaghetti sauce into the air and exclaimed: "He can have a flying stick in the Neighborhood of Make-Believe, but I can't ask where a tool goes in a belt!"

And though Fred Rogers could often seem like a perfectionist, he was never wedded to the outcome. According to the cinematographer Joe Seamans, who did camera work and production for the *Neighborhood*, Rogers was accepting of things in ways that often surprised his crew.[25]

Once when Seamans (Elizabeth's husband) was filming the fish in the *Neighborhood* fish tank eating their food, the fish wouldn't eat. Everyone except Fred thought they would have to reshoot: "Fred had his own fish tank and he used to feed the fish, so we rehearsed it. The guy [production assistant] went back and he put all his fish food in there and all the fish came and ate. Fred looked at it and we had to get rid of the glare on the glass and stuff, so we were ready to go. So then we roll the tape; the guy goes back there and he puts the fish food in there and the fish just stare at it as it floats to the bottom of the tank. Because they were full."

Everyone on the set assumed they were in for a long day, shooting and reshooting, waiting for the fish to get hungry again. "Fred just looked at it," recalls Seamans, "and he looked at the camera and said, 'I guess the fish aren't hungry right now; you know, sometimes we're not hungry.' "[26] Rogers understood that the very young children viewing his show would find that a perfectly sensible explanation.

As they were filming other scenes over the ensuing years, the crew members would frequently remind themselves, as Joe Seamans puts it, "Well, do the fish really need to eat?" Seamans himself became a believer that if one is accepting, serendipity can often produce better programming for children.[27]

But Fred's intense care for shaping the program wasn't universally admired or understood, at least by some adults. Basil Cox, a former executive with the Rogers nonprofit Family Communications, recalls that Fred Rogers always had doubters as well as supporters: "Fred was very controversial, for most of his career. There were always a significant number of people who just didn't believe him . . . thought it was an act. Thought that he was somehow phony. That they just couldn't buy that there was somebody who had that persona . . . and who just didn't like him. You know, just really were offended by him almost.

"He was not a saint. . . . He was recognized by some as a saint, but by the general world, he was a host of a kiddy television show, and that's it. And he was no more sanctified than Captain Kangaroo.

"He was constantly having to persuade people that he was real, in those days—constantly. Even later on, he always had his detractors, but—then I hesitate to say it, but I think early on they were in the majority, not the minority. He was just not believable to people."[28]

ONE REASON ROGERS FELT that his television work could speak for itself was the strong faith he always put in showing reality—even harsh reality—on the screen. When he produced an entire show about death in 1970, he used careful language but didn't spare his young viewers.

As this episode opened, Fred looked particularly dapper in a double-breasted blue blazer and a bright red tie, a more corporate and less avuncular image than typical. He was about forty-two years old, but still looked as if he was in his late twenties: slim and fit, his face smooth and boyish, with a full head of dark hair. And he projected a perfect image of the calm, centered, Zen master of childhood: fully inhabiting the child's world, the world of the simple, the innocent, the imaginative, and the playful. He finished singing "It's a Beautiful Day in the Neighborhood" and opened the closet door on the set to hang up the blue blazer and replace it with a baby-blue zippered cardigan sweater. He held up a small panel of wood to the camera, his four fingers and thumb emphasizing the five corners of the pentagon, and explained the meaning of this new word to the watching children.

Then he turned to "Picture-Picture," a screen-within-the-television-screen of the program itself, a device Rogers used to capture the attention of his viewers. Today, Picture-Picture showed a lovely, colorful, and soothing shot of swimming fish. Things were still at their usual calming, soothing pace as Fred turned to the fish tank on the set and invited his viewers to join him feeding the fish.

Then the jolt: Floating upside down at the bottom of the tank was a dead fish—an alarming little mess that turned the tenor of the show to the ominous. Fred was quieter now, even more earnest, but he plowed ahead into an exceptional scene for three- and four-year-old children: parsing the living from the dead. What followed was a truly extraordinary exploration of death, loss, pain, and the meaning of life, all delivered simultaneously on two levels: the child's level of innocent, sometimes agonizing questioning of the meaning of things, and a powerful existential level of inquiry that never defaults to the easy answer. It was Fred Rogers at his very best as teacher and philosopher.

"Oh, what's that down there?" he asked, looking deadpan into the camera to the watching children. "Do you see a dead fish? A dead fish would be one that isn't breathing or swimming or anything at all. Look down there and see."

Down at the bottom of the aquarium was a small, silvery dead body lying on the pebbles. Fred got a small net and reached gingerly into the tank to lift out the dead fish. He told the children watching that he'd read that sometimes if you put a dead fish in heavily salted water, it can shock the fish back to life. He put the fish in a waterproof bag, pulled a container of salt off a shelf, and sprinkled it into the bag. Nothing.

"I guess the salt isn't going to help us," he said softly. He got a paper towel, folded the body into a little origami coffin made from the paper, and retrieved a trowel from a drawer on his way back out the door to the yard. There Fred Rogers carefully dug a small hole in the soil near an evergreen, put the body in this ad hoc grave, and patted the soil down.

Mister Rogers took his viewers on this little journey to show that even in the face of death, things move ahead. That's the essential message as he sits by the fish grave. Rogers never told grieving children that everything will be all right: no such simplistic reassurances. Instead he shared his feelings about death and loss, and the extraordinary truth, reaffirmed repeatedly throughout the program, that life does go on. Delivered by this Presbyterian minister-educator who was so childlike himself, his message brought poignancy far beyond the trite bromides usually served to little children.

As Mister Rogers sat next to the little pile of earth marking the grave of a dead fish, he talked shyly about a death he won't forget from his own childhood. He described his friendship with his dog Mitzie and how "she got too old and died. She and I were good pals. And when she died, I cried. And my grandmother heard me cry." Rogers, who never thought of himself as a performer, gave a great performance in part because it was so genuine, but also because the pacing and the tone of the storytelling were so skillful and engaging.

"My dad said we'd have to bury Mitzie. And I didn't want to. . . . I thought I'd just pretend that she was still alive. . . . But my dad said her body was dead, and we'd have to bury her." Long pause. "So, we did."

He walked back slowly into the house on his set. "Even now, I can still remember Mitzie's prickly fur, and her curly tail." He brought out an old photo of Mitzie the mutt, scraggly, with floppy ears, and proudly displayed it to his viewers. And then he looked directly into the camera and sang, "Sometimes people get sad . . ."

The message of the song is that the same people who get sad also, later, get glad. Life goes on.

After a respite that takes the viewers to the Neighborhood of Make-Believe segment of the show, we're back in the house for a visit from Fred's neighbor Bob Trow, a skilled carpenter. They make a grave marker out of the pentagonal piece of wood from the show's opening—everything comes together on *Mister Rogers' Neighborhood*—then go outside and place it on the fish's grave.

Then Fred Rogers sings about all the other questions, beyond death and sadness and the loss of a pet or a friend, that inhabit the life of the child: "Why does it have to get dark? Why won't the day always stay? . . . Someday, oh someday, I'll know what to say."

Mister Rogers speaks directly into the camera to the little children who are quietly, intently watching: "It helps to say that you're sad. Often it even helps to cry . . . let people know how you feel." This is Rogers's signature message: feelings are all right, whatever is mentionable is manageable, however confusing and scary life may become. Even with death and loss and pain, it's okay to feel all of it, and then go on.

A program for preschoolers exploring the question of death was a radical departure in 1970s television. Eliot Daley posits: "*Mister Rogers' Neighborhood* could never get on the air today, because it's too subtle. But fortunately, it came along at a time when the medium was hungry for programming. Fred was able to self-fund a lot of his own dedication, because he had some independent wealth, and people weren't being very critical, and there weren't a lot of watchdog groups.

"But I suspect that today it'd be different. There'd be people who would say: This is nothing but pediatric psychotherapy. And they're messing with our children's minds, you know. Get them off the air."[29]

Following Margaret McFarland's dictum that "anything mentionable is manageable," Fred Rogers tackled difficult topics not addressed on most shows for adults, let alone children. For example, he wrote a special segment of the *Neighborhood* literally overnight after Robert Kennedy's assassination, an episode that aired on June 7, 1968, in black and white. In it, Mister Rogers is in his house at the outset, and dressed in a suit. He never changes into his sweater and sneakers.

Most striking, he seems to be speaking not only to his young "neighbors," but also to their parents, about his concerns about the graphic displays of violence shown on mass media: He pleads for "your protection and support of your young children. There is just so much that a very young child can take without it being overwhelming."

In the Neighborhood of Make-Believe segment (no trolley this time), the kindhearted Lady Aberlin (Betty Aberlin) talks about a shooting with Lady Elaine and X the Owl (both puppets). She suggests that the man who did the shooting was very angry about something; but she assures X that the angry wishes he may have harbored about people didn't come true. Later in the show, Daniel asks her what "assassination" means—amazing subject matter on a show for children.

Toward the end of the program, Mister Rogers talks about the need to grapple with anger, and he sings "What Do You Do with the Mad that You Feel?" He stresses that some families might be comforted by watching the funeral on TV, but that for others, a long walk in the woods might be the best way to cope.

In a speech to a National Symposium on Children and Television in Chicago in October 1971, Rogers explained: "When President Kennedy, Dr. King, and Senator Kennedy were assassinated, I felt that I had to speak to the families of our country about grief. So many families and children were taking these catastrophes personally. Among many things, my main point in mounting such a program was to present a plea for families to include children in their own ways of coping with grief—a plea not to leave the children isolated and at the mercy of their own fantasies of loss and destruction, which tend to be much more frightening than any reality. On the Emmy citation for that particular program it is written that 'Mister Rogers was the only one on television to think of the children's needs at this time of national mourning.' What does that say about our industry?"[30]

HEDDA SHARAPAN REMEMBERS how strong Fred's instinct was to stick with reality, no matter how challenging. On a series of shows about noise, for which she was a producer, part of the production involved the noise of garbage trucks and how disruptive that can be in a neighborhood.[31] Lady Elaine, the sharp-tongued puppet who always acted as a provocateur, suggested that the noise could be avoided by just dumping the garbage in the ocean. Fred wanted to show how beautiful the ocean is and how horrible it would be to dump garbage in it. But the theme was "Noise," so he also wanted to produce footage that included underwater noise of the sea.

Fred engaged an eminent marine biologist, Sylvia Earle, the first female chief scientist of the National Oceanic and Atmospheric Administration. She used a device called a hydrophone to record underwater sound to accompany the film footage. It was a very expensive undertaking, involving a film crew, Earle and Rogers snorkeling together in the ocean, a marine sound team, and a lot of travel. When the shoot finally took place, the ocean looked beautiful, but there was no sound. Everything was still and quiet, with no noise whatsoever. Fred showed the segment anyway, explaining how quiet the sea can be. Later Sylvia Earle brought the hydrophone to Mister Rogers's house to listen to the fish in the on-set aquarium, but they weren't making any noise at all.

In another instance recounted by Sharapan, Fred begins his regular program routine by putting on his cardigan and buttoning it up, only to discover he had started at the wrong buttonhole; he was one button off. It came at the very beginning of the show, so the crew expected

Fred to simply start the whole thing over. Instead, he gave Sharapan a look and then ad-libbed the dialogue, explaining to the children how easy it is to make a mistake and showing them how to correct it.[32]

Rogers's embrace of reality also included breaking one of the established rules of television, a prohibition against footage that is essentially empty. While *Sesame Street* used fast pacing and quick-cut technique to excite and engage young viewers and keep them glued to the screen, Fred Rogers deliberately headed in the opposite direction, creating his own quiet, slow-paced, thoughtful world, which led to real learning in his view.

Elizabeth Seamans observes that on the show with guests, "Fred didn't allow talking constantly through whatever they were doing, even if it was twirling a hula-hoop. If Yo-Yo Ma comes on, let him play. Watch his hands. Move on his body with the camera so you can get so close that you can see his hands on the fret board—not just a cutaway, but a real look."[33]

Silence—Fred's willingness, as a producer and as a person, to embrace quiet, inactivity, and empty space—and his calm demeanor were completely unexpected in television in the 1970s. They were qualities that captivated children and their parents.

As soon as the *Neighborhood* gained a national audience, experts in child development applauded Rogers's approach. Dorothy G. Singer, senior research scientist in the Department of Psychology at Yale University and codirector of the Yale University Family Television Research and Consultation Center, gave credit to the combination of Fred's direct, personal approach and the very real issues on which he focused: "I think because he dealt with issues that children were dealing with: divorce, he dealt with death . . . he dealt with jealousy. All through that little kingdom of make-believe—and that was very important—all these social and emotional issues came out. Fred was there to explain anything you didn't understand, acting like the parent who really clarifies things for you. All of the characters really expressed their feelings—jealousy, anger. It was as if he was having a conversation with the child.

"And there was silence on the program, time for you to think about what Fred said and time for you to answer him. He really was interested in the child as a developing person. That was appealing to us because that's what I'm interested in, in preschool children. The numbers and letters will come later."[34]

A key to Rogers's direct connection to children was his own childlike nature. A favorite saying of his was, "The child is in me still and sometimes not so still."

Dr. Singer recalled that Fred's manner worried some parents, who thought, "Oh, he's a sissy. I don't want my kids watching that."[35]

He never heeded the doubters. Fred Rogers had absolute clarity about the techniques and messaging that were appropriate for his young viewers, which translated into a determination to control the content of *Mister Rogers' Neighborhood*. Given that he was the chief scriptwriter, the songwriter, the producer, the singer, the puppeteer, the host, and the creator of the show, and had to work with dozens of other actors, producers, writers, and directors to achieve his vision, it's not surprising that most of them found him to have a strong will and a determined focus.

"When you're an only child," observes one of his producers, Margy Whitmer, "competition is hard. I think that he clearly had a vision of what he wanted to say and do with kids, so he didn't want to be influenced by this 'outside' world, and he didn't want to compete. He didn't watch a lot of other children's shows. He didn't watch television, period."[36]

Still, he maintained a friendly relationship with Bob Keeshan, Captain Kangaroo, and called him every New Year's Day to wish him a happy New Year. And *Sesame Street*'s Big Bird was a guest on the *Neighborhood* in a charming 1981 sequence on, appropriately, "Competition." But the episode's lesson was about overcoming the fear of losing friends, and of being ignored when a new family member arrives.

Sesame debuted on PBS in the fall of 1969, just a year and a half after the *Neighborhood*. Fred Rogers was always very careful not to criticize *Sesame Street*'s more fast-paced, high-intensity approach in any public way. In fact, Mister Rogers himself appeared on *Sesame* in 1974, looking dapper in a white suit.

On the relationship between two of the most influential children's shows ever produced, "Speedy Delivery" mailman and longtime Rogers associate David Newell notes: "*Sesame Street* had a much bigger budget. We were more of an intimate show, though our budget increased over the years. They were sort of hip, and we were sort of . . . geeky. But Fred stuck to his guns."[37]

Neighborhood guest Wynton Marsalis points out the futility of comparisons between numbers for *Mister Rogers' Neighborhood* and *Sesame Street*: "I was once complaining to a mentor of mine about how little our music is listened to, and how much anything that has ignorance or minstrel-show imagery and degrades black people—how many millions of people love that. They might have fifty thousand people, and we only have a thousand.

"He listened to me complain, and when I got finished complaining, he said: 'Who are the thousand?'

"*Sesame Street* came on, and it was a phenomenal show, deserving of the praise. And Mister Rogers, he had his show; he had his concept. People who looked at that show (the *Neighborhood*), they were informed by it. They were more productive in their lives. *Sesame Street* had impact of one kind; Mister Rogers had his own impact.

"[Comparing them], it's like telling me, 'Man, my grandmother can cook. And there's a great restaurant in my neighborhood, and I can go eat at it.' And I tell you, 'Well, McDonald's can serve twenty million.'

"That's not even a good analogy, because, okay, *Sesame Street* is better than McDonald's. But it's like saying you like Five Guys, or whatever it is that you like. And then someone else might say, 'Yeah, I like Five Guys, but I also like Hamburger Heaven. But they don't sell as much as McDonald's.' I'm not telling you they did.

"Fred Rogers was fantastic; he was not fantastic in relation to what? He was fantastic to himself."[38]

13.

MISTER ROGERS, BOSS AND TEACHER

ONCE IN THE EARLY YEARS of the *Neighborhood*, Mister Rogers opened the closet door to hang up his jacket; but instead of his cardigan sweater, he discovered a blow-up sex doll. Michael Keaton, who started his television and movie career on *Mister Rogers' Neighborhood* and was an indefatigable prankster, had put the doll in the closet to throw Fred into confusion. The producers and crew, in on the joke, thought they'd have a good laugh and then reshoot the scene.

But Fred surprised them, grabbing the doll in his arms and waltzing out of the closet to a Fred Astaire dance routine across the set. He never missed a beat, dancing the doll back to the closet and closing the door. Then he emerged from the closet and pulled his crew back together for a reshoot. No one was more surprised, or more delighted, than Keaton, a stagehand who was also part of a troupe of stunt performers on the *Neighborhood* called The Flying Zookeeni Brothers Daredevil Circus.[1]

In a taped interview, Fred Rogers also looked back at a moment when the young Keaton was operating the machine behind "Picture, Picture." As Mister Rogers reached in to put a tape into the opening, a suspiciously familiar voice told him: "I'm ready to hear your confession, my son!"[2]

In addition to displaying a good sense of humor, Fred Rogers was artful in drawing from his own life to provide the substance and detail of the *Neighborhood*. The zip-up cardigan sweaters he always wore on the program came from his mother; she had knitted them for years for Fred, and kept giving him a new one each year for Christmas. The sneakers he put on at the beginning of each show derived from his experience on *The Children's Corner*, where he had learned to wear sneakers so he could run from the piano to the puppet stage without making distracting noises.

Most importantly, the sweaters and the sneakers and the whole notion of changing his attire at the beginning of each program was a way of expressing Margaret McFarland's rule of providing clear transitions for young children so they could absorb and adapt to the action (a rule not followed by most competing children's programs). The transition was also incorporated into the show by the trolley that transported viewers and players on *Mister Rogers' Neighborhood* from the reality part of the program to the Neighborhood of Make-Believe. Fred and Dr. McFarland wanted each child to be very clear about where reality ended and playful make-believe picked up.

Johnny Costa's beautiful, light tinkling music that floods the screen when Mister Rogers feeds the fish is just one example of the musical "triggers" that alerted kids to a segment they anticipated in the routines of their television neighbor. Then the music would help young viewers transition easily to the next segment. In "talking" as the trolley, for instance, the music is in effect another actor on the show.

Cast members both participated in the "real" segments of the program and interacted with the puppets in the Neighborhood of Make-Believe. Fred Rogers had a keen eye for local talent. One of the first members of a de facto *Neighborhood* repertory company was Don Brockett, who played Chef Brockett of Brockett's Bakery, a key stop in many a "real world" segment on the *Neighborhood*, which also highlighted trips to Bob Trow's multifaceted repair shop and Joe Negri's music shop. Most of the actors in the "real world" segments of the show were very skilled musicians or singers.

Joe Negri observes: "Occasionally Fred would want me to walk through the Neighborhood with a guitar wrapped around my neck; but that's not the kind of musician that I am. I was a jazz musician then, as I am now. I used to leave the show and go play musical jobs—jazz jobs, you know. I wasn't a handyman in real life by any means."[3]

Negri, who appeared in three hundred episodes of the *Neighborhood* over thirty-five years, notes with amusement that he is not handy at all: "My wife is handier than I am. When Fred called me and asked, 'How would you like to be a handyman?' I said to him, 'you gotta be kiddin'. You're picking the wrong guy here, because I'm not handy at all.'"

Rogers assured him that "It's just going to be pretend."

"So that's the way we did it. I really wasn't an actor," Negri says, "and I never tried to be one. I just played myself. I remember once reading about Spencer Tracy: He said, 'I just play myself.' And I thought, 'That's what I do, too.'"

He adds: "We had a couple of funny incidents where the plumbing, everything, in the Neighborhood got messed up. King Friday put me on the job, and I had to call real plumbers. I thought, 'Whoa, this is getting a bit heavy for me.' The plumbers and electricians would come on and wind up talking to King Friday about their occupations."

Joe Negri did enjoy the music shop: "That was a kind of a natural for me because since I was six or seven years old, I'd been going to music shops and taking guitar lessons. It was something I was very familiar with."[4]

Fred Rogers, son of an industrialist and a successful businessman, maintained a lifelong—some would say childlike—sense of curiosity about how things worked, which seeped into various aspects of the strolls Mister Rogers took around the Neighborhood once he left his living room or his front porch. His sister, Laney, observes: "He was like a sponge. He could just get interested in something, and want to know all about it. He encouraged that in other people, too."[5]

She recalls her mystification about her older brother's whereabouts on a trip she took to Paris with Fred and Joanne when she was thirteen or fourteen years old. Every day, Fred would disappear with no explanation.

"Finally, on the last day before we left, he said, 'I will take you and show you what I've been doing with my vacation.' And he had found a man on the Left Bank who was teaching him how to bind books. We went up into this turret with the old French gentleman [who] had very large pieces of equipment, and he was teaching Fred how to manipulate the papers and things. . . . Throughout his life, [Fred] was inquisitive about how to do things, and what more there was to learn."[6]

Rogers made such operations a highlight of early *Neighborhood* programs. In addition to Brockett's Bakery, Betty's Little Theater showcased shows within the *Neighborhood*, organized by fresh-faced, sweet-voiced ingenue Betty Aberlin, dubbed Lady Aberlin for the Make-Believe segments of the program. New York native Aberlin was a mainstay of the program from 1968 to the year the *Neighborhood* went off the air, 2001—a thirty-three-year run. Her tender exchanges with the puppet Daniel Striped Tiger are some of the most-watched and most-loved episodes in the *Neighborhood*'s archives.

Michael Horton, who voiced puppets on the show, observes: "In the scenes with Betty and Daniel, Betty was the mother and Daniel was the child. I think that Fred never really grew up. The things that affect most children never affected him. And the things that affected him never affected most children."[7]

One charming early episode (1972) featured Betty Aberlin as the host of a variety show at "BLT," as she called Betty's Little Theater. Among other memorable acts, Mister Rogers appears in a tux and plays an accordion duet with Johnny Costa, and Betty herself performs a Chaplin-esque silent hide-and-seek with Bob Trow. Mr. and Mrs. McFeely join local tap-dance whiz Joey Hollingsworth for a concluding dance number.

Aberlin also contributed ideas to many scripts. Michael Horton observes: "It would never have occurred to me to say anything to Fred during the taping of the show—to interject something. We were extremely, extremely close friends. I knew I'd be eating dinner with him and his family that night. I was also very young.

"Betty was the one who spoke up. She knew the characters much more than I did. Betty Aberlin is a brilliant person; the program would not have worked without her. There were a couple of times when Betty felt that she knew Fred enough to say, 'This might be offensive to handicapped people,' 'This might be offensive to women,' 'This might be offensive to gay people.'"[8]

Michael Horton was a young man from Alabama with a fundamentalist Christian background when he first met Fred Rogers through a friend who was the organ master at the church where the Rogers family worshipped. "Fred wanted to help me. I remember that he said to me one time, when we were just joking around in his living room: 'You have a talent.' No one had ever said that to me before."[9]

Neighborhood stalwart Don Brockett was a local impresario with a notably ribald sense of humor who wrote, produced, and directed revues and industrial shows at a time when Pittsburgh was the third-largest corporate headquarters in America, behind New York and Chicago, with companies like Alcoa, Mellon Bank, US Steel, and Westinghouse.

In a Pittsburgh summer-stock production of a revue called *Berlin to Broadway with Kurt Weill*, Fred Rogers first saw Chuck Aber, whom Fred later dubbed Neighbor Aber. Rogers had come to see Betty Aberlin, who was in the show, too. Chuck Aber was also employed in several of Don Brockett's industrial productions. One thing—or person—led to another in the world of the arts in late 1960s and early 1970s in Pittsburgh. By 1972 Aber, who started on the *Neighborhood* as a puppeteer, was a regular, like Brockett and Aberlin. Eventually Aber was cast as assistant mayor to Maggie Stewart, the mayor of Westwood, a neighborhood adjoining the Neighborhood of Make-Believe. He notes: "It was really kind of ahead of its time, to have a female mayor—let alone a woman of color."[10]

Former producer Margy Whitmer, who joined the program later, observes that the show's topics evolved to reflect changes in society: "In Fred's perfect world, there would be a mother and father and kids—the nuclear family. We really had to convince him that it was important to do materials on childcare, because kids were going to daycare. And before I started, they did a week about divorce. That was something he really didn't want to touch with a ten-foot pole, but reality made it so that he had to."[11]

And sometimes, Whitmer recalls, Rogers would take things he observed in daily life and work them into the show: "Our computer guy who would come in and do tech stuff gave Fred one of those laser pointers as a present. He wrote it into a script. A year or two later, we found out that they can blind you, so we had to redo that segment."

Though Elizabeth Seamans donned a wig and played Mrs. McFeely in addition to writing scripts, she never felt comfortable as an actor. Fred Rogers was disappointed when she quit not once, but twice: "It's a complicated thing, talking through these characters that are in someone else's head. They have their own vocabulary, they have their own syntax, they have their complete personalities. Creatively, you can't do that forever if they aren't your characters."[12]

Though working to Fred Rogers's exacting standards had challenges, Seamans and others found him an empowering boss, despite his flaws—self-absorption and stubbornness among them.

His staff also respected him as a bold leader. Arthur Greenwald observed that Rogers's wealth gave him a certain "level of security. . . . He chose to dedicate himself to making the world better. He was always focused on 'What good can come of this? Where do people need help?'

"There's a consistent theme in Fred's career of people underestimating him. I don't think that it's widely understood . . . what a powerful intellect he had, and . . . for lack of a better term, what a tough guy he was. He had a passion about helping children that his famous gentle manner belied, and he had a really steely core."[13]

Elizabeth Seamans found him to be an empathetic if sometimes exasperating boss: "He was not proud or arrogant. He didn't take anything or anybody for granted, ever. He was flawed, but he was a really, really great man, and a good man."[14]

David Newell—Mr. McFeely—notes that "Fred really wanted people to grow; that was a big word in his vocabulary. He was always growing—growing emotionally, growing educationally. He would never sit and twiddle his thumbs. Fred was always doing something with the finite time we have here."[15]

Rogers's office at WQED Pittsburgh famously did not have a

desk, only a sofa and armchairs, because Fred Rogers thought a desk was "too much of a barrier."

Staffers at Family Communications were told to take as much time as they needed to deal with their issues: "I can't come into work today, my cat's sick." "I've got to leave because I'm really sad." Fred Rogers's respect for the people who worked for him made it a comfortable place to work.

Rogers paid his staff what was considered a fair salary, especially in public television, though he was noted for his own frugality, and for running the *Neighborhood* on a shoestring budget.

At Christmas, the staff received bonuses and exchanged gifts at a Christmas lunch. One year, producer Margy Whitmer got her boss's name in the draw. She decided to give him, playfully, a salt-and-pepper-shaker snow globe from her "cheesy" collection: "The salt was the globe, and it was sitting in this chair painted to represent the moon and the stars. So I said to Fred, 'What do you give somebody who has everything? I guess I'll have to give you the world, and the moon and the stars.' A couple years later, Fred got my name. What did I get? The salt-and-pepper shaker back: he regifted me. People gave him all this stuff, so it was easy for him to regift. But he was never about material things; he really just gave you himself."[16]

Though Rogers made a show based on his Christian values, he never tried to impose his beliefs on staff members who were Jewish or not particularly religious. Longtime staffer Hedda Sharapan, a student of child psychology whose mentor was Margaret McFarland, comes from a family in which "My father found his own father in a concentration camp after the war was over. . . . So the Holocaust was a very important part of my family.

"Fred Rogers's . . . faith and ministry was based in Christianity. And yet, I always felt very comfortable in his sense of spirituality and openness to Jewishness. . . . Spirituality was in the air. It was in the walls. It was in Fred's office and it was in my office, because Fred brought it with him. And I don't know how I would describe spirituality except as kind of goodness, thoughtfulness.

"There's a story that when Fred walked into the studio each day, he said a silent prayer. 'Dear Lord—let some word of this be Yours.' I have actually taken that on as my mantra."[17]

Margy Whitmer adds: "I think faith in a greater being was what's important to Fred. And most religions have all the same tenets of kindness, and taking care of your neighbor."

Still, she noted, "Fred wanted to surround himself with a competent staff, and he wanted them to have confidence. But we always said, 'Whose *Neighborhood* is it? Not yours.'"[18]

FRED ROGERS had the final word on any directorial decision. His range of contributions to the *Neighborhood* was astounding: He wrote most of the approximately nine hundred program scripts (and edited the others); he wrote all two hundred songs performed on the *Neighborhood* (as well as thirteen operas); he played the piano in most of the musical performances, and sang in many; he created all of the characters on the program; he played most of the major puppet roles; he played the role of host on every episode; he produced the programs; and although there were official directors of the programs, he approved every detail of every show.

In addition to very talented guests ranging from local folksinger Ella Jenkins to famous performers like Yo-Yo Ma and Wynton Marsalis, regular cast members such as François Clemmons, the first African American person to appear in a recurring role on a children's TV series, often burst into song on the *Neighborhood*, frequently accompanying Mister Rogers.

Former producer Margy Whitmer observes: "Whenever we could write in a part for a woman that was traditionally a man's part, I tried to do that. If you look at the old shows, even though the main characters are basically white people, Fred also had handicapped people, black people, Asian people in small roles. He had them on in those early shows in the late sixties and early seventies. I don't think he gets the proper credit for that, mainly because the main neighbors were white people—the core crew. Mayor Maggie was brought in later; François Clemmons was added. It reached a plateau, and then we had to really try and crank it up, and whenever possible, get people of color."[19]

Michael Long, author of *Peaceful Neighbor: Discovering the Countercultural Mister Rogers*, notes that by the time the *Neighborhood* went national in 1968, racial issues dominated the headlines: ". . . white backlash against the civil rights movement, the Black Power Movement, and urban violence had taken the form of 'white flight.' Against this backdrop, the first week of *Mister Rogers' Neighborhood* saw Mister Rogers enjoying a home visit from Mrs. Saunders, an African American teacher, and a small interracial group of her students. It was a simple visit with a hard-hitting message: Whites and blacks live, study, and play together in the *Neighborhood*."[20]

In the 1972 episode featuring a variety show at Betty's Little Theater, dancer Joey Hollingsworth taps up a storm to a boogie-woogie tune, dressed in a military-style jacket, and sporting a substantial Afro—not a common sight on children's television of the era. In the same episode, African American mother and daughter Elsie and Debbie Neal recite a poem and sing, respectively. Fred Rogers's interest in, and dedication to, music on the *Neighborhood* often led him to feature talented artists and performers from Pittsburgh's black community, whose rich cultural legacy is most famously celebrated in the work of playwright August Wilson. In fact, Fred Rogers is mentioned in Wilson's "memoir in monologue," *How I Learned What I Learned.*

In the wake of the riots that erupted in 1968 after Martin Luther King Jr. was assassinated, the *Neighborhood* greeted a black policeman who kept everyone safe, played by accomplished opera singer Clemmons. He went on to appear on the show for twenty-five years. He also appeared as other characters in several of Rogers's operas.

As François Clemmons told Story Corps interviewer Karl Lindholm in 2016, Fred Rogers approached Clemmons after hearing him singing in church. At first, Clemmons was reluctant to take the role as a police officer: "I grew up in the ghetto. I did not have a positive opinion of police officers. Policemen were siccing police dogs and water hoses on people. And I really had a hard time putting myself in that role. So I was not excited about being Officer Clemmons at all."²¹

In due course, this accomplished artist with music degrees from Oberlin and Carnegie Mellon changed his mind. In one of his most memorable scenes, in a 1969 episode just after the first anniversary of the assassination of Martin Luther King Jr., Officer Clemmons is invited to sit alongside Mister Rogers in a little wading pool on a hot summer day: "He invited me to come over and to rest my feet in the water with him," Clemmons recalls. "The icon Fred Rogers not only was showing my brown skin in the tub with his white skin as two friends, but as I was getting out of that tub, he was helping me dry my feet."²²

The scene—which the two revisited in 1993 in their last episode together—touched Clemmons in a way he hadn't expected: "I think he [Fred Rogers] was making a very strong statement. That was his way. I still was not convinced that Officer Clemmons could have a positive influence in the *Neighborhood* and in the real-world neighborhood, but I think I was proven wrong."

When he traveled to help promote the *Neighborhood*, Clemmons heard from viewers who felt that *Sesame Street*, set in an urban neighborhood populated by both kids and adults of color, was more attuned to a diverse audience.²³ This was partially true, and may have reflected Fred Rogers's desire to avoid overt political expressions on the show. In addition, he was reflecting the Latrobe, Pennsylvania, he grew up in, not the New York–like cityscape of *Sesame Street*.

By 1975, François Clemmons had been joined by Maggie Stewart, an African American actress who played Mayor Maggie in the Neighborhood of Make-Believe's adjoining town, Westwood. Her associate mayor was blond, blue-eyed Chuck Aber.

And as noted by producer Margy Whitmer, Rogers was not credited with adding diverse cast members because many were in smaller roles, reflecting again, perhaps, the world of Latrobe as he knew it.²⁴

François Clemmons tried to talk Fred Rogers into casting an interracial couple in one of the operas he showcased on the *Neighborhood*.

As Clemmons tells it, "Fred was never hostile [to the idea]. . . . He just never did it." Clemmons assumed that Rogers was concerned about alienating socially conservative viewers.[25]

Married for a time when he started on the *Neighborhood*, Clemmons later came out as gay, though not overtly on the show. Rogers apparently encouraged Clemmons to focus on his singing career; Rogers evidently believed Clemmons would tank his career should he come out as a gay man in the late 1960s.[26]

As Michael Long notes in the book *The Peaceful Neighbor: Discovering the Countercultural Mister Rogers*: "But—and this is a crucial point—Rogers later revised his counsel to his younger friend. As countless gays came out more publicly following the Stonewall uprising, Rogers even urged Clemmons to enter into a long-term, stable gay relationship. And he always warmly welcomed Clemmons's gay friends whenever they visited the television set in Pittsburgh."[27]

This underscored the significance of another element of the 1993 "wading pool" episode, which reprised the 1969 original. At the end of the episode, when Mister Rogers takes his sneakers off and hangs up his sweater, as usual, he says, "You make every day a special day just by being you, and I like you just the way you are."

François Clemmons looked over at Rogers as he said it. As Rogers walked over, Clemmons asked: " 'Fred were you talking to me?' And he said, 'Yes, I have been talking to you for years. But you heard me today.' It was like telling me I'm okay as a human being. That was one of the most meaningful experiences I'd ever had."[28]

Rogers himself was often labeled "a sissy," or gay, in a derogatory sense. But as his longtime associate Eliot Daley put it: "Fred is one of the strongest people I have ever met in my life. So if they are saying he's gay because . . . that's a surrogate for saying he's weak, that's not right, because he's incredibly strong." He adds: "He wasn't a very masculine person, he wasn't a very feminine person; he was androgynous."[29]

In a 1975 interview for the *New York Times*, Rogers noted drolly: "I'm not John Wayne, so consequently, for some people I'm not the model for the man in the house."[30]

In conversation with one of his friends, the openly gay Dr. William Hirsch, Fred Rogers himself concluded that if sexuality was measured on a scale of one to ten: "Well, you know, I must be right smack in the middle. Because I have found women attractive, and I have found men attractive."[31]

Michael Horton, the voice of *Neighborhood* puppets and a close Rogers-family friend for decades, notes that he is always asked first about Fred Rogers: "Was he really like that?"

"I say, 'Do you mean, was he a nice, kind person off-camera, the way he comes across?' The answer is always yes."

Then the follow up: "People don't say to me, 'Was he gay,' but 'Isn't he gay?' To me, that's very revealing in a way, because of how presumptuous people can be. In other words, 'Isn't he gay?' sort of leads you to think that maybe Fred had a double life or something."[32]

There was no double life. And without exception, close associates concluded that Fred Rogers was absolutely faithful to his marriage vows.

IN EXPOSING CHILDREN to art forms like opera, in addressing serious social issues, and in integrating Margaret McFarland's child-development research into a program for preschoolers, Fred Rogers changed the landscape of children's programming and strongly influenced the television medium itself. Ellen Wartella, professor of communication studies and psychology at Northwestern University and a leading scholar of the role of media in children's development, explains: "Fred Rogers and the educational shows on public television were able to demonstrate that [television was not inherently bad], that there was a market for quality children's television, and now you see a lot more quality."[33]

Wartella adds that, at the point at which *Mister Rogers' Neighborhood* and *Sesame Street* came on screen, there was great concern over the impact of violent programming on children, and the medium itself was seen to hold little educational value. Only a few years earlier,

Federal Communications Commission Chairman Newton Minow had described television as a "vast wasteland."

Rogers and *Sesame Street*, according to Wartella, helped restore the medium's reputation: "There wasn't inherently anything in the medium that required TV to be violent to attract an audience . . . and concern about the audience, particularly the child audience, from someone who had Fred Rogers's understanding of developmental psychology, his inherently compassionate nature, and his concern about taking care of children—that he would produce a program that would be an icon of a different model of TV at the same moment that violence was so much the topic of discussion about television—it's really quite remarkable."[34]

Wartella also emphasizes the importance of Rogers's distinctive approach to social and emotional learning: "It's not that he didn't introduce knowledge—all those tours of how you make ice cream—and there were lots of things that he had that were very important in introducing children to the world. But he did it within a context that he was very much concerned with the social and emotional wellbeing of children, and that was in contradistinction to the time."[35]

This emphasis came, of course, from Fred's work with McFarland and the Arsenal Center. She and Benjamin Spock and Erik Erikson and the other researchers there had been learning that very young children simply don't learn very well in a cognitive sense unless their social and emotional development is advancing effectively. *Sesame Street*, by contrast, focused initially on learning words and numbers. It was decades before the field of early education and children's television caught up to Rogers.

Though not persuasive to some, for the most part Fred Rogers's gentle, childish qualities came across well to parents. And his presentation was applauded by experts in education and child development.

In a 2007 interview, Ellen Galinsky, president of the Families and Work Institute and author of *Mind in the Making*, said: "He's authentic. He's genuine. He connects on an intellectual and a social and emotional level all at once. He does care about people. That song about 'you're special' is real for him. He retained his childlike self. Particularly for teachers that's very important, because they care about that childlike self in themselves. He told stories. He would get louder, softer, pause. He was not afraid of silence. . . . That really brought you in emotionally.

"He would tell a story from different perspectives. If he was doing something on superheroes, he'd bring a superhero there and show how they got into their costume, and ask them what it was like for them. He shared the grown-up world with [children]. . . . He had a way of weaving in a subject that was an exercise in learning.

"What Fred did was include the things kids need to learn, but the subject was integrated into real stories. [This] process of engaged learning was fundamental to him."[36]

As Rogers himself put it: "There are many people in the world who want to make children into performing seals. And as long as children can perform well, those adults will applaud. But I would much rather help a child to be able to say who he or she is."[37]

Fred Rogers's brand of magic, though understated by comparison to *Sesame Street*, was very powerful. Elizabeth Seamans reflects on "an enormous gift" he gave his staff: "Permission to step back the typical vocabulary of television, and to say there can be a whole other vocabulary, a whole other pace, even a whole other relationship to the camera. You can think carefully about an audience, and meet the needs and the pace and the interests of that audience very narrowly, and still have an enormous impact and an enormous viewership.

"Fred Rogers was absolutely unfazed by expectations about television. What drove a lot of television in general was anxiety and the fear that viewers would turn away. We'd continually show things that are not necessarily interesting, but riveting because they are scary. Artists like Fred Rogers dredge into the light what we all acknowledge and recognize, but are too busy barreling down the road of life. There was no barrier to what Fred was willing to think about or accept."[38]

Margy Whitmer sums up the appeal of the man in the cardigan sweater: "It's really quite simple: The man you saw on the show, that's who he was. His respect and passion for children was real. . . . What he put out to the world was so important to us. It struck a real note in our hearts and our souls.

"Everything he set out to do, he set out to do the best way possible. There's a poem he liked called 'Be the Best of What You Are.' If you're a janitor, be the best janitor—or whoever you are. Whatever you do, do it the best way you know how.

"He encouraged me to speak my mind. He was like a father figure who allowed me to blossom and be creative. He really helped me think about other people and get a bigger global perspective. He taught me to think about my neighbor . . . to step outside of myself and embrace otherness, and always try and think about what the other person's going through."

She remembers: "Fred wanted to nurture, and set an example as a caring adult. That was always the message."[39]

Chuck Aber stresses the same point as he recalls a taping he witnessed one day in the *Neighborhood*'s studio: "The story line was a . . . Hansel and Gretel sort of thing. Lady Elaine Fairchilde had this little cottage in the forest, and she had taken Bert Lloyd (Mr. Allmine) . . . kidnapped him, if you will.

"Between one of the takes, I was standing with Fred, and one of the crew, Nicky Tallo, came over and showed Fred that they could get smoke to billow out of the chimney of this house in the forest.

"Without a pause, Fred said, 'I really appreciate that. But I just want a little sliver of smoke, because I don't want the television friend to think that she's [Lady Elaine] cooking Bert Lloyd with her cookies.' He was always looking at it from his television friend's perspective."[40]

14.

PUPPET WORLD

SUSAN STAMBERG was a busy woman, host of the popular radio program *All Things Considered* on National Public Radio, the first woman in the US to host such a national news program. And she had a young son, Josh.

Still, when she got a call from one of Fred Rogers's producers asking her to work with Rogers on a new television program for the Public Broadcasting Service, she was intrigued. Josh watched *Mister Rogers' Neighborhood* regularly on PBS. Although her family's television wasn't often used, "I would specifically tune in so that he would have a chance to see *Mister Rogers' Neighborhood*, because it was so full of wonderful values. You'd see plenty of children sitting glommed in front of the television set, inert and not responding. But Josh always reacted to Fred. He was laughing and smiling, really engaged."[1]

Rogers's producer told Stamberg: "Fred's ready to move his message to an older audience."[2] He wanted to know if she'd be interested in getting involved. He wanted Stamberg to moderate a series of discussions on a variety of topics that affect families.

As she recalls: "He'd have experts sitting on the set with him. I was to be there, too, to interview them all, and then go out into the audience with a handheld microphone and be Phil Donahue . . . to work the crowd."

At first, Stamberg was excited about the idea. Then she got worried: "There would be a live audience. I do a live broadcast every night. I thought, 'Oh, really?'— and then I panicked."[3]

She called Rogers's producers at WQED to tell them she just didn't have the confidence to do live television. She didn't think she could manage a panel of experts, interact with a live audience, follow a teleprompter for questions, and do all this in front of four cameras when she was really accustomed to radio. The producers were disappointed, but understanding.

When her phone rang a few hours later, Stamberg thought it might be Rogers calling to plead his case. But when she answered, she found herself talking with the soft voice of Daniel Striped Tiger, the famous *Neighborhood* puppet, who was very well known to her son.

"I can tell you're very upset about something," Daniel said. "I think you're just frightened and uneasy about this. I can hear that, but I know you can do it. I know you can do this, and I will give you every possible help I can provide to you—and it will go very well."[4]

Daniel Striped Tiger—Fred Rogers speaking as Daniel Striped Tiger—persuaded Stamberg to do the series of PBS specials with him. "I had seven interviews to do for that night's radio broadcast of *All Things Considered*. Nonetheless I sat on the telephone listening, practically sucking my thumb. And in the end, you can guess the result. I said, 'Okay, Daniel. I'll do my best.'"

After Stamberg did seven of the programs, she came to appreciate Fred Rogers as much as her son did: "He can speak to our fears as he did with me on the telephone, and he can speak to our great joys, our apprehensions, our puzzlements, the things that we don't understand."[5]

It wasn't the only time Rogers used a *Neighborhood* puppet to pursue something he wanted. The tactic often worked because, to a significant extent, Fred Rogers was Daniel Striped Tiger, and King Friday XIII, and Queen Sara Saturday, and Lady Elaine Fairchilde, and all the other puppets he created and performed over the years. He had inhabited many of those characters since his childhood, and each of them embodied some facet of himself.

According to Fred's son Jim, his father identified so completely with the puppets that from time to time he would drop into a puppet persona at home. "The puppets were works of art, first of all," says Jim. "We were allowed to look, but not to touch. I remember thinking, 'God forbid I'm the one that knocks a chip out of King Friday's nose.'

"They were real extensions of him, and they enabled him to say some decidedly un-Mister-Rogersish things, even sitting around the dinner table. If it was something a little bit racy or risqué, he would say it in Lady Elaine's voice.

"There was mean-spirited Lady Elaine Fairchilde, and then the shy, quiet little boy Daniel, and the blustery, self-important King Friday. They were all little pieces of him."[6]

Many people assumed that Lady Elaine was based to some degree on Fred's sister, Elaine (Laney) Rogers. Not so, according to Jim Rogers: "That's where the name came from, I'm sure, but I think that the personality was mostly him. He would trot out her voice to say things that he felt he shouldn't be saying."[7]

In contrast, "If he [Fred Rogers] had to be the authority figure, he was King Friday, who would tell us it was time to go to bed."

The King also appeared sometimes when Fred was mad at his sons, Jim remembers: "If it was King Friday's voice, that meant I hadn't really stepped too far out of bounds. If it was his own voice, that was tough: 'I'm disappointed in you,' or something along those lines. You didn't want to hear that." His father "wasn't really as much a disciplinarian as Mom was," Jim adds, "but when he had to, he could do pretty well."[8]

The puppet characters provided useful channels for Fred to express parts of himself both at home and at work. And sometimes, as with Susan Stamberg, they could give him a tactical advantage. In the early 1980s, he needed to find a manager to be the executive director of Family Communications, Inc. (FCI), his production company. He needed a number two who would be tough enough to run the business while possessing the *Neighborhood* sensibility about children, plus other qualities Rogers cared about, such as kindness and consideration.

Fred Rogers thought he'd found the perfect candidate in Bill Isler, an official in the Pennsylvania Department of Education, who had a strong background in early education and family issues accompanied by a great sense of humor. Isler had the right résumé, and he had a reputation as a tough and savvy operator who could deal with little children, top business executives, and even the most jaded politicians.

Isler had gone through the interview process and discussed his potential role at FCI with Rogers. The two men were in the process of making up their minds. Then Isler got a call from the sensible, level-headed Queen Sara Saturday. It was Sara who offered him the job at Family Communications, and it was she who outlined the compelling reasons why Isler should say yes.[9]

The puppet Queen Sara—named for Rogers's wife, whose full name is Sara Joanne Byrd Rogers—was very familiar to Isler from his years in Pittsburgh and his work in early childhood education. She easily persuaded him to take the job. In coming years, Isler was key in the success of Rogers's work, and he became president of FCI.

Fred Rogers's relationship with his puppets, and his use of their personas in his own life, began in childhood, on the small stage he created in the attic of his parents' home in Latrobe. His schoolmate and frequent playmate Peggy Moberg McFeaters later realized she'd seen a seminal moment in the evolution of Rogers's creative work in the puppet theater—though at the time, she thought he just wanted some company.[10] He played with his puppets almost daily and wanted someone with whom he could share that experience. The puppets were essential expressions of his creativity.

By the time Fred reached high school, he was focused on music, and he set the puppets aside. When he and Joanne Byrd dated in college, he owned a ventriloquist's dummy—an odd creature named Hisher Boop Truck—but Joanne knew nothing about the other puppets. They weren't gone, though. Rogers had put them in storage, and they wound up in the attic of the couple's Pittsburgh house. Joanne was still unaware of their existence until Fred needed them at WQED.[11]

Hisher Boop Truck didn't survive beyond the first year at WQED. "Truck" was to be featured in a new program being created by Josie Carey. But the dummy didn't pass critical review. Eventually, when

Rogers evolved into the role of puppeteer on *The Children's Corner*, he became exclusively focused on hand puppets—to some extent because he never did master the art of "throwing" his voice as ventriloquists do.

On the new show, Rogers began to build his repertory company of puppets: "I think the puppets saved us," he said later. "Daniel made his appearance that very first day, but after a while he became such a part of the show because he and Josie would [talk]. So the next one we tried was a king. I had this king puppet at home. The king was very sad because he had lost his country."[12]

King Friday XIII was born, and the children and parents who watched *The Children's Corner* helped him find a new home and a name for his new country. Others followed: Queen Saturday, Prince Tuesday, X the Owl—all of them combinations of Rogers's childhood inventiveness and his grown-up imagination about television.[13]

OVER THE YEARS, on *The Children's Corner*, on *Misterogers* in Canada, and on *Mister Rogers' Neighborhood*, Rogers brought to life a host of puppet characters. They inhabited the Neighborhood of Make-Believe, the home of storytelling and fantasy in *Mister Rogers' Neighborhood*, and included an extraordinary variety of personalities.

Fred Rogers's longtime associate Hedda Sharapan notes that Rogers kept his puppets simple and unchanging over the years on purpose: "They are simple. They are rather crude. I think Fred also wanted to make the point that they don't have to be magnificent puppets for you to have your own puppet stories.

"He brought the puppets now and then to his television house and said, 'Here's how I do King Friday. And here's how I do Daniel.' . . . Fred has said, 'These puppets are all facets of us.'

"So it wasn't the outer stuff that was resonating with people. It was the personalities and the way they handled situations. . . . They must have all been important parts of Fred's personality for him to have made them so believable."[14]

Daniel Striped Tiger was the first and is in many ways the most important puppet. Voiced by Rogers, Daniel lives in a large, nonfunctioning clock, out of which he pops to announce the time. He represents the shy and anxious side of his creator, but is also the source of a great deal of wisdom and common sense.

Hedda Sharapan recalls the seminal program in the week about mistakes: "Daniel sings to Betty [Lady Aberlin], 'Sometimes I wonder if I'm a mistake / I'm not supposed to be scared, am I? / Sometimes I cry. / Sometimes I shake, wondering, isn't it true that the strong never break? / I'm not like anyone else I know.' We wept in the studio . . . and the whole place broke out into applause."[15]

At the center of things is King Friday XIII, the rather temperamental and imperious monarch of the Neighborhood of Make-Believe. The King is often autocratic and peremptory, but he isn't really a bad ruler, and he can become more tractable, particularly when influenced by his wife. He is given to pomposity and long-winded speeches, but is likable anyway.

Queen Sara Saturday is as reasonable and even-keeled as her husband is not. She is thoughtful and caring in ways reminiscent of Rogers's mother and his wife. Sara first appeared as a commoner, and it was a big *Neighborhood* moment when she and the King were married. The King and the Queen were both voiced by Rogers.

Their son Prince Tuesday came along in the third season of the *Neighborhood* and is named for the day of the week on which he was born. He is always interested in learning about whatever is going on, but he worries sometimes about family dynamics and growing up. Prince Tuesday was voiced by a number of performers over the years, but not by Rogers.

X the Owl was the third puppet introduced on *The Children's Corner*. Along with Daniel Striped Tiger and the King and Queen, X is one of the four puppets who most closely embody Rogers's creative psyche and who play critically instructive roles on the *Neighborhood*. Voiced by Rogers, X displays an adolescent personality; he is cheerful and willing but can be a bit tentative and bashful. He lives in an oak tree and was a favorite of many young viewers of the show.

Perhaps the most unusual of the puppets is Lady Elaine Fairch-ilde, who can be devious, scheming, and difficult. When there's trouble in the Neighborhood of Make-Believe, Lady Elaine usually makes it. She provides much of the drama and conflict. The success of other puppets in dealing with Lady Elaine and instructing her provides the basis for some of the important emotional education in *Mister Rogers' Neighborhood*. As Jim Rogers explains, Lady Elaine is a window into the more mischievous side of Fred Rogers, who provided her voice.

The fourth puppet to appear was Henrietta Pussycat, also voiced by Rogers. She serves as governess for several mice, who live with her in a small yellow-and-orange schoolhouse supported by the same tree in which X the Owl lives. Henrietta can be anxious, even jealous, but she has a charming side as well.

And then there is Cornflake S. Pecially, who looks like a beaver and operates a factory that makes rocking chairs as well as other things like dolls and trolleys. "Corny," who was introduced on *Misterogers* in Canada, became a staple of Rogers's educational programming. The Platypus Family, early arrivals in the Neighborhood of Make-Believe, include Dr. Bill Platypus, voiced by Rogers's close friend Rev. William Barker in a rich Scottish brogue, and his wife, Elsie Jean Platypus, also voiced by Barker.

Over time, many other puppets came to inhabit Fred Rogers's television world, including Grandpere Tiger (voiced by Rogers), Harriet Elizabeth Cow, Edgar Cooke (the castle chef), H. J. Elephant III (a reference to Rogers's friend Sen. H. John Heinz III), Betty Okonak Templeton-Jones (Betty Okonak was Fred's cousin and friend, voiced by Michael Horton), James Michael Jones (also voiced by Horton), Carrie Dell Okonak Templeton-Jones, Old Goat and New Goat, Hilda Dingleborder, Donkey Hodie (his name, a reference to Don Quixote, is one of several wordplays in the *Neighborhood* that only parents would understand), the Frogg Family, Audrey Duck, and Mr. Skunk.

Susan Linn, a psychologist at the Harvard Medical School and the cofounder and director of the Campaign for a Commercial-Free Childhood, is an accomplished puppeteer in her own right (as well as the voice of Audrey Duck). She points to the psychological power of puppetry: "The freedom we get from speaking through this creature that is us and not us at the same time makes [puppets] such incredibly powerful tools for therapy. Children—and adults—say things with puppets they absolutely wouldn't say otherwise."[16]

When Linn appeared on the *Neighborhood* early in the evolution of the program, Rogers had only one suggestion for her: "Somehow you must remember what it was like to be a child."

She marveled at how effectively Rogers's puppets carried a childhood connection into their relationship with the program's viewers: "In Fred's hands, with love and gentleness, the puppets draw forth the underside of childhood. By 'underside,' I don't mean macabre, warped, or seamy; they tap into the vein of fear, anger, and awkwardness, and unadulterated self-centeredness that lies beneath the sunny surface of childhood.

"In direct contrast to most of the other puppets and fantasy creatures seen on children's television, the inhabitants of the Neighborhood of Make-Believe are complex, complicated, and utterly honest beings housed in rather rudimentary bodies."[17]

As illustration, she recalls the episode in which Lady Aberlin (a human) tells Daniel Striped Tiger that the Neighborhood of Make-Believe is about to get a visit from Santa Claus. Daniel is not thrilled; he is alarmed. He has heard the lyrics to songs about Santa, and he is afraid of someone who knows so much: when you're sleeping and when you're awake, when you've been good or bad.

"Santa Claus? What's he going to do to us?" Daniel asks. "Oh, I try to be good. But I'm not always good. I think I'm afraid of Santa Claus. I wish he weren't coming here."

Lady Aberlin does not dismiss Daniel's feelings; she takes the boy tiger seriously. Then when Santa Claus does come, and Daniel blurts that he is not always good, Santa replies, "Good people aren't always good. They just try to be."

When Daniel finds the courage to ask Santa if he can see people when they're sleeping and learn whether they're good or bad, Santa is surprisingly direct: "Of course not. Someone made that up about me. I'm not a spy."[18] The exchange tellingly illustrates Rogers's capacity for empathy and his ability to use the puppet theater to speak bluntly to children's real fears.

Indeed, children's television advocate Peggy Charren has been quoted as saying that the first time she saw *Mister Rogers' Neighborhood*, she said to herself, "Oh, a singing psychologist for children!"[19]

Rogers used the lyrics of his songs to deliver lessons for children. The song "Fancy on the Outside" ("Some are fancy on the outside / Some are fancy on the inside") deals with children's sexual interest and gender awareness. Timid Daniel Tiger's song in which he wonders about being a mistake lets kids know it's okay to be yourself. When Prince Tuesday sings to his mother, Queen Sara, that he's going to marry her, she gently responds, "You're going to marry somebody like me." "What Do You Do?" offers a list of anger management tools for all ages.

PUPPETEERING IS AN ANCIENT ART. We can easily imagine an early hominid crouching in the flickering light of a cave fire, hand wrapped in a small animal skin, playing out some ancient parable for small children huddled in the cave. Perhaps the most famous puppet theater is Punch and Judy, an English form that dates to the seventeenth century. Italian antecedents go back to a time well before that.

The typical Punch and Judy puppet show is unscripted, and the narrative has evolved over the centuries as different puppeteers have advanced their own story lines. But the commonalities include fairly obnoxious characters, a lot of poor behavior on the part of Mr. Punch, and usually a violent beating of Mr. Punch by his wife, Judy, when she discovers he has failed to take care of their baby. Punch and Judy themselves are loud and unpleasant. Often the audience would jump into the action, cheering or jeering the puppets' antics and even throwing food or other items at them.

In one script for the show, written in 1832, Punch enters singing to the audience, followed soon thereafter by the dog Toby. Although Punch greets the dog in a friendly manner, it is not long before Toby has bitten him on the nose and, holding on, torments Punch until the puppet finally frees himself. As soon as Toby leaves, its owner, Scaramouche, comes out onto the stage and begins to beat Punch with a large stick, punishing him for supposedly mistreating his dog. Punch grabs the stick and hits Scaramouche so hard that the puppet's head flies off.

Punch laughs and says, "How you like that tune, my good friend? That sweet music, or sour music, eh! He! he! he!" As soon as Punch has thrown away the stick, Judy enters the stage and, getting a quick kiss from Punch, slaps him across the face.

When Judy brings a baby onto the stage, Punch plays with the baby for a moment before it begins to cry. Punch boxes the child on the ear, and then—the crying growing louder—he suddenly throws the baby off the front of the stage into the audience, shouting, "There! There! There! How you like that? I thought I stop your squalling. Get along with you, nasty, naughty, crying child."[20]

Because of the violence, the obnoxious behavior, and the mistreatment of a child, it is a pretty good bet that Punch and Judy horrified Fred Rogers. Nonetheless, it played a seminal role in the development of many other puppet acts for hundreds of years and continues today as an important influence on puppeteering. And there is at least one similarity between Fred Rogers's puppets and Punch and Judy: The typical Punch and Judy puppet is a fairly unsophisticated, simple figure with stationary features, as are the puppets from Fred Rogers's Neighborhood of Make-Believe. But the behavior of the two types could not be more different.

On television, the first successful use of puppets came several years before *The Children's Corner* and, like the *Corner*, featured an empathetic female host talking with charming puppets. *Kukla, Fran and Ollie* went on air in Chicago in 1947 and gained a national audience at NBC in 1949.[21] Another key characteristic it shared with the *Corner* was the lack of a script: The creator of *Kukla*, Burr Tillstrom, and the show's host, Fran Allison, never used one during their ten years of NBC television together. They were as spontaneous and appealing to children as Fred Rogers and Josie Carey.

Although Tillstrom won over fifty major television awards, including five Emmys, he couldn't sustain a national television presence for *Kukla, Fran and Ollie*.[22] The rejection of such high-quality children's programming by commercial broadcasting seemed to ratify Fred Rogers's early-1950s decision to move his work to educational television. Burr Tillstrom took *Kukla* to PBS briefly at the end of the 1960s, but it was overtaken by *Mister Rogers' Neighborhood* and *Sesame Street*.

Fred Rogers's most important rival in the world of puppeteering and children's television, *Sesame Street*'s creative genius Jim Henson, had made the same move as Fred Rogers, taking his talents from the commercial world to PBS. *Sesame Street* was conceived in 1965, when Lloyd Morrisett, a vice president at the Carnegie Corporation with a PhD in psychology, wondered if his daughter's fascination with television could be harnessed to a good educational end. At a dinner party at the Manhattan apartment of Tim and Joan Ganz Cooney (a producer at PBS's Channel Thirteen) that very question was discussed at length. After months of intense research, Ganz Cooney conceived *Sesame Street* as "edutainment." Jim Henson joined the Children's Television Workshop in 1969. His puppets provided the "delicate balance of fun and learning," as Henson once put it.

Jim Henson was born in Mississippi and grew up there for a while before his family moved to Hyattsville, Maryland, a suburb of Washington, DC, in the late 1940s. Although he was raised as a Christian Scientist and even taught Sunday school for a time, he later wrote to the church to tell them he had ceased practicing that religion. Henson graduated from the University of Maryland, where a class in applied arts introduced him to puppets. His talents were so strong that, shortly after graduation, he launched a career in puppeteering and television.

And Henson, who remembered the arrival of television in his parents' house as a highly important event in his young life, later said he was strongly influenced by the ventriloquist Edgar Bergen, by puppeteers Bill and Cora Baird, and by Burr Tillstrom.

"Burr Tillstrom and the Bairds had more to do with the beginning of puppets on television than we did," Henson said in a 1979 interview. "But they had developed their art and style to a certain extent before hitting television. Baird had done marionette shows long before he came to television. Burr Tillstrom's puppets were basically the standard hand-puppet characters that went back to Punch and Judy. But from the beginning, we worked watching a television monitor, which is very different from working in a puppet theater."[23]

Sesame debuted on PBS in the fall of 1969, just a year and a half after the *Neighborhood*. But, unlike Rogers, Henson kept close ties to commerce, marketing his *Sesame* Muppets to children, partnering with the commercial-programming behemoth Walt Disney Company, and eventually negotiating to sell the puppets he controlled (as opposed to those controlled by *Sesame*) to Disney.[24]

Henson's Muppets and Rogers's *Neighborhood* puppets occupied comparable niches on educational television for decades, and each attracted loyal audiences of children and their parents. But Henson clearly won the ratings competition, if there was one.

Although the *Neighborhood* reached as many as seven million households during its peak years in the 1980s, *Sesame Street* exceeded that, with an audience of about ten million by 1985. *Sesame* continued to air after the *Neighborhood* ceased production and is now shown in more than a hundred countries around the world. After its first season, *Sesame Street* won three Emmys and a Peabody and was on the cover of *Time* magazine. Since then, there have been scores of Emmy awards among the hundreds of accolades showered on Henson and *Sesame*.

The genius of Jim Henson was that his puppets—Kermit the Frog, Bert and Ernie, Miss Piggy, and all the rest—were charming, funny, and very appealing to little children and to their parents. The grown-ups watched *Mister Rogers' Neighborhood* with their children because they understood the value of sharing this important experience, and because they were attracted to Rogers's slow, childlike pacing.

But they watched *Sesame* because its fast-paced, hip messaging was fun, and funny, for the parents, too. Somehow Henson found a universal language that seemed to draw everyone into the good times.

Certainly, *Sesame* was controversial, particularly at the very beginning, because its pacing and quick-cutaway style seemed too close to the frantic world of commercial advertising. But, just as clearly, Henson had a gift for creating characters that had the charm, the authenticity, and the joy to convey learning to millions of children. Throughout the decades, millions of kids learned their numbers and their ABCs from Big Bird, Bert and Ernie, and the others.[25]

When Henson died unexpectedly (from a streptococcus infection) in 1990 at the age of 53, the television world was plunged into mourning. Joan Ganz Cooney, the creative force who had organized the people, the funding, and the thinking that gave birth to *Sesame Street* and the Children's Television Workshop, said at the time: "He was our era's Charlie Chaplin, Mae West, W. C. Fields, and Marx Brothers, and indeed he drew from all of them to create a new art form that influenced popular culture around the world."[26]

Though Fred Rogers's legacy has not been as strong and durable as that of *Sesame Street* and the Muppets, there is no question that Fred Rogers's puppets were an essential ingredient not only in his creative expression but also in his outreach to young viewers. His secretary Elaine Lynch recalled that, despite Rogers's aversion to allowing children on the set while he was working (because he knew they would claim his attention), he sometimes invited a group of them from the Make-A-Wish Foundation, an organization that arranges exciting experiences for children with serious medical conditions. Many of these children would ask if they could meet Mister Rogers, and the foundation and Rogers's staff periodically arranged for visits to the *Neighborhood* set while the program was being produced.

One day, said Lynch, a group of such children included a twelve-year-old boy who was autistic: "I tried to get as much information from the family as I could so Fred had an idea of what their problems were. This was a mother and father, and the autistic boy was, I think, the oldest of three. He had a sister, and he also had a younger brother, all of whom, they claimed, had never heard him speak. He grunted—'Mmm, mmm'—what he wanted, pointed to what he wanted."[27]

Lynch noticed that the father was the one shooting video of the event, and she maneuvered herself over near him to help him get positioned properly to get the best footage.

"But Fred, when he came out to visit with the family, had the King and Queen puppets on his hands, and he started talking to the family, and he finally got to the boy, who was almost as tall as Fred at that point. The child started speaking in full sentences to the King and Queen. Well, I don't know whether you can imagine what the family was going through at that point, hearing their son speak for the first time. The father started blubbering to the point where he could no longer hold the camera, and I took the camera gently from him."

Lynch got a *Neighborhood* crew member to film the rest of the encounter between the puppets, the boy, and his family. Rogers said nothing as himself. He stayed in character as the voices of King Friday XIII and Queen Sara Saturday. And Lynch—who later referred to the whole exchange as a "miracle"—rushed upstairs to get the family their own King and Queen puppets from Rogers's office.[28]

PART IV

You rarely have time for everything you want in this life,
so you need to make choices. And hopefully your
choices can come from a deep sense of who you are.

—FRED ROGERS

15.

ON HIATUS

FRED ROGERS is in a blue blazer and a dark blue tie. As he enters the room—a living room that looks similar to his "television house" on *Mister Rogers' Neighborhood*—soft music plays that also seems in keeping with the show's theme. He sits down and starts sorting through the day's mail, showing viewers some of the letters and pictures sent in from his many correspondents. Then he even shows a home movie from one of his admirers. The letters, the pictures, and the movie all illustrate the theme of this show, which is about memories—how they are made and how much they mean to us.

Then Rogers shows pictures of his own family: the young Fred with his mother and father and grandfather. Making a subtle transition from the memories of his viewers to those from his own childhood, he features pictures of his grandfather, Fred McFeely.

Rogers talks about his childhood: "I remember being dressed up a lot of the time." He shows pictures of himself looking chubby and shy in a suit, with his mother and father. He tells the TV audience that he loved his grandfather because Fred McFeely let Fred relax and be natural. "He loved fun. And encouraged me to be myself."[1]

Gradually, it dawns on the viewer that this isn't *Mister Rogers' Neighborhood*. This isn't a program for children. Although it is the same soft-spoken, gentle-mannered, avuncular Fred Rogers onscreen, he is clearly talking to an adult audience. It is different from the television Fred Rogers made for children; but it is also very different from most of the television programming made for adults.

After showing a picture of his grandfather's house from years earlier, Rogers plays a video of himself as an adult, standing behind the ruined foundation. He explains that since his grandfather died, the house has been torn down, and all he has left are the memories. Then the viewers see Buttermilk Falls, near his grandfather's house. Young Fred often played outside with his grandfather, he told the television audience, and the memory of Fred McFeely still sustained him. It was his grandfather who taught Fred Rogers how to enjoy the freedom to explore, and who helped him grow from a shy, hesitant boy into a more confident and accomplished young man.

Then the video shifts to a contrived reenactment of a scene from Fred's youth when he was climbing on a high stone wall and his mother and grandmother, fearful for his safety, admonished him. His grandfather steps in and tells the two women to let the kid climb the wall as young Fred needs to learn to do things for himself. The adult Fred tells the audience how much he loved his grandfather for the timely intervention. He goes on to offer a thought on the importance of memories: "Our memories are ours to share or not to share. We have the right to make that decision."[2]

This is painful television: By the standards of programming made for adult audiences, it seems awkward and self-conscious. The gentle, almost childlike style of Mister Rogers may have been fine when Fred was producing television for young children, but it comes across as somewhat hokey, almost, for an adult audience.

Although Fred still has the direct openness that makes him so appealing, the content, the format, and the tone of the show seem to fall somewhere between children's television and the sort of earnest programming that might appear in an educational film made for a high school audience. The pacing and the overly simplistic messaging just don't seem to work for adults, even back in the mid-1970s.

What we are watching here is something called *Old Friends . . . New Friends*, a public television series written and produced by Fred Rogers after he abruptly dropped *Mister Rogers' Neighborhood* in 1975. After seven years of producing the most popular show on PBS, Fred had decided that he had covered much of the terrain he thought was important for young children, and he was ready for something else.[3] According to those who knew and worked with Fred back then, that something else was intended to include television programming for adults and perhaps even a radio talk show.[4]

David Newell, who played the part of Mr. McFeely on the *Neighborhood*, remembers that Rogers was inspired in part by the knowledge that many older viewers watched and enjoyed *Mister Rogers' Neighborhood*; Fred felt that these older viewers might form the base for a larger audience for his proposed programming for grown-ups.[5]

His former producer Margy Whitmer explains: "Fred loved to interview people. But he was quite troubled by what was happening in this country in terms of taking care of children. That was when drive-bys and gangs were prominent in the news. He was troubled by this whole breakdown. He said, 'But there's got to be people out there who are taking care of kids. Who are those people? They are the people that should be on television. You know, we always hear all the bad news. What about the good news?' I think that was really where that came from."[6]

This is the same impulse behind today's *CNN Heroes*, the original *People* magazine, and NBC News's "Making a Difference" segment. As usual, Fred Rogers was ahead of the curve.

And perhaps Fred Rogers just needed a new challenge. In a May 8, 1975, interview with Kenneth Briggs of the *New York Times* entitled "Mr. Rogers Decides It's Time to Head for New Neighborhoods," Rogers says he is looking forward to his "first respite in twenty years," and a chance to write new operas as well as shows for adults. He explains that he would still commune with his television neighbors, but in reruns, as he pares down 455 episodes of the *Neighborhood* to comprise a "well-rounded cycle" to run on the 237 PBS stations that carried his show then.[7]

On the last day of taping the *Neighborhood*, Rogers tells Briggs, "I think this has been a good vehicle, and I won't say we won't use it again." Fred Rogers goes on to note that writing and producing the *Neighborhood* has also helped him "become more comfortable with who I have become. For a time, I had real difficulty with the little boy who had so many limits inside."[8]

One can conjecture that this newfound comfort also fueled Rogers's desire to reach out in new directions.

This move by Fred Rogers—abandoning the themes that had made him such a success on public television and delivering a surprising segue into adult fare—caught many of his coworkers and supporters off guard.

According to Basil Cox, the manager of Family Communications, Inc. (FCI) back then, the decision was made entirely by Fred Rogers: "I don't really remember the genesis of it. But he wanted to talk to families. He wanted to talk to adults. He wanted to explore what that would feel like to him, I think, and what kind of television that would make."[9]

Basil Cox adds: "The decision to stop producing children's programming left everyone at the production company questioning each other about the future. "What's next? You know: What are we doing next?" was the common refrain.

"There was some—there was a feeling of anxiety, I think, for sure. . . . So there was a certain amount of shuffling off of people. We became a smaller company. We're not making as many programs. I don't actually remember what the difference in revenue was, but [it] probably shrank by a million dollars a year, or something like that."[10]

In addition to the documentary series *Old Friends . . . New Friends* (1978), there were special programs and another PBS series, *Fred Rogers' Heroes* (1994), portraits of a wide and wild variety of people from across the country. Margy Whitmer produced and directed both: "My favorite was about sculptor Edgar Tolson, one of the great American folk artists of the last century. The days we spent with him and his family in rural Kentucky—including introducing Edgar to Fred Rogers and seeing them take each other's measure—were among the most memorable of my life.

"One of our specials got wonderful reviews, but it aired on some weird night, like Labor Day. We couldn't get them to schedule it at a better time. People were coming back from vacation, or getting ready for back to school."[11]

Old Friends . . . New Friends was designed to take advantage of Rogers's strength—his ability to make direct connections with people and translate that to a television audience. Aired in 1978, the twenty-episode program, filmed and recorded on location, featured Fred Rogers asking people about the meaning of life; it positioned him as an interviewer of interesting public figures in a format that allowed him to interject himself and his thinking. And some programs were essentially just Fred being philosophical Fred.

Rogers's interviewees on *Friends* included the famous (Hoagy Carmichael, Helen Hayes, Milton Berle, baseball's Willie Stargell) and inspirational figures such as Father William Wasson, who established Nuestros Pequeños Hermanos, a home for orphaned and abandoned children in Cuernavaca, Mexico, where Fred Rogers talks with some of the children about what it means to be part of this caring "family."

Part of the problem with shows like *Friends* was that Fred Rogers, who had an extraordinary instinct for the power of conversational television, had already established a childlike style and persona during his twenty-plus years in children's television, and he wasn't able to escape it. And this adult showcase for Rogers as minister lacked the entertainment value his music and, most importantly, the puppets imparted to *Mister Rogers' Neighborhood*. Without an outlet for his whimsy, the adult Rogers fails to channel his most valuable resources.

Though *Friends* captured many of the ingredients that had made *Mister Rogers' Neighborhood* so successful, it never escaped the gentleness of Rogers's earlier work to translate effectively to an adult audience. In a television world growing ever more intense and overheated, Rogers on *Friends* lacked edge.

This was, after all, the era in which shows like *All in the Family* were shaking up the television landscape with jarringly honest depictions of the very social conflicts Fred Rogers decried. He held on to a thoughtful, sensitive, slow-paced approach just as most television programming was speeding up, reflecting the culture of the time.

Rogers's former colleague Elizabeth Seamans observes: "When you are talking to somebody, they will give you an answer. Instead of moving on to the next question, you let them say that thing that isn't so obvious. Then if you're Fred, you probably wait again. Not only would he get more beautiful and much more nuanced and sometimes more intimate answers, but often just more interesting, complex, unusual ones—the unexpected, the thing you don't ask. Pretty soon, they'd begin volunteering things you would never have known to ask, and Fred would allow us to show those things in television time."[12]

Some of the programming Fred developed in the mid-1970s, though it was high-minded and serious, simply seemed to lack a complete understanding of what makes compelling television. A case in point is an *Old Friends . . . New Friends* episode on Republican Senator John Heinz of Pittsburgh and his family.[13]

It opens with John and Teresa Heinz and their son André talking about a recent boating accident in which André was injured. There is real drama in the offing: André had been hit in the head with an outboard-motor propeller and could easily have been killed. What's more, his mother, philanthropist Teresa Heinz, seems inclined to be surprisingly direct and honest in this program.

But then, just as we are warming to the possibility of listening to André and his mother talk about this frightening and powerful episode in their lives, poof, they are gone, and Fred takes us into a long and turgid journey through endless videotape of Senator Heinz campaigning. The senator knows he is being filmed for a show that will be on national television, and he is not about to give us anything like candor.

Then after a long scene in which the senator tells a group of potential supporters a classic noblesse oblige story about his great-grandfather building churches all over town, we are suddenly back with Teresa Heinz again. Soft-spoken and deadly serious, she is very straightforward about political life: "Campaigning is a special kind of tension and pressure," says Mrs. Heinz. "It's awful, in the sense of what it does to one's family life."[14]

Teresa Heinz is as candid and blunt and honest about Washington and politics as her husband has been guarded and cautious. But just as we are focusing on Teresa's frank assessment of political life, she is gone again, and we are back with the senator's very guarded and politically careful description of his public life. When the program finally returns to the drama of André's near-death experience, it is almost at the end of the shoot, and even André seems to have become bored with it.

To put it succinctly, Fred Rogers is working outside his métier. He can't seem to focus in a way that delivers compelling documentary, conversational television for grown-ups. *Mister Rogers' Neighborhood* is marvelously thoughtful and thematic, always responding in perfect harmony with the children it serves. But *Old Friends . . . New Friends* is the opposite: It seems to have little awareness of what its adult audience may be interested in, and it manages to bring out a preachy side of Fred that the *Neighborhood* always skillfully steered away from.

Despite laudable intentions, Rogers's "television time" was just too slow for most adults. There were powerful exceptions, like Rogers's interview with the iconic theater director and acting teacher Lee Strasberg, a part of the *Old Friends . . . New Friends* series that is often cited as the high point in Fred's four years of producing adult programming.[15]

"Lee Strasberg . . . there's a guy who's, you know, defended with five inches of bulletproof armor," said Basil Cox. "He [Rogers] got through to him; and he got him to talk about things that were really personal. He had a—he had a gift, just an extraordinary gift, to get to people."[16]

Rogers's gift wasn't enough to make *Old Friends . . . New Friends,* or the other adult programming produced by Fred, successful enough to be sustained. The funding wasn't secure enough, or the programming good enough, to win over the PBS hierarchy, nor were the ratings high enough to dazzle potential supporters.

Elizabeth Seamans observes: "*Old Friends . . .* didn't come from inside of Fred the way other stuff did, and I don't think it ever had a chance. I'm not sure Fred really knew why he was doing [it]. The way the subjects came up was kind of pell-mell. They didn't come out of his marrow the way *Mister Rogers' Neighborhood* did, over time.

"I think it's too bad [it] didn't have time to evolve. Fred's children's show had a long gestation period, all through the 50s. Television today doesn't often give you that time or opportunity.

"Look at Jim Henson's work: In his early twenties, Jim Henson was on some little local program with his goofy puppets. He's doing what Fred was doing in his twenties: fooling around on TV and having a lot of latitude because there wasn't that much on. The concept of television time is something to conjure with as it has gotten more and more powerful: the cost of the second, the cost of the television minute."[17]

Of course, to some extent Fred didn't care. He never had produced, nor ever would produce, television for money or ratings. He produced it for himself; to meet the standards he envisioned and to do some good in the world. Elizabeth Seamans explains: "I don't know how much he watched ratings. I never heard him talk about ratings; I never even knew him to be aware of them, though he probably was. But the letters that came to him [were important to him], and the response was very personal. He thrived on the fan mail."[18]

Rogers's commitment to this audience was essentially a pastoral one, she adds: "He saw that people were given heart and courage, and an outlook toward children and families that he really believed in."

In fact, in a 1978 letter to a friend, Rogers shares the hope that church groups will watch *Old Friends . . . New Friends* and use it as the basis for discussion groups afterward.

Fred Rogers saw the television producer as having a special, ennobling mission: "Our job in life," he said at a graduation ceremony at Thiel College in Greenville, Pennsylvania, early in his career, in 1969, "is to help people realize how rare and valuable each one of us really is—that each of us has something that no one else has—or ever will have—something inside which is unique to all time. It's our job to encourage each other to discover that uniqueness, and to provide ways of developing its expression."[19]

TV executives like James Thomas Aubrey Jr., the notorious president of CBS during the formative 1960s, known to associates as "the smiling cobra," didn't share Fred Rogers's aspirations for the medium. Aubrey earned the label of "barbarian" for his relentless pursuit of schlocky programming to propel higher ratings and profits.[20] Aubrey managed to drive down the intelligence of television programming in the early sixties, while driving up ratings, profits, and his own compensation. He was finally fired by CBS after the FCC (Federal Communications Commission) began an investigation of charges that he was taking kickbacks from producers who wanted to get their shows on CBS channels around the country.

Ironically, it wasn't until right before Fred Rogers died in 2003 that commercial television began making a significant amount of high-quality programming. When cable television producers (and later, Netflix, Amazon, and Hulu) began to produce such outstanding serial programs as *The Sopranos*, *The Wire*, and *Breaking Bad*, critics began comparing such television fare favorably to the best feature movies. But even if Fred Rogers had lived to see that level of quality on commercial television, he would undoubtedly have had little use for the cynicism and violence of shows like *Breaking Bad*.

In addition to *Old Friends . . . New Friends*, Rogers and his crew at FCI produced other programs for PBS aimed at grown-ups, including some that used the talk-show format to explore important societal issues. Most notable was the series of specials on issues affecting parents and children moderated by Susan Stamberg, then the host of NPR's highly popular program *All Things Considered*.[21]

On February 15, 1981, for instance, Stamberg hosted "Mister Rogers Talks with Parents About Divorce," featuring Fred Rogers and family counselor Earl Grollman. This was followed on May 3, 1981, by "Mister Rogers Talks with Parents About Competition," a program that focused on the arrival of a new baby in the family and showcased not only the

commentary of Harvard psychologist Tom Cottle but also a short interview with Pittsburgh Steelers wide receiver Lynn Swann. Interestingly,
pamphlets on the topics from Family Communications were offered
halfway through the shows.

Rogers played both an on-air and a producing role on these specials. Certainly, they had many moments of high-quality television,
though they were not popular enough to gain a life of their own and
continue on PBS.

In a few of the specials he produced for PBS in those years, Rogers brought back the crew from the *Neighborhood,* but in prime time.
On December 17, 1977, at 8:00 P.M., he presented his first-ever "Christ-
mastime with Mister Rogers," featuring Betty Aberlin, François Clemmons, Audrey Roth, Joe Negri, Elsie Neal, David Newell, and Elizabeth
Seamans planning a holiday gathering. A young ballerina scheduled to
perform is concerned that her family, stranded with car trouble, may not
make it to see her dance, but it all works out in the end.

Notably, on the special, Mister Rogers doesn't say much about
the birth of Christ. Instead he talks about families with different tra-
ditions for Christmas and Chanukah, as well as those who celebrate
neither. The trolley features a banner that reads "Merry Christmas"
on one side and "Happy Chanukah" on the other. At one point, Mister
Rogers plays with a dreidel as he sings "The Dreidel Song."

He summarizes his holiday message as he thinks about a gift for
all of his television neighbors: "I suppose the thing I'd like most to be
able to give you is hope. Hope that through your own doing and your
own living with others, you'll be able to find what best fits for you in
this life. . . . I, for one, wish you good memories of this holiday. And I
hope you'll be able to look for all the different ways that people have of
showing that they love you."

The *Bangor Daily News* of Maine noted at the time: "'Christmas-
time with Mister Rogers' is a quiet show. It is a kind of lullaby, dropped
in the middle of the hullabaloo."[22]

Fred Rogers always advocated for a noncommercial approach
to the holiday. In the early 1970s, Hallmark approached him about

contributing to their annual display for the store in midtown Manhattan. He and his colleague Eliot Daley went to New York to "case the joint and come up with a plan," as Daley remembers it.[23]

"There were all kinds of phantasmagorical decorations that more garish celebrities had concocted, which Hallmark was preparing to execute. But the idea that we hatched together was this: a Norfolk Island pine tree, about the height of a three- or four-year-old, which was to be left entirely natural and undecorated. It was to be a live tree, planted in a clear/transparent Lucite cube so that the roots would show. And on the plaque or whatever label they put on it, [it] said, 'I like you just the way you are.' "

Though Daley is unsure if Fred and Joanne Rogers made it to New York to see the tree in the Hallmark store, he did: "It was perfect."[24]

TO HIS CREDIT, Fred Rogers was evidently one of the first to acknowledge that his programming for adults was failing to hit the mark. According to Basil Cox, just as Rogers had cooled to children's television in 1975, he began to cool to his new assignment as a creator and producer of television for adults: "I didn't sense any, you know, enormous amount of grieving on Fred's part that *Old Friends . . . New Friends* was over. I think he appreciated the experience. . . . But I think he was ready to go back to *Mister Rogers' Neighborhood*."[25]

Ellen Galinsky, the president of Families and Work Institute in New York, recalled in an interview in 2007 that Fred almost seemed withdrawn when they were working together around 1980 on a program called "Mister Rogers Talks to Parents." On the advice of consultants hired to advise FCI about the style of the program, it was faster paced, with shorter, quicker frames than the television Fred was used to doing.

Galinsky said: "The show that I did was, I think, ultimately uncomfortable for Fred. One of the things that the staff will tell you is that every time anyone from the audience asked him a question, he would turn to me, and they would have to stop the camera and say, 'Fred! I'm sure Ellen can answer it, but they're also wanting to hear from you, too.' He's a slow, contemplative person. I think the program was jarring for him."[26]

Fred's instinct for talking with children with joy and natural grace just didn't translate to adult television. His secretary Elaine Lynch remembers that when *Old Friends . . . New Friends* was ending, Rogers felt a pang of disappointment that there seemed to be so little interest in this programming: "The shows were wonderful. And they aired once and—poof!—they're on our shelves, which always disappointed him."[27]

Still, observes Basil Cox: "After experiencing being away from the *Neighborhood* for a while, and being relieved of the pressure of having to produce for it—he [Fred] took some pleasure in thinking about going back to it again. And I think he came to terms with who he was. He was Mister Rogers. You know, and there was no need to look for a new persona, that was who he was."[28]

But if Fred was disappointed in his four years of making programs for grown-ups, he was also looking forward. He remained in constant conversation with his mentor and teacher, Dr. Margaret McFarland of the University of Pittsburgh. They continued their conversations about children and early childhood education, and eventually they began to explore the idea of a new kind of *Mister Rogers' Neighborhood*, one that could focus on some of the most difficult themes of childhood.

16.

HE'S BACK!

THE NEW CONCEPT formulated by Fred Rogers and Dr. Margaret McFarland focused on shows that spanned a full week, integrating programs that would be watched from Monday through Friday in a way that would weave together narrative storytelling and instruction. They felt they could carry a story line, and an important theme from childhood, through a full five days, and that they could create the most powerful and sophisticated children's television yet produced. Most importantly, they wanted to tackle the toughest questions young children might encounter.

By the end of 1979, Rogers was lining up support for a new round of *Mister Rogers' Neighborhood* programming—a round that would extend through to the end of the century and cement Fred's reputation as the most thoughtful, sensitive, and courageous creator of children's television.

IT ALL CAME TOGETHER in Hawaii, of all places.

In the late 1970s, David Newell and Fred Rogers were traveling together to Honolulu, where Fred was scheduled to make a speech. David Newell handled public relations for Fred Rogers and his production company, Family Communications, Inc. (FCI), as well as playing Mr. McFeely, the "speedy delivery" mailman character on *Mister Rogers' Neighborhood*. Rogers hated traveling by himself—in fact, he hated traveling at all, just as he hated giving speeches. But he was often called on to speak at colleges and universities, as well as to early childhood education groups and broadcasting organizations, and most often it was Newell who traveled with him. Newell enjoyed the chance to have long, discursive conversations with Fred, something they were usually too busy to do back at FCI.[1]

In a taxi to the speaking engagement, Rogers was lost in thought about his upcoming speech. Newell recalls: "In the newspaper, I came across this little blurb that a child had jumped off a roof with a towel—the Superman thing."[2]

Newell interrupted Rogers's reverie to tell him the shocking news that a little boy who'd watched Superman on television had decided he would try to fly, and was terribly injured falling from a rooftop. One of the few things that could raise anger—real, intense anger—in Mister Rogers was willfully misleading innocent, impressionable children. To him, it was immoral and completely unacceptable.

His feelings extended to programming of any kind, including advertising and entertainment watched by very young children. In a speech given at an academic conference at Yale University in 1972, Fred Rogers said, "The impact of television must be considered in the light of the possibility that children are exposed to experiences which may be far beyond what their egos can deal with effectively. Those of us who produce television must assume the responsibility for providing images of trustworthy available adults who will modulate these experiences and attempt to keep them within manageable limits."[3] Which is exactly what Rogers himself had tried to do with the production of *Mister Rogers' Neighborhood*.

In a now-famous Rogers dictum, delivered in speeches and in his books, he advises adults: "Please, think of the children first. If you ever have anything to do with their entertainment, their food, their toys, their custody, their day care, their health, their education—please listen to the children, learn about them, learn from them."[4] When Fred Rogers and David Newell learned about the child who hurt himself trying to be a superhero, they came up with an idea: a special program to help kids grasp just what a fictional superhero is. In the cab, they talked about whether one special program would be enough, or would they need a whole week on the topic? They started to plan a week of programs to explain superheroes to children, to help them separate fact from fantasy, just as Rogers had on the *Neighborhood* in the late 1960s and early 1970s.[5]

Mister Rogers' Neighborhood was about to be reborn in a second phase. After a hiatus of almost five years, it came back stronger and more sophisticated than ever. It was the most ambitious concept Fred Rogers had yet come up with, one that would tackle the toughest questions young children might encounter. He wanted to risk talking about divorce, separation from parents, sickness, violence, and some of the other fears that could be most daunting for very young children. It would take exceptionally skilled scriptwriting to sustain a story over a full week, and to weave in and out of explication through which Mister Rogers would try to address the concerns of his young viewers.

By the time he got back from Hawaii, Fred Rogers had concluded that the sort of programming he was planning could best be handled in the *Mister Rogers' Neighborhood* format: using the segments from the Neighborhood of Make-Believe to advance a narrative employing fantasy storytelling to raise important issues, and using the segments that focused on Fred's "real television neighborhood" to bring in experts and guests to explore the meaning of these issues.

He and Margaret McFarland began deliberations on some of the most challenging topics imaginable for an audience of children, including theme weeks on superheroes, divorce, discipline, mistakes, anger, competition, and absent parents who are at work all week.[6]

Fred and his staff lined up support from PBS and the Sears-Roebuck Foundation for the theme-week concept, and production got underway in 1979, starting with a week on superheroes that highlighted the professional bodybuilder and actor Lou Ferrigno, who played the Incredible Hulk on the television show of the same name.[7] The week, which aired in February 1980, starts with Rogers using wooden blocks to demonstrate that, though each person may seem the same as others, everyone is distinctive and different in important ways.

In the Neighborhood of Make-Believe portion of the first show, the puppet Prince Tuesday shows Lady Aberlin a trick; then, convinced by his own skill with the trick, Prince Tuesday begins to think he can do almost anything: that he has something like superpowers.

When the show returns to Mister Rogers's "real neighborhood," Fred tells the viewers that pretending can be a problem when a child comes to believe what he is pretending. The show ends with Mister Rogers getting a phone call from Bill Bixby, the actor who plays Dr. David Banner on *The Incredible Hulk*. Bixby and Rogers promise the viewers that they'll go on the set of the *Hulk* later that week to see how the show is made. A major goal of Rogers was to demystify the creation of a superhero by taking his viewers behind the scenes to see the details by which the fantasy is created.

Through the course of the week, Rogers used the Neighborhood of Make-Believe to explore the fantasies of children: the puppet Ana Platypus thinks she can fly, and has to be caught by Lady Aberlin; Prince Tuesday alternates between delusions of superpower and fears. Rogers uses the "real neighborhood" to patiently explain reality. As scriptwriter, he took great pains to ensure that his young viewers could distinguish between the reality and fantasy sections.

When Mister Rogers and Mr. McFeely go to the set of *The Incredible Hulk*, they get to interview Bill Bixby and Lou Ferrigno about their roles "pretending" to be characters, and about their real lives. Rogers and McFeely want to illustrate how different these actors are from the characters they pretend to be. Mister Rogers manages quietly and gently to show viewers the behind-the-scenes creation of the Hulk, based on the comic-book story by Stan Lee and Jack Kirby about a widowed physician and scientist, Dr. Banner, who turns into the Hulk when he gets angry.[8]

During the whole week, Mister Rogers manages to slow the world down and reduce some of the most confusing and troubling apprehensions of children to calm, thoughtful, and simple explication. The Hulk show was a more in-depth treatment of a topic explored in an earlier 1975 *Neighborhood* episode featuring Margaret Hamilton, the

Wicked Witch in *The Wizard of Oz*. As she donned the witch's costume, and then took it off to go back to street clothes, children could see that it was all part of a show—not something scary or real.

Academics who've studied Rogers's work often marvel at how young children calm down, pay attention, and learn so much from this television production—and at how they remain calm and centered for some time after watching the *Neighborhood*. Rogers himself put great care into the pacing of the program to help children slow down and steady themselves.

One of Rogers's film editors, Pasquale Buba (who went on from the *Neighborhood* to Hollywood to edit dozens of feature films), explains that Rogers deliberately lengthened scenes as the theme week progressed, so that the children would get used to an environment that extended their attention spans as they became more and more familiar with the story line.[9]

Many of the academics who studied early learning became advocates for the *Neighborhood's* thoughtful, gentle approach.

Some of the advocates for giving children creative freedom—like Vivian Gussin Paley, author of *A Child's Work: The Importance of Fantasy Play*—decried an education format that pushed children toward rote learning. Story-based learning gives kids the freedom to explore fantasy and can help advance social and emotional development: "With the growth of nursery schools and childcare centers came the notion that there was too much play," said Paley.[10]

"Furthermore, these early years were designated as the optimum time to introduce the shapes and sounds of letters rather than the shapes and sounds of characters in a story. . . . Further confusing our logic and common sense, children labeled 'at risk,' who often had less opportunity for play and talk at home, were allowed less time for these activities in school as well."

The debate was not just about education and pacing. It was about childhood itself. Fred Rogers was viewed as the champion of slow pacing and a free-flowing approach allowing young children to play, to fantasize, to make up stories, and to take lots of time to process learning: the most likely way to enable them to develop appropriately. *Mister Rogers' Neighborhood* was viewed as the great exemplar of this relaxed approach. *Sesame Street* came to be viewed—sometimes to an unfair extent—as an example of a frenetic, intense, information-age approach that put cognitive learning first, cranked up the pressure, and foreshortened childhood in favor of learning letters and numbers. The pacing was set to be as fast as the times, with some emulation of *Rowan & Martin's Laugh-In* and the television serial *Batman*.

As the years went by, *Sesame Street* slowed down and tried a more balanced approach to learning, but the focus on intense pressure to accomplish rote learning at younger and younger ages still colored the common perception of the show. Dorothy Singer of Yale University speculated that a kind of competition had grown up between the slow-paced *Neighborhood* and other children's programming: "I think he [Rogers] has a lot of competition with these jazzed-up shows because I think that's what our world is like today . . . many of them that try to be slow-paced, producers won't even look at. They want something that's very quick, fun, excitement, a lot of music, and a lot of zip. . . . And I think there is going to be a turnaround. I'm seeing a backlash right now of parents demanding more playtime, parents demanding more recess.

"Look what happened to *Sesame Street*. . . . They are a very fast-paced program. But . . . because of Elmo, their largest audience . . . is two, two and a half, and three instead of fours and fives. The Elmo segment is now a longer segment, and slower-paced. And they know that young children can't process as quickly as older children. So, we're seeing some changes."[11]

According to Dr. Singer, "We have spoken to the *Sesame Street* people again and again. I've timed that program so many times where I can find twenty-three different elements in one hour, and none of them really lasts more than a minute, minute and a half, or three minutes. They've slowed that down a little bit, while with Fred Rogers there's one theme that goes through his whole program in thirty minutes.

Fred Rogers seesawing with Marilyn Barnett, a physical education teacher and later a school principal, who came on the show to teach Mister Rogers exercises, 1992

Fred Rogers with puppeteers Carole Switala and Lenny Meledandri, 1992

Fred Rogers greeting a child, 1970s

Fred Rogers and children, 1979

Fred Rogers with guest Jeff Erlanger, 1981

Fred Rogers with oceanographer Sylvia Earle, 1990

Fred Rogers with the musical Marsalis family, 1990

Fred Rogers on his daily swim at the Pittsburgh Athletic Association

Fred Rogers with François Clemmons in a
famous scene from the *Neighborhood*, 1993

Fred Rogers with Joanne Rogers on Nantucket Island, Massachusetts, 1990s

Fred Rogers at the Crooked House in Nantucket, 1990s

FOOD

We eat different parts of plants.
Corn for instance - how neatly the seeds are arranged.
Did you ever eat sunflower seeds? Birds love
to eat them.

TUESDAY

(1)

MR ENTERS WITH DIFFERENT ELEMENTS
FOR ASSEMBLING GRANOLA. (+ gift bags
(really seeds)   or jars)

Change to sweater. + APRON.

KITCHEN
WASH HANDS — PUT ON APRON
SHOW Different ingredients
Assemble granola.
Make into bars for presents.
One of MR's favorite things
to eat is granola.
Another one is TOFU

⭐. (Either GO to TOFU making place
      or   see it on P. Picture)

(Banana
 sandwich)

NOM

X is thrilled because his seeds
have grown -
He shows them to Henrietta.
He'll certainly have enough
for dinner !!! for both of the
He's going to go find L.A. so
she can   see. it.
Hen goes into her house to wash her paws.

Old Goat comes and eats all of
X's seedlings.

B.D.
✖ & L.A. enter together.

B.D. ✖. Wait 'til you see. Those seeds
were really .... Oh no !

Outline for the script of Food Week on *Mister Rogers' Neighborhood*, 1984

MR's PLACE

Different kinds of foods.
We've been thinking a lot about
food for the body, and that's
very important because when
a person is very very hungry
he or she can't think of any
other kinds of food.

BUT THERE ARE OTHER KINDS

i.e.   MUSIC   (PIANO)   food for the   ears (?)
                        + something in "NATURE."
        P.P. PAINTINGS ^   "   "   eyes
        BOOK   (Reading stories)   "   "   soul
        LOVING OTHER PEOPLE   "   "   spirit

SONG: "MANY WAYS"
                Reading
                eating
                hugging
                etc.

        GIVING / RECEIVING   (FOOD)
                                        SHOWING
        BOTH WAYS OF ^ LOVE

SONG: GOOD FEELING.

Final page of the outline of the script for Food Week on *Mister Rogers' Neighborhood*, 1984.
Included is Fred Rogers adapting the song "Many Ways" to fit the theme.

Fred Rogers crossing the bridge at Idlewild Park, an amusement park in Ligonier, Pennsylvania, near Latrobe, 1990s. Scenes from *Mister Rogers' Neighborhood* were sometimes filmed there.

Miniature set of the Neighborhood

"He has various ways of approaching that theme, but it's one theme, while *Sesame Street* could have many, many themes going on. That's very hard for a child to remember. . . . They [*Sesame*] have also introduced more imaginative elements. They've also tried to do more pro-social behavior. Those are influences [from *Mister Rogers' Neighborhood*]. I'm pretty sure that if you asked them, they might say no, but I think they came from Fred."[12]

In truth, the evolution of *Sesame Street* and the Children's Television Workshop in New York was every bit as high-minded, idealistic, and ambitious as the birth of *Mister Rogers' Neighborhood*. Joan Ganz Cooney worked with Lloyd Morrisett of the Carnegie Corporation to try to find a way to use television to provide an educational boost to young children, particularly those from disadvantaged backgrounds. And she brought in Dr. Gerald S. Lesser, a psychologist from the faculty of the Harvard Graduate School of Education, to help shape programming approaches with quick-witted humor and the techniques of advertising to capture the attention of young children and provide instruction on the alphabet, numbers, and reading, to help them get ready for their formal schooling. It was a brilliant idea, and it resulted in programming that has run longer and probably done more good, in telecasts all over the world, than anything else in television.

Fred Rogers himself was always very careful not to criticize *Sesame Street* in any public way. Privately, though, he shared with some staff members his concern that the hip pacing of the show could make it harder, rather than easier, for young children to learn. And Rogers, who had always believed it was more important to help young children deal with social and emotional development than it was to just cram facts into their heads, worried that *Sesame*'s unrelenting emphasis on cognitive learning left it too thin on the social and emotional.

Early in the evolution of *Mister Rogers' Neighborhood*, Rogers offered this definitive observation to a meeting of the American Academy of Child Psychiatry: "It's easy to convince people that children need to learn the alphabet and numbers. . . . How do we help people to realize that what matters even more than the superimposition of adult symbols is how a person's inner life finally puts together the alphabet and numbers of his outer life? What really matters is whether he uses the alphabet for the declaration of war or the description of a sunrise— his numbers for the final count at Buchenwald or the specifics of a brand-new bridge."[13]

Language, and the best way to develop language skills in young children, became a centerpiece of this debate about early childhood education. In a classic academic study, two researchers from the University of Kansas, Drs. Todd Risley and Betty Hart, spent years following the lives of a very large number of families to gauge the difference and importance of developing language skills in very young children. They discovered that parents in economically disadvantaged households had much less informal discourse with their very young children than did middle-class families.

The conversations in poor families tended to be more perfunctory—"don't do that, come here, put on your coat"—while in middle-class families they were richer, more discursive, and exploratory, employing a dramatically larger number of words. The result: The poor children in the study, published in 1995, had little more than a quarter of the vocabulary of the middle-class kids by the time they got to public school, and they arrived at kindergarten far behind and far less ready to learn.

Most significantly, many of these kids never caught up: It was game over by kindergarten, just because they hadn't evolved rich and modulated language skills.[14]

Fred Rogers understood this. He had learned it from his studies with Dr. McFarland and Dr. Benjamin Spock and Eric Erikson and others at the University of Pittsburgh. He had learned it from his own experience teaching children and creating programming for them. He had learned it as a little boy, lonely and unsure of himself, but with a mother and father and grandparents who gave him unconditional love and talked to him. Most importantly, Rogers had been given the freedom to play, to develop his own creative fantasies. He had been given the gift of language by his mother. He learned that creativity is far more important than rote learning.

These debates about education—emotional and social learning versus hard-edged cognitive development, slow- or fast-paced, feelings or facts—are as old as the art of teaching itself. And there have been plenty of critics of Rogers's approach as naive, hopelessly idealistic, and not geared to the vicissitudes of adult life. As early as the late 1960s, *Mister Rogers' Neighborhood* was sometimes chided for being too much about feelings. Rogers's critics often derided him for being too soft and undemanding, and not emphasizing the sort of painful cognitive rigor needed for success in the real world.

Most researchers credit *Sesame Street* and *Mister Rogers' Neighborhood* together with raising the absolute standard for all children's programming in the second half of the twentieth century. Moreover, Rogers and Cooney joined together to try to deflect any notion of competitive bad blood between the two:

"There were two schools of thought in preschool education," said Cooney in an interview. "One school thought you did not teach cognitive skills, you only worked on the affective side—the 'whole child,' as it was called. Fred and I had no such problems at all, and we just refused—I don't think we ever talked about it, but maybe we did on the phone. We refused to be pitted against each other by people like the Singers, who were always attacking us for being cognitive. Fred and I just stood firm and said, 'We are two sides of the same coin.' . . . We were great admirers of each other. You know, Fred was unique. There had never been a Fred Rogers, and there wasn't going to be another Fred Rogers."[15]

Rogers himself couldn't have cared less about engaging the debate. He wasn't much interested in academic wrangles, and throughout his life he was more often repelled, rather than attracted, by the strife of ideological battle. He believed in his approach, he believed in his teachers—McFarland, Spock, Erikson, Brazelton—and he was determined to pursue his vision of transformative children's television based on slow pacing, the elegance of simple explanations of the world's

complexity, and his distinctive focus on human kindness. Rogers's supporters argue that the proof is in the pudding: Children raised on the
ethic of the *Neighborhood*, though less likely to make millions on an
innovative hedge-fund scheme on Wall Street, are more likely to grow
up with the kind of social and emotional understanding that can lead
to a happily balanced life.

CHILDREN COULD NOT GET ENOUGH of Mister Rogers, as producer Margy Whitmer discovered on her very first location shoot. She
learned a real lesson: "When *Mister Rogers' Neighborhood* started, I was
a little bit too old to watch, so I never really got it. At a program at the
National Zoo, we were breaking for lunch, when all of a sudden, I saw
a horde of preschool kids running toward Fred. It was like he was the
Mick Jagger of the preschool set.

"I said, 'Stop! Mister Rogers has to eat his lunch!'" She adds, "It
was so inspiring to work with Fred, but sometimes there were frustrations. When he didn't get what he wanted, he could act like the only
child who always wants to get his way."[16]

Margy Whitmer came to the Neighborhood as an associate producer in 1980 after working on a radio call-in show at WQED, and she
stayed on as a producer until *Mister Rogers' Neighborhood* went off the
air in 2003. She still works for the Fred Rogers Company as director of
video production and special events.

Whitmer feels that it was "pretty amazing" for a man of Rogers's
generation to have a woman producer, years younger than him. She and
Fred Rogers had both grown up in small towns: "My sensibilities, some
of my quirks and hang-ups, come from that era of 'children are seen
and not heard.' I think that's why Fred spent so much of his life trying
to help kids talk about their feelings, about who they are. Because his
background didn't allow him to do that as much as he thought kids
should be able to do."[17]

One of the many ways in which Fred Rogers was ahead of his
time was in his transparency, and his straight-on relationship with his

very young audience. Not only does he address his "television neighbors" directly at the start and end of each half-hour show, he even aired a segment in 1984 called "Behind the Scenes," during a week of episodes on work, in which the cameras pan to encompass the entire studio, including Johnny Costa and members of the *Neighborhood* orchestra.

Then Mister Rogers cradles his beloved puppets and demonstrates how he manipulates Prince Tuesday and Queen Sarah and Daniel Striped Tiger and the rest of the gang from behind a little stage in the Neighborhood of Make-Believe.

Similarly, Rogers didn't want children to think that Picture, Picture was a magical device. Hence, he started having Mr. McFeely bring in tapes, so that Mister Rogers could show his television neighbors that behind the picture frame was a projector and a videotape machine. In breaking the theatrical "fourth wall," Fred Rogers is engaging in very "meta," strikingly sophisticated exercises for an audience of preschoolers. Yet it also jibes with his carefully considered attempts to help children differentiate between the man who comes onto the set in his suit and the man transformed into their friendly neighbor once he dons his signature cardigan and sneakers.

He believed in being as honest about the workings of the show as he was about family dynamics or children's fears. Fascination with the practical aspects of the "television house" prompted queries such as this one from Rebecca, age four: "Does it ever rain in your neighborhood?"

Mister Rogers responded by letter, explaining, "Dear Rebecca: Our television Neighborhood is set up inside, in a big room called a television studio. Of course, it doesn't rain inside, but sometimes we make it look like it's raining. It takes a lot of work to make it look like it's raining in the studio, and we don't do it very often. But once in a while we do. I like to talk to my television neighbors about different kinds of weather. I know it's not always a 'beautiful day' outside, but I like to think we can make it a 'beautiful day' inside because we enjoy having a television visit together."[18]

When Meaghan, age ten, asked: "What is the purpose of feeding the fish every day? To demonstrate responsibility?" Mister Rogers wrote back, "Dear Meaghan: When we feed the fish, we're showing that we 'take care of' other living things, and being taken care of is something very important to children. They know they need grown-ups to provide them with food, like the fish in our tank need us to feed them. It does have a lot to do with responsibility, as you mention. I also like to watch anything that swims!"[19]

Probably the most effective theme week in the 1980s iteration of *Mister Rogers' Neighborhood*, and certainly some of the most powerful programming ever developed for children's television, was Fred Rogers's week on divorce. It represented the best of this new second phase in the evolution of the *Neighborhood*: courageously confronting one of the most pressing and complex fears of childhood—the breakup of the family.

When Fred Rogers's parents were growing up, divorce was a relative rarity. By the time he finished his television career in 2001, around half the marriages in America ended in divorce. Just a few years later, the US passed another watershed: Over 40 percent of babies were being born out of wedlock; and for women in their twenties—a harbinger of future trends—the percentage of babies born outside of marriage was 60 percent.[20]

As someone devoted to family and community, Fred Rogers was clearly disheartened by such trends. But he was careful in his programming not to be strident or judgmental, but simply to explore and explain what this must mean and feel like for the children involved. Rogers fervently believed in the power of communities and families to help young children grow. He knew that young children learn less from books or movies or television than they do from caring adults.

But he was not a crusader. As much as Fred Rogers worried about American trends—more geographic mobility, more emphasis on individual latitude, potentially disrupting traditional responsibility to community and family—he knew his job was to try to understand the effects of these trends on children, to understand the children themselves, and how to help them. In his conversations on the topic with Margaret McFarland, she reminded him that every time parents quarrel, children fantasize that they might separate—the children's greatest fear.

The first program in the *Neighborhood*'s weeklong special on divorce, which aired in 1981, starts with the host opening a bag of pretzels and examining the contents. The pretzels will reappear as illustrations of the idea that a group of things that may look alike—pretzels, people—can on closer examination be quite varied and different. Rogers is preparing his audience to react thoughtfully when the trolley takes them to the Neighborhood of Make-Believe, and they encounter puppet characters, who, though they may seem the same, behave quite differently.

In the make-believe segment, we see King Friday XIII, the authority figure among the puppets, succumb to a slick sales pitch from a young woman (a human) who proffers a new royal jet plane tailor-made for the King's needs.

She "proudly presents" the XIII Special, "designed especially for you, King Friday, through special arrangement with our top-flight engineers."

It's a hard sell, the kind of advertising that usually made Fred Rogers cringe. "You and your royal family," she says, "will be able to soar into limitless altitudes while enjoying the comfort of your own castle." And she promises "not one, not two, but thirteen fuel tanks. Yes, sire, this is your plane."

Then Queen Sara Saturday arrives to remind the King that they'd decided not to purchase another plane. But King Friday says, "You may have decided, Sara, but I want to hear this person out."

Queen Sara turns to the saleswoman and says she thinks this sales pitch may be a big waste of time. Then the King and Queen quarrel about the fuel consumption of the new plane.

The King fumes, "Well, it's purple, and it has thirteens all over it." Suddenly he says, "Well, I'm the King."

Queen Sara replies, "Well, I'm the Queen." She storms away, and the King seems temporarily flummoxed. He excuses himself, saying, "Perhaps I should speak further with the Queen." He seems to slink away in uncertainty.

Then the saleswoman and Lady Aberlin, a human (rather than a puppet) figure who sometimes plays the role of hostess on make-believe segments, hear crying in the background. It is Prince Tuesday, who comes out from a hiding place to say, "I don't like it when my mom and dad are mad at each other." He asks, "Is it my fault . . . that they're fighting?"

The Prince confesses that he once wished he had a jet airplane, but he didn't say anything about it. Suddenly he says, "I sure wish I didn't have any feelings," afraid that his feelings have caused upset in the family. After everyone leaves, we see Prince Tuesday lift a small suitcase over the wall and carry it under the trolley tracks; he is running away. Soon, everyone in the Neighborhood is scurrying around frantically looking for the missing little boy.

Then the trolley takes the viewers back from the land of make-believe to Mister Rogers's house. Fred tells his young viewers: "Prince Tuesday is afraid that his mother and dad's fighting is all his fault. A lot of Prince Tuesday's worries are on the inside. Do you suppose his mother and dad know that he's worried? They might not know if he doesn't tell them."

At the end of this program, Rogers carefully puts the different-size pretzels away, feeds his fish, and sings good-bye to his viewers. He changes into his jacket and shoes, picks up his pretzel tin and starts to leave. Then he pauses and says, "Sometimes children wonder if other people know what they're thinking. People don't know what you're thinking if you don't tell them. So, if you're worried about something, it can really help to tell the people you love what you're worried about."

Each person is different; like the pretzels, they may look the same, but they are individual and distinct. If you want someone else to understand what you are thinking and feeling, you must tell them. He waves good-bye. "We'll have time to do more things tomorrow."

This is vintage Mister Rogers: detailed, consistent, gently spaced and timed, richly interwoven with narrative, fantasy, a touch of the lecture—a mix of great storytelling, parable, and gentle explication.

The rest of the weeklong series on divorce follows the same pattern. Rogers even brings in an expert on the effects of divorce on young children to help him explore the meaning and the feelings of things. Fred was always hopeful that parents would watch with their children, and the thoughts of this expert—Dr. Earl Grollman, author of books on divorce and grief and feelings—seem aimed as much at the parents as the kids.[21]

Finally, the week ends on a high note, with King Friday and Queen Sara Saturday and Prince Tuesday reconciled, and Rogers himself singing to his viewers about the critical importance of being able to talk about one's feelings with others. This is what has helped Prince Tuesday resolve his situation, and Mister Rogers gently explains that the pain of divorce is real, that there is nothing magic that will make it disappear, but that the ability to talk with those we love about feelings will bring us through something difficult. As usual, Fred Rogers offers no easy, quick fixes, and his message for children is that their feelings will be okay if they can share them.

This theme week, like most of the others, has delivered a surprising amount of information and cognitive learning, but has done so in ways that are always processing opportunities for social and emotional learning as well. It is the distinctive Rogers blend, and it came to be deeply appreciated by millions of children, as well as many experts on communications and education. As George Gerbner, dean emeritus of the Annenberg School for Communication at the University of Pennsylvania, wrote in a 1996 essay about Fred Rogers and his work:

"His dreams, his stories, offer ways to control the chaotic life of the streets and neighborhoods in which many children live. Children are starving for story, the kind that builds on hope, the kind that echoes for a lifetime. We need story in our lives, not dreams based on greed. Mister Rogers turns to the viewer and says quietly, 'Believe you. It is your story that is important. It is your mind and heart that can make things possible—just because of who you are.' "[22]

Fred Rogers had made the leap to addressing issues in the world around him that affected kids, thereby ensuring the *Neighborhood*'s run through to the end of the century, and cementing his reputation as the most thoughtful, sensitive, and courageous creator of children's television.

17.

BEHIND THE SCENES IN
THE *NEIGHBORHOOD*

IN 1975, Jeffrey Erlanger, a five-year-old boy from Madison, Wisconsin, confined to a wheelchair, asked his parents, Howard and Pam, if he could meet Mister Rogers rather than going to Disneyland. It was the family's own version of "Make-A-Wish," proposed on the eve of major surgery to fuse Jeff's spine. When asked in an interview why Jeff chose Fred Rogers, Howard and Pam explained that their son "always said that Mister Rogers told him that he was special and that he was just fine the way he was, and it gave him confidence and it made him feel good, and Mister Rogers just seemed to love him."[1]

Jeff and his sister, Lisa, both watched the *Neighborhood* so often that they knew all the words to Fred Rogers's songs. Pam and Howard Erlanger wrote a letter to the television star about Jeff's desire to meet him, and they got a handwritten answer that led to a breakfast meeting at a hotel in Milwaukee, where Fred Rogers was visiting to promote the local PBS station. Later they continued to correspond; Mister Rogers wrote to say how glad he was that Jeff's surgery had gone well.

The years passed, and even if the growing Jeff didn't watch the *Neighborhood* quite as often as he had when he was younger, he kept a place in his heart for Mister Rogers. Then in 1980, Fred Rogers decided he wanted to have a child in a wheelchair on the show for a theme week on all things mechanical and electrical:

"He remembered Jeff, and he told his staff to get Jeff. The staff said, 'There're handicapped kids in Pittsburgh. We don't have to fly somebody here from Wisconsin and go through all that. We could just go down the block.' No. Fred insisted it had to be Jeff," recalled Pam and Howard Erlanger.[2]

Reasonably enough, the staff at the *Neighborhood* thought the family lived in Milwaukee, not in Madison. And Fred Rogers remembered them as the Ehrlingers. When they couldn't be located, Rogers instructed the staff to put the project on hold. But in cleaning out some files, the *Neighborhood*'s staff found letters from the Erlangers about their older daughter, Lisa, not Jeff. Lisa was worried about the fact that in her mind, the show "didn't have any strong female role models."

Rogers had written to say that the *Neighborhood* was made of modules, and some of the segments dated from the 1960s; he was trying to remedy the situation. In fact, a song from a very early show included these lyrics: "My daddy's strong and drives a car and my mommy's pretty and cooks." For all his humanistic impulses, Fred Rogers was also a man of his times.[3]

Once the Erlanger family had been located, they were all flown to Pittsburgh for the taping. Jeff was now a preternaturally intelligent ten-year-old. When asked if there was any special preparation for Jeff, his mother, Pam, said: "Absolutely not. The first time Jeff heard anything about what was going to happen was when we arrived on the set a few minutes before they started rolling the cameras. At that point Fred said to him, 'Jeff, I'm just going to ask you some questions, and then we'll sing a song together.' He did say, 'Remember, we're talking to very young children so don't use any words that are too big.'"[4]

Jeff Erlanger didn't quite heed Mister Rogers words. In one of the *Neighborhood*'s most memorable broadcasts in 1981, Mister Rogers asks Jeff straightforwardly about the mechanics of his wheelchair, and how he wound up in it. The young boy explains his medical condition (resulting from a spinal tumor) in sophisticated detail, including even his urinary functions.

Mister Rogers listens intently and says simply: "Your parents must be very proud of you."[5]

This was the Zen of Fred Rogers's radical acceptance: There was no topic he wouldn't address on air, no matter how difficult. "We don't fudge things," he said once when asked about the sources of the show's popularity. "People long to be in touch with honesty."

Producer Margy Whitmer recalls Jeff Erlanger's appearance on the *Neighborhood*: "It was one of the most stunning moments. . . . Here's this child who has multiple disabilities, and Fred said, 'Talk to me about that wheelchair. Talk to me about what's wrong with you.' And this extraordinary kid talked about it in a matter-of-fact way. Fred . . . presented it to kids watching the show, as 'this is just the way he is.' "[6]

Jeff's parents felt completely comfortable allowing their son to speak this way on television because, as Howard Erlanger explained: "In our own way, we felt totally analogous to how the kids felt, that Fred Rogers was part of our family, that he was just a regular person. And we saw that everything that happened on the show was very warm and nurturing and supporting, so whatever it was that Jeff was going to do was going to be nurturing and supporting. There was no risk whatsoever that there could be anything that would be embarrassing or that we would be unhappy.

"We just felt totally comfortable, like we were going to a relative's for an evening."[7]

Jeff Erlanger and Fred Rogers didn't meet again until nearly twenty years later, when Fred Rogers was being inducted into the Television Hall of Fame in 1999. When Jeff rolls onstage to surprise him, Rogers runs up to the stage and hugs him as if they are the only two people in the auditorium. "On behalf of millions of children and grown-ups," says Jeff to Fred Rogers, "It's you I like."[8]

There wasn't a dry eye in the well-dressed house.

THE SECOND ITERATION of the *Neighborhood*, which showcased the Erlanger episode in 1981, was in production three seasons of the year: fall, winter, and spring. The scripts for the Neighborhood of Make-Believe were comprised of individual dramas that began on Monday and had to be resolved by Friday. Fred Rogers continued to incorporate daily life into scripts, as he always had.

Chuck Aber (Neighbor Aber) recalls: "Sometimes you had to be careful what you said to Fred, because it would end up in the program. One of my favorite theme weeks . . . was 'Alike and Different.' Somewhere along the line, I guess I mentioned . . . that I had this 1958 Corvette, a beautiful car. . . .

"Next thing I know, I got a script, and [in it] there was going to be a car show up at Idlewild Park, which is near Latrobe, where Fred grew up. My car is in that program.

"Fred comes along, and I'm cleaning my car for the show. He's already shown the television viewer that this other car has a wooden steering wheel and spoked wheels. Then he gets to mine, and it has a plastic steering wheel and metal wheels. So they're alike, but they're very different at the same time.

"That's an example of where you innocently mention something to Fred, and next thing you know, it's in the program."[9]

Every summer Fred Rogers went to Nantucket on his yearly sojourn with his family. But he was still working: The staff would give him ideas about themes and segments to work on while he was away. Rogers's longtime secretary Elaine Lynch describes the process: "Fred enjoyed Nantucket, but he also had a private office up there, and a piano. He did have a typewriter, but he didn't use it much. He still liked handwriting the scripts on eight-and-a-half-by-fourteen legal pads, and he would use a whole pad for five programs. Most of the time he'd mail them back to me from Nantucket, and I would start typing them. . . .

"Then I would mail him a copy of the typed scripts, and after he had checked them, he would call me and say, 'Go ahead and distribute them' to the . . . crew. Then they would start doing what they needed to do to make the production happen when he got back."[10]

A production period for five programs, one week's programming, was about four weeks. Location pieces were shot first, as the art crew was simultaneously making props for interior shoots. A segment on visiting a crayon factory, or Chef Brockett in his bakery, for example, might come to just over six minutes after editing.

Budgets were always modest. Betty Aberlin notes: "It was so low-budget, in a way, it was as close to live TV as you've got. There was no rehearsal time, so you basically learned your lines and then sometimes you had to do something tricky with a puppet or a prop. At which time you got the prop and puppet, and the lines went out of your head. I mean, we did our own hair, our own makeup, we miked ourselves, we dressed in a toilet—a very nice toilet, but still, the toilet."[11]

On a typical day in the studio, the crew would arrive at 8:00 or 8:30 A.M. The Neighborhood of Make-Believe was taped first, in equally timed segments for all five programs. Rogers always found the Neighborhood of Make-Believe part of the show easier because he was behind the scenes, manipulating the puppets.

After filming the make-believe segments, it was on to the set where Mister Rogers enters his television house, including the kitchen and the porch. Due to time considerations, the introductions often changed dramatically from what Rogers had originally written in the script. Programs had to be exactly twenty-eight minutes long, so the interiors were often rewritten to fit that requirement.

Producer Margy Whitmer explains: "Fred started out in television as a floor man, so he understood continuity; it would make him nuts if it wasn't just quite right. Shooting it in this order helped eliminate the element of surprise or error. Fred was a pretty linear person: beginning, middle, end."[12]

While Whitmer was setting up the lights and tracking down the props person and art crew to make sure everything was in place for the first scene, Fred Rogers was on set with visitors such as kids from the Make-A-Wish Foundation, in what was slotted to be a ten- or fifteen-minute encounter.

Sometimes this became a headache for his staff. Whitmer recalls: "People would say, 'Can I bring my daughter?' Then they would decide to invite their neighbor. All of a sudden, a party of three people was six. I tried to put my foot down and limit it to fifteen people per day. The hard part was that Fred would genuinely get into talking to the kids, and having his picture taken with them. My main job then was to say,

'Time to go.' Though people understood, sometimes it was hard for me to be diplomatic. It was my fault if we went into overtime because we didn't get started on time."[13]

Margy Whitmer would do Mister Rogers's makeup at around 9:30 A.M. He hated getting into makeup because it involved putting in his contact lenses, which he never learned to do himself. Pepper Mallinger, Fred Rogers's ophthalmologist, or the eye doctor's assistant, put them into his eyes in the morning and took them out at night.

Though she wasn't a trained makeup artist, Whitmer enjoyed the sessions with Fred Rogers: "It was a wonderful time for me to spend with him, talking about the script, and reminding him of details for the shoot. I could judge if he was tired: Did he sleep well? Did he get his swim in? What's on his mind?"[14]

Every day Fred Rogers would rise early, read his Bible, and then go down to the Pittsburgh Athletic Association building for a long swim before he went to work. When Rogers traveled, he asked his staff to book him into a hotel with a pool, so he could continue exercising daily.

On set at 10:00 A.M., one or two takes of *Mister Rogers' Neighborhood* usually did the trick. Whitmer observes: "The actors knew that because Fred was demanding on himself, he'd be on them, too: They knew they needed to get their act together. And for the most part, they did."[15]

When Mister Rogers presented a special show on music in 1985, he went down into the *Neighborhood* studio to introduce viewers to Johnny Costa on piano, Bobby Rawsthorne on drums, and Carl McVicker on bass. Each played his part of the show's theme song separately on his instrument before they played the signature *Neighborhood* introduction together, so that kids in the audience could get a sense of how they "communicate" with their fellow musicians.

In addition to the show's instantly recognizable theme, the trio played the trolley whistle, Mr. McFeely's frenetic "Speedy Delivery" piano plonks, vibraphone sounds and flute toots on a synthesizer as Fred fed his fish, dreamy celesta lines, incidental music, and Rogers's entrance and exit tunes.

Chuck Aber, whose training included the Pittsburgh Civic Light Opera, observed in an interview that Johnny Costa and Fred were considered an odd couple in terms of personality, but certainly not in their musicality or insistence on the highest quality of production: "Johnny was a very ebullient, outgoing kind of guy, and just the most incredibly talented musician I've ever met. . . . He and Fred had a wonderful relationship."[16]

Aber recalls that rehearsal time for musical segments in the Neighborhood of Make-Believe was minimal: "If we had a song to do, we'd rehearse it with Johnny Costa. He made sure the key was right and everything was good. . . . You'd get one or two run-throughs with him, and that was it.

"That's a tribute to the director in the studio, in the control room, as well as Fred, and those of us . . . who worked so hard on the scripts. Studio time was so expensive. The professionalism of all those . . . crew guys that were there with Fred forever, like Nicky Tallo and Jimmy Seech, Frank Warninsky, Art Vogel. . . . You'd get a couple of run-throughs, and they'd say, 'Roll tape. Underway.' "

As Chuck Aber recalls, "Johnny would occasionally speak up. I remember watching a replay of one of the scenes we'd done. Fred would say, 'Everyone okay with that?' Because if you said, 'No, I didn't think—' very often, he'd say, 'Let's do it again.'

"Other times, Margy [producer Margy Whitmer] would say, 'No. . . . We just have to keep going, and deal with it.' But at this one occasion, we're watching the playback . . . Fred said, 'I think that was good. Let's move on.'

"Johnny went, 'They always use the one after my best take.' Now, of course, none of us would have noticed anything, but in Johnny's mind, that one wasn't as good, or maybe the next one would be. I think he was often a little dissatisfied. I don't know how he could possibly have improved it. But if Johnny had insisted, Fred would have said, 'Let's do it again.' "[17]

Rogers's son Jim notes that *Neighborhood* floor manager Nicky Tallo was short and heavy, wore a Fu Manchu mustache, and had tattoos up and down his arms: "He looked like a biker. He and Dad got along like two peas in a pod."[18]

In an interview with writer Daniel Kellison in the now-defunct web magazine *Grantland,* Michael Keaton provides an additional illustration of the relationship between Fred Rogers and Nicky Tallo: "So one day, we were taping, and Fred comes in, and starts singing, 'It's a beautiful day in the neighborhood, a beautiful day . . . ,' puts the shoes down here, goes to hang up the sweater in the closet. And he's singing, and he opens the door—and there's his floor manager, Nick, this big guy with his long goatee, pierced ears, hair all over the place, totally nude, just standing there naked in the closet. Well, Fred just fell down; it was the most hysterical thing you've ever seen. He was totally cool."[19]

AFTER TAPING EACH SHOW (and even the thirteen operas Fred Rogers wrote had to fit into the twenty-eight-minute format), everyone would break for lunch. Fred Rogers would often go to his office to read his mail, or perhaps do a little meditating. Then he'd come back down to carry on. Producer Margy Whitmer recalls that as he started to slow down, "Towards the end, he wouldn't tape two days in a row. We didn't realize how lucky we were, working three days a week, 10:00 A.M. to 4:30 P.M."[20]

One of the challenges of her job was to find practical applications for Fred Rogers's sometimes wacky ideas: "Weekly staff meetings were the bane of my existence. Once Fred wanted Prince Tuesday, the puppet, to get a bicycle. Prince Tuesday doesn't have legs. So how do you make a bicycle, and how does the puppeteer manipulate it? Fred would come up with flying trolleys and flying carpets, or he'd want it to rain in the Neighborhood of Make-Believe but not all over the studio floor."

Other problems arose because, as Margy Whitmer saw it, "He couldn't really visualize what he wanted until he saw something, and then he would know that he didn't want that, or he'd want it changed. The hardest part was that he had such respect for the art crew, their talent, their whimsy, and their wackiness, that it was hard for him to tell them he didn't like something. So sometimes I would have to go in and say, 'Fred, that learning machine that they came up, they didn't do such a great job on it. Tell me what you think.'

"Then he would agree: 'Well, I really didn't like it that much.'

"I'd have to go back and ask the crew to change it, with them not really knowing that it was from Fred."[21]

Chuck Aber remembers Rogers's directing style as similarly indirect. Aber debuted as the voice of H. J. Elephant III, named after Fred's friend Senator H. John Heinz III. As he recalls Rogers's directive: "He wanted H. J. to be a little—not too much, but a little—streetwise, and have maybe a Southern accent."[22]

Other than that, Rogers gave Aber very little instruction or direction: "Fred's attitude was, let the muse take you . . . not as a puppet, but as Neighbor Aber. Whenever I would ask him a question, maybe about the script . . . sometimes he would say, 'We'll have to ask the writer about that.'

Of course, Rogers *was* the writer. The way Chuck Aber figures it: "I don't know that Fred necessarily separated himself from that process. He knew he was the writer, of course. But I think it was just part of his whimsy."

He adds: "Fred didn't always want to tell you . . . what things meant. Whatever it means to you, that's more important."[23]

Sometimes Rogers wrote scripts with specific performers in mind. Once he wrote a set of scripts about dance for Tommy Tune, who turned out not to be available. So Margy Whitmer had to find another dancer: "It was fine, because we weren't really about stars, like *Sesame Street*; we were about having good talent.

"I think there was a real fear of rejection in Fred: To have to ask Tommy Tune first, and have Tommy Tune say, 'No, I'm not interested in being in the show,' would have been really hurtful. It was much easier to write the script, and say: 'He wasn't available. What can I do?' There was an insecurity there."[24]

The staff had to find ways to allow Fred Rogers to be Mister

Rogers—to keep up his image, and not show any flaws. There were times when he didn't want to cooperate: "That was the part of him someone in the office called 'Baby Fred,'" recalls Margy Whitmer.

She felt that her role included being Fred Rogers's protector, so that he could save his energy. If he was talking to someone on the phone and wanted to get off, Whitmer would pretend to be his secretary Elaine, who needed Mister Rogers's immediate attention.[25]

Lots of times David Newell had to be Fred Rogers's shield, as the de facto "Number Two" on the show and the public relations director. If someone wanted to interview Mister Rogers, it was Newell's job to massage the request, sometimes for weeks.

Newell observes: "It was never Fred Rogers's goal to be a television star. Television was a vehicle for Fred, to reach children and families; it was sort of a necessary evil."[26]

Still, his staffers often noted that he could "glow" onscreen. As Hedda Sharapan puts it: "Fred wasn't an actor, but he loved the camera . . . and he loved the fact that he was able to communicate through television."[27]

David Newell feels that Rogers did enjoy aspects of being famous: "I think he enjoyed the respect he got for good work. It was about all those years of child development, and music, and his discipline—his investment."[28]

By its second run in the early 1980s, the *Neighborhood* was such a cultural touchstone that it had inspired numerous parodies, notably Eddie Murphy's *Saturday Night Live* sketch "Mister Robinson's Neighborhood," which aired over numerous episodes of the sketch comedy series in 1983 and 1984. Set in an urban ghetto, the parody was "not always G-rated," as David Newell put it.[29]

SNL was filmed upstairs from David Letterman's show in NBC's Studio 8H, where Rogers worked in his first television job as a floor manager, decades earlier. Right before Fred Rogers's appearance on the popular talk show, he and David Newell took a special elevator to the *SNL* outpost and found Murphy in his dressing room.

As Newell related the story in January 2017 on the *The Moth Radio Hour,* "Eddie Murphy was truly surprised, and stepped back at first."[30]

But he recovered quickly, and exclaimed, "Here's the real Mister Robinson!" before giving Fred Rogers a big hug. David Newell noted: "Eddie Murphy had grown up watching *Mister Rogers' Neighborhood,* and it was obvious that there was a real connection."

Shortly thereafter on *Letterman,* Fred Rogers held up a Polaroid just taken of him with Eddie Murphy. Most of the parodies of the *Neighborhood* were done "with kindness in their hearts," Rogers told David Letterman.[31]

DESPITE ROGERS'S AMBIVALENCE about fame, his staff was aware that when you were with Fred Rogers, unexpected things happened. Margy Whitmer recounts a time when the show was shooting in colonial Williamsburg, Virginia: After the staff got on the plane in Pittsburgh, she realized that she'd left the signature Mister Rogers sweater and sneakers back in the airline's club lounge. Since the plane wasn't ready to take off, Whitmer asked the attendant if she could go back to retrieve the essential props. But the flight attendant said she couldn't reopen the plane door. Instead, she proposed that she put the sweater and sneakers on a flight to Roanoke that left shortly thereafter.

A relieved Whitmer planned to take Fred Rogers to Williamsburg and then drive back to the Roanoke airport to get the sweater and sneakers. But a woman behind the Rogers team on the flight overheard the exchange and offered to do it herself. Whitmer noted: "I trusted this woman, even though I'd never seen her before in my life."[32]

But there was another wrinkle: How would the staff at the airport know that this volunteer was authorized to pick up the Rogers props? Unable to get the airport on the phone, Whitmer finally dialed the US Airways 800 number to describe what awaited in Roanoke: "The woman who answered said, 'I can't do that for you.'

"I said, 'Listen, lady, this is Mister Rogers's sweater and sneakers, and if we don't have these tomorrow, we can't shoot.'

"She said, 'Oh my gosh. Hold on a second. I'll make this happen for you.'"

When Margy Whitmer got back from dinner, the sweater and sneakers were on her bed.[33]

Rogers's quirks came to the forefront on a trip to the Soviet Union in 1987, during the perestroika era. David Newell initiated the visit after watching *Nightline*. Host Ted Koppel likened the gentleness of Mister Rogers to a Russian show called *Spokoynoy, nochi malyshi!* (*Good Night, Little Ones*), on in prime time. In a time of building bridges, Newell and Whitmer suggested that the *Neighborhood* crew do a cultural exchange with the cast of the Soviet show.

At the time, Rogers and the staff were working on a week about "alike and different." He wrote to *Good Night* host Tatiana Vedeneyeva about an exchange between the two shows. As a lead-in, the *Neighborhood* staff composed a segment about television shows from different countries.

By the fall of that year, the complex preparations had been completed. Once they got to Russia, Fred Rogers never changed his watch to local time. He stayed on his usual schedule, getting up at four o'clock in the morning and going to bed at eight o'clock. So the staff had to finish shooting by the middle of the day, Russian time.

Margy Whitmer recalls: "We only shot two segments, and it took us two weeks. We didn't even get to go anywhere. It took forever to do anything. Poor Fred was tired. We got followed by the cops once; all we needed was to have Mister Rogers get arrested in Russia."[34]

But she was struck by the fact that the Russians knew all about *Mister Rogers' Neighborhood*, because it had been pirated there. At the first production meeting, Rogers's staff was on one side of the table, and the Russians were on the other side.

She observes: "At one point, Fred was thinking, this is not good. So he pulls out Daniel Striped Tiger the puppet, and Daniel warms everybody up, even though they don't really understand what he's saying. Then Fred pulled out X the Owl. The beak was broken. The Russian art director takes the puppet, and we're thinking: 'Uh-oh, we're never going to see that again.' About half an hour later he brings back X, with the beak fixed perfectly.

"These puppets were a way for Fred to break the ice. And the crew couldn't have been more wonderful. We all cried and cried when we left. Our interpreter came to visit me a few years later. But I think this set of shows was more PR for who Fred was, for his philosophy."[35]

For the kids in the TV "neighborhood," Russia could have been down the street. As wonderful as it had been, the trip was an exhausting experience Fred Rogers vowed never to repeat.

HEDDA SHARAPAN NOTED: "There was a wonderful, thoughtful intensity . . . in the studio of *Mister Rogers' Neighborhood*: 'Let's do this really well.' But there was also wonderful playfulness . . . warmth, playfulness, and respect."[36]

Fred Rogers's great sense of humor, and his sense of timing, often came out in unexpected ways. Arthur Greenwald recalls an incident while driving Rogers to the airport after a conference on early childhood development at Yale, also attended by Dr. Margaret McFarland: "I ran out of gas in this borrowed car, and finally flagged down a state trooper. I was really embarrassed. I said to Fred, as the state trooper took him and Margaret and their belongings into the car with the flashing lights, 'Oh, Fred, what would Lady Elaine say at a time like this?'

"And through the darkness, Lady Elaine's voice came back: 'She'd say, 'Oh, shit!' '"[37]

Fred Rogers's humor could be subversive in its own way. When Katie Couric was traveling the United States one summer, she did her *Today* show openers in different cities. Broadcasting from Pittsburgh, she set up next to "this beautiful fountain at the headwaters of the Ohio" and went on to introduce Rogers: "This is a premier citizen of Pittsburgh, Mr. Fred Rogers.

"Good morning, Mister Rogers. Do you have anything in particular to say to our viewers?"

Fred said, "Well, I just think it's really appropriate, because I am so interested in young children, that you're interviewing me next to this fountain, because you know, the control of bodily fluids is so critically important to children. And this fountain is so exuberant, and yet it contains all the fluid."

Katie Couric just looked at the camera and said, "I think we're going to go to a commercial."[38]

Fred Rogers was completely deadpan. As usual, he was thinking about children, and not so much about Katie Couric and her show.

18.

FRED ROGERS, MUSICIAN

MUSIC WAS ALWAYS A LIFELINE and an inspiration for Fred Rogers. As a young man, he'd often retreat from his parents' parties upstairs to his room, to his puppets and music. Rogers had the opportunity to infuse his show with music on nearly every level. His signature opening song, "Won't You Be My Neighbor," one of his most iconic and lasting achievements, is still sung today by longtime fans.

As he wrote to a viewer in 1984: "I think that of all the things I do, the thing I like best is composing music for the program. And I've liked musical expressions ever since I was a young boy. I remember playing the organ every Christmas Eve at our house on Weldon Street. Dad always put the soundbox out on the street so that people driving or walking by could hear the Christmas carols and other music I was playing. I have such good musical memories from childhood. That's probably one major reason why I enjoy music so much today: The adults in my young life helped me to know what value there was in things musical."[1]

For thirty-three years, Fred Rogers asked millions of "television neighbors" if it was a beautiful day in their neighborhood. The many other songs he wrote for the show, two hundred in all, as well as the musical interludes, weren't just for the children in the audience: They were key outlets for Fred Rogers's emotions, as well as a creative wellspring.

The crew on *Mister Rogers' Neighborhood* reported that when Fred became frustrated, even a little angry—most often when technological glitches would interfere with producing just the scene or sequence he was looking for—he would leave the puppet stage, move over to the piano, and just start playing. Sometimes it was quiet music, sometimes loud and powerful.

Rogers's longtime secretary Elaine Lynch recalls an incident that caused Fred Rogers to erupt in a most uncharacteristic manner: "I remember specifically when Dr. McFarland's health was failing, one of the things that Fred did was to audiotape their sessions so that he would have them to refer to. And he came in one afternoon, and he was so angry, and he was punching the machine and he was saying words I won't even repeat. And he was just upset because . . . one of the most important parts in their conversations together—and he did not know it until he tried to play it back—was not coming through on the tape. So I took the recorder and the tape from him, and I said, 'Let me see what we can do.' "2

Lynch managed to get a transcript of that part of the conversation from a local audio-recording company. And Fred took solace in his music.

From time to time, Johnny Costa would come over and play the piano with Fred. Always the crew and staff listened raptly, enjoying the break. And everyone understood that this was Fred's way of coping.

Rogers once replied to a young viewer's letter with an explanation of how important managing one's feelings can be: "You wondered if I ever get angry.

"Of course I do; everybody gets angry sometimes. But, Alex, each person has his and her way of showing angry feelings. Usually, if I'm angry, I play loud and angry sounds on the piano. . . . I think that finding ways of showing our feelings—ways that don't hurt ourselves or anybody else—is one of the most important things we can learn to do."3

As an adult, Rogers reflected on the fact that music was his emotional refuge growing up: "I was always able to cry or laugh or say I was angry through the tips of my fingers on the piano. I would go to the piano, even . . . when I was five years old, and start to play how I felt. It was very natural for me to become a composer."4

Dealing with anger was a topic Fred Rogers addressed frequently. As he explained in a 1974 letter to a brother and sister in Pennsylvania, "If I couldn't allow myself to feel angry, then I would never be able to let out the happy feelings when I am happy.

"Sometimes children think that feeling angry with another person can hurt them, but it can't. It's only the things we *do* when we are angry that can hurt."[5]

Then he sends the young fans a song called "Freedom."

In a tribute documentary about Rogers hosted by Michael Keaton that aired on PBS in 2004, Fred Rogers observes that he found solace and an outlet for his emotions in music, because he didn't want to voice things that would make him "a bad boy."[6]

Rogers often spoke in more personal and revelatory terms in speeches, perhaps because of his ability to connect to an audience, as a preacher might from the pulpit. He used his own life experiences to illuminate his many very human struggles.

For example, when he finally addressed the traumatic incident in which he was bullied and chased home from school, he shared the moment full of feeling: "I resented the pain. I resented those kids for not seeing beyond my fatness or my shyness, and what's more I didn't know that it was all right to resent it, to feel bad about it, even to feel very sad about it. I didn't know it was all right to feel any of those things, because the advice I got from the grown-ups was 'just let on you don't care, then nobody will bother you.'

"Let on you don't care! . . . I felt I had no friends, and I was told to let on that I didn't care."[7]

Fred told this story in two speeches, first in 1995 at the Saint Vincent Archabbey in Latrobe, and then in 1997 at the Memphis Theological Seminary—trusted settings. In these addresses, he has chosen to lower his guard, and he uses the story of Fat Freddy to talk about the ways in which he was shaped by the experience of suffering: "What I actually did was mourn," he continues. "I cried to myself whenever I was alone. I cried through my fingers as I made up songs on the piano. I sought out stories of other people who were poor in spirit, and I felt for them."[8]

Latrobe's richest child, with prominent parents, found common ground with others in far less advantageous material circumstances. The emotional release and comfort Fred Rogers found in music propelled many of his creative choices.

Besides the many songs Rogers wrote for *Mister Rogers' Neighborhood*, he also composed thirteen operas over the show's thirty-three-year run. And his delight in hosting performers like Tony Bennett, Rita Moreno, Mabel Mercer, and Van Cliburn was palpable in special "guest" segments. In Bennett's surpassingly charming 1975 appearance on "MGR-TV" (Lady Elaine Fairchilde's mock television studio in the Museum-Go-Round, where she interviews special guests in the Neighborhood of Make-Believe), Bennett sketches Lady Elaine, dolled up in a pink boa, before launching into a hard-swinging rendition of "It's You I Like." She swoons appreciatively.[9]

When Wynton Marsalis and the *Neighborhood* band tear into an instrumental version of the same song in a 1985 show, it's clear that Fred Rogers's music stands alone brilliantly, even without his heartfelt lyrics.

Joe "Handyman" Negri, the show's first musical advisor, notes that Fred Rogers's emphasis was often on a song's "lesson": "Fred wrote in a very simplistic harmonic way. For 'It's You I Like,' he would write chords in C major.

"Johnny [Costa] and I would do it differently, with chord changes that made it totally sophisticated, with a jazz quality to it. If I would play you 'It's You I Like' in a folk style, it would be very simple. Johnny would add chords, and I would get my shot to add sophisticated harmonies, which really changed the whole picture, and made it much more of a jazz composition.

"There's a song that he [Fred] wrote—and I think Josie Carey might have had a hand in this one—'Once Upon a Lovely Day': 'Once upon a lovely day / Your song comes along . . .' It's one of my favorites. And again . . . Fred wrote it with a very, very plain—as we say in the music business, 'vanilla' harmony—meaning just basic chords, no substitutions, nothing fancy added. Johnny and I would take that song and we would make it a lot richer with the harmonic changes."[10]

Special musical guest Wynton Marsalis grew up watching Fred Rogers's show: "It was always on a few of the PBS channels in New Orleans, Channel 26. He [Fred Rogers] was love.

"You thought that the show was not real, you know, just a show. He's not actually like that. But when I came to Pittsburgh, when I arrived, from the person who picked me up, till I came to the show . . . I'd never heard that many people speak positively, with such genuine love and kindness, toward a person that they worked for. I'd never experienced that . . . even to this day. From my initial contact with the show to being on the set, everybody else would talk about how great Fred was. And it wasn't like they were programmed; it was so honest and open.

"Then when I met him . . . it was an unbelievable pleasure to see that he was exactly as he was on the TV show. He was patient, calm, generous."[11]

Joe Negri also notes that jazz trombone player Joe Dallas came into his music store on the *Neighborhood*, as did Nathan Davis, head of jazz at the University of Pittsburgh at the time: "So there was a lot of jazz, even besides Wynton."[12]

A noted composer, virtuoso performer, and college instructor of jazz guitar, Joe Negri says: "I really would have liked to have done a lot more musically on the show. In fact, I asked specifically if I could be part of Johnny's combo . . . but I was turned down. I honestly think that it was a matter of money. If I would have done that, they would have had to pay me two salaries, an actor's salary, and a musician's salary. They didn't want to do that: that's my own personal feeling as to why I was turned down."[13]

Wynton Marsalis has a different take on whether Fred Rogers should have featured musicians like Joe Negri and Johnny Costa more prominently: "That's like when you serve me spaghetti, and I say, 'Man, it sure would be nice if we had sushi.'

"Or I go for some sushi and then I say, 'Well, sushi is great, but I thought we were having a hamburger.'

"First of all, his show [the *Neighborhood*] was so original, expos- ing people to the music, with the greatest musicians he could find, and the players that he found were fantastic. They functioned on the show the way that no other group functioned on a TV show then, except maybe on *The Tonight Show*. They had a lot of great musicians on there before Johnny Carson. What other kids' show had music on that level?

"So I would never go to that. I would say it was fantastic that he featured them."[14]

A few years after Wynton's 1986 appearance, his father, Ellis, and three of Wynton's musician brothers also appeared on the *Neighborhood* on an episode about fathers and music. With Ellis on piano, Branford on sax, Delfeayo on trombone, and a very young Jason on drums, the Marsalis family, accompanied by Joe Negri on guitar and Carl McVicker on upright bass, rip into a swinging version of another Fred Rogers composition, "Something Isn't Always."

Oldest brother Branford also reflects on the lessons they learned from their father, not necessarily about music per se, but about how to treat other people, and how to carry themselves in the world. "This has a profound effect on what we play musically," he tells Mister Rogers, who says approvingly: "You're playing from your heart."[15]

In the thirteen operas he composed for the *Neighborhood*, truly inventive flights of lyrical fancy, Fred Rogers had an opportunity to show the full range of his creative whimsy. Every winter he would go down to Florida to work with Johnny Costa on new material. Rogers wrote the music as well as the lyrics, but as noted by Chuck Aber, "Johnny put it all together."[16]

The two would compile audio tapes to send back to the cast in Pittsburgh, with Rogers singing the songs. Aber observes that "those of us who read music didn't necessarily need the tapes. But you would hear how it all would come together, and what Fred was looking for."

The two men, Rogers and Costa, from vastly different class and ethnic backgrounds, got along swimmingly. As Betty Aberlin observes,

"He [Johnny] was like pepper, and Fred was salt."[17] (In 1996, beloved musical director Johnny Costa died of cancer. For the rest of the *Neighborhood's* run, the role was taken on by Michael Moricz.)

Fred Rogers's operas, often wacky and highly imaginative, showcased his musical abilities as well as the talents of his cast. Early productions such as *Babysitter Opera* (1968), *The Three Bears* (1968), *Campsite Opera* (1968), and *Lost and Found Teddy Bear* (1969) were set in the Neighborhood of Make-Believe, presented by the usual mix of puppets and cast members. In *Campsite Opera*, for example, X the Owl is given the role of a visiting Ben Franklin. And the lost teddy bear in the 1969 production is Daniel Striped Tiger, playing the lead.

The rotating casts included John Reardon, an accomplished baritone with the Metropolitan Opera in New York, who'd known Fred Rogers since their student days at Rollins College in Florida, as well as other members of the *Neighborhood's* core troupe, such as Betty Aberlin, Don Brockett, Chuck Aber, Joe Negri, Audrey Roth, Bob Trow, François Clemmons, and Michael Horton, a trained opera singer who was behind the scenes doing puppet voices.

In an opera called *Grandad for Daniel*, Horton's puppet Betty Okonak Templeton-Jones played a starfish: "In her puppet voice, I had to explore upper registers that weren't in my normal voice."[18]

Horton reflects on the camaraderie that developed among the key players on the operas: "The fun for me was working with Audrey [Roth] and Don Brockett, although they complained incessantly about being stuck in those costumes. [I valued] any chance I had to be around the people that worked on the program—especially Betty, whom I met and became very close to, very early on. We traveled back and forth together from New York. . . .

"It was interesting to see just the process of how it worked, being a musician, because all Fred ever did was write down melody lines. In many ways, it was pretty much an improvisation, because everyone would get together at a table read, and then when it came time for you to sing your part, Fred had worked it out ahead of time with Johnny and the trio, knowing what direction he wanted it to go in. It was this great collaborative process that sort of unfolded in real time. There was no one standing there with a stopwatch, as there [was] during the taping of normal programs."

Horton clarifies the nature of the improvised element to the operas: "If there was a word that needed to be changed, sometimes—not all the time—Fred would be open to changing words. The music, it wasn't so much improvised as far as changing actual notes that people sang. . . . In the collaborative process, everyone was able to offer what they thought—though instances of that were few and far between.

"You'd normally have to have a piano in an opera rehearsal, before the orchestra shows up. But the improvisation came from them [Johnny and other musicians]. The whole musical process, aside from the actual notes and rhythms, and words on the page, was somewhat improvisational."[19]

He also notes the method in what seemed to be Fred Rogers's over-the-top whimsy. In *Grandad for Daniel*, Daniel's father is a professional polisher of the dusty leaves of plants: "Polishing, polishing, I'm polishing in the jungle," goes one of the songs.

Horton recalls: "At the time, I thought to myself, 'Wow, he [Fred] is really out there.' I'd never heard of anyone polishing leaves in the jungle. Well, up until last year, my partner and I owned a flower shop in western Maryland. We learned very quickly that all leaves have to be polished! I immediately thought back to the opera and Fred, when I thought that was crazy. I'd just never heard of it.

"It's still a weird thing to write a song about. But if your characters are in a jungle, I guess it's an accessible thing for children to think somebody does."[20]

Perhaps the most famous opera on the *Neighborhood* was *Windstorm in Bubbleland*, which appeared on May 23, 1980. The actual opera was part of a weeklong exploration called Making an Opera, in which Mister Rogers instructs his television neighbors in how stories in song are put together. A spirited song from Officer Clemmons opens one of the introductory episodes, after which Mister Rogers ambles over to Chef Brockett's bakery for instructions in how to make things with bananas, including a "banana boat," a slice of white bread spread with peanut butter and then folded around a whole banana, with pretzels inserted into the sides as oars. In a subsequent episode in which the full opera is performed, Don Brockett plays the captain of a banana boat.

Windstorm features John Reardon as an amiable television news reporter named Robert Redgate, who is always sure there's never, never, never any trouble in Bubbleland. Lady Aberlin plays Betty of Betty's Better Sweaters. Dressed in an elaborate gray costume, François Clemmons portrays a weather-forecasting porpoise, and Lady Elaine Fairchilde is Hildegarde Hummingbird, who thinks a windstorm is approaching Bubbleland, but no one believes her.

In fact, a terrible storm is brewing, thanks to the latest product on the market: Spray Sweater, created by W. I. Norton Donovan (Handyman Negri), which is the wind in disguise. Once his plan goes into effect, the wind attempts to demolish Bubbleland completely. Joe Negri notes that it was "the only time in my life that I ever had to play a bad guy. I really had to act on that—to come off like a meanie. They hooked me up to a contraption that Peter Pan used on Broadway, so that I could fly. Oh, it was a weird time."[21]

A most unlikely heroine, Hildegard Hummingbird, saves the day.

In another memorable opera, the 1982 production *Spoon Mountain*, Bob Trow plays a character called Wicked Knife and Fork, who lives atop Spoon Mountain dressed in a burlap-like costume emblazoned with a crossed knife and fork on his chest; the insignia also appears on his knit cap. But by the end, it's revealed that he's not wicked. He sings: "All I ever I wanted was a spoon, a spoon. A spoon was all I ever wanted. But all they ever gave me was a knife and fork."

Don Brockett, the local king, and Audrey Roth, the queen, finally give him a spoon. Chuck Aber, in vaguely Tyrolean attire, and Betty Aberlin as Betty Green, a park ranger, fall in love as they climb Spoon Mountain to try to rescue Purple Twirling Kitty, played by Jeff Shade, a local baton-twirling champion. Their exploits, reported on the Alpine News by a reporter played by a bearded John Reardon, are aided by a heroic commodore (François Clemmons).

Despite the somewhat outlandish story, framed by a troubadour/ storyteller (Joe Negri), the soaring, melodic score carries the opera, whose ultimate lesson is that people have a lot more in them than we may realize at first. Chuck Aber observes: "I don't know where any of that came from. It's Fred's whimsy and creativity."[22]

Adapted for the stage as well, *Spoon Mountain* was presented by the Vineyard Theatre in New York in 1984.

In a 2006 interview with arts blogger Bill Madison, Betty Aberlin notes that the operas were her favorites: "Considering that I starred in all of them, I liked them the very best," she says, tongue not far in cheek. "And because they were whimsical, they were not straitjacketed by child-development concerns."[23]

She observes: "The operas were Fred at his whimsical best. The operas still focused on the beautiful themes that were pertinent to children, but Fred was allowed to be more expressive. For some reason or another, he said that PBS was not so fond of them, but I thought they were it. I loved them."

Critic Joyce Millman noted on *Salon.com* in 1999: "These trippy productions about windstorms in Bubbleland and Wicked Knife and Fork Man's tormenting of the happy Spoon people were a cross between the innocently disjointed imaginings of a preschooler and some avant-garde opus by John Adams."[24]

Josephine the Short-Neck Giraffe, the last opera on the *Neighborhood*, was also the longest, occupying not the usual Friday slot but a Wednesday, Thursday, and Friday, in May 1989. Fred Rogers had originally written the charming story in French, as a student at Rollins College.

It's ironic that it took Fred Rogers so long to mount what became his last opera on the show. Years before, even before he debuted on the CBC, he was pitching *Josephine*, not only to Fred Rainsberry in Toronto, but also to the well-known puppeteer Bill Baird in New York City. As he sat in the waiting room at LaGuardia Airport in the spring of 1961 on his way home to Pittsburgh, Rogers wrote to answer questions that had arisen in his meeting with Baird. The puppeteer has asked about the meaning of Josephine's sadness that her neck has not grown. She wants to look like all the other giraffes.

Fred Rogers explained: "I have come to the conclusion that Josephine's neck is really a symbol—a symbol of growing up, and how difficult maturing really is. . . .

"Josephine and her short neck is really every child; for every child feels small beside his elders. And every child reacts in his own particular way to this temporary inferiority."[25]

In the version of *Josephine* presented on the *Neighborhood* in 1989, a friend of the young giraffe, Hazel, an elephant, tries to talk her into attending a school where Hazel is learning to play the trombone. Josephine's friends Bird, Butterfly, and Bee encourage her to make a short visit first to Sunflower, Frog (Aber), and Tree (Bob Trow). Chuck Aber recalls: "We're trying to convince Josephine that she's fine; we like her. But she has to figure that out from the inside out."[26]

Finally, Josephine and Hazel head off for the school, where Mr. Bulldog (Don Brockett) is the dean, and the teaching staff includes a striped elephant and a spotted elephant. Among the fellow students is J. R. Giraffe (Chuck Aber), a shy giraffe. Josephine and Hazel meet all sorts of other animals, too, including a snake that doesn't know how to hiss. Josephine attends the "Attractive Active Animals" class.

On day three of the opera, J. R. finally works up the nerve to tell Josephine that he thinks she's pretty nice. She says, "Well, I have a short neck." He says, "I just think you're nice." There's a song about it. And Sam Snake even learns to hiss.

The themes of the operas were always cleverly foreshadowed and then reinforced in the on-set segments of the show. Back at the house, Mister Rogers feeds the fish and sings an "attractive active fishes" version of "Attractive Active Animals." Then he wraps up by reemphasizing how we are all more than what we look like, punctuated by the song "You're Much More."

Thus did Fred Rogers come to demonstrate that after all these intervening years, Josephine can accept herself "just the way she is."

YO-YO MA'S SON, Nicholas, was two when his famous musician father was approached to play his cello on the *Neighborhood* for the first time, in 1985. Yo-Yo Ma appeared on the show in a sweater and jacket, given the Pittsburgh winter. He found the television lights very hot, yet Fred Rogers was in his usual cardigan, sitting close to Ma: "He sat closer and closer and closer until his face was maybe three inches from my face, and he said, 'It's so nice to see you.' The usual social distance between people was suddenly crossed into a very intimate space. Being already hot, I was totally taken aback. And I said, 'It's really nice to see you, too.' "[27]

Even this simple exchange made the thoughtful Ma reflect afterward: "One of the things that I think Mister Rogers does in such an amazingly disarming . . . way is to take away all the socialized behavior that we adopt as we become older. . . . I remember children, babies, going for your teeth, and looking really close, taking your glasses away . . . because there's no sense of that kind of social distance. By essentially relieving himself of the years of adult social behavior, Mister Rogers becomes in the same space orientation as a child."

Ma starts his first visit to the *Neighborhood* in 1985 with a warm-up rehearsal in Joe Negri's music shop. In an unscripted moment, Mister Rogers asks Yo-Yo Ma about the kind of music the world-class cellist might perform on the *Neighborhood*: "What do you feel? What would you play if you were sad, or happy, or angry?"

"So," Ma notes, "context gets to content."[28]

Ma proceeds to demonstrate these emotions in some short pieces, followed by two straight minutes of gorgeous, uninterrupted Bach, for an audience of two- and three-year-olds.

Yo-Yo Ma recalls that twenty-four years after he appeared on the *Neighborhood*, he still retains the notion that "children have an incredible capacity to concentrate on things if they are interested. It would be awful to say, 'Okay, now you're going to sit there and listen to something,' versus getting people first curious about something, and not making them come to my world, but actually going into their world. This is their show. This is what they watch. . . .

"I think that's the genius of Fred Rogers. He's the guide for the children into many, many different worlds and many, many different thought processes and feelings and fears. It's all okay.

"He never talks down to kids. It's a relationship that's based on love and respect, with boundaries."[29]

From his appearance on the *Neighborhood*, Ma feels he learned a great deal about what was behind outwardly very simple behavior. For instance, the time it takes Mister Rogers to take off his coat and put on his sweater and his sneakers "is actually the time and space it takes when a parent comes home, and you change your clothes, you feed the fish, you talk. It's in slo-mo, but that's also the time that a parent or child is open to questions and answers and familial interaction. Creating that kind of time-space relationship in the media, I thought that was really, really interesting."

In an interview, Ma called the *Neighborhood* a "safe show," in that the musical transitions provided children in the television audience with a kind of safety net: "Going from the unfamiliar, the foreign, to the familiar, is a lifelong enterprise and a lifelong sense of habits that we hopefully practice. I think Mister Rogers 'gets it' by creating the safe place on television, [so as] to actually make sure that the unsafe feelings that one has, well, let's say, in exploring music or in exploring life, [are] in context of something that is supported, that is as basic as—well, the most precious thing, unconditional love. . . .

". . . Some people are beautiful on the outside, and some people are beautiful on the inside. Somehow both the external and the internal are always part of the package and inseparable. . . . In those two simple ways, he addresses many people's fears about 'Well, I don't look good' or 'I don't feel good.' But maybe if you know you're beautiful on the inside, that actually makes you beautiful on the outside.

"I think these things are extremely basic, and yet hard to actually practice. The fact that he unabashedly is able to say these things is an incredibly important thing in our society, not just for young people, but for adults also."[30]

Yo-Yo Ma appeared on the *Neighborhood* a second time, in 1990, with his son, Nicholas, who joins him and Mister Rogers on piano for a spirited rendition of "The Skater's Waltz," composed in 1882 by Frenchman Emile Waldteufel.

In the ultimate accolade, Ma says that if someone asks him what he's really proud of, it would be appearing on Fred Rogers's show: "He really influenced kids to say—if music happened to be the thing that struck, so to speak, a chord in their lives, they actually would ask for it and get it. Twenty years later they're musicians, and they trace it back to a *Mister Rogers' Neighborhood* show. That's pretty amazing."

Another lesson Ma learned on the *Neighborhood*: "Very little of what I think about when I work with professional orchestras is about—it's never a hierarchical proposition. We're all on the same level playing field trying to do something together, and I think that's straight out of the Fred Rogers playbook."

Yo-Yo Ma and his wife remained friends with Fred and Joanne Rogers for years. After Rogers's death in 2003, says Ma, he remembered not the many memorials and tributes. Instead, "I remember Fred very vividly as a person that is incredibly alive. I remember palpably the words, the tone, the attitude, the gentleness."[31]

Wynton Marsalis also reflects on the way his appearance on the *Neighborhood* made an impact that stays with him, many years later: "Going on his show, and seeing the respect in how he treated people, the way that the show operated, and the type of respect and love people had for him—it's something that I've worked on throughout my career. And I definitely always think of that in terms of him. That's the thing that stuck with me the most of everything. Wow, this guy . . . this is really how he is. To be congruent that way . . .

"There's that gospel song, 'I'm Gonna Live the Life I Sing About in My Songs' . . . You know, like that."[32]

A few years after Marsalis appeared on the *Neighborhood*, in 1992, he and Fred Rogers both received honorary doctorates from Boston University. As he recalls, "I was always the youngest person receiving a doctorate. I got a lot of honorary doctorates. I was almost always the favorite of the students, you know, if they'd heard of me. You think, okay, young, this jazz guy. But for Mister Rogers, the type of love, the spirit, the energy that those students had for him: 'Mister Rogers, Mister Rogers . . .' Here were all these college kids from the counterculture, trying to be hip.

"Boy, it was unabashed love everywhere he went. It was so deserved. I was part of the crowd! They all wanted to see him, get their pictures taken with him."[33]

FRED ROGERS WAS ENCHANTED by all aspects of music and performance. On one of the very first shows, in 1968, when the *Neighborhood* was still in black and white, Mister Rogers hosts an experimental electronic musician and inventor named Bruce Haack and his cohort Esther Nelson, a dancer, who leads kids through exercises that echo the sounds of Haack's homemade analog synthesizer, constructed from household objects.

Pianist André Watts, violinist Itzhak Perlman, and the cast of the off-Broadway percussion-based show *STOMP* also made visits to the *Neighborhood*. Mister Rogers made a game attempt to stomp along with the cast. He even tried a few moonwalks with young break-dancer Jermaine Vaughn, who appeared to pop and lock on the *Neighborhood* in 1985.

Also in 1985, Rogers devoted a week's worth of shows to "making music," including a visit to a factory that makes cellos and other stringed instruments; a stop into a rehearsal of the Empire Brass Ensemble, whose members demonstrate the different sounds made by a tuba and a French horn; and a look at the exotically populated studio of an instrument collector, whose pieces span the globe.

In a Neighborhood of Make-Believe sequence that spans the entire week, King Friday orders all his subjects to attend a bass violin festival—a celebration of his own instrument.

All his subjects strive to address the theme, while also remaining true to their own special skills. Several violin puppets join the fray. Lady

Aberlin dances with a large bass violin, and Miss Paulifficate (Audrey Roth) tap dances wearing an elaborate costume that culminates with a bass violin on her head. A trio of girl "pages" wearing violins on their heads, too, plays a fanfare that fulfills King Friday's desire for a most royal occasion.

Whimsical, often hilarious, the week's story lines all circle back to a basic theme: You can be a master of "the mad that you feel" by expressing your special talent, whatever it may be. Mister Rogers wants you to know, as always, that he likes you just the way you are—bass violin specialist or not.

19.

MISTER ROGERS'S FAMILY VALUES

THROUGHOUT HIS LONG CAREER, Fred Rogers allowed advertising only to adults. His attitude toward advertising to children had always been consistent. Commercial exploitation of children's TV dated back to the 1950s, when Dr. Frances Horwich, Miss Frances as host of NBC's *Ding Dong School*, damaged her teaching credibility in the eyes of many child development specialists with overt hucksterism of sponsored products, including Wheaties and One A Day vitamins.

Rogers's ban on commercials sprang from the teaching of Margaret McFarland; the immorality of advertising to young children became one of his ironclad beliefs. He never allowed advertising on the *Neighborhood* that targeted kids, for fear that young viewers couldn't tell the difference between product pitches and the educational content of the show.

But as Family Communications, Inc. (FCI) executive Basil Cox points out, Rogers didn't object to the marketplace per se, given that the *Neighborhood* needed to subsidize the grants it received for many years from PBS and Sears-Roebuck. And Fred Rogers wanted the largest possible audience for his books, records, videos, and other materials as long as his standards were observed: "Fred was very anxious to have his products in the marketplace, very anxious to have his ideas in the marketplace, and to have his representations of his characters in the marketplace. But under very defined circumstances."[1]

In fact, when Cox first joined FCI in 1974, Hoagy Carmichael Jr., then director of public relations for the *Neighborhood*, had initiated a newsletter called *Around the Neighborhood*, sold directly to subscribers.

Cox notes: "Fred was very enthusiastic about it. It was aggressively advertised through direct mail . . . and Fred did not have a problem with that." Still, it didn't work commercially and was shut down.[2]

Rogers's aversion to turning children into consumers was unique in American television. Operating in a free-market system, protected by the First Amendment, advertisers felt no constraint about going after young children who could push their parents to buy things. *The Howdy Doody Show* sold souvenirs and artifacts through the 1950s, including T-shirts, lunch boxes, and comic books, generating millions in revenue for NBC.

Humorist Dave Barry wrote: "They could have advertised the official Howdy Doody edition of all sixteen volumes of *Remembrance of Things Past* by Marcel Proust in the original French, and we would have begged our parents for it."[3]

Even Jim Henson, creator of *Sesame Street*'s Muppets, made a deal with the Walt Disney Company to market his characters to kids. *Sesame Street* spun off a variety of products. As Basil Cox notes: "Nothing that *Sesame Street* did commercially was offensive. It was just much more successful, because it was much more widely watched, and much more widely appreciated by adults."[4]

One notable exception in avoiding commercial product lures was Burr Tillstrom, creator of *Kukla, Fran and Ollie*, who turned down multiple offers in the 1950s to convert his beloved puppets, as real to him as people, into toys; he had no desire to see replicas on store shelves.

Though Fred Rogers later approved the sale of replicas of some of the *Neighborhood* puppets and other artifacts to adults—parents, grandparents, teachers—he remained adamant that they not be marketed to kids. Eliot Daley, who joined Rogers's staff in the early 1970s, initiated a Mister Rogers Toy of the Month Club. But as he recalls, the toys "just turned out to be garbage. I don't know whether I got seduced by the big money up front . . . and whether I needed the money for working capital. I was so grateful when it turned out to be a complete disaster, and nobody bought them [the toys]."[5]

For the most part, any product associated with Mister Rogers had to meet Fred Rogers's usual high standards. According to Bill Isler, who joined FCI in 1984 and later became its president, "Fred was really a Good Housekeeping Seal of Approval as far as companies were concerned."[6]

In 1983, Fred Rogers had just donated one of the cardigans his mother made him to the collection at the Smithsonian. When Isler arrived, he teased Rogers about his newly iconic status, calling him "a franchise." But even when "the franchise" approved a product, Rogers was a highly reluctant marketer whose promotional appearances—predictably mobbed by fans—suffered logistically from the amount of time he felt compelled to give each child.

Fred Rogers's longtime colleague and friend David Newell notes that Rogers wasn't comfortable going on national tours to promote his videos and books and records: "His marketing views again reflected his respect for his audience. He would rather spend his time creating another program or writing music that would directly help his audience than being out on the road."[7]

Successful Mister Rogers products like the Plan and Play vacation guide for kids helped to augment the *Neighborhood*'s steady support from Sears and PBS, but if Fred Rogers had been a more active and enthusiastic promoter, "It would have been a different ballgame," observes former FCI president Bill Isler.[8]

Interestingly, for home videos and other deals, Fred Rogers was represented by the powerhouse talent agency IMG, contacted via his old Latrobe friend and former classmate Arnold Palmer.

Still, Rogers's integrity barred him for the rest of his life from profiting from any enterprise that involved selling directly to children. According to Joanne Rogers, even though Fred was courted several times by national television networks, the talk ended as soon as the network executives "knew how he felt about selling cereal."[9]

Rogers's antipathy to advertising extended to anything that might be construed as fooling a child; he viewed himself as a powerful mentor who must never abuse children's trust by pretending to be something else. He once told David Newell about a conversation he had with a network executive that went sour when the executive asked what Rogers would wear as host of a network show.

"The executive wanted some sort of costume," says Newell. "Fred said, 'Well, then, it looks as if this interview is over.' "[10]

In the spring of 1984, Burger King used Rogers's image in a commercial featuring an actor called "Mister Rodney," who dressed in a cardigan and sneakers to attack the product of their rival, McDonald's. In the spot, Mister Rodney holds up a flashcard with the word "McFrying," which is what McDonald's does to their burgers. Mister Rodney was clearly more in favor of Burger King's flame-broiled method.

As Fred Rogers's former colleague Eliot Daley notes: "This guy was so good that the first time I saw it, I thought: God, they must have just pirated some videotape of Fred, and cut and stitched, and put this thing together, and did a dub, or something. Because this guy was—he was Fred. It was just chilling."[11]

The executives at Burger King had not contacted Rogers's company, FCI, before airing the ad. Once Fred Rogers's staff told him about it, he called a press conference to state unequivocally that he did not endorse the company's use of his character or likeness.

Daley adds: "Fred was a rabid vegetarian, and the notion of selling hot, dead cow meat to children was just—you know, it was the most distressed, I think, I've ever seen him."[12]

Rather than suing Burger King, Fred Rogers preferred a direct approach, and contacted Don Dempsey, Burger King's senior vice president for marketing, who produced the ad with the agency J. Walter Thompson.

As recalled by Eliot Daley: "As I understood it later from both parties, Fred opened the conversation by introducing himself, and asking this guy, 'Are you by any chance a father?' And the guy said yes, he is. And he says, 'Do your children know what you do?'

"And he said, 'Well yes, they've got some sense that I come here to work, and they like to go into Burger King stores,' and so forth.

"Fred said, 'Well that's wonderful. It must feel great to have them know and appreciate, and be proud of what you do.' He said, 'What do you think it would be like if they misunderstood what you do? Actually, if they thought that what you do was something bad, or you know, harmful to people, or the food that you were selling them was not good for them? And if they lost respect for what you do?'

"They chatted on a little bit more about what a bad thing that would be. So they hung up. About ten seconds later, the phone rings at J. Walter Thompson, and it's this guy saying, 'Pull those damn commercials off the air. I want them erased, destroyed. I don't ever want them seen again.'"[13]

Within seventy-two hours, an ad campaign that cost Burger King 150,000 dollars and had been on the air for only a week was pulled.

In 1990, Fred Rogers took a different approach, joining Family Communications, Inc., in suing the White Knights of the Ku Klux Klan and three men to stop them from using tape-recorded telephone messages that imitated the theme music on *Mister Rogers' Neighborhood* and Rogers's voice. It was one of the few times Rogers took legal action against people and organizations that used his popularity to advance their own agendas and causes.[14]

Fred Rogers's refusal to abide by the rules of the marketplace, along with his gentle, slow approach to programming overall, left him open to criticism that he was coddling children and giving them unrealistic expectations of the harsh world they would someday enter.

Don Feder, a nationally syndicated columnist for the *Boston Herald*, summed it up: "For over twenty-five years on his PBS series, Fred Rogers has been filling the innocent heads of children with this pap. . . . Under a self-esteem regime, America is becoming a nation of feel-good mediocrities."[15]

But Rogers's critics are guilty of ignoring great volumes of his work that emphasize personal responsibility and discipline on the parts of children and their parents and teachers. Fred Rogers always believed in a balance between cognitive and emotional content, and he tried to give appropriate weight to the need for discipline and focus. In fact, he produced an entire theme week of episodes just on the topic of discipline. In all his books, his speeches, his letters to children and parents, his scripts, even the lyrics to his songs, Fred repeatedly emphasized personal responsibility.

The difference is that Rogers honed in on the cultivation of self-discipline rather than an emphasis on parents and teachers dropping the proverbial hammer. Fred Rogers felt very strongly—backed by the research of child-development mentors—that the most effective gift to young children is nurturing the capacity for self-discipline rather than the imposition of it. He recognized the importance, and the value, of outside discipline, but he thought lasting benefit for the child came from developing the ability to concentrate and hold yourself accountable for your own actions. Fred Rogers was committed to helping young children find and evolve their own capacities, including that of self-discipline, because he believed it would make them stronger adults.

He famously declared: "I think of discipline as the continual everyday process of helping a child learn self-discipline."[16] His Family Communications, Inc., production company even created a training workshop—complete with guides, videos, handouts, and DVDs— entitled "Learning Discipline—Connecting Discipline, Communications and Relationships." It reflects Rogers's layered approach to learning, always examining the connections that help children reach their own potential. His work stands as a stark contrast to the simplistic, black-and-white perspective of many of his critics.

AND WHAT OF Fred Rogers's philosophy about discipline when it came to his own children? It changed a great deal once they became teenagers—a time of life with which he was far less comfortable. Joanne Rogers's recollection of Fred's parenting style is that he almost always was, as he was on *Mister Rogers' Neighborhood*, quiet and gentle and understanding with his two sons, particularly when they were very little. But as they grew into their teenage years, Fred was often mystified about how to handle them.

One day in the mid-1970s, Joanne Rogers saw a sliver of light coming from a blocked-off area in her basement where she hadn't even known there was a space. She and Fred and the boys had moved into the big old Pittsburgh house—some would call it a mansion—on Beechwood Boulevard when they returned from Toronto. The basement seemed enormous, containing room after room. Puzzled, Joanne found her way to the small enclosure and was amazed to discover "grow lamps" installed by her teenage sons, Jim and John, for the marijuana plants they were cultivating right there in the basement.

Joanne was stunned, but also a little amused: She later speculated that at least it showed some entrepreneurial energy on the boys' part. Their father was not so easygoing. "He was furious," says Joanne. "It was illegal, for one thing . . . many people would have loved to have that story out there and . . . he was really, really angry and he went up and got them."[17] Fred didn't get angry very often, and he didn't stay angry very long. But he did make the boys clean up the basement garden and destroy the plants in the backyard.

Though Jim and John weren't happy to lose the crop, they felt their father was fair with them.

John later recounted how angry Fred got when John—driving his girlfriend home on an icy winter night in Pittsburgh—wrecked the car his father had given him to drive himself back and forth to school. "I have never seen him that angry. I didn't think he got angry," said John years later.[18]

Fred and his son "yelled and screamed at each other for an hour," John added. After they quieted down, Fred Rogers told his son, "You know, I feel much better now," and the two agreed they had gotten a much-needed release of tension that had been building between them. John also said he was pleased that his father trusted him enough to get angry.

John also got into trouble cruising in a twenty-two-foot-long black Cadillac limousine that he borrowed from an aunt and later purchased from his grandmother's estate. While a high school senior, he and a crew of friends drove to West Virginia to buy beer. In an interview, he admitted: "We had about five, six, seven people in the thing [the limo] smoking a little bit of something. . . .

"Well, a policeman comes up and this thing is full of smoke . . . I lowered the window and the smoke went right in his face. He said, 'You are going to have to leave now, the park is closed.' And that's all he did. We lucked out."[19]

After another encounter with a cop when John plowed into some parked cars after he'd been drinking, John Rogers began to wonder if his luck was wearing thin.

After one or the other of the boys got into a scrape, they'd convene with Fred and Joanne for a family meeting. All four of them would sit down to hash out the offending incident. John remembers that Joanne told the boys once when they were in their early teens: " 'You know, we are just four different people living in the same house.'

"I was thinking, yes, you are probably right. Of course, then my brother and I would go out on the roof and smoke and things."[20]

Joanne was the parent who delivered punishment in the Rogers family. "Fred would be very, very patient," recalls Joanne, "and I wasn't."[21] She adds that she was not opposed to spanking when the boys were young. Both Rogers boys went to private schools: both to St. Edmund's Academy in the Squirrel Hill neighborhood of Pittsburgh, where the family lived, then Jim to Shady Side Academy outside Pittsburgh, and John to Sewickley Academy in Sewickley, Pennsylvania, after a stint in the public schools of Latrobe.

Joanne reports that although Fred never blamed her or himself for the boys' struggles in adolescence, "I think he saw this as, well, they're adolescents, and what are you going to do about it."[22] When Jim went off to college, to Rollins, he stopped communicating with his parents for a time.

The rift became public knowledge when an article appeared in *People* magazine in May 1978 under the headline, "Fred Rogers Moves into a New Neighborhood—and So Does His Rebellious Son."

It noted: "Most kids rebel against their parents sooner or later. But Jim Rogers is having a harder time than other 18-year-olds telling his father to buzz off. Jim's pop is not just any Mister Rogers. He's the Mister Rogers, for 24 years the gentle host of public TV's *Mister Rogers' Neighborhood* and a paragon of parental understanding. A freshman at his dad's alma mater, Rollins College in Florida, Jim has stopped writing his folks or even returning their phone calls. 'He's flown the coop,' sighs his father."[23]

Joanne saw Jim's behavior as a continuation of adolescent rebellion: "It's been a difficult year. There's real hostility."[24]

But Fred, always the intellectual when it came to children and parenting, sought to support his son. "It's been painful, and it's rough on Jamie," he said. "But if we don't allow him to go off and have this time for himself, he'll never come back to the nest."[25]

Neither Rogers son finished college, but both have grown up to be family men as committed to their children as Fred and Joanne were.

Fred Rogers always did his best to be an involved parent, despite his rigorous schedule. When he was just starting out in television, he took great pains to be home for supper. His older son, Jim, remembers that sometimes Fred was so rushed that he came in still wearing his pancake makeup. As his sons grew, though, he often had to travel, and both boys missed him. Joanne reported that later in life he worried he'd let them down by being so absorbed in his work. Staffers also worried about the amount of time Fred Rogers gave to people they called "birds with broken wings," needy people who took up a lot of his time.

Joanne Rogers observes that for Fred, "The work never ended. He had three or four people who called . . . oftentimes they were young people that he felt might need his advice, and they were almost always long-winded. Needy people were attracted to him; I do think that that was part of his ministry."[26]

Dr. William Hirsch, a great family friend who often had holiday dinners with the family, recalls that Fred once confided in him, "My life would have been so different if the boys had just had a more easy time going through that part of their life."[27] (Rogers was referring to his sons' adolescent years.)

Fred Rogers put in long hours at the studio. Joanne observes: "It was hard work. And he would be very tired by the time he got home. And I, of course, had been driving the kids, and running around with them. So I would be pretty worn-out, too."[28]

Jim Rogers recalls the family's routine: "When Dad was in the studio, that would be hectic in the evening because he was rushing home from work, in order to sit down with us for dinner. But on days that he wasn't in the studio, he would come home from the office around five o'clock and that would be quiet time, and we all went to our rooms and Dad took a nap. We were told, 'You don't have to take a nap; it's not nap time, it's just quiet time. You can do whatever you want, but you do it quietly.'

"That would last, as I say, from about five o'clock till about six o'clock, and then it would be dinnertime. And then we'd be just as raucous as we wanted to be until it was bedtime. But that was a staple in the house, quiet time."[29]

Dinner could sometimes be less than quiet, especially from Joanne Rogers's perspective: "At dinner, I think they [their sons] knew exactly which buttons to push, and they would say, 'Yuck,' when they saw the food."[30]

Fred Rogers did not force his vegetarianism on the rest of the family. Jim recalls: "We had a woman who cooked for us for years, Dolores Johnson, and I know that she would tear her hair out every time he'd come up with something else that he didn't want to eat. . . . But she got to be quite a wizard with the tofu. Dolores would cook one thing for Mom and John and me and then something else for Dad."[31] Fred Rogers did have a sweet tooth, and he was a fan of the plum pudding (prune whip) at Stouffer's as well as ice cream at Baskin-Robbins.

Never having had siblings, Joanne had no way to gauge if her sons' behavior at the dinner table was particularly bad for two young boys less than two years apart in age. She notes: "I thought sometimes they were going to kill each other. They tussled, and roughhoused so much. . . . And they could get me right down to their level sometimes. But Fred was so patient with them. He was extremely patient."[32]

Joanne would wait to see if Fred Rogers would chide the boys for their behavior: "It didn't come, and I'd end up saying, 'OK, that's it, you've had it.' Or worse."

Jim Rogers, who saw his paternal grandfather as a "stern, kind of austere man," speculates that Fred Rogers's own upbringing had a lot to do with his unwillingness to crack down more on his sons: "I guarantee you that the way he was treated growing up, was, 'Say hello to the nice people and then go back upstairs.' You didn't hear about a whole lot of horseplay in that household."[33]

Ironically, John Rogers, the younger son, observed in an interview that "Maybe there was a little too much self-discipline in our family, for my brother and me. Meaning that we weren't ready for the self-discipline that maybe was exuded upon us. . . . I often feel that—I don't know if we want to use the term—the hammer should have come down a little harder; more limits should have been set."[34]

Overall, "I consider them both good parents, and both parents that were involved in their kids' lives. And of course, Dad was very busy. But he was also around a lot, and Mom was around a lot."

Growing up, the two Rogers sons dealt with their father's notoriety in somewhat different ways. When they were little, Jim and John Rogers would see their father on television and point to the set and say, "Other Daddy."

As Joanne Rogers describes it, "John, the younger one, was always very ready to tell people who his daddy was."[35]

John has happy memories of "going to the studio to watch them tape the show. I knew the whole staff there. It was a like a big family, a huge family."[36] He recalls visiting the set of the *Neighborhood* often from around ages eight to fifteen, and sometimes wondering how his dad could stand the heat from the lights on set. Henrietta Pussycat was his favorite puppet.

Jim Rogers notes that the two boys could differentiate the television Mister Rogers from their father since they could see what went into making the *Neighborhood*: "I saw it much more as, 'This is my dad at home. That's my dad at work.' It's all so seamless when you watch the episode on television, and yet if you go to the studio and you see them screaming, 'Cut,' every five minutes . . . and everything being shot out of sequence. . . . From a very early age, I realized this is my dad working. Watching it on television, it would be the final product of the work."[37]

Jim's favorite part of visiting the set was looking at the miniature model of the town shown at the start of every episode: "It was about, I would say, four feet by four feet and was up on a table. It had all these little cardboard houses . . . and little, tiny Matchbox cars on the little streets."

He remembers moving the miniature cars from one side of the model street to the other: "Being small . . . it was kind of like being a giant . . . a sort of Godzilla feeling."

When asked about the misconceptions people may have had about Fred Rogers, Jim cites the mistaken impression that his father was in any way intellectually slow, because of his manner of speech as Mister Rogers: "I think he can come off sounding slow, almost simple, if you will, and yet he was one of the most quick-witted people I've ever known. People always say, 'Boy, is he really like that when he comes home?'

"And for the most part, 'Yeah, what you see is what you get, except that he's not talking to a three-year-old anymore now; now he's talking with us.' He was very quick-witted, very funny, very down to earth."[38]

At home, the whole family often watched Rogers's older shows, such as *The Children's Corner*, on sixteen-millimeter film.

Fred Rogers mined family life for ideas for the *Neighborhood*. Jim recalls: "There were times that I would tell Dad . . . about something that was bothering me, and six months later you'd see it on TV. . . . It was strange. Again, it's sort of that life-in-a-fishbowl thing. But it was always honest, and it wasn't a mockery of anything, it wasn't a parody. . . . It was genuine and heartfelt, so I always took that as, okay, that's a good thing, then."[39]

As Dad, Fred Rogers would proclaim: "I don't like television. We need to limit the television in this house." The regimen was one hour of TV a day. The one show they watched as a family was *The Waltons*, every Thursday night at 8:00 P.M. The family even visited the show's set in Hollywood. Sometimes *Dr. Quinn, Medicine Woman* was also on the very limited viewing list. Later, in 1996 when the boys were grown, Fred Rogers made a guest appearance on *Dr. Quinn*, the only time he adopted a fictional role on television. In an episode called "Deal with the Devil," he plays, appropriately enough, a frontier minister.

Jim Rogers recalls his father's unusual enthusiasm for a new show that he previewed one night for the family: "I can remember being probably ten or eleven, and Dad came home from work one day with a videotape. He said, 'I have something you have to watch.' "[40]

WQED was considering offering it, and program director Sam Silberman had asked for Fred Rogers's input for a show featuring six guys from England—the first four or five episodes of *Monty Python's Flying Circus*. "Well, we just howled watching this," Jim recalls. "It was just so up his alley."

"As gentle as Dad was, this was one of those paradoxes. *Monty Python* is not particularly gentle. They think nothing of dropping a sixteen-ton weight on somebody to end a skit. For some reason, [the parrot sketch] just tickled Dad so much—a man waving a parrot around and talking about how he wanted his money back because he had bought this dead parrot.

"At the same time, he had no use for what you would call today satire or making jokes at the expense of other people. . . . He never saw anything funny in that, and yet something ridiculously silly would just put him on the floor."

Listening to music was much more encouraged for the Rogers sons than TV viewing. Fred Rogers was attuned to both music and the lack of it. Jim Rogers describes his father as "aggressively quiet. He often spoke very softly and slowly, and it was a way, I think, of getting people to really pay attention. We would go to restaurants sometimes and there would be Muzak playing in the background. More often than not he would ask the manager . . . if they could possibly turn off the Muzak, because he felt that that undercurrent of noise took away from conversation and from communication with other people."[41]

Usually when they were out in public, Fred Rogers tried to maintain a low-key profile, taking a table in restaurants off to the side or in the back. When recognized, he was too honest to deny his identity, but, said Jim, "it wasn't that he craved the attention, but if the attention came his way, he certainly acknowledged it, and was as gracious as he could be with people."

At some point, Fred Rogers realized that rather than give autographs, it was more meaningful to get people to write their name and address on a piece of paper, and then send them a photograph that he would take of them. This became a signature part of his typical exchange with fans, who were pleased to get photos of themselves shot by Fred Rogers.

Both sons were often asked if Fred Rogers wore his cardigan sweater around the house. John replies: "No, no, no. He wore a little jumpsuit. That's what he wore a lot of the time. You know, he had comfy clothes. He either had those on, or he was in a suit. Dad always wore a suit: mainly either a tie and a shirt—bow tie, mainly [. . .] or a turtleneck and a jacket. He kept some of that formal feel."[42]

Jim Rogers describes his father's style: "It ran the gamut from understated elegance to the jumpsuits. They were zip-up in varying odd colors because he was color-blind and he couldn't really tell—everything looked sort of brownish to him. He'd have these powder-blue jumpsuits: 'Dad, what are you doing?' But if it wasn't the jumpsuit, then it was a pair of slacks and a shirt with a tie, a bow tie sometimes."[43]

Once on an airplane, Rogers was sitting in his blazer and his bow tie when a flight attendant came over and tapped him on the shoulder and said, "I don't mean to disturb you, but I just wanted to tell you how much I like your popcorn." She thought he was Orville Redenbacher.

"For somebody that is recognized all the time, he just thought it was wonderful to be recognized as somebody else. He never got tired of telling that one," Jim Rogers remembers.

For part of his high school years, John Rogers went to Latrobe High School, staying during the week with Fred Rogers's cousins. But complications arose: "The Latrobe Die Casting Company, which was my grandfather's company years prior to that, was having a strike. It was a wildcat strike, and they were burning people in effigy." John Rogers switched schools, coming back to Pittsburgh.[44]

Both Rogers sons have memories of many happy times in the Crooked House on Nantucket.

When Fred Rogers was composing during the summers on Nantucket, John recalls that "you could hear the music through the windows . . . right into the garage area." Rogers often asked his family for input on his new compositions. John's favorite was music from the opera *Josephine the Short-Neck Giraffe*. He and his father collaborated on a simple song called "Tree, Tree, Tree" when John was only three.

Jim remembers his father always being confident about the music, but less so about the words: "It was the lyric that he wanted input on."[45]

Though there were visits at their home in Pittsburgh from famous family friends like Bill Bixby, John describes a "pretty normal" upbringing: "Dad always raised us in a way that we didn't have to feel like fancy people. We needed to feel like we were comfortable people. And just comfortable."[46] Despite the fact that they had help at home cleaning and cooking, "Mom got out the Hoover, once in a while. We all did." The boys had chores, like cutting the grass at their grandparents' home in Latrobe, and received small allowances.

Joanne notes that Jim, the older son, never mentioned his father's television fame: "He [Fred] went to visit him at college one time—the first time he went down to visit him at college—and they were all just, you know, like that [makes a surprised face], because he hadn't told a soul."[47]

Jim tells it a little differently: "The way I treated it was it was much more about, this is what he does for a living. This is his job. Your dad's a doctor, your dad's a lawyer, and my dad's on television. The only difference being you don't get to go home and watch your dad on TV, watch him lawyering or doctoring or whatever . . . that carried on, too, as I got older."[48]

When people he worked with, or went to school with, asked him why he hadn't told them about his dad, he would say: " 'Well, I don't know. It just sort of never came up, I guess. You didn't tell me what your dad did, either.'

"It's not that I wasn't proud of him; it's just that, again, it wasn't who he was; it was his job. And unlike a lot of people, he was able to put a lot of who he was into his job. But it wasn't a be-all and end-all."

Joanne Rogers points out that though Fred was a vegetarian who swam every day ("He did so many things in a healthy way") he didn't know how to take a vacation "without having an agenda. He just wanted everybody to be busy, and constructively doing something. He didn't understand about just sitting there and looking at the ocean. I'm just completely opposite . . . that's why I think we got along, probably."[49]

Jim Rogers recalled that his father feared not being as responsive to children—his own or any others—as much as they needed. Once, Ben Carson, the famed neurosurgeon at Johns Hopkins Hospital in Baltimore, asked Fred to talk on the phone with a little girl who was about to undergo surgery. Rogers did so; then after the conversation ended, impulsively he took a plane to Baltimore to comfort the child in person. Having a parent subject to such compulsions must have bemused his sons on occasion, but they knew their father loved them.

When interviewed by a *New York Times* reporter who asked what it was like to be Fred Rogers's son, John replied: "Well, it's hard to make a comparison, because he's the only father I have."[50]

He added, "I thought, 'I hope you don't think that's smart-alecky.' . . . Dad's very normal and natural. He's not a Clint Eastwood or some high-powered actor. He's himself. He's himself, and he wants us all to be ourselves, and . . . to be comfortable. He's not a fancy person."

Like many children of well-known people, John Rogers struggled to establish his own identity. But the message from Fred Rogers was lived as well as told: "Dad was a very 'fancy on the inside and not fancy on the outside' type of person. One of his quotes to me [was] 'The richer we are, the less we need,' meaning stuff—that we're richer if we don't need much."

John also cited an example of Fred Rogers's notorious frugality: "When he could park his vehicle at a meter for twenty-five cents, versus paying two dollars and fifty cents at the parking lot at the PAA [Pittsburgh Athletic Association], where would he park? He'd park at the meter. He was the most laid-back, unfancy type of person you can think of, for being in his position."

Fred Rogers didn't discuss his good works or television successes with his sons. As John puts it, "Dad never talked too much about his accomplishments. He always wanted to hear about yours."[51]

In New York City, Fred and Joanne Rogers owned a condo on West Fifty-Sixth Street between Eighth and Ninth Avenues. Father Douglas Nowicki told John Rogers the story of how Fred looked out the window and saw a man being beaten on the street. Rogers went down to the street, and went over to the man as he was about to limp away. Fred Rogers handed the man a hundred-dollar bill and told him, "I just want you to know that somebody in this world loves you."

John Rogers sees his family's heritage as one of compassion: "I hear a lot of these stories about my grandmother and my grandfather, so I know that Dad got a lot of that from them. They may have been more fancy on the outside, but they also did a lot of fancy-on-the-inside stuff . . . they did some fabulous things for people."[52]

Both Jim and John Rogers have sons of their own. Jim notes that Fred Rogers "loved being a grandfather. I think it was very liberating for him. I can remember him chasing Alex [one of Fred Rogers's grandsons] around a tree when we lived in Squirrel Hill. . . . It was almost as though he was a kid again. . . .

"He always used to tell me, 'Thank you for allowing me to remember what it's like to be a child.' He was reconnecting again with his childhood."[53]

Whatever his personal foibles, Jim Rogers observes, his father had only one real touchstone: "Being who you are was so important to him that the only thing that would really upset him was phoniness. As long as I was being genuine and honest, he respected that."

He adds: "I think all Dad really ever wanted for John or me was to be happy and pleased with who we are."[54]

20.

FEARLESS AUTHENTICITY

IN HIS OFFICE at *Esquire* magazine on Fifty-Fifth Street between Seventh and Eighth Avenues in Manhattan, Tom Junod was working on a profile of Fred Rogers for a special 1998 issue on "new American heroes." A self-described "bad-boy journalist" who had cultivated a reputation for controversy, Junod was uncomfortable about tackling such a goody-goody, and wasn't sure how to approach the article.

"When I called, I heard that unmistakable voice. What was amazing about Fred was that he was the exact same person he was on TV. There was no show, no act—that was him."[1]

Junod was discovering the same thing everyone did: Fred Rogers *was* Mister Rogers—the identical, authentic person in every setting. And he treated everyone the same, from the president of PBS to the doorman at his apartment building in New York to the little girl who stopped him on the street to get his autograph. All were met with kindness, hospitality, and respect.

But Tom Junod also discovered that Fred Rogers was not quite as simple as the man on television who spoke so slowly to preschool kids: "Though his [Rogers's] trust was absolute, his ability to draw a person in on his own terms was an incredibly powerful thing.

"I look at Fred as a complicated person who chose simplicity, but at the same time, Fred was a powerful, powerful person. He was spiritually powerful, but he was also interpersonally powerful. It wasn't as if Fred was continually deferring to you. It was not like that at all. Fred was very, very active in engaging you, but in the way he wanted to engage you."[2]

When Junod called, Fred Rogers pointed out that he was not in Pittsburgh, but in his Manhattan apartment near the *Esquire* offices; why didn't Tom just come on over? Never mind the fact that Rogers was still in his bathrobe, and no one at Family Communications, Inc., in Pittsburgh had vetted Junod.

Years later, Junod recalled that when he got to the building where Fred Rogers lived when he was in the city, "Fred was waiting at the door . . . in his [flimsy, old] bathrobe . . . with his white skinny legs and his socks pulled up, with this big smile on his face."

After this totally disarming introduction, Junod unexpectedly found himself at the other end of the interviewing process. Successful journalists try to get people to reflect on themselves, but Fred Rogers had other ideas: "Fred was incredibly artful at deflecting questions. . . . It was impossible to get him to answer a question. He always threw it back to you."

Soon Tom Junod was telling Fred Rogers about Old Rabbit, his "special friend" when Junod was a kid. Then Joanne Rogers called. Fred introduced Junod to her on the phone, and Junod had his picture taken by the man he was supposed to be profiling: "All of a sudden, it was as if I was a character on one of Fred's shows."[3]

By the time Junod had finished a long series of interviews with Rogers and everyone around him, he was ready to write the most positive profile he'd ever written about anyone—one of the most positive *Esquire* ever published.

At the end of their time together, Junod concluded in a later interview: "People, I think, spoke of Fred as a childlike person. I don't think so. I think that Fred was very, very grown up in that he protected that childlike aspect of him. He was obviously not an unsophisticated man by any stretch of the imagination, but I think there was a vulnerable side of Fred . . . that was always off to the side. It informed and empowered what Fred did, and the so-called childlike side of Fred's personality that he allowed you to see sort of protected that other side of his personality."

In the end, the hotshot "bad-boy" journalist concluded that

Rogers had agreed to the interview for Fred Rogers's own reasons: "Once I sort of got in his sights, I think that he was looking to minister to me."

For the *Esquire* piece, Junod observed the on-set activity on the *Neighborhood*. In a later interview, he noted of longtime cast members: "In their way, they were strangely kind of vulnerable folks, too. I mean, they were kind of total local Pittsburgh people who had really settled in and had had their artistic and creative home there. Yet their artistic and creative home was doing this show for very young children, and they had stayed there for a long time doing that. There was an acceptance of limitation there. It wasn't like they were out there fulfilling their own wild ambitions doing that show. It was not that at all. It was like they were there because they had found a home there."[4]

Joe Negri notes that a musician of Johnny Costa's talent could have gone anywhere, as Negri could have. For a time, Costa worked in New York City, as did Negri. After leaving the *Neighborhood*, Betty Aberlin appeared in several films by the noted indie director Kevin Smith.

In the end, Costa and Negri preferred Pittsburgh. Negri says: "I've just remained here. And I've been happy with it. I made a good living. . . . All in all, I have great memories of *Mister Rogers' Neighborhood*. It was fun. I enjoyed the people; we all got along beautifully."[5]

Tom Junod saw the way Rogers's perfectionism affected the staff overall: "Fred, of course, was an amazing perfectionist who didn't—I wouldn't say drove those people, that's the wrong word—but absolutely knew what he wanted when he wanted [it] and would not leave that day until he saw it.

"Fred's vision was always, always about what a child would grasp and understand, and I didn't know the brilliance of that and the power of that until I had a child of my own."[6]

Mister Rogers' Neighborhood won four Emmy awards, and Rogers himself was presented with a Lifetime Achievement Award at the 1997 Daytime Emmys, a scene that Junod describes movingly in his profile. After Fred Rogers went onstage to accept the award, he bowed and said into the microphone, "All of us have special ones who have loved us into being. Would you just take, along with me, ten seconds to think of the people who have helped you become who you are? . . . Ten seconds of silence."

Then, as Tom Junod recounted, "He lifted his wrist, and looked at the audience, and looked at his watch, and said softly, 'I'll watch the time,' and there was, at first, a small whoop from the crowd, a giddy, strangled hiccup of laughter, as people realized that *he wasn't kidding*, that Mister Rogers was not some convenient eunuch but rather a *man*, an authority figure who actually expected them to do what he asked . . . and so they did.

"One second, two seconds, three seconds . . . and now the jaws clenched, and the bosoms heaved, and the mascara ran, and the tears fell upon the beglittered gathering like rain leaking down a crystal chandelier, and Mister Rogers finally looked up from his watch and said, 'May God be with you' to all his vanquished children."[7]

ROGERS'S UNIQUE BRAND OF AUTHENTICITY was an anomaly in show business. He wouldn't engage in derogatory or even slightly mean or cynical comments; he mirrored back something far more decent and caring and loving. Despite Rogers's reluctance to be interviewed on television talk shows, usually he would charm the host with his quick wit and ability to ad-lib on a moment's notice. His ability to remain adamantly himself, even out of his Mister Rogers "costume," showed both his stubbornness and a flair for the dramatic, no matter how low-key.

Producer Margy Whitmer observes: "I guess it was about control—him not wanting to share his vulnerabilities . . . even though he flipped it around on the show. He wanted kids to talk about their angry feelings, or their sadness, or their insecurity. You know, in some way, he fiercely protected his own. When different writers would come in to interview for articles, they would often walk out and say, 'He interviewed me.'"[8]

Fred Rogers also hated to have his picture taken, and preferred to take pictures of other people. According to Whitmer: "He was not in these pictures himself, so you'd have to write on the back, 'taken by Fred Rogers.' It was his chance to not be in the spotlight."

"It was kind of his way of working through, 'I'm going to take your picture before you can take mine.' I also think it was part of him just loving to document things. But a lot of it had to do with, 'Let me see what it's like to be the photographer for a while.'"

When Arsenio Hall got in touch, the *Neighborhood*'s staff worried that Fred Rogers wouldn't even know who he was. But after much coaxing, Rogers did the show in 1992 and was a big hit. Hall's questions were respectful, serious, and probing. He asked Mister Rogers directly how to cope with the violence some kids experience in LA neighborhoods. In reply, Fred Rogers quoted his mother, Nancy McFeely Rogers, with advice he would repeat on several occasions of national trauma: "Look for the helpers. You will always find people who are helping."[9]

Later he would reiterate: "To this day, especially in times of disaster, I remember my mother's words and I am always comforted by realizing that there are still so many helpers—so many caring people in this world."

Fred Rogers also tells Hall the story of George Allen, who came to live with the Rogers family when he was eleven and Fred was three, after Allen's mother had died. When Fred was in high school, Allen taught Fred to fly a Piper aircraft, and went on to train African American airmen at Tuskegee Institute in Alabama. "So you see, I had a black brother even then," Rogers tells a surprised Hall, reaching over to grasp the host's hand.

Later Fred Rogers dons a special jacket to match Arsenio's, a lavishly decorated bomber with garish embellishments that couldn't be further from his own style. But he wears it with seeming delight.[10]

It was the same story with the notoriously hard-bitten comedienne Joan Rivers, who was filling in for Johnny Carson on *The Tonight Show* in 1983 when Fred Rogers observed the thirtieth anniversary of his career in public television and the publication of *Mister Rogers Talks with Parents.* Rivers starts a spirited and obviously affectionate repartee with Rogers with the line: "Enough with the charm—do you ever get hate mail?"[11]

Fred smiles and moves on to ask how many members of the studio audience grew up with the *Neighborhood*, as Joan's daughter Melissa did. He gets a rousing response.

Later in their exchange, Rogers describes the effort that goes into creating the show. You don't make children's programming by stringing together a bunch of cartoons: "I am not a babysitter. Children are to be respected," he says with a serious mien. The audience erupts with applause.

As they wind down, Fred Rogers sings "It's You I Like" directly to Joan as he looks into her eyes. The caustic comedienne beams adoringly and is so nonplussed that she's forced to pull her sweater over her head to hide her embarrassment.

The lively sequence ends with a special rendition of "Row, Row, Your Boat," by King Friday, who substitutes hilariously pretentious "kingly" lyrics of his own, rowing "ecstatically, ecstatically, ecstatically; existence is but an illusion."[12]

Joan Rivers invited Fred Rogers back on *The Tonight Show* a few years later in 1986, an appearance marked by a marvelous rendition of the song that closes every episode of the *Neighborhood*, "Good Feeling." Fred and Joan join in for Johnny Costa's jazzed-up version, with Joan snapping her fingers in unison with Fred at the conclusion.[13]

Rogers's appearances on *The Tonight Show* with regular host Johnny Carson were less warm and fuzzy. In fact, Carson played Rogers in a 1978 parody in which he donned a bad wig and found only a dead fish in the famous tank on a simulated *Neighborhood* set. Instead of sneakers, Carson donned white shoes of the sort gamblers might wear in Vegas. And holding Barbie and Ken dolls, speaking in a slow and seemingly child-friendly cadence, Carson's Mister Rogers, full of sly innuendo, shows the audience how the two dolls get under the bed covers to make a baby.[14]

Despite the canned laughter he elicited then, even Carson

admitted the Rogers parody sketch was a dud. Years after it aired, he burned the script, in a 1984 broadcast celebrating *The Tonight Show*'s twenty-second anniversary. "Not all of them work out," he admitted to Ed McMahon as the flames rose.

After Johnny Carson played a little segment of a spoof called "Mister Codgers Neighborhood," David Newell got in touch with the show's producer, Fred De Cordova, and asked for equal time. Fred Rogers appeared in his sneakers, looking nervous. The audience started to snicker before he even got into his chair.

As described in the *Washington Post* by Paul Hendrickson in a November 18, 1982, article: "That's when a funny thing happened: Carson turned protective. He seemed ashamed of his audience's bad manners.

"It was as if some atavistic Midwestern compassion came suddenly welling up. We may be urban-cool and all, Carson seemed to be telling his audience, but in some other, deeper, feeling way, we're all losers. During the break, Carson leaned over and told Rogers that the first show he had on TV back in Omaha . . . was a kids' show, and that he knew you couldn't dare be a phony, not with kids."[15]

At one point, when Carson tried to get a rise out of him, Fred responded, "Most of the people I know like fun just as much as you do." Carson kept having him back.[16]

Even as Fred Rogers's staff felt protective of him, they also enjoyed the parodies of the *Neighborhood*, particularly the 1982 *SCTV* sketch in which a skinny Mister Rogers stand-in wearing black socks dukes it out with a busty Julia Child. Ultimately Mister Rogers is triumphant by bopping Child on the head with the puppet King Friday, as a Howard Cosell lookalike provides color commentary on the sidelines.

ROGERS'S IDIOSYNCRASIES were at the heart of his charm. For his whole adult life, he weighed exactly 143 pounds. Chuck Aber points out: "One, four, three. It's the number of letters in I, which has one letter; LOVE, which has four letters; and YOU, which has three letters.

"One program, Lady Elaine Fairchilde had on her Museum-Go-Round all these different streamers that we pulled out, in all these different languages: *love* and *peace*. And I believe the name Fred was on there, which was appropriate."[17]

Tom Junod adds: "Fred's email address was zzz143@aol.com. Zzz meant simply that he slept soundly at night, which he did, eight hours a night. And one hundred forty-three referred to two things." First, "his weight. Every morning Fred weighed himself before he went to swim, and every morning he weighed one hundred forty-three pounds . . . that's remarkable to the extent of near insanity. In another person, it would seem like obsessive-compulsive disorder, but in Fred it didn't seem that way.

"In Fred, it seemed this remarkable willed simplicity and consistency from which he decided to make his stand to the world. One-four-three was also reference to the . . . letters it took to say I love you. One, I. Four, love. Three, you.

"That's how Fred approached everything. His email address . . . seems simple, but it was full of all these interesting revelations."[18]

EVERYONE AT FAMILY COMMUNICATIONS, INC., and in Rogers's circle of friends came to deeply appreciate Fred-time, that slow-paced world of quiet with Rogers at its center.

When Dan Fales, an executive producer for WQED in Pittsburgh, got an emergency call from the studio two floors below his office that production was being held up on a public-service program, he was upset. Fales had two other crises to deal with and four important phone calls to return. He stalked out to the elevator and punched the call button as hard as he could. One floor down, the elevator stopped, and Fred Rogers came aboard. When Rogers saw Fales's angry face, he hit the stop button and turned to speak quietly: "Dan, remember what is important—your wonderful family, your sense of joy, and that wit that we all like. I hear that you work things out very well." Fales left the elevator feeling calm, focused, and quite good about himself.

As soon as he had smoothly defused the crisis in the studio, he looked over to floor manager Nicky Tallo to see if the crew was ready to proceed. Tallo winked and whispered to Fales, "Pure Fred—it works every time."[19]

Fred Rogers, writer Tom Junod concludes "was about grace. Fred was about bringing grace to people's lives, everybody that he met that I can tell. And more amazingly, and . . . through much greater difficulty, and against much higher odds, through the medium of television, a graceless medium if there ever was one—and Fred insisted that this could be a medium of grace. That's revolutionary."[20]

Though Tom Junod had interviewed famous people of all stripes, Fred Rogers was something special: "I've met a lot of interesting people. I've met great actors. I've met great writers. I've met great this, great that. But Fred's the only person that I would call a great man."

Junod observes that when you saw Fred Rogers on TV, you could tell that "he was looking to have a relationship with the people who watched it. I don't think it was that he ever meant to be this abstracted figure on high. He was as human on TV as he was in his life, because I think that Fred understood that if there is to be grace, it begins right in this space, and I think what Fred was really brave about was that he decided that this space could exist from an electronic medium, that this space was holy space, and that that's where it all happened. And that's Fred, and he did it with children. He did that with everybody he met. Anybody who sort of ventured into this space was in for a ride."

Junod also notes that "Fred liked to shock people." Indeed, Junod's piece for *Esquire* begins with Fred Rogers completely disrobing in front of his interviewer at the pool where he swims. "Well, Tom," he says, "I guess you've already gotten a deeper glimpse into my daily routine than most people have."[21]

In fact, this is both a show of the ultimate vulnerability and a dare—a seemingly passive aggressive act, even, preempting the journalist's curious gaze.

Fred Rogers wasn't perfect: Sometimes he failed the expectations of his associates. In 1979 and 1980, during a long and bitter strike at a company that had been owned by his family, he wrote a public letter to Latrobe's residents denying rumors he was the owner of the company. In fact, though, he was chairman of the board of Latrobe Die Casting, and president of the McFeely-Rogers Foundation, which did own the company. Some of the residents of Latrobe felt betrayed by what they saw as Rogers's disingenuous message.

Still, Fred Rogers was that unique television star with a real spiritual life. His values came to him not only through his Christianity but also through his careful study of other religions and cultures.

As his colleague Elizabeth Seamans describes it, "Fred was willing to float in what psychoanalysts describe as the place between sleep and wakefulness, which allows for a kind of a listening beyond literal listening. This breathing with the unseen viewer comes from trusting himself, trusting his own creativity; it was deeply original."[22]

As time went on, this characteristic became more telling in distinguishing Rogers's work from that of others in television or other media. While communication technology proliferated, becoming ever faster and more complex, Rogers used it in ways that were slow, thoughtful, and nuanced. Among the values he represented to viewers was the unusual one of patience.

He told Charlie Rose of PBS in a penetrating 1994 interview: "The white spaces between words are more important than the text, because they give you time to think about what you've read."[23] All his career, he emphasized the importance of listening; he felt that silence is a gift, as is what he called "graceful receiving." He worried about the lack of silence in a noisy world, and pondered how those in the field of television could encourage reflection. Today these ideas may seem quaint, yet they can also be seen as radical and more pressing than ever.

Rogers's views were the culmination of years of study. Beside his bed in his Pittsburgh apartment was a tall revolving bookcase with several shelves of books he wanted handy to read and reread either in the evening or in the early morning, when he also read the Bible before starting his day. The titles reflected his broad interest in religion and spirituality: *The Book of Common Worship of the Presbyterian Church*;

Zen Lessons: The Art of Leadership; The Way of Chuang Tzu; Dhamma-
pada: The Sayings of the Buddha; The Ragamuffin Gospel; A Grammatical
Analysis of the Greek New Testament; The Loving and Beloved Superego in
Freud's Structural Theory; The Diving Bell and the Butterfly; Three Scien-
tists and Their Gods.

Though Rogers was an ordained Presbyterian minister devoted
to the teachings of Jesus of Nazareth, he was equally a spiritualist, in
the sense that he had a broad, inclusive view of the human spirit and
how to reach it.

The Reverend Clark Kerr, pastor at Latrobe Presbyterian Church,
saw Rogers as having gained both strength and humility from the
breadth of his studies: "He was revered at the seminary and [by] professors who had come into contact with him. I think it was for his gentleness and his humility, his kindness . . . You know they say the meek
shall inherit the earth? I think Jesus meant people like Fred."[24]

One of Rogers's greatest friends, and one of his favorite thinkers, was the Catholic theologian and author Henri Nouwen. Rogers
frequently visited Nouwen, a charismatic Dutch-born priest who wrote
thirty-nine books about spirituality and had a large and loyal following
internationally. The two enjoyed extended discussions about God and
the human condition.

Joan Kroc, heir to the fortune of Ray Kroc, the founder of
McDonald's, also sought spiritual guidance from the very thoughtful
and highly sensitive Henri Nouwen. In fact, Rogers once joined Nouwen
on a trip to California to visit Joan Kroc. Both of these very spiritual men
hoped Kroc might support some of Nouwen's philanthropic work with
disadvantaged and disabled populations, but the trip was not productive.

Despite Rogers's religious studies and his devotion to human
spirituality, he was sometimes seized by terrible doubts about his work,
human nature, and the course of events. In 1979, struggling to write
a script for a weeklong series on "Going to School," he wrote in a note
to himself: "Am I kidding myself that I'm able to write a script again?
Am I really just whistling Dixie? I wonder. Why don't I trust myself?
Really that's what it's all about . . . that and not wanting to go through

the agony of creation. AFTER ALL THESE YEARS, IT'S JUST AS BAD AS EVER. I wonder if every creative artist goes through the tortures of the damned trying to create? GET TO IT, FRED! But don't let anybody ever tell anybody else that it was easy. It wasn't."[25]

Producer Margy Whitmer remembers coming into his office one day when Family Communications was filming public-service messages for PBS during the first Gulf War, in 1990: "I went to bring him down to the studios, and he was almost in tears. He said, 'Why am I doing this? What good is this going to do?'

"Fred was a father figure to so many people. Now the roles were reversed as I took him in my arms to support him.

"I said, 'Fred, think of all the people who watch this show—all the people who love you. How can you not think this is going to make an impression?' He carried so much responsibility on his shoulders. Though I didn't say this, I was thinking, 'It's not up to you to save the world. But you can certainly help people get through this time.' "[26]

21.

SWIMMING

FRED ROGERS'S GOAL of keeping his weight to 143 was of course tied to his lifelong avocation for the water. And swimming was an important part of the strong sense of self-discipline he cultivated. In his theme week on discipline on *Mister Rogers' Neighborhood,* he tried to create a contrast for children between self-discipline and the imposition of outside discipline, so they could see the values of each in action.

In one 1982 segment, he shows young viewers where he swims each day and explains that this physical routine is part of the structure and self-discipline of his regular day.[1] A 1997 show features Mister Rogers swimming with a teenage Paralympian; the two glide through the water with equal grace. In the later Neighborhood of Make-Believe segment, King Friday goes swimming and loses his crown.[2]

Fred Rogers got up every morning between 4:30 and 5:30 A.M. to read the Bible and prepare himself for the day before he went to the Pittsburgh Athletic Association to swim. But Rogers's preparation was not so much professional as it was spiritual: He would study passages of interest from the Bible, and then he would visualize who he would be seeing that day, so that he would be prepared to be as caring and giving as he could be. Fred's prayers in those early morning sessions were not for success or accomplishment, but rather for the goodness of heart to be the best person he could be in each of the encounters he would have that day.

Rogers's first experiences with swimming were with his family at their weekend and vacation home outside Latrobe on the side of Chestnut Ridge, where the family had a pool. But he developed his aquatic skills on the many winter trips his family made to Florida when he was a boy. His sister, Laney, recalls, "he was a very proficient swimmer as a young boy. Of course, we had gone to Florida every winter for many, many years . . . we went to a hotel. The swimming teacher was Mr. Wetherell."[3]

Austin Wetherell had qualified as a swimming competitor for the 1928 Olympic Games in Amsterdam, but opted not to go so he could marry his fiancée, and then became a swimming teacher at one of the hotels that the Rogers family frequented in Florida.

Back in Latrobe, Fred's sister, Laney, remembers Fred would often jump into the pool in back of the Rogers' country place at Tudor Manor, where she still lives: "Swimming was always something that Fred really enjoyed doing."[4]

Swimming and playing the piano became lifelong passions of the young Fred Rogers. Both gave him a chance to feel capable and in charge of his destiny.

OVER FORTY YEARS AGO, when he was a young man, Jeff Varion was riding the bus from his family's home in Dormont, a small town just outside Pittsburgh, when a woman traveling on the bus pointed out a newspaper ad for a position as locker-room attendant at the Pittsburgh Athletic Association in the Oakland area of the city. Varion needed a job, and he went over to the Athletic Association to apply.[5] And he got the position, which gave him employment for decades and provided one of the great friendships of his life, with Fred Rogers.

As an adult, Fred Rogers arrived at the Athletic Association either at the early-morning men's-only period, or the men's swim session later, around noon. Swimming was almost an obsession for Rogers—his chosen way to stay fit— and he tried to find time to swim most days, even when he was traveling for productions of *Mister Rogers' Neighborhood* or to make a speech or appear at a conference.

Varion remembers Fred's preference for the early morning, and that he would sometimes choose to swim naked, with just his goggles and a bathing cap. In the early-swim period, Rogers would do multiple twenty-five-yard laps for up to forty-five or fifty minutes, then shower and head to work at WQED, just up Fifth Avenue. Varion remembers Rogers as very "fit . . . he had a great body," slim and strong from his aquatic routine.

Over time, they became good friends. Jeff Varion describes himself as "working poor" and recalls that at first it seemed remarkable to be making friends with someone famous: "I says, how can he be on TV, and he's here swimming?" But Rogers was always open and friendly and natural, according to Varion: "And we started talking, and talking. And we became good friends, and everything."[6]

Typical of Rogers's natural affinity for people, although Varion describes Rogers as seeking privacy during his swim, he never refused to talk with those who came up to him, including parents with little children: ". . . he had a lot—when people come here with some children— 'Oh, wait, Mister Rogers!' "[7]

Fred was renowned for being just as likely to make friends with a locker-room attendant as the president of a local bank or the head of one of the foundations that provided funding for his program. Bill Isler, former president of Family Communications and, later, the Fred Rogers Company, tells a story about Rogers walking down the sidewalk in New York on his way to an expensive television shoot, with a union film crew waiting for him there.

Rogers happened upon a homeless man begging on the sidewalk, says Isler, and knelt down beside him to contribute a bill to the money he was collecting. And then he began to talk . . . and talk . . . and talk, all while poor Isler tried in vain to move him along to the site of the shoot.[8]

Fred Rogers's friendship with Varion became so strong over the years that he invited the young man to come up to the Rogerses' vacation home on Nantucket, where there would be good swimming for both of them in the ocean. Varion never made the trip, but he kept up his friendship with Rogers for decades.

In 2001, in a graduation speech at Marquette University, Rogers described his appreciation of Varion's character: "Early in the morning of every workday before I even get to my office, I see someone who influences me greatly. This person has a job which many people might consider unglamorous and tediously mundane. He's the locker-room attendant in Pittsburgh where I swim each day. His name is Jeff. We recently celebrated Jeff's twenty-fifth anniversary working at the pool— twenty-five years cleaning sinks and sorting towels and caring about everybody. For his anniversary, some of us regulars got him a cake and a book about New York because Jeff loves New York."[9]

When Rogers died two years later, Varion was one of the employees of the Pittsburgh Athletic Association who made the case for leaving Rogers's locker vacant, with his name plate still on it, as a memorial. It had always been swimming, and their shared enthusiasm for the pool, that provided the bond for Fred and Jeff.

AFTER THE LATE 1950S, when Fred's parents helped Joanne and Fred buy the Crooked House in Madaket, on Nantucket Island, Fred did much of his summertime swimming from Madaket Harbor out to the end of Smith's Point, the westernmost tip of the island. He would write scripts and music in the morning, then go to the beach right in front of his house, clad in a brief swimsuit and a bathing cap, and plunge into the Madaket Harbor waters. Joanne recalled that Fred would swim for about forty-five minutes toward Smith Point, then wade out of the water and walk back along the beach to their house.

Sometimes the swim could take even longer; if the tide was coming into the harbor, Fred would be working against it. Even so, occasionally the walk back from Smith Point could take even longer still, depending on how many people stopped Fred along the beach to talk about *Mister Rogers' Neighborhood*. Fred couldn't sign autographs, of course: No one had pen and paper at the beach. But that would lead to even longer conversations as beachgoers told Fred how much the *Neighborhood* meant to them and he responded, as he always did, by asking them about their lives and their families.

Sometimes, Rogers's fans and others would swarm across the family's large piece of land that surrounded the Crooked House. And once, when a local member of the Board of Selectmen said he and his family had been ordered off the beach by one of Fred's sons, a mini controversy brewed up. Most townspeople thought the selectman was grandstanding for attention, and they sided with Rogers. Fred settled the issue by donating nineteen acres of his land and part of the beach (much of the land that went with the former Valentine Small Farm) to the Massachusetts Audubon Society.[10, 11]

Everyone on the island was able to enjoy a nature preserve and access to the beach next door to the Crooked House. And Fred went on swimming, and talking with all who stopped him along the beach.

PART V

———

When I was a boy I used to think that strong meant having
big muscles, great physical power; but the longer I live,
the more I realize that real strength has much more to do with
what is not seen. Real strength has to do with helping others.

—FRED ROGERS

22.

THE LEGACY

FRED ROGERS ARTICULATED his philosophy in written form, as well as in broadcasts. He wrote, coauthored, or contributed to almost three dozen books published during his life, and a few that were released immediately after his death in 2003. Many were service books meant to help parents and children (*The New Baby*, 1996; *Making Friends*, 1996; *Going to the Potty*, 1997; *Going to the Hospital*, 1997; *When a Pet Dies*, 1998; *Let's Talk About It: Divorce*, 1998).

But some of the later books were the offerings of a sage: *You Are Special: Words of Wisdom from America's Most Beloved Neighbor*, 1994; *The World According to Mister Rogers: Important Things to Remember*, 2003; and *Many Ways to Say I Love You: Wisdom for Parents and Children from Mister Rogers*, 2006. Many of these are still in print and available online through the Fred Rogers Company website and in major retail outlets.

The Giving Box (2000), which taught children lessons of generosity and community, came packaged with a tin bank in which kids could save coins to donate. The book contains fables from around the world that convey a tradition of giving (e.g., the Hebrew tale "The Brothers," about two siblings who secretly help each other without the other's knowledge, and Aesop's "The Lion and the Mouse").

In his writing, Rogers was homespun in his wisdom and quite elegant in his wording, sometimes simultaneously. The art that won him honors for homiletics at the Pittsburgh Theological Seminary often shines through.

Former Family Communications, Inc., executive Basil Cox

observes: "My theory . . . is that Fred became an iconic figure . . . when people began to experience him through words—written words, rather than through his spoken words. When people started to write extensively about him, and write at length about the genius of the man, and when his own books started to come out for adults, with his own words on the page, to be read, not to be heard.

"You can't read that stuff without thinking: My God, this is amazing. I mean this is so true. . . . I'm sure many think that: I can't believe that that guy [Mister Rogers] wrote this. This is what he's been saying all along, you know. It was kind of a huge eye-opener, I think, for people who just could not ever get through that persona that he had— just couldn't ever buy it, just never—never could penetrate it, never could believe it, never could accept it."[1]

Rogers gave scores of interviews over the years and made about one hundred fifty major speeches. For decades, invitations for speaking engagements poured into the offices of Family Communications: Would Mister Rogers speak, preach, make a brief appearance, cut a ribbon, give a blessing, or receive an honorary degree?

A perfectionist, Rogers accepted only a few such invitations each year, and devoted weeks and weeks to his drafts. "He would agonize over a speech," says David Newell.[2]

"There wasn't a spontaneous bone in that man's body," observes Elizabeth Seamans. "He really hated to go into anything unprepared."[3]

Yet ironically, it was often in his speeches that he was most unguarded in a public forum. Many of the speeches were about children, education, and television; but many others focused on his view of the world, and how to make it a better place. Though his tone always remained quiet and informal, something in his manner commanded attention. Some of his associates remember when he spoke to an audience of PBS administrators and station managers in 1989. At first the audience was loud and distracted, with dozens of conversations going on throughout the hall. But as Rogers spoke, the crowd gradually quieted until all that could be heard in the hall was his singsong, nasal twang.

He explained why he felt so strongly about presenting himself as a real person on television: "We found out that what makes television accessible to its viewers is a human being . . . a person who believes in—who loves—what he or she is doing and wants to share it with somebody else."[4]

In many of Rogers's commencement speeches, he talked about the way his quest for self-knowledge ultimately brought an exhilarating kind of freedom and focus: "I'll never forget the sense of wholeness I felt when I finally realized what I was—songwriter, telecommunicator, student of human development, language buff—but that all those things and more could be used in the service of children's healthy growing. The directions weren't written in invisible ink on the back of my diploma. They came ever so slowly for me; and ever so firmly I trusted that they would emerge. All I can say is, it's worth the struggle to discover who you really are."[5]

In his last commencement address, to the faculty, students, and parents of Dartmouth—the college he had dropped out of half a century earlier—he said: "I'm very much interested in choices, and what it is and who it is that enable us human beings to make the choices we make all though our lives. What choices lead to ethnic cleansing? What choices lead to healing? What choices lead to the destruction of the environment, the erosion of the Sabbath, suicide bombings, or teenagers shooting teachers? What choices encourage heroism in the midst of chaos?"[6]

These were the same questions he'd tried to address in his programs for adults in the four years that the Neighborhood was on hiatus. Even if those shows didn't reach a large audience, Fred Rogers continued to engage with vital questions of how to live a life with meaning. Above all, he stressed the need to allow children to express their creativity.

In a 1969 speech at Thiel College in Greenville, Pennsylvania, entitled "Encouraging Creativity," he told the audience about his delight in a letter he'd received from a PBS station manager in Dallas, Texas. Attached were eleven pages of music paper containing an opera by a six-year-old who'd been inspired by the ones he saw on the

Neighborhood. The boy's story line concerned an owl and a king and an archaeologist who finds out that what others thought was a monster was just a blinking flashlight found in a tunnel.[7]

"Most children don't write operas," observes Rogers. "Nevertheless, each child is born with a unique endowment which gives him an opportunity to make something entirely different from anyone else in the world." He goes on to decry anything that would hold kids back from self-expression: "Children, like laboratory rats, can learn quickly not to experiment with wrong answers."

Finally, Fred Rogers states his central thesis: "One of the major goals of education must be to help students discover a greater awareness of their own unique selves, in order to increase their feelings of personal worth, responsibility, and freedom."[8]

For all his long career, Rogers reveled in his relationship with his young audience. In nearly four decades on television, Mister Rogers heard from thousands of viewers. And he always answered.

Hedda Sharapan, who helped him answer many of the letters, observes: "What I loved about the fan mail was what people gave to us about how their lives were enriched by the program. And to think that a half hour of this simple communication, this loving, simple communication, could help people, who are still writing to us and saying the power of what he said and how he said it has stayed with them and that—to think that he's become an icon and that this legacy has lasted and people are still using it and working on it. That's just remarkable."[9]

Such was the depth and strength of Fred Rogers's commitment to his audience that he started out answering every letter by hand when the CBC was producing and hosting the precursor to *Mister Rogers' Neighborhood* in Toronto. Because he wanted to personally answer every single letter—and the trickle of letters was turning into a stream—he and his wife Joanne devoted themselves to long evenings at the kitchen table after their sons were in bed, poring over missives from children and parents, and handwriting the responses.

By the time Rogers got back to WQED in Pittsburgh, and the *Neighborhood* had gone national on educational television, the stream was a torrent. He couldn't keep up, so he hired Hedda Sharapan to help him; but he never let the answers go out without reading and editing and signing each one, acting out a pastoral duty of sorts in addressing themes that covered every aspect of a child's life, especially those that might seem scary as he or she ventures beyond the immediate world of home and family.

These included going to daycare; going to the doctor or dentist, or to the hospital; what to do when your best friend moves; imaginary friends; taking a trip on an airplane; managing feelings like anger; why it's okay to cry; and even joyful themes, such as why grandparents are so special. Nothing affecting the lives of children was off the table.

Hedda Sharapan explains the sensitivity of Mister Rogers's method in writing back to *Neighborhood* viewers, his perspective honed during long and extensive conversations with child-development specialists like Dr. Margaret McFarland: "If a parent wrote, Fred would send something for the child. If a child wrote, Fred would sometimes send something to the parent, also. One of my most treasured mothers was one who'd written to us just before Christmas one year saying that her teenagers and she and her husband lived in a trailer. They had no money and really needed help with Christmas presents; could Fred autograph pictures for her kids?

"Fred sent back the autographed pictures and a letter saying, 'How fortunate your children are to have such a caring mother.' She wrote back a letter that was so incredibly touching, how she cried because she never thought of her children as being fortunate to have her as a mother."[10]

In 1996, Rogers published a volume of letters called *Dear Mister Rogers, Does It Ever Rain in Your Neighborhood?* In one, five-year-old Timmy was puzzled. He couldn't figure out the truth about Mister Rogers, one of his favorite television figures.

> *Mister Rogers, are you for real, or are you under a mask*
> *or costume, like Big Bird? For my birthday wish, I want to*
> *know if you are for real.*

Mister Rogers replied: "Dear Timmy: I am a real person, just the way you are. There are some things on television that aren't real—the monsters and scary things. Your television set is a special way that you can see the picture of me and hear my voice. I can't look through the television set to see or hear my television friends, but I think of them whenever we make our television visits."[11]

One young man wrote to say that as a boy, he'd once run around to the back of his TV at the end of an episode of the *Neighborhood* and cupped his hands under the set, hoping to catch Mister Rogers as he came out. And Nicholas, age three, wrote: "Dear Mister Rogers: I wish you could be on Earth."[12]

Viewer confusion about Mister Rogers, television presence, and Fred Rogers the man was also at the heart of one of the funniest letters he ever received:

Dear Mister Rogers,

While putting [my son] to bed last night, he said, "Mister Rogers doesn't poop." I said that of course you did. He denied it vehemently. I asked where his certainty came from and he said, "Well, I've never seen him poop." I pointed out that there were lots of people he hadn't seen poop, and they all still did. He accepted that others [adults and kids did], but denied it about you. I kissed him goodnight and left the room. Five minutes later I was summoned to his bedside.

"Daddy, I know Mister Rogers doesn't poop."

"How?" I asked.

"Because I've seen his house and he just has a closet, a living room, a kitchen and a yard."

Sincerely,
Isaac's father

Fred Rogers wrote back:

Dear Isaac,

Your father told me you had an interesting talk with him about whether I "poop." It's good that you and he were talking about that. I know it can be hard to understand that I do. I am a real person. And one thing for certain is that all real people "poop." That is an important part of how our bodies work. Little by little as you grow, you will learn more about how our bodies work. And it is good that you are thinking about that now.

    On some of our programs I show the bathroom in my television house. It is off to the side of the kitchen. We don't often show the bathroom of our television set because that is not my real house. I think of it as my "television house." That is a place where I stop by during my workday to have a television visit with my friends. When I am at work, I use the bathrooms in the building where we make our programs.[13]

But Fred Rogers wasn't satisfied just writing to Isaac. He also sent a letter to Isaac's father: *"Your letter was absolutely refreshing! Thank you for all that you shared with us, especially for the conversation you had with Isaac about my bodily functions. That's such a wonderful story to attest to young children's focus on 'bathroom' concerns. But what particularly struck me was the way you were so sensitive to your son's questions and that you were willing to help him think the issues through, even with a subject that can be as sensitive as that. Your son is indeed fortunate to have a father like you."*

Rogers always seemed to bring his explanations back to the world of the child, so that the "lesson" embodied in his letters could be used in a concrete way.

An example: Joe, identified simply as "toddler," asks, "Why aren't there any hands on Daniel's clock?"

Rogers replies:

Dear Joe;

. . . We decided not to have hands on Daniel's clock because
his clock is in the Neighborhood of Make-Believe, and that's a
place where we pretend things can be any way we want them
to be. We decided that we could pretend there was no time
in Make-Believe, like the timelessness of love. If you were
making up a pretend place, what kind of things would you
have there? Would you have hands on your pretend clock?
For your pretending, things can by any way you want them
to be!"[14]

Even if Joe's parents might have to fill him in on the nature of
"timeless love," he can see in Mister Rogers's reply that he can be king
of his own pretend domain.

IT ISN'T HARD to guess how Fred Rogers would have reacted to the
current plight of migrant children, for example, or the degradation of
the physical environment. As he concluded the 1969 speech at Thiel
College on "Encouraging Creativity," he told the students in the audience: "You know, it may well be that our planet, Earth, is the only spot
in the entire Universe which can sustain human life. Of all the worlds,
we may be the only one where there has ever been—or ever will be—
people! That's sort of like someone saying to you that that there is only
one square inch of soil on this Earth that can grow anything—and that
square inch happens to be in your own backyard. You look at that soil of
yours with infinitely greater appreciation when you become aware how
rare and valuable it is."[15]

At Kenyon College's 2016 graduation, John Green, the bestselling author of young adult books such as *The Fault in Our Stars*, asked
the new graduates to pause for ten seconds—as referenced by Rogers
in an acceptance speech at the Emmys—to think about everyone who'd

helped them get to that point.[16] As Fred would have put it: "Who in your life has been a servant to you, enabling you to grow?"

In the May 2017 issue of the Jesuit magazine *America*, a teacher named David Dark, from Tennessee, wrote of the reaction of his students when he showed them the video of the 1969 Pastore hearings: "I watched this marvel of a video with most of my classes during the presidential election, and we reached the general consensus that 'what you do with the mad that you feel?' is probably the kind of question we would do well to put to anyone seeking public office. We are also right to put the question to ourselves as often as possible."[17]

"Fred Rogers has been doing the same small good thing for a very long time . . ." This was the sub-headline of Tom Junod's 1998 *Esquire* piece about Fred Rogers, American hero.[18] But what is small about reaching millions of kids, day after day for decades, and shaping their views for the rest of their lives?

Even Mister Rogers's gestures, seen by millions for years, became a form of ritual. He took off his street clothes and donned the sweater his mother had made, then took off his shoes and put on a pair of navy-blue canvas boating sneakers "at the beginning of 865 television programs, over a span of thirty-one years." This was in 1998.[19]

Rogers's simple routine was articulated in some unexpected quarters. One of Fred Rogers's most loyal fans was Koko, a famously communicative gorilla who appeared on the *Neighborhood* in 1998. Since Koko had been a faithful viewer of Rogers's program for years, Fred visited her at the Gorilla Foundation in Redwood City, California, in his sweater and sneakers. When she saw him, Koko immediately folded him in her long, black arms, as though he were a child, and took off his shoes. Then they conversed in American Sign Language, shared a hug, and took pictures of each other.

Fred was particularly delighted when Koko told him she loved him as well as loving her television visits with him.[20]

In a bizarre coda, Fred Rogers's death coincided with the rise of internet culture and the proliferation of "urban myths" about this saintly seeming man. One of the most widely circulated, and the most outlandish, was that Rogers had been convicted of child molestation early in his career, and had created his show as community service as part of his sentence. Didn't he have a character with the suggestive name of "Mr. McFeely"?

Snopes.com, "the definitive fact-checking and Internet reference source for urban legends, folklore, myths, rumors, and misinformation," set readers right about Fred Rogers's training at NBC and the identity of his grandfather. And as the site's writers noted: "It stretches credulity to the breaking point to believe that the host of an extremely popular children's program on public television could have remained in that position for thirty-three years without having been hounded off the air amidst howls of condemnation from thousands of outraged parents."[21]

Another myth repeated thousands of times on the web was that Mister Rogers had in fact been a Navy SEAL sniper during the Vietnam War, and had many "kills" to his credit. Rogers never served in the military at all, let alone in a hyper-macho, elite unit.

Fred Rogers was also much too old to have been drafted, given that the draft started in 1969, when his show was just getting established. Nor did he wear long-sleeve shirts on the *Neighborhood* to hide tattoos—another rumor. It's almost as if people, afraid of the influence of such a gentle, soft-spoken, and popular man, had to turn him into his opposite—a figment of fevered imagination.

As Rogers's former colleague Basil Cox notes, for his whole career, Fred Rogers perplexed people who couldn't believe that he was "for real."[22]

Widely disseminated images of Fred Rogers supposedly "flipping off" his audience during the taping of his final show in December 2000 were in fact taken from a program in 1967 when he was leading children through a song called "Where Is Thumbkin?" which, notes Snopes, "is traditionally accompanied by the participants' holding up the corresponding fingers as they are each named in the song."[23]

On the converse side is the story of how Mister Rogers's old Oldsmobile was stolen from a street near WQED, but then returned by contrite thieves. According to a piece in *TV Guide*, Rogers filed a police report, which was picked up by every media outlet in Pittsburgh. But within a few days, the car was supposedly back in the spot from where it was taken, with a note on the dashboard that said: "If we'd known that it was yours, we never would have taken it."[24]

An article in the *Wall Street Journal* reported: "Children aren't the only ones with a soft spot for Mister Rogers. Two weeks ago, his Oldsmobile sedan was stolen while he was babysitting for his grandson. After looking over papers and props he had left in the car, the thieves apparently realized who the owner was. Mister Rogers found the car parked in front of his house a day or so later. All that was missing was a director's chair with his name on it."[25]

The only problem is that Fred Rogers himself never seems to have mentioned the story. Still, it's a heartwarming notion that even thieves had a heart for the man Koko the gorilla folded so lovingly in her arms.

23.

THE END OF THE *NEIGHBORHOOD*

FRED ROGERS was not motivated by many of the things that keep other people hard at work year after year. As they grew older, Fred and Joanne were less and less interested in money and what it could buy. They had sold the big brick house in Pittsburgh's East End and moved into a three-bedroom apartment near the campus of Carnegie Mellon University. Fred drove a light-blue Honda Accord coupe and dressed in old khakis and slightly worn jackets. He seemed to ignore his staff's comments on the shabbiness of his outfits.

Producer Margy Whitmer recalls: "He'd always been thrifty. When we went on the road, he'd tell us, 'Look at all the money I'm saving by eating yogurt and crackers in my room for dinner.'"[1]

Once in Los Angeles with David Newell, Rogers found a jacket he really liked at a thrift store. Newell observes: "I think he loved the conquest of getting something as a bargain. But it was more about, you don't need to spend a lot of money on clothes. His faith, his religion, came through in the song 'It's You I Like': 'It's not the things you wear / It's not the way you do your hair / But it's you I like . . .' He could have bought five-thousand-dollar suits, but he never did."[2]

As former Family Communications executive Basil Cox notes: "Fred was . . . far from an extravagant man. But there's nothing about Fred that's consistent. I remember once Fred hired a jet to take him to New York. Fred had lots of money. He always lived in kind of luxurious surroundings. His apartments were very beautifully decorated, and he lived in a huge house, before he moved into an apartment. At one point, he had three houses. I think that as he got older, he probably narrowed down his expenses. He went from driving a BMW to driving a Chevrolet Celebrity.

"He dressed like a member of the upper class. He always wore a white shirt and a tie . . . if he was dressing up. His hair was always perfect—perfectly combed, and perfectly brushed.

"I think that it would not be accurate to say that Fred tried hard not to seem like a member of the upper class. Now, I don't think he ever would have used those words. I don't think he would think in those terms. But I don't think that he was embarrassed by who he was . . . or by his upbringing, which was ridiculously upper class. . . . He never felt that his parents were, you know, robber barons, or . . . that he'd been brought up in ridiculous luxuriousness."[3]

He and Joanne never fixed up the Crooked House, their vacation home on the western end of Nantucket. It remained a spare, unfinished, unheated wooden cottage on an island increasingly dotted with the mansions of rich traders, financiers, bankers, and fund managers from New York and Boston. (It really is crooked. The floors and walls are uneven, and the whole place seems to tilt precariously.)

Speaking about fame and fortune in an interview, Rogers once said: "How many clothes can you wear? How many cars can you drive? How big of a shelter do you really need? Some people get so caught up in the trappings of life, I feel they lose what is real." A bit later, he added: "Deep and simple—that's what matters."[4]

On Charlie Rose's show, he added: "Fame is a four-letter word, like tape or pain or zoom or life or love. What matters is what we do with it. People in television are in a service role, to meet the needs of those who watch. In the one life we have to live, we can choose to demean this life, or to cherish it in creative, imaginative ways."[5]

As the 1990s progressed, Rogers still loved his work. Though he still enjoyed spending most of his time with the cast and crew of *Mister Rogers' Neighborhood*, he was slowing down. Margy Whitmer recalls that in the last few years of production, Rogers's energy level "was less and less. It became more and more important to him to get his rest."[6]

Fred Rogers had been thinking about retirement for several

years. Bill Isler, the former president and CEO of Family Communications, recalls: "He'd said in his early sixties that it was going to be sixty-five—a good time to go. It never happened."[7]

In an interview, Joanne Rogers recalls that by the time Fred reached his sixties, he had finally become able to say "no" a bit more readily: "He got to be very good at it. He was about sixty-one or -two when he came to me, and he said, 'You know, I just don't like to do those programs with orchestras, where I'm entertaining.'

"And I said to him, 'If you don't like it, then the audience is not going to like it. And I think you've done your bit. And if that's something you don't like, quit doing it. . . .

"He never felt like an entertainer. He felt much more like an educator. And he was. He was very, very good with people, and was able to be very entertaining. . . . He had produced a lot of things that were entertaining. But that wasn't who he was, essentially."[8]

It suddenly became clear to Fred Rogers when he was just over seventy that the moment to retire had really arrived. Isler observes: "He said, 'An opera singer knows when it's time. I really think it's time, so we should think about how to handle this.' "[9] Rogers brought in an old friend, advertising executive George Hill, who'd helped him find funding for the *Neighborhood* in the earliest days of the program. Now Hill helped create elaborate public relations plans. Still, once the 2001 retirement was announced, Rogers and his crew at Family Communications were overwhelmed by hundreds of requests for interviews. Rogers tried to shift the focus from his retirement to the durability of *Mister Rogers' Neighborhood*. In an earlier interview, he'd said: "These programs are timeless, sort of like *The Wizard of Oz*. They can be seen in any epoch."[10]

In fact, after his retirement, the programs were broadcast less and less often; parents who wanted their children exposed to the *Neighborhood* had to buy it on DVD, or download episodes from the web. Joanne Rogers recalls that Fred was somewhat depressed after he left the production company, and he lamented that he missed his friends there.

After production on the show had ceased, Fred wasn't spending as much time at Family Communications with his staff. Joanne was worried that he seemed uncharacteristically unsure of himself, and full of doubts. But over time, particularly when he read a good deal about religion and spirituality, he recovered his spirits and reengaged more with life after work. And eventually, he became increasingly enthusiastic about a project that would carry on his legacy: working with Archabbot Douglas Nowicki, the chancellor of nearby Saint Vincent College in Latrobe, on plans for a children's media center that would bear his name.

The final episode of *Mister Rogers' Neighborhood* aired on August 31, 2001, in the thirty-third season of the show. This season was the shortest, comprised of only five episodes, entitled, appropriately, "Celebrate the Arts." In the final episode, Mr. McFeely shakes Mister Rogers's hand before he exits the stage, something he'd never done before. David Newell explains: "That handshake is for me. I was saying a lot to Fred in that handshake. Thank you, and it's just been wonderful knowing you for thirty-five years."[11]

In an interview for the *Pittsburgh Post-Gazette,* television critic Rob Owen asked Fred Rogers why he decided to end the program. "It was a fairly simple, straightforward decision," Fred Rogers replied. "Of course, I prayed about it."

"I don't like to be spooky about stuff, but I do think that sometimes you feel inspired to make certain decisions," Rogers added. "I've never tried to make a decision that had to do with selfishness. I think we certainly have done the kind of work I have wanted to do for children and one of the avenues has been the *Neighborhood.* That will always be a part of who I am, and I trust it will always be a part of those who have grown up with it, and will continue to."[12]

Fred Rogers explained that he didn't plan to retire, but to focus on new developments at Family Communications: "When I started, television was the new medium . . . well, there are some new media now and they're taking more and more of my time." He was referring to his company's website. Later in the interview, Rogers pointed to a photo on the wall, showing his favorite sign at Rollins College, "Life is for Service," the one he once jokingly altered to read "Life is for vice."

He concluded: "Those of us in broadcasting have a special calling to give whatever we feel is the most nourishing that we can for our audience. We are servants of those who watch and listen."[13]

After the last taped show was aired that summer, the plan was to recycle it, along with three hundred others of the seventeen hundred Rogers made, in an endless loop. In his "retirement" office, Fred Rogers had fifteen employees, including such longtime stalwarts as David Newell. In the spring of 2001, *New York Times* reporter Doreen Carvajal found Fred Rogers in his office in WQED, with a "familiar pair of blue sneakers . . . tacked [to the wall] like a rare butterfly in a plexiglass shrine."[14]

Carjaval reports that when Roger and his wife, Joanne, took a stroll around their "real-life" Pittsburgh neighborhood, strangers greeted them with spontaneous renditions of "It's a beautiful day in the neighborhood"—something that also happened to Rogers when he rode the New York City subway.

Joanne Rogers observed: "He doesn't miss the show. I think he misses the Neighborhood of Make-Believe because he enjoyed working with people around him. He really loves all of them, and he'll keep in touch. But he did not enjoy what he called 'interiors,' the beginning and endings of the program. He had gotten where he had really dreaded it so."[15]

Rogers had grown to loathe wearing makeup and contact lenses for the segments. As he explained, "I don't know why. It has something to do with I like to give myself as I am. In the early days, you could do that."

Fred Rogers had been contemplating retirement ever since Johnny Costa's death in 1996, but kept going out of concern for longtime staff and cast members. Hedda Sharapan, then an employee for thirty-three years, described how Rogers went with her when she had to put her cat to sleep.

The *Times* account ends with the story of two college students who drove cross-country from Seattle to Pittsburgh to see the "real Mister Rogers' Neighborhood." Casey McNerthney, twenty, a sophomore at Western Washington University, tells the reporter: "If you grow up watching *Mister Rogers' Neighborhood*, you can really connect it with your childhood.

"The topics that Fred takes on are themes that only come up after a long car ride or after a discussion real late at night. And I think those lessons of trust and appreciation for other people can be applied to your everyday life."

"These kids give you such hope," said Rogers, reflecting on their visit. "Maybe they realize that you don't have to be macho to be acceptable, and that everybody longs to be loved and feel that he or she is capable of loving. I would hope that is one of the major influences of the *Neighborhood*."[16]

THE PROOF OF FRED ROGERS'S influence is in the adult lives of the "neighbors" who grew up with the man in the grandad sweater. Over the years, Fred Rogers grew fearful that the dominance of television and the computer would overwhelm the simple human values he held most dear.

Excerpts from two university speeches he made in midcareer capture his concern: "It really has been very effectively communicated in many circles that computers and their relatives are more clever, are much quicker, make fewer mistakes and are more to be valued than human beings. But without human beings there never would have been a computer or anything else that we call advanced technology. That's something I like to help children remember: that, no matter what the machine may be, it was people who thought it up and made it, and it's people who make it work.

"And as we . . . find ourselves being concerned about the conditions that make life on Earth possible, we will recognize the need to make people more important than things, and we will join hands with young and old alike by putting our dominant energies into developing a sane design for living."[17]

He even suggested, only somewhat tongue-in-cheek, one answer to all this complexity: Turn off the machine. In an appearance at the opening of a Fred Rogers exhibit at the Pittsburgh Children's Museum in 1998, he said, simply: "I've always said the best time for our program is once it's over and the television is turned off."

24.

AMERICA'S FAVORITE NEIGHBOR

ELIOT DALEY RECALLS a fateful day about a year and a half after Fred Rogers's retirement: "Every November twenty-sixth the phone would ring, wherever I was, and it would be King Friday the Thirteenth wishing me glorious felicitations on my natal day. . . . King Friday the Thirteenth was Fred's alter ego. He was everything that Fred wasn't: imperious, insensitive, demanding, and egotistical.

"This went on for thirty-two or -three years, I guess—unbroken. And it became a matter of pride to track the other person down. I tracked Fred down once on a boat, on a ship-to-shore telephone on a boat off Galveston Bay. And he tracked me down once in Ireland. . . .

"On November 26, 2002, I didn't get a call from the King. And after thirty-some years, I knew something must be up."[1]

In the summer of that year, Fred Rogers's stomach distress had become so bad that his secretary at Family Communications, Elaine Lynch, had started to notice. Joanne Rogers said Fred had suffered from an upset stomach for several years, but he had always been reluctant to see a doctor. By July and August 2002, though, both women could tell it was getting worse.

Although Fred Rogers did keep up with his medical care, he just didn't like being examined and poked and prodded and tested at the doctor's; and he didn't like to think he needed much attention—after all, he ate well, swam and took walks almost every day, and he kept his weight at exactly 143 pounds his whole adult life. He just didn't think he needed to worry that much with doctors.

Also, Rogers was very busy planning for the new center at Saint

Vincent College, making public appearances, and traveling. Yes, he was retired, but he was as busy as ever. He spent a good deal of time working with Archabbot Douglas Nowicki, chancellor of Saint Vincent College, making detailed plans for the children's media center at the college. Fred intended to spend a significant part of his retirement working at the center developing programs for parents and kids that could advance his early childhood education legacy and continue his work helping families cope with the modern world.

He was looking forward to being based at the center as he continued to make public appearances around the country. When he and the Archabbot were working with the architects to design the new center building, Fred had them put in a small bathroom just off a meeting room called the "Gathering Space," where he felt he would spend time working and meeting with students and colleagues. And he and Douglas Nowicki even talked about a sleeping room for Fred in the monastery where he could stay overnight when he didn't want to make the hour-long drive back into Pittsburgh between workdays at the center.

He put off a full doctor's examination until October. Complicating matters was his scheduled trip early that fall to Scotland with his friends Bill Barker, a fellow Presbyterian minister, and the Archabbot. Fred had been excited about the prospect of that trip for months, and now he didn't want to miss it. He went ahead, traveling with his friends, even though the pain in his stomach was persistent and sometimes overwhelming, according to the later accounts of both Barker and Rev. Nowicki.

When he got back at the beginning of October, both Joanne Rogers and Elaine Lynch pressed Fred hard to see a physician. When he finally agreed to go in to see his doctor and get a full examination, an endoscopy revealed stomach cancer.

Still Rogers put off treatment. He had promised to appear as a grand marshal at the January 2003 Rose Bowl Parade in Pasadena, California, with friends Bill Cosby and Art Linkletter, and he didn't want to let them down. As always, Fred Rogers's sense of duty and discipline came first.

By Christmas of that year, close friends knew something was afoot. Basil Cox remembers: "Every Christmas morning, at nine o'clock or so, there'd be a knock on the door—it would be in the middle of a blizzard—didn't matter—and it'd be Fred, with gifts of one sort or another for the family. . . . Every Easter, at nine o'clock, would be Fred with a knock on the door, and he'd have an Easter lily . . . he never missed one.

"And even the very last Christmas of his life, when he could, I bet, barely walk from the pain of his stomach, he still trudged up the hill to our house. And it was icy. At one point, he called—I think he called on Christmas Eve, and he said, 'You know I'm really not feeling very well, and so I may not be able to see you tomorrow. So that'll be the first time that I haven't been there for—you know, I just want you to know I love you all.' But he was there anyway."[2]

Cox adds: "One word that characterizes Fred almost as much as anything, or more than anything, is that discipline, that sense of duty, that sense that, I will see this list of the people that I love every Christmas and every Easter. Nothing will keep me away from that."

After the Rose Bowl Parade in Pasadena, Bill Cosby told some of his other friends that Rogers was in such pain that he gripped Cosby's leg throughout the parade—tightly enough to leave bruises. But he wouldn't miss that obligation; only after the parade would Rogers go in for surgery. When Fred Rogers returned to Pittsburgh, he revealed to his associates at Family Communications that he needed surgery for cancer. But he was careful not to alarm them.

Elaine Lynch says most of them stayed optimistic: "He told us they were going to take half of his stomach. I knew a woman who sang with my mother and had half of her stomach removed. She lived fifteen or twenty years more, so Fred's announcement didn't hit me then."[3]

Joanne Rogers recalled later that Fred seemed to worry more about the feelings of those around him than he did about himself. And she shared a note she had written to herself at the time of Fred's scheduled surgery becoming public: "Fred . . . spoke to his staff at FCI [Family Communications, Inc.] today to let them be the first to know that he'll be entering the hospital here on Monday to undergo surgery. In early December, he began a battery of tests, and a malignant, ulcerated tumor (about three centimeters in size) was located in the upper [section] of his stomach. The surgery on Monday will be exploratory in nature and will likely be a partial gastrectomy—to remove the entire area around the tumor. It is expected to give him relief from the severe discomfort he's had lately—that is, after the initial discomfort of the surgery itself. While an endoscopy and a CT-Scan can be very effective in locating the problem, we are told that there's no substitute for the surgeon's eyes and hands to complete the diagnosis. There was, in addition, a bone scan which was clear and normal."[4]

But the hint of potential good news in the note Joanne wrote was not to be realized. When the surgery was performed, the results were disastrous: The surgeons found that the cancer had spread beyond Rogers's stomach, which they removed in its entirety. Dr. Bill Hirsch, a close family friend, was with Joanne when the doctors told her how far the disease had spread. When Hirsch started to cry, Joanne knew the end was probably near.

Dr. Hirsch took time off from his work to be with Joanne and Fred once Fred came home. He later recalled: "He [Fred] had the surgery, and I can remember when the surgeon came out partway through the operation and he said, well, you know, it's so advanced, we don't really have to take his stomach out. And Joanne said, well I think Fred really wants it out. . . . So they went on and completed the surgery then, in the hospital."[5]

Hirsch added that because Fred was struggling with pain when he and Joanne got him back to the Rogers apartment, he had to strictly limit the number of people who could visit: "He was just so exhausted. And he said I hope they don't think I'm being elitist to not have them visiting; and he cried when he said that because he didn't want to hurt their feelings, but he just didn't have much to give at that point. There were certain individuals that I think he wanted to email, but he would start writing an email and he would just fall asleep or something. It was very, very frustrating for him. . . . Joanne sat on the bed once and said, 'Fred, I know the boys are going to be okay. I'll try to be,' she said. And he said 'Oh, Joanne, you don't know what a relief that is for me to hear that.' "[6]

Family friend Michael Horton was one of the ones who saw Fred Rogers right before he died. He reflects on what he learned from Rogers: "One time I said something unkind about someone. . . . And I said, 'Oh, I'm sorry. I'm horrible.'

"And he'd say, 'No, you're not horrible. What you said is not horrible. Nothing about you is horrible—except how you treat others. What you do.'

"Fred believed in the goodness in everyone. . . . Really, Fred and Joanne were the most marvelous people—the most loving, and giving, people I've ever met in my life."[7]

According to Dr. Hirsch, one of Fred's major preoccupations in his final days was making sure he was not a bother to anyone else at the end of his life. He told Hirsch he was relieved to get a catheter, so he would not have to wake up Bill or Joanne to help him get to the bathroom in the middle of the night. Often, when he would wake up at night, he would sit by himself and read one of the numerous books on his nightstand that dealt with many of the world's religions—Fred reminding himself of the spiritual things that were dearest to him.

The three of them struggled to get the pain medication just right, to balance Fred's need for relief with his wish to be alert enough to make contact with people.

Hirsch recalled: "He wanted to have his thinking clear. He wanted that because there were so many people he wanted to talk to, but he was in terrible pain. So we did this thing for a couple of weeks where we were trying to give him just enough to relieve the pain, and then he would have an hour or two where he was coherent, but it didn't work. Basically, it was too far along . . . then he would be in such pain and so distressed. Then you would give him the painkiller, and then he was asleep."[8]

After days upon days of nursing Fred and working with hospice services, Joanne and Bill were exhausted by the awful burden of helping their friend and trying to skillfully manage his medications. One day in the kitchen, Joanne recalls, they were almost giddy with weariness, working out the right dosage of Fred's powerful pain medicine. "I said to Bill, 'Well, they said to give him such and such. And he said, 'Oh, do you think that much?'

"I said, 'Well, they said he really needs a lot.' Then I looked at Bill and said, 'The worst it could do is to kill him.'

"Then we sat on the floor, and laughed and laughed. It was the most painful thing I can remember. . . . And yet, it was funny."[9]

When Joanne was helping Fred get back in bed, and trying to make him comfortable, sometimes he would smile sheepishly and ask for a hug. Joanne recalled later that as she gave Fred a heartfelt hug, it seemed so poignantly sad to her that she could hardly bear it.

Their younger son, John, recalls his last visit with his father: "I felt terrible for him near the end. I'm glad it didn't last too long, because here's a guy who never took a drug or a drink in his whole life and swam every day from age forty on. He can't swim anymore. He's having to wear these patches so that he's not in complete pain, and at first, I think he was hallucinating. . . . He just wasn't Dad anymore. But you have to make people comfortable. It's the only right thing to do."[10]

Fred Rogers died on February 27, 2003, just a month before he would have turned seventy-five. He was in his own bed, in his apartment, in Pittsburgh, the city where he had made children's television programming for half a century.

Rogers's eclectic embrace of religion served him to the very end. As he lay comatose shortly before he died, his friend Archabbot Douglas Nowicki, chancellor of Saint Vincent College, came to the Rogerses' apartment in Pittsburgh to administer the last rites of the Catholic Church.

How would Rogers have felt about that? Joanne later explained that because of Fred's embrace of all faiths—he frequently prayed with those of other faiths—he would have been pleased to receive Catholic last rites just before dying as a Presbyterian.

Right after he died, the presents started arriving at the homes and offices of his friends and associates. During the last few months of his life, Rogers had thought about which of his personal belongings would be right to give to each of his many friends. Archabbot Nowicki got a pair of cufflinks. The journalist Tim Madigan, author of *I'm Proud of You: My Friendship with Fred Rogers*, got photographs commemorating their association. Jeannine Morrison, a college friend from Rollins, got a check, which she and her husband used to buy a car—a Honda, like Fred's.

Rogers had arranged for his cousin Jim Okonak, executive director of the McFeely-Rogers Foundation, to mail these gifts out after his death. There was very little written communication. In effect, the gift itself was the message: a note of caring, kindness, and thoughtfulness from the master of benevolence.

While he was mustering his gift list, Rogers worried he might die before he had done everything he could to be a good person. His doubts caught up with him, and he worried that he had somehow let down his God. But then he consulted with Joanne and his sister, Laney, and with Archabbot Nowicki, and he prayed. He came to the conclusion that he'd used his gifts to the best of his ability. And Fred decided that, imperfect though he knew himself to be, he really had done his best, and that God, to whom he had dedicated his life, would accept him into heaven.

Eliot Daley, Fred Rogers's old friend and former executive at Small World Enterprises, says: "I would describe him as the ultimate 'what you see is what you get,' with one exception. What most people couldn't see in Fred was his enormous power. Power. Capital P. Fred is the most powerful person I have ever known in my whole life. . . . I've dealt with a lot of people whom the world regards as powerful. None of them could hold a candle to Fred's power. . . .

"His power derived from a really unique place. It was his absolute self-possession, which is very different from self-interest or self-satisfaction, or selfishness. He didn't need anything from you or from me. He welcomed it, but he didn't need it."[11]

Joanne Rogers adds: "Fred was a wonderful husband. And he was interesting and fun, and loving. I can't think of ever having a better relationship. And I do miss him. Whenever I do miss him, I think about the times when he was so sick. And I think: No, I wouldn't have wanted him to stay on in that condition. In a way—you know, we were fortunate that his illness was not that extended, although it seemed like ten years, even if it was only two months.

"I knew that he was ready any time. Some of us, when we talk about him, you'd think sainthood wouldn't even be good enough. But he was a very special person. Very special. The most special person I ever knew."[12]

Michael Horton reflects on his long friendship with Fred Rogers: "One word that defines my friendship with Fred is *laughter*. All of our phone calls, all of our visits, all of our interactions non-studio, non-work, were full of laughter. His sense of whimsy was unparalleled. Early on, I asked him to write a couple of letters of recommendation for me; and even those were just wonderful.

"I miss him so much; I need that laughter. He gave unconditional love—no matter what you did or what you said. He always loved you. I can make my husband cry to this day by singing 'It's You I Like.' He'll never let me finish. I never quite get to the end of it because I don't want to cry."[13]

Fred Rogers's death was such a significant event that the next day, the *Pittsburgh Post-Gazette* devoted the entire front page of the paper to him. His longtime friend Rev. Bill Barker presided over a public memorial at Heinz Hall in Pittsburgh on May 3, 2003, attended by over twenty-seven hundred people, including former *Good Morning America* host David Hartman, Teresa Heinz Kerry, philanthropist Elsie Hillman, PBS President Pat Mitchell, *Arthur* creator Marc Brown, and *The Very Hungry Caterpillar* author-illustrator Eric Carle.

In the lobby of the hall, guests could write farewell messages to Fred Rogers in suede-covered books; colored pencils were also provided. His newest grandson, Ian, slept peacefully during the service.

An old Rogers friend, the famed violinist Itzhak Perlman, made a surprise visit to play in Fred's memory; and renowned cellist Yo-Yo Ma played via videotape since he had another performance that conflicted with the service. Speakers remembered Rogers's love of children, devotion to his religion, enthusiasm for music, and quirks. Teresa Heinz Kerry said of Rogers, "He never condescended, just invited us into his conversation. He spoke to us as the people we were, not as the people others wished we were."[14]

Fred Rogers is interred at Unity Cemetery outside Latrobe, not far from where he grew up, and just a mile from the Fred Rogers Center for Early Learning and Children's Media, the institution that was conceived to carry on his legacy and work, located on the campus of Saint Vincent College. Soon after he died, Joanne Rogers sent his concert grand piano back to the Steinway factory in New York to be rebuilt, then made a gift of it to the center.

It remains there, part of the history of Fred Rogers, *Mister Rogers' Neighborhood*, and the generosity of Fred's grandmother, "Nana" McFeely. The piano is occasionally played by one of the Saint Vincent College music students. Sometimes it is moved across the hall from the Rogers Center to a large meeting hall in the same building. There the piano rings out again with songs from the *Neighborhood* at special events.

On New Year's Day, 2004, Michael Keaton hosted a PBS special entitled *Fred Rogers: America's Favorite Neighbor.* Later, to mark what would have been Fred's eightieth birthday, the Fred Rogers Company sponsored several events to memorialize him, including "Won't You Wear a Sweater Day," during which fans and neighbors were asked to wear their favorite sweaters in celebration of Rogers's life.

Rogers received the Presidential Medal of Freedom, over forty honorary degrees, and a Peabody Award, as well as a Lifetime Achievement Emmy. He was inducted into the Television Hall of Fame, was recognized by two Congressional resolutions, and ranks No. 35 among *TV Guide*'s Fifty Greatest TV Stars of All Time. Several buildings and artworks in Pennsylvania are dedicated to his memory, as is the asteroid 26858 Misterrogers, named by the International Astronomical Union on May 2, 2003, by the director of the Henry Buhl Jr. Planetarium & Observatory at the Carnegie Science Center in Pittsburgh. And the science center worked with Rogers's Family Communications, Inc., to produce a planetarium show for preschoolers called "The Sky Above Mister Rogers' Neighborhood," which plays at planetariums across the United States.[15]

Some longtime staffers like Hedda Sharapan continue to work with the Fred Rogers Company and the Fred Rogers Center. In the wake of his death, she observed: "This is something kind of strange, but I use Fred's work so much in my everyday life that he's still here for me. Sometimes, I have trouble talking about him in the past tense."[16]

A little more than a month after Fred's death, the Gorilla Foundation shared a tribute to Fred from Koko in a rebroadcast of their visit together.

In a short video released by PBS a few months before Fred Rogers's death, he says good-bye. Looking distinguished in a sharp suit and tie and glasses, he addresses his "television neighbors" directly, as he always does: "I would like to tell you what I often told you when you were much younger. I like you just the way you are. And what's more, I'm so grateful to you for helping the children in your life to know that you'll do everything you can to keep them safe. And to help them express their feelings in ways that will bring healing in many different neighborhoods. It's such a good feeling to know that we're lifelong friends."[17]

25.

MISTER ROGERS LIVES ON

TODAY, the Fred Rogers Company produces programs like *Peg + Cat*, *Odd Squad*, *Through the Woods*, and *Daniel Tiger's Neighborhood* that make use of Rogers's techniques. They've all achieved critical and commercial success with approaches that incorporate some of Fred's style and substance, as well as his emphasis on human values.

Angela Santomero, the creator of *Blue's Clues*, remembers watching *Mister Rogers' Neighborhood* as a three-year-old and talking back to Mister Rogers on television. Later, she came back to Rogers's work in creating her own show: "It really was paying tribute to the Mister Rogers show, because . . . I took many of the formal features he used—speaking directly to the camera, this idea that there is this intimacy of talking directly. And in having a world of imagination. Fred used the trolley to transition you to the land of the make-believe, and we used a little skidoo dance that transitioned you into a skidoo world."[1]

Like Rogers, Santomero bases her work heavily on research in the fields of education and child development. In developing *Blue's Clues*, she worked closely with Dr. Alice Wilder, a leading thinker on media and child development who has a EdD in educational psychology from Columbia University. "The research piece is very important to me," says Santomero, "so in our production budget we carved out a little bit of money just for research, which nobody had done before within a production."[2]

The creator of *Wonder Pets*, Josh Selig, recalls the power of Rogers's approach and its influence on his own creative work: "There's something about the rhythm of Fred Rogers that is very calming and soothing, and I know that this was very deliberate on his part. He really understood children's minds and the pace at which they could receive information comfortably. *Wonder Pets* does have a lot of what we would call formal features, meaning that in every episode certain things always happen. . . .

"That level of predictability, I think, is very comforting to young children. Similarly, Mister Rogers had certain structures, but within that there was always a lot of originality."[3]

Like Rogers, Selig decided to incorporate live music into his show, and he wove operatic themes into the program in ways that are reminiscent of Rogers's use of opera and song: "I'd learned from years watching Fred that music has power in storytelling. I see this as almost a child's interpretation of opera. It shouldn't be sophisticated opera that's going to leave them behind, but a very playful way of singing dialogue that helps the child understand the emotion of a scene or the arc of the whole show."[4]

Selig and Santomero have received numerous accolades. Selig was awarded a Daytime Emmy for *Wonder Pets*, as well as numerous other nominations. Santomero's work was also nominated several times for Daytime Emmys. In addition, Santomero won a Peabody Award for *Blue's Clues*.

One of the fundamental things that Fred Rogers understood, that brought the sort of power to his work that attracted Selig and Santomero and others, is that it is perfectly appropriate for children to be utterly different from grown-ups. They are not little adults, just like their parents, but smaller. They have a unique perspective, and they have a special job to do: learning. But this idea—that children have an utterly different and completely important place separate from adults—didn't begin to germinate until the nineteenth century, and then it grew slowly as research into childhood advanced.

In 1996, Lynette Friedrich Cofer, a professor of psychology at the University of New Mexico, wrote that since she conducted a 1975 study of the effects of *Mister Rogers' Neighborhood* on young viewers with a colleague at Penn State, Aletha Huston-Stein, things had gotten much worse in content aimed at young children: "Children's television is . . . strewn with war toys, insipid cartoons, and over-sweetened cereals. We seem unable to halt a technological and commercial expansion that has invaded the lives of children and families."[5]

She looks back with regret at how little Fred Rogers's power has been appreciated: "And what of the children who saw the quiet and complex *Mister Rogers' Neighborhood* programs? They showed significant changes in behaviors that require self-control: increased persistence or the amount of time spent concentrating on projects, greater ability to carry out responsibility without adult intervention in tasks like helping with cleanup, and greater patience waiting to take their turn or to be served at juice time. We also found significant changes for children from lower social-class homes in the quality of their play with other children—increased cooperation, ability to express feelings, and sympathy and help for others."[6]

Fred Rogers appeared before audiences of millions of young children and their parents, grandparents, and teachers over a forty-year period, including long after the *Neighborhood* finished production three years before the death of its creator. At the height of its appeal in the mid-1980s, nearly 10 percent of American households tuned into the show.

Historian and bestselling author David McCullough notes: "Mister Rogers was the greatest teacher of all times. He taught more students than anyone else in history."[7]

To aid parents and teachers, the Fred Rogers Company now also maintains an online store that offers instructional materials on topics such as what to do when your baby cries or how to protect the environment (activity books along with DVDs). There is even a book and workshop on what to do with "mad feelings," and a compilation of four episodes of the *Neighborhood* that deal with kids with autism. In addition, the company sells branded merchandise featuring beloved *Neighborhood* characters like Mr. McFeely, plush versions of popular new characters like the animated Daniel, and materials to encourage creativity in children (such as the book *A Piece of Red Paper*, about using construction paper).

FRED ROGERS'S WORK shaped not only television in new and exciting ways; he also left his mark on the technology that drives it by testifying before the Supreme Court in 1983. Universal Studios, backed by the Motion Picture Association of America (MPAA) had sued the Sony Corporation, manufacturers of the VCR (MPAA head Jack Valenti called the ability to record TV shows "savagery"). Fred Rogers testified on Sony's behalf, saying he had no objection to the taping of his shows because, "I just feel that anything that allows a person to be more active in the control of his or her life, in a healthy way, is important."[8] The Supreme Court ruled in Sony's favor, and the case would later serve as precedent for similar technologies such as Netflix and Hulu.

Ironically, the computer that worried Rogers has in fact given him, and *Mister Rogers' Neighborhood*, a new lease on life. After the 2016 election, Fred Rogers's now-adult "neighbors" looked for a voice of kindness and compassion. In May 2017, Twitch, a video platform for gamers, mounted a *Mister Rogers' Neighborhood* marathon of all 886 episodes that garnered over a million views in the first few days of streaming. The marathon was repeated in late May 2018.

In turn, Twitter "blew up" (over ten thousand "likes" in a matter of days, retweeted by caustic comedian Sarah Silverman, among others) with a story by Anthony Breznican, a senior writer at *Entertainment Weekly* (*EW*), later reprinted in *EW* and even picked up by *USA Today*. In it, he agonized about what to tell his four-year-old son in the wake of the bombing in Manchester, England, that endangered so many innocent children and young adults.[9] Then he recounts a seminal incident from years earlier, when he encountered Rogers in an elevator at the University of Pittsburgh. When they got off together, Breznican broke down and told Rogers about the recent death of his grandfather. Fred Rogers comforted the young man with a story about how much he was affected by the death of his own grandfather. Yes, concludes Anthony Breznican, Rogers personified the "helping" ethos his mother taught him. All over the internet, the "meme" of Fred Rogers encouraging his viewers to "look for the helpers" offers solace.

Fred Rogers continues to elicit as much interest as he did when he was alive, and he seems as current, as relevant, and even as controversial as at any time in his career: when education is discussed, when the rearing of children is considered, when the uses of technology or the value of funding for public television are debated, and whenever another spasm of violence shakes the world.

Whenever a great tragedy strikes—war, famine, mass shootings, or even an outbreak of populist rage—millions of people turn to Fred's messages about life. Then the web is filled with his words and images. With fascinating frequency, his written messages and video clips surge across the internet, reaching hundreds of thousands of people who, confronted with a tough issue or an ominous development, open themselves to Rogers's messages of quiet contemplation, of simplicity, of active listening and the practice of human kindness.

Still, the question of Fred's legacy is not so easily resolved by a biography, or the work of the Fred Rogers Center, or the productions of the Fred Rogers Company. Rogers remains controversial to some who think of him as too soft, too likely to coddle the young and weaken their moral and intellectual fiber. In July 2007, Jeffrey Zaslow (most famous for later coauthoring the book *The Last Lecture* with dying Carnegie Mellon University professor Randy Pausch) wrote in the *Wall Street Journal*: "As educators and researchers struggle to define the new parameters of parenting, circa 2007, some are revisiting the language of child ego-boosting."[10]

Though Zaslow criticized Rogers directly for being too undemanding in his support of children, he was relatively measured in his commentary. But not all who followed suit were so genteel. In the spring of 2010, the Fox News Channel devoted part of its daily newscast to a segment entitled "Is Mr. [sic] Rogers Ruining Kids?" *Fox & Friends* took it all the way, describing Rogers as "this evil man" who taught kids that they are special, thereby sapping their will to work hard in school, or to improve themselves.[11]

A highly publicized and notably controversial shot in this philosophical war was the 2011 publication of *Battle Hymn of the Tiger Mother* by Amy Chua, professor of law at Yale Law School, who humorously and thoroughly explores the implications of a very tough, demanding style of parenting.[12]

Like many other writers before her, Professor Chua sees virtue in the role of a very exacting parent who emphasizes hard work and discipline. Her book rekindled the debate, with some criticizing her for advocating a harsh parental regimen, and others applauding this shot across the bow of wimps like Rogers. In fact, philosophers of parenting like Fred Rogers and Professor Chua are almost always far more nuanced and thoughtfully balanced than their provocative critics would have us believe. Professor Chua's book is full of humor and self-deprecation, and the approach she advocates, while demanding of her children, is not nearly so draconian as her critics would suggest.

The fact that the internet—and popular culture—continues today to resonate with so much interest in Fred Rogers and his message is less puzzling when we consider what he represents in the context of our times. On one level, Fred is a gentle, reserved old man in a fading cardigan sweater whose principal contribution to society has been in the field of childcare. But on another level—and this is the level on which he is so often appreciated today—he is a powerful cultural avatar in an age that seems sick with rage and conflict.

Whether it is the overwhelming pace of change, the baffling complexity of communications technology, the disruptive force of a globalizing economy, or the rise of populist political anger, Fred Rogers offers a counterpoint.

After all, the dominant trend of our time is the steady, relentless increase to the pace of change, the inexorable drive toward complexity in all aspects of our lives: in communication, information, technology, commerce, education, employment, even warfare. The pace of change is unyielding, and its ability to disrupt our lives in myriad ways is equally relentless. Of course, change can—and does—make life better in so many ways. But even when it is delivering improvement, it can be disruptive and unsettling.

Inevitably, we look for someone or something to blame: It must be government, interfering with our lives and putting chocks under our wheels. Or we blame the *other*: those other countries or peoples or ethnic groups that are not like us and may be competing for advantage.

Fred Rogers doesn't offer an answer to today's profound dilemmas, nor does he offer an escape from them. But he does offer a philosophy, an approach, that can enable us to better manage through the struggle. He offers the idea of slowing down . . . way down to *Fred-time* . . . to get to a calmer place from which to work. He offers the idea of simplicity: of reducing things to their most constructive and most elemental, to *Freddish*—a base from which to build understanding. He urges us to value our global citizens "just the way they are," no matter their skin color or religious affiliation.

Looking back on his career in his retirement, he said in a speech: "In our makeshift ways, those of us who were producing felt that what we were doing was somehow a gift. We felt that by way of educational television, we were giving a life-enriching gift. If that sounds lofty to you, remember we were a little band of ecstatic pioneers—you know, to be 'ecstatic' literally means 'to be outside of a static place.' Well, we were on the move, and we had to feel that our work was a valuable gift; otherwise, we couldn't have produced all the hours and days and months and years of television that we did."[13]

EPILOGUE: A PERSONAL NOTE ON THE IMPORTANCE OF FRED ROGERS

FRED ROGERS AND I were sitting in his office at Family Communications, Inc., in the WQED building on Fifth Avenue in Pittsburgh. His staff had arranged for the two of us to get together and talk, back when I was president of the Heinz Endowments, one of the larger foundations in the country, chaired by Fred's longtime friend and supporter Teresa Heinz. But we didn't talk about the foundation or funding; we talked about everything else: Fred's grandchildren, Pittsburgh, journalism, and our vacation houses on Nantucket Island.

Fred sat on a large sofa along one wall, and I sat in a big, comfortable easy chair facing him. Over Fred's head was a needlepoint picture of Nantucket. When I remarked on it, we discovered that we each owned a small, run-down, unheated fisherman's shack on the island, Fred's at the western end in Madaket, and mine to the east in Wauwinet. Fred explained that the needlepoint map of Nantucket had been done by his mother.

"Where is your mother now?" I asked.

"She is in heaven," he said. No sheepishness, no smile, no half-hearted apology for believing.

As so many had discovered before me, in person, Fred Rogers was just as he was on television: simple, childlike, earnest, and charming. I saw him only one other time: a year later, on the street, and we simply said hello. Not long afterward, he was suddenly gone—lost to cancer at too early an age.

I had come to appreciate Fred during my years in Pittsburgh; it seemed that almost everyone there had a deep understanding of his commitment to children and to the value of human kindness. But it wasn't until five years later, when I was retiring from the Endowments, that I reconnected with his work and his world. At the same time as I was leaving Heinz, my term as chairman of the board of the National Council on Foundations was expiring. With two jobs ending at once, I was in a bit of a panic. When Archabbot Douglas Nowicki, chancellor of Saint Vincent College in Latrobe, Pennsylvania, asked me to help with the establishment of the Fred Rogers Center for Early Learning and Children's Media at the college, I joined up.

I made myself a student of Fred and his work. Over time, I came to appreciate that in addition to being one of the most important champions of early childhood education in America, Fred was a fascinating and admirable character in many ways. During the two years I spent as director of the center, I often talked with Douglas, and with Fred's widow Joanne Rogers, about the need for a biography of Fred. They explained that while Fred was alive, he didn't want a biography; he didn't want attention to be on him instead of the children.

I pointed out that things were different now: If we were going to advance Fred's legacy, we needed a biography.

Besides, the world needed to know the story of this extraordinary, important, and exemplary man. Finally, they acceded. And when they did, Joanne convinced me that I should take on the job of writing that biography. The project got underway when I stepped down as director of the center in 2010. One of the first things I did was to call David Black, the literary agent in New York. I knew David from my time at *The Philadelphia Inquirer*, when several of the writers at the paper had engaged him as their agent.

I went on for a while on the phone, telling David about my connection to the Rogers Center, and my hope to write a biography of Fred. Silence on the other end of the line. I continued, elaborating on my intended approach to the book. Silence.

Finally, I blurted out, "David, what's the matter? This could be a good book, and I'm getting nothing back from you."

David said he had been stunned into silence by the irony of getting a call about a Rogers biography. Ten years earlier, he had traveled to Pittsburgh with Tom Junod, the talented writer who had done an acclaimed profile of Fred in *Esquire* magazine in 1998. Black and Junod spent two hours with Rogers, trying desperately to get him to agree to have Junod write a biography. But Fred was adamant: He didn't want the spotlight on himself.

A decade later, I popped back into David Black's life to offer another chance at the Rogers story. Tom Junod's story about his friendship with Rogers is now being made into a feature film starring Tom Hanks as Fred.

There are, essentially, two compelling reasons why I believe the reading public should care about Fred and his work: First, he recognized the critical importance of learning during the earliest years. No one better understood how essential it is for proper social, emotional, cognitive, and language development to take place in the first few years of life. And no one did more to convince a mass audience in America of the value of early education.

Second, he provided, and continues to provide, exemplary moral leadership. Fred Rogers advanced humanistic values because of his belief in Christianity, but his spirituality was completely eclectic; he found merit in all faiths and philosophies. His signature value was human kindness; he lived it and he preached it, to children, to their parents, to their teachers, to all of us everywhere who could take the time to listen.

Two organizations are dedicated to carrying on Fred's work: the Fred Rogers Company (www.fredrogers.org), formerly Family Communications, Inc., which still produces superb children's programming for television; and the Fred Rogers Center for Early Learning and Children's Media at Saint Vincent College (www.fredrogerscenter.org), which manages a broad series of programs to help parents, families, teachers, and media producers with the education and development of young children.

The Fred Rogers Company still leads the children's television world with such programs as *Daniel Tiger's Neighborhood* and *Peg + Cat.* The company made a remarkable resurgence since Fred Rogers's passing, and it is now again one of the leading producers of quality children's media in the country.

The Fred Rogers Center, where I served as a senior fellow during the researching and writing of this book, was planned during the last few years of Fred's life. By design, it is located at Saint Vincent in Latrobe, where Fred grew up. The college is committed to advancing Rogers's legacy through the work of the center, which focuses on the uses of communications technology, language development, and early childhood education.

The center is committed to sustaining the most rigorous standards of programmatic excellence, just as Rogers was. He hoped that support for the center would come from across America, not only from charitable foundations, but also from individuals who appreciated his work and his standards. Information about the center's work, and how to support it, can be found on its website.

Fred Rogers illuminates the way to integrity, respect, responsibility, fairness, and compassion, enshrined in most of the world's religions and philosophies.

And of course: the children. Always, the children. Think first of the children, the lifeblood of our future.

As Fred Rogers summed it up: "Childhood is not just clowns and balloons. In fact, childhood goes to the very heart of who we all become."

When Terry Gross on NPR's *Fresh Air* interviewed Fred Rogers in 1984, she concluded by asking him if he ever wanted to be a child again: "Do you ever wish you were five or ten or twelve?"

To which he replied: "Yes. But I'd like to be that with what I know now. And I think I'd like that because there are many significant people in my life that I have lost through death, and I'd like to be able to talk to them again, and tell them some things that I wasn't able to tell them then. In fact, I'd like to be able to tell them, you are special."

ACKNOWLEDGMENTS

To Patricia Mulcahy, whose artful editing, good counsel, and writing assistance have made all the difference in the quality of this book. Without her skill as an editor and as an accomplished storyteller, the manuscript for *The Good Neighbor* would have fallen short of its potential. I am grateful for her assistance and her friendship.

To the leaders of the Apex Foundation in Bellevue, Washington, for their early support, their deep appreciation for this project, and their encouragement. At the very beginning, chairs Bruce and Jolene McCaw and director Craig Stewart saw the potential of the biography to advance their deep commitment to early learning and good parenting. They supported research work for the project with a generous grant to the Fred Rogers Center at Saint Vincent College. And to the Buhl Foundation and the Fisher Fund, both in Pittsburgh, for their early and generous funding to the center in support of the research for this project.

To Joanne Rogers, whose sharp intelligence, patience, and good humor made our long interviews together such a joy. Without Joanne's candor and hard work at bringing the details of Fred's life and her life into vivid focus, this book could not be a success. Her wonderful strength of character made the process of getting to know her, and getting to know Fred through her, a complete joy.

To Archabbot Douglas Nowicki, chancellor of Saint Vincent College and Monastery, whose powerful understanding of Fred Rogers and his work has enriched this book, as it enriched the life and work of Rogers himself. The Archabbot's commitment to Rogers's legacy has been the force behind the Fred Rogers Center for Early Learning and Children's Media and a catalyst of this book project.

To Elaine Rogers Crozier, Fred's beloved sister, Laney, who gave generously of her time and her strong recollections of her brother.

Laney's insightfulness and thoughtfulness, about Fred and Latrobe and the extended Rogers family, helped me understand the environment that shaped Rogers's life. And to Fred Rogers's sons, James and John, who provided great detail and clear thinking about their father and their family.

To Jamison Stoltz, whose passion for Fred Rogers's story and great skill as an editor have helped me achieve a book that just may have a chance of being worthy of its subject. Jamison's depth of engagement and understanding of good narrative have helped push this project to success.

To Alicia Tan, for her careful attention to detail as the manuscript moved from text to final book.

To copyeditor Jean Hartig, whose fine attention to style and detail helped greatly in shaping the final draft.

To David Black, whose unrelenting drive to improve this project, and to improve me as a writer, contributed in the most substantive ways toward our common goal of producing a worthy book. His talents as an agent and a critic have been invaluable to me.

To archivist Emily Uhrin of the Fred Rogers Center at Saint Vincent College, who provided so much intelligent support and assistance for this project. Time and again, Emily pointed me in the right direction, gently warned me off the wrong direction, helped with research, and gave critical feedback at key moments.

To the staff members of the Fred Rogers Center at Saint Vincent College who provided so much help, support, and important feedback throughout this process: Theresa Noel, Cindy Scarpo, Rita Catalano, Rick Fernandes, Junlei Li, Sandra Frye, and Karen Myers.

To Elizabeth Deane, who contributed importantly to this project at a time when it was in danger of stalling out. Elizabeth's well-honed skill as an award-winning documentary filmmaker helped her fashion important contributions to key portions of this book.

To Mary Lowe Kennedy, who helped with editing and revising this manuscript early enough in the process to make a significant difference in approach, pushing the text from exposition to narrative in ways that have made it more compelling.

To Kathryn Klawinski and Teresa Noel of the Fred Rogers Center at Saint Vincent College, whose thoughtful help with organizing and verifying footnotes for this book is much appreciated.

To my wife, Margaret Ann, and my sons, Ned and Will, for all their support and intelligent feedback on this project over such a long period of time.

To all those who have given freely and generously of their time to recollecting the power of *Mister Rogers' Neighborhood* and Fred Rogers: Elizabeth Seamans, Joe Seamans, Eliot Daley, Basil Cox, Margy Whitmer, Hedda Sharapan, David Newell, Bill Isler, Betty Aberlin, Chuck Aber, Cathy Droz, Margot Woodwell, Elaine Lynch, Joan Ganz Cooney, Roberta Schomburg, Rev. Clark Kerr, James R. Okonak, Linda McKenna Boxx, Jane Werner, Patricia Neeper, Ed "Yogi" Showalter, Peggy Moberg McFeaters, Anita Lavin Manoli, Richard "Puffy" Jim, Rudolph Prohaska, Jeannine Morrison, Arthur Greenwald, Arnold Palmer, Rev. William Barker, Jean Barker, Kirk Browning, Milton Chen, Dr. Margaret Mary Kimmel, Nancy Curry, Bill Strickland, Rev. George Wirth, Yo-Yo Ma, Joe Negri, Michael Horton, Wynton Marsalis, Dr. Jerome Singer, Dr. Dorothy Singer, Dr. Susan Linn, Jeff Varion, Dr. James Hughes, Dr. William Hirsch, Danforth Fales, Rev. Burr Wishart, David Hartman, Rev. Lisa Dormire, Barry Head, Howard Erlanger, Pam Erlanger, Sam Silberman, Dr. Bernard Mallinger, Stephanie Mallinger, Pasquale Buba, Paul Taff, Tom Junod, Kate Taylor, George Hill, Nancy Gruner, Susan Stamberg, Francis Chapman, Dr. Andrew Purves, Jerlean Daniel, Alice Cahn, Josh Selig, Angela Santomero, and Tim Lybarger.

And, finally, to Marianne Cola of The Pittsburgh Foundation, who has been invaluable to me in sorting through the demands of running a major charitable organization while finishing the writing of a complicated biography.

NOTES

CHAPTER 1

1. *The Heritage of a Commonwealth.* [Biographical sketches] W. Palm Beach, FL: The American Historical Co., Inc., 1969. Page 449. Print.
2. Okonak, James R. Personal Interview. 12 October 2010. Audio.
3. Crozier, Elaine Rogers. Personal Interview. 4 October 2010. Audio.
4. Rogers, Fred. Interview by Charlie Rose. *Charlie Rose.* 20 September 1994. Video.
5. Crozier, Elaine Rogers. Personal Interview. 9 January 2012. Audio.
6. *The Latrobe Bulletin,* Latrobe, PA. November 1981. Print.
7. "The Benefactor." Latrobe Area Hospital Charitable Foundation. Fall 1996. Print.
8. Chapman, Francis. Interview by Jessica Wiederhorn. The Narrative Trust. Fred Rogers Oral History Collection. Fred Rogers Center for Early Learning and Children's Media at St. Vincent College. 16 July 2008. Video.
9. "Some Ancestors of Fred McFeely Rogers." Kapp, Deborah. Prepared for the Fred Rogers Center for Early Learning and Children's Media at St. Vincent College. November 2011. Print.
10. Showalter, Edward. Interview by Jessica Wiederhorn. The Narrative Trust. Fred Rogers Oral History Collection. Fred Rogers Center for Early Learning and Children's Media at St. Vincent College. 20 July 2009. Video.
11. Manoli, Anita Lavin. Interview by Jessica Wiederhorn. The Narrative Trust. Fred Rogers Oral History Collection. Fred Rogers Center for Early Learning and Children's Media at St. Vincent College. 20 July 2009. Video.
12. Kerr, The Rev. Clark. Personal Interview. 15 March 2011. Audio.
13. Crozier, Elaine Rogers. Personal Interview. 27 September 2010. Audio.
14. Okonak, James R. Personal Interview. 24 May 2011. Audio.
15. Crozier, Elaine Rogers. Personal Interview. 27 September 2010. Audio.
16. "Latrobe, Pennsylvania." Greater Latrobe Centennial Corporation. June 1954. Print.
17. Ibid.
18. "Some Ancestors of Fred McFeely Rogers." Kapp, Deborah. Prepared for the Fred Rogers Center for Early Learning and Children's Media at St. Vincent College. November 2011. Print.
19. Manoli, Anita Lavin. Interview by Jessica Wiederhorn. The Narrative Trust. Fred Rogers Oral History Collection. Fred Rogers Center for Early Learning and Children's Media at St. Vincent College. 20 July 2009. Video.
20. Ibid.
21. Crozier, Elaine Rogers. Personal Interview. 24 September 2010. Audio.
22. Prohaska, Rudolph. Interview by Jessica Wiederhorn. The Narrative Trust. Fred Rogers Oral History Collection. Fred Rogers Center for Early Learning and Children's Media at St. Vincent College. 20 July 2009. Video.
23. Ibid.
24. Mencken, H. L. *The Baltimore Sun.* Baltimore, MD. January 1935. Print.
25. Okonak, James R. Personal Interview. 24 May 2011. Audio.
26. McFeaters, Peggy Moberg. Interview by Jessica Wiederhorn. The Narrative Trust. Fred Rogers Oral History Collection. Fred Rogers Center for Early Learning and Children's Media at St. Vincent College. 21 July 2009. Video.
27. Ibid.
28. Crozier, Elaine Rogers. Personal Interview. 27 September 2010. Audio.
29. Crozier, Elaine Rogers. Personal Interview. 4 October 2010. Audio.
30. Prohaska, Rudolph. Interview by Jessica Wiederhorn. The Narrative Trust. Fred

Rogers Oral History Collection. Fred Rogers Center for Early Learning and Children's Media at St. Vincent College. 20 July 2009. Video.

31. Crozier, Elaine Rogers. Interview by Jessica Wiederhorn. The Narrative Trust. Fred Rogers Oral History Collection. Fred Rogers Center for Early Learning and Children's Media at St. Vincent College. 18 October 2007. Video.

32. Rogers, Alberta Vance. Interview by Mike Pacek. Latrobe Area Historical Society. 23 July 1991. Print.

33. Palmer, Arnold. Personal Interview. 16 May 2011. Audio.

34. Ibid.

35. Rogers, Fred. Speech. Opening Ceremonies Sesquicentennial. Saint Vincent Archabbey and College. Latrobe, PA. Fred Rogers Archive. Fred Rogers Center for Early Learning and Children's Media at St. Vincent College. 25 April 1995. Print.

36. Ibid.

37. McFeaters, Peggy Moberg. Interview by Jessica Wiederhorn. The Narrative Trust. Fred Rogers Oral History Collection. Fred Rogers Center for Early Learning and Children's Media at St. Vincent College. 21 July 2009. Video.

CHAPTER 2

1. Crozier, Elaine Rogers. Interview by Jessica Wiederhorn. The Narrative Trust. Fred Rogers Oral History Collection. Fred Rogers Center for Early Learning and Children's Media at St. Vincent College. 18 October 2007. Video.

2. Ibid.

3. Crozier, Elaine Rogers. Personal Interview. 27 September 2010. Audio.

4. Collins, Mark, and Margaret Mary Kimmel, editors. Mister Rogers Neighborhood: Children, Television and Fred Rogers. Pittsburgh: University Of Pittsburgh Press. 1996. Page 23. Print.

5. Crozier, Elaine Rogers. Personal Interview. 27 September 2010. Audio.

6. Rogers, Joanne. Interview by Jessica Wiederhorn. The Narrative Trust. Fred Rogers Oral History Collection. Fred Rogers Center for Early Learning and Children's Media at St. Vincent College. 14 June 2007. Video.

7. Crozier, Elaine Rogers. Interview by Jessica Wiederhorn. The Narrative Trust. Fred Rogers Oral History Collection. Fred Rogers Center for Early Learning and Children's Media at St. Vincent College. 18 October 2007. Video.

8. "The Historic Beginnings of Latrobe." Around Latrobe. Latrobe Historical Society. 2003. Print.

9. Crozier, Elaine Rogers. Interview by Jessica Wiederhorn. The Narrative Trust. Fred Rogers Oral History Collection. Fred Rogers Center for Early Learning and Children's Media at St. Vincent College. 18 October 2007. Video.

10. Okonak, James R. Personal Interview. 12 October 2010. Audio.

11. Eliot, Marc. Jimmy Stewart: A Biography. New York: Random House, 2007. Print.

12. Hatano-Worrell, A.W. "Fred Rogers, The Kindly Neighbor (1928–2003)." 2006. www .project-files.net/gratefulness/giftpeople/ fred_rogers.htm.

13. Crozier, Elaine Rogers. Personal Interview. 27 September 2010. Audio.

14. Old Friends, New Friends. Program 105, "Memories." The Fred Rogers Company. 13 April 1978. Television.

15. Ibid.

16. Neeper, Patricia. Personal Interview. 26 January 2011. Audio.

17. Kirkland, David. Steinway and Sons. Telephone Interview. 2 November 2011. Audio.

18. Neeper, Patricia. Personal Interview. 26 January 2011. Audio.

19. Crozier, Elaine Rogers. Interview by Jessica Wiederhorn. The Narrative Trust. Fred Rogers Oral History Collection. Fred Rogers Center for Early Learning and Children's Media at St. Vincent College. 18 October 2007. Video.

20. Rogers, Joanne. Personal Interview. 14 September 2011. Audio.

21. Ibid.

22. Manoli, Anita Lavin. Interview by Jessica Wiederhorn. The Narrative Trust. Fred Rogers Oral History Collection. Fred Rogers Center for Early Learning and Children's Media at St. Vincent College. 20 July 2009. Video.

23. Ibid.

24. Jim, Richard "Puffy". Interview by Jessica Wiederhorn. The Narrative Trust. Fred

Rogers Oral History Collection. Fred Rogers Center for Early Learning and Children's Media at St. Vincent College. 20 July 2009. Video.

25. Ibid.

26. Fred Rogers Interview, by Karen Herman on July 22, 1999 for *The Interviews: An Oral History of Television*. Visit TelevisionAcademy .com/Interviews for more information.

27. Kimmel, Maggie. Personal Interview. 16 September 2010. Audio.

CHAPTER 3

1. Fred Rogers Interview, by Karen Herman on July 22, 1999 for *The Interviews: An Oral History of Television*. Visit TelevisionAcademy .com/Interviews for more information.

2. "Some Ancestors of Fred McFeely Rogers." Kapp, Deborah. Prepared for the Fred Rogers Center for Early Learning and Children's Media at St. Vincent College. November 2011. Print.

3. Ibid.

4. Crozier, Elaine Rogers. Interview by Jessica Wiederhorn. The Narrative Trust. Fred Rogers Oral History Collection. Fred Rogers Center for Early Learning and Children's Media at St. Vincent College. 18 October 2007. Video.

5. Leffler, Mark. "House Rules: Chris Miller Takes Us Back to the Real Animal House." *The Review*. Issue 626. 16 November 2006. Print.

6. Fred Rogers Interview, by Karen Herman on July 22, 1999 for *The Interviews: An Oral History of Television*. Visit TelevisionAcademy .com/Interviews for more information.

7. Rogers, Joanne. Personal Interview. 27 July 2010. Audio.

8. Fred Rogers Interview, by Karen Herman on July 22, 1999 for *The Interviews: An Oral History of Television*. Visit TelevisionAcademy .com/Interviews for more information.

9. Ibid.

10. Rogers, Joanne. Interview by Jessica Wiederhorn. The Narrative Trust. Fred Rogers Oral History Collection. Fred Rogers Center for Early Learning and Children's Media at St. Vincent College. 14 June 2007. Video.

11. Ibid.

12. Ibid.

13. Fred Rogers Interview, by Karen Herman on

July 22, 1999 for *The Interviews: An Oral History of Television*. Visit TelevisionAcademy .com/Interviews for more information.

14. Morrison, Jeannine. Interview by Jessica Wiederhorn. The Narrative Trust. Fred Rogers Oral History Collection. Fred Rogers Center for Early Learning and Children's Media at St. Vincent College. 21 July 2009. Video.

CHAPTER 4

1. Rogers, Joanne. Personal Interview. 19 July 2010. Audio.

2. Ibid.

3. Ibid.

4. Ibid.

5. Ibid.

6. Rogers, Joanne. Interview by Jessica Wiederhorn. The Narrative Trust. Fred Rogers Oral History Collection. Fred Rogers Center for Early Learning and Children's Media at St. Vincent College. 14 June 2007. Video.

7. Ibid.

8. Rogers, Joanne. Personal Interview. 19 July 2010. Audio.

9. Ibid.

10. Ibid.

11. Ibid.

12. Rogers, Joanne. Interview by Jessica Wiederhorn. The Narrative Trust. Fred Rogers Oral History Collection. Fred Rogers Center for Early Learning and Children's Media at St. Vincent College. 14 June 2007. Video.

13. Ibid.

14. Ibid.

15. Rogers, Joanne. Personal Interview. 2 November 2010. Audio.

16. Rogers, Joanne. Interview by Jessica Wiederhorn. The Narrative Trust. Fred Rogers Oral History Collection. Fred Rogers Center for Early Learning and Children's Media at St. Vincent College. 14 June 2007. Video.

17. Morrison, Jeannine. Interview by Jessica Wiederhorn. The Narrative Trust. Fred Rogers Oral History Collection. Fred Rogers Center for Early Learning and Children's Media at St. Vincent College. 21 July 2009. Video.

18. Rogers, Joanne. Interview by Jessica Wiederhorn. The Narrative Trust. Fred Rogers Oral History Collection. Fred Rogers Cen-

ter for Early Learning and Children's Media at St. Vincent College. 14 June 2007. Video.

19. Ibid.

20. Ibid.

21. Fred Rogers Interview, by Karen Herman on July 22, 1999 for *The Interviews: An Oral History of Television*. Visit TelevisionAcademy .com/Interviews for more information.

22. Rogers, Joanne. Personal Interview. 27 July 2010. Audio.

23. Ibid.

24. Ibid.

25. Ibid.

26. Rogers, Joanne. Interview by Jessica Wiederhorn. The Narrative Trust. Fred Rogers Oral History Collection. Fred Rogers Center for Early Learning and Children's Media at St. Vincent College. 14 June 2007. Video.

27. Morrison, Jeannine. Interview by Jessica Wiederhorn. The Narrative Trust. Fred Rogers Oral History Collection. Fred Rogers Center for Early Learning and Children's Media at St. Vincent College. 21 July 2009. Video.

28. Rogers, Joanne. Interview by Jessica Wiederhorn. The Narrative Trust. Fred Rogers Oral History Collection. Fred Rogers Center for Early Learning and Children's Media at St. Vincent College. 14 June 2007. Video.

29. Morrison, Jeannine. Interview by Jessica Wiederhorn. The Narrative Trust. Fred Rogers Oral History Collection. Fred Rogers Center for Early Learning and Children's Media at St. Vincent College. 21 July 2009. Video.

30. Crozier, Elaine Rogers. Personal Interview. 4 October 2010. Audio.

31. Ibid.

32. Morrison, Jeannine. Interview by Jessica Wiederhorn. The Narrative Trust. Fred Rogers Oral History Collection. Fred Rogers Center for Early Learning and Children's Media at St. Vincent College. 21 July 2009. Video.

33. Ibid.

34. Ibid.

35. Fred Rogers Interview, by Karen Herman on July 22, 1999 for *The Interviews: An Oral History of Television*. Visit TelevisionAcademy .com/Interviews for more information.

36. Ibid.

37. Morrison, Jeannine. Interview by Jessica Wiederhorn. The Narrative Trust. Fred Rogers Oral History Collection. Fred Rog-

ers Center for Early Learning and Children's Media at St. Vincent College. 21 July 2009. Video.

38. Crozier, Elaine Rogers. Personal Interview. 27 September 2010. Audio.

39. Fred Rogers Interview, by Karen Herman on July 22, 1999 for *The Interviews: An Oral History of Television*. Visit TelevisionAcademy .com/Interviews for more information.

40. Rogers, Joanne. Interview by Jessica Wiederhorn. The Narrative Trust. Fred Rogers Oral History Collection. Fred Rogers Center for Early Learning and Children's Media at St. Vincent College. 14 June 2007. Video.

41. Ibid.

CHAPTER 5

1. Rogers, Joanne. Interview by Jessica Wiederhorn. The Narrative Trust. Fred Rogers Oral History Collection. Fred Rogers Center for Early Learning and Children's Media at St. Vincent College. 14 June 2007. Video.

2. Browning, Kirk. Interview by Jessica Wiederhorn. The Narrative Trust. Fred Rogers Oral History Collection. Fred Rogers Center for Early Learning and Children's Media at St. Vincent College. 10 April 2006. Video.

3. Rogers, Joanne. Personal Interview. 14 September 2011. Audio.

4. Ibid.

5. Ibid.

6. Ibid.

7. Ibid.

8. Ibid.

9. Rogers, Joanne. Interview by Jessica Wiederhorn. The Narrative Trust. Fred Rogers Oral History Collection. Fred Rogers Center for Early Learning and Children's Media at St. Vincent College. 14 June 2007. Video.

10. Ibid.

11. Crozier, Elaine Rogers. Personal Interview. 4 October 2010. Audio.

12. Browning, Kirk. Interview by Jessica Wiederhorn. The Narrative Trust. Fred Rogers Oral History Collection. Fred Rogers Center for Early Learning and Children's Media at St. Vincent College. 10 April 2006. Video.

13. Ibid.

14. Ibid.

15. Ibid.

16. Rogers, Joanne. Interview by Jessica Wiederhorn. The Narrative Trust. Fred Rogers Oral History Collection. Fred Rogers Cen-

ter for Early Learning and Children's Media at St. Vincent College. 14 June 2007. Video.

17. Ibid.

18. Ibid.

19. Edgerton, Gary R. *The Columbia History of American Television*. New York: Columbia University Press, 2007. Page 158. Print.

20. Ibid., 26.

21. Ibid., 44.

22. Ibid., 45.

23. Ibid., 159.

24. Ibid., 159.

25. Ibid., 168.

26. Fred Rogers Interview, by Karen Herman on July 22, 1999 for *The Interviews: An Oral History of Television*. Visit TelevisionAcademy .com/Interviews for more information.

27. Edgerton, Gary R. *The Columbia History of American Television*. New York: Columbia University Press, 2007. Page 156. Print.

28. Browning, Kirk. Interview by Jessica Wiederhorn. The Narrative Trust. Fred Rogers Oral History Collection. Fred Rogers Center for Early Learning and Children's Media at St. Vincent College. 10 April 2006. Video.

29. Crozier, Elaine Rogers. Interview by Jessica Wiederhorn. The Narrative Trust. Fred Rogers Oral History Collection. Fred Rogers Center for Early Learning and Children's Media at St. Vincent College. 18 October 2007. Video.

30. Fred Rogers Interview, by Karen Herman on July 22, 1999 for *The Interviews: An Oral History of Television*. Visit TelevisionAcademy .com/Interviews for more information.

31. Browning, Kirk. Interview by Jessica Wiederhorn. The Narrative Trust. Fred Rogers Oral History Collection. Fred Rogers Center for Early Learning and Children's Media at St. Vincent College. 10 April 2006. Video.

32. Ibid.

33. Ibid.

34. Fred Rogers Interview, by Karen Herman on July 22, 1999 for *The Interviews: An Oral History of Television*. Visit TelevisionAcademy .com/Interviews for more information.

35. Yaconielli, Mike. "Door Interview: Mr. Fred Rogers." *The Wittenberg Door,* June/July 1997. Pages 8–15. Print.

36. Fred Rogers Interview, by Karen Herman on July 22, 1999 for *The Interviews: An Oral History of Television*. Visit TelevisionAcademy .com/Interviews for more information.

37. Ibid.

38. Ibid.

39. Browning, Kirk. Interview by Jessica Wiederhorn. The Narrative Trust. Fred Rogers Oral History Collection. Fred Rogers Center for Early Learning and Children's Media at St. Vincent College. 10 April 2006. Video.

40. Ibid.

CHAPTER 6

1. Fred Rogers Interview, by Karen Herman on July 22, 1999 for *The Interviews: An Oral History of Television*. Visit TelevisionAcademy .com/Interviews for more information.

2. Ibid.

3. Ibid.

4. Silverman, Sam. Interview by Jessica Wiederhorn. The Narrative Trust. Fred Rogers Oral History Collection. Fred Rogers Center for Early Learning and Children's Media at St. Vincent College. 28 February 2007. Video.

5. Hazard, Leland. "Educational Television." *The Atlantic Magazine.* 1 November 1955. Print.

6. Fred Rogers Interview, by Karen Herman on July 22, 1999 for *The Interviews: An Oral History of Television*. Visit TelevisionAcademy .com/Interviews for more information.

7. Josie Carey Interview, by Karen Herman on July 23, 1999 for *The Interviews: An Oral History of Television*. Visit TelevisionAcademy .com/Interviews for more information.

8. Ibid.

9. Owen, Robb. "Obituary: Josie Carey/TV Pioneer, Star of *The Children's Corner*." *Pittsburgh Post-Gazette.* 29 May 2004. Print.

10. Ibid.

11. Josie Carey Interview, by Karen Herman on July 23, 1999 for *The Interviews: An Oral History of Television*. Visit TelevisionAcademy .com/Interviews for more information.

12. Fred Rogers Interview, by Karen Herman on July 22, 1999 for *The Interviews: An Oral History of Television*. Visit TelevisionAcademy .com/Interviews for more information.

13. Ibid.

14. Josie Carey Interview, by Karen Herman on July 23, 1999 for *The Interviews: An Oral History of Television*. Visit TelevisionAcademy .com/Interviews for more information.

15. Woodwell, Margot. Interview by Jessica Wiederhorn. The Narrative Trust. Fred Rogers Oral History Collection. Fred Rog-

ers Center for Early Learning and Children's Media at St. Vincent College. 12 June 2007. Video.

16. Fred Rogers Interview, by Karen Herman on July 22, 1999 for *The Interviews: An Oral History of Television*. Visit TelevisionAcademy .com/Interviews for more information.

17. Rogers, Joanne. Interview by Jessica Wiederhorn. The Narrative Trust. Fred Rogers Oral History Collection. Fred Rogers Center for Early Learning and Children's Media at St. Vincent College. 14 June 2007. Video.

18. Josie Carey Interview, by Karen Herman on July 23, 1999 for *The Interviews: An Oral History of Television*. Visit TelevisionAcademy .com/Interviews for more information.

19. Woodwell, Margot. Personal Interview. 25 February 2011. Audio.

20. Josie Carey Interview, by Karen Herman on July 23, 1999 for *The Interviews: An Oral History of Television*. Visit TelevisionAcademy .com/Interviews for more information.

21. Ibid.

22. Ibid.

23. Fred Rogers Interview, by Karen Herman on July 22, 1999 for *The Interviews: An Oral History of Television*. Visit TelevisionAcademy .com/Interviews for more information.

24. Josie Carey Interview, by Karen Herman on July 23, 1999 for *The Interviews: An Oral History of Television*. Visit TelevisionAcademy .com/Interviews for more information.

25. Fred Rogers Interview, by Karen Herman on July 22, 1999 for *The Interviews: An Oral History of Television*. Visit TelevisionAcademy .com/Interviews for more information.

26. Josie Carey Interview, by Karen Herman on July 23, 1999 for *The Interviews: An Oral History of Television*. Visit TelevisionAcademy .com/Interviews for more information.

27. Edgerton, Gary R. *The Columbia History of American Television*. New York: Columbia University Press, 2007. Page 158. Print.

28. Wakin, Daniel. "Frances R. Horwich, 94, Host of 'Ding Dong School' in 50's." *New York Times*. 26 July 2001. Print.

29. Josie Carey Interview, by Karen Herman on July 23, 1999 for *The Interviews: An Oral History of Television*. Visit TelevisionAcademy .com/Interviews for more information.

30. Ibid.

31. Ibid.

32. Ibid.

33. Ibid.

34. Fred Rogers Interview, by Karen Herman on July 22, 1999 for *The Interviews: An Oral History of Television*. Visit TelevisionAcademy .com/Interviews for more information.

35. Josie Carey Interview, by Karen Herman on July 23, 1999 for *The Interviews: An Oral History of Television*. Visit TelevisionAcademy .com/Interviews for more information.

36. Fred Rogers Interview, by Karen Herman on July 22, 1999 for *The Interviews: An Oral History of Television*. Visit TelevisionAcademy .com/Interviews for more information.

37. Josie Carey Interview, by Karen Herman on July 23, 1999 for *The Interviews: An Oral History of Television*. Visit TelevisionAcademy .com/Interviews for more information.

CHAPTER 7

1. Daley, Eliot. Personal Interview. 15 August 2011. Audio.

2. Rogers, Joanne. Interview. Christianbook. com. 2013. Website.

3. Josie Carey Interview, by Karen Herman on July 23, 1999 for *The Interviews: An Oral History of Television*. Visit TelevisionAcademy .com/Interviews for more information.

4. Ibid.

5. Rogers, Joanne. Personal Interview. 4 December 2017. Email.

6. Sharapan, Hedda. Interview by Jessica Wiederhorn. The Narrative Trust. Fred Rogers Oral History Collection. Fred Rogers Center for Early Learning and Children's Media at St. Vincent College. 27 February 2007. Video.

7. Hughes, Jim. Personal Interview. 5 March 2012.

8. McKim, Donald K. *Ever a Vision: A Brief History of Pittsburgh Theological Seminary*. William B. Eerdmans Publishing Company, 2009. Page 111, 114–120. Print.

9. Rogers, Joanne. Interview by Jessica Wiederhorn. The Narrative Trust. Fred Rogers Oral History Collection. Fred Rogers Center for Early Learning and Children's Media at St. Vincent College. 14 June 2007. Video.

10. Purves, Dr. Andrew. Personal Interview. 28 April 2011. Audio.

11. Dillard, Annie. *An American Childhood*.

New York: Harper and Row, 1987. Pages 133–134, 191–193. Print.

12. McCullough, David. Personal Interview. 31 August 2010. Audio.

13. Rogers, Fred. Speech. Memphis Theological Seminary. Memphis, Tn. 10 May 1997. Print.

14. Barker, William P. Interview by Jessica Wiederhorn. The Narrative Trust. Fred Rogers Oral History Collection. Fred Rogers Center for Early Learning and Children's Media at St. Vincent College. 4 April 2006. Video.

15. Ibid.

16. Fred Rogers Interview, by Karen Herman on July 22, 1999 for *The Interviews: An Oral History of Television*. Visit TelevisionAcademy .com/Interviews for more information.

17. Dormire, Lisa. Personal Interview. 19 July 2011. Audio.

18. Hollingsworth, Amy. *The Simple Faith of Mister Rogers: Spiritual Insights from the World's Most Beloved Neighbor*. Nashville: Integrity Publishing, 2005. Page 80. Print.

19. Wirth, George. Interview by Jessica Wiederhorn. The Narrative Trust. Fred Rogers Oral History Collection. Fred Rogers Center for Early Learning and Children's Media at St. Vincent College. 24 April 2008. Video.

20. Hirsch, William. Personal Interview. 7 November 2011. Audio.

21. Wirth, George. Interview by Jessica Wiederhorn. The Narrative Trust. Fred Rogers Oral History Collection. Fred Rogers Center for Early Learning and Children's Media at St. Vincent College. 24 April 2008. Video.

22. Dormire, Lisa. Personal Interview. 19 July 2011. Audio.

23. Rogers, Fred. Sermon. Sixth Presbyterian Church of Pittsburgh. Pittsburgh, PA. 27 August 1972. Print.

24. Rogers, Fred. Speech. Annual Convention of the National Association for the Education of Young Children. Los Angeles, CA. 10 November 1993. Print.

25. Fred Rogers Interview, by Karen Herman on July 22, 1999 for *The Interviews: An Oral History of Television*. Visit TelevisionAcademy .com/Interviews for more information.

26. Barker, William P. and Jean. Personal Interview. 5 April 2011.

27. Ibid.

28. Barker, William P. Interview by Jessica Wiederhorn. The Narrative Trust. Fred Rogers

Oral History Collection. Fred Rogers Center for Early Learning and Children's Media at St. Vincent College. 4 April 2006. Video.

CHAPTER 8

1. Flecker, Sally Ann. "When Fred Met Margaret." *Pitt Med Magazine*. Publication of the University of Pittsburgh School of Medicine. Winter 2014. Print.

2. McFarland, Margaret. Interview by Family Communications, Inc. Early 1988. Video.

3. Ibid.

4. Rogers, Fred. "Margaret McFarland Remembered as Teacher, Advisor, Friend". *Saint Vincent College Alumni News*. Latrobe, PA. Fall 1988. Print.

5. McFarland, Margaret. Interview by Dr. Margaret Mary Kimmel. University of Pittsburgh. 21 October 1983. Video.

6. Ibid.

7. Ibid.

8. Ibid.

9. Flecker, Sally Ann. "When Fred Met Margaret." *Pitt Med Magazine*. Publication of the University of Pittsburgh School of Medicine. Winter 2014. Print.

10. Curry, Nancy. Personal Interview. 6 December 2010. Audio.

11. Sharapan, Hedda. Personal Interview. 9 November 2010. Audio.

12. Curry, Nancy. "The Reality of Make-Believe." *In Mister Rogers' Neighborhood: Children, Television and Fred Rogers*. Edited by Mark Collins and Margaret Mary Kimmel. Pittsburgh: University of Pittsburgh Press, 1996. Pages 51 and 52. Print.

13. Ibid.

14. Ibid.

15. Newell, David. Personal Interview. 7 January 2014. Email.

16. Curry, Nancy. Personal Interview. 6 December 2010. Audio.

17. Daley, Eliot. Personal Interview. 15 August 2011. Audio.

18. McFarland, Margaret. Interview by Family Communications, Inc. Early 1988. Video.

19. McCullough, David. "American History and America's Future." Lecture. Hillsdale College National Leadership Seminar. Phoenix, AZ. 15 February 2005. Print.

20. Flecker, Sally Ann. "When Fred Met Margaret." *Pitt Med Magazine*. Publication of the

University of Pittsburgh School of Medicine. Winter 2014. Print.

CHAPTER 9

1. Chapman, Francis. Interview by Jessica Wiederhorn. The Narrative Trust. Fred Rogers Oral History Collection. Fred Rogers Center for Early Learning and Children's Media at St. Vincent College. 16 July 2008. Video.
2. Ibid.
3. Ibid.
4. Rogers, Joanne. Interview by Jessica Wiederhorn. The Narrative Trust. Fred Rogers Oral History Collection. Fred Rogers Center for Early Learning and Children's Media at St. Vincent College. 14 June 2007. Video.
5. Rogers, Fred. Letter to F. B. Rainsberry. Fred Rogers Archive. Fred Rogers Center for Early Learning and Children's Media at St. Vincent College. 1958 May 12.
6. Rogers, Fred. Letter to F. B. Rainsberry. Fred Rogers Archive. Fred Rogers Center for Early Learning and Children's Media at St. Vincent College. 1961 February 2.
7. Chapman, Francis. Interview by Jessica Wiederhorn. The Narrative Trust. Fred Rogers Oral History Collection. Fred Rogers Center for Early Learning and Children's Media at St. Vincent College. 16 July 2008. Video.
8. Ibid
9. Fred Rogers Interview, by Karen Herman on July 22, 1999 for The Interviews: An Oral History of Television. Visit TelevisionAcademy.com/Interviews for more information.
10. Note to Fred Rogers from Rainsberry's son-in-law Andrew Heap on the Death of Fred Rainsberry. Fred Rogers Archive. Fred Rogers Center for Early Learning and Children's Media at St. Vincent College. April 1996. Print.
11. Fred Rogers Interview, by Karen Herman on July 22, 1999 for The Interviews: An Oral History of Television. Visit TelevisionAcademy.com/Interviews for more information.
12. Chapman, Francis. Interview by Jessica Wiederhorn. The Narrative Trust. Fred Rogers Oral History Collection. Fred Rogers Center for Early Learning and Children's Media at St. Vincent College. 16 July 2008. Video.
13. Ibid.
14. Ibid.
15. Ibid.
16. Ibid.
17. Ibid.
18. Hughes, Jim. Personal Interview. 5 March 2012. Audio.
19. Newell, David. Personal Interview. 22 September 2011. Audio.
20. Rogers, James. Interview by Melanie Shorin. The Narrative Trust. Fred Rogers Oral History Collection. Fred Rogers Center for Early Learning and Children's Media at St. Vincent College. 15 October 2007. Video.
21. Rogers, Joanne. Personal Interview. 2 November 2010. Audio.
22. Ibid.
23. Rogers, James. Interview by Melanie Shorin. The Narrative Trust. Fred Rogers Oral History Collection. Fred Rogers Center for Early Learning and Children's Media at St. Vincent College. 15 October 2007. Video.
24. Rogers, John. Interview by Jessica Wiederhorn. The Narrative Trust. Fred Rogers Oral History Collection. Fred Rogers Center for Early Learning and Children's Media at St. Vincent College. April 24, 2008. Video.
25. Rogers, Fred. Speech. Association of Family and Conciliation Courts. Latrobe, PA. 15 May 1991. Print.

CHAPTER 10

1. Hill, George. Interview by Jessica Wiederhorn. The Narrative Trust. Fred Rogers Oral History Collection. Fred Rogers Center for Early Learning and Children's Media at St. Vincent College. 26 February 2007. Video.
2. Ibid.
3. Ibid.
4. Negri, Joe. Personal Interview. 8 July 2017. Audio.
5. Lynch, Elaine. Interview by Jessica Wiederhorn. The Narrative Trust. Fred Rogers Oral History Collection. Fred Rogers Center for Early Learning and Children's Media at St. Vincent College. 6 April 2006. Video.
6. Ibid.
7. Hill, George. Interview by Jessica Wiederhorn. The Narrative Trust. Fred Rogers Oral History Collection. Fred Rogers Center for Early Learning and Children's Media at St. Vincent College. 26 February 2007. Video.
8. Sharapan, Hedda. Personal Interview. 9 November 2010. Audio.

9. Ibid.
10. Newell, David. Personal Interview. 11 February 2012. Email.
11. Rogers, Fred. Interview by Karen Herman. Academy of Television Arts & Sciences Archive of American Television. 22 July 2000. Video.
12. Ibid.
13. Taff, Paul. Interview by Melanie Shorin. The Narrative Trust. Fred Rogers Oral History Collection. Fred Rogers Center for Early Learning and Children's Media at St. Vincent College. 28 June 2007. Video.
14. Ibid.
15. Rogers, Fred. Interview by Karen Herman. Academy of Television Arts & Sciences Archive of American Television. 22 July 2000. Video.
16. Hill, George. Interview by Jessica Wiederhorn. The Narrative Trust. Fred Rogers Oral History Collection. Fred Rogers Center for Early Learning and Children's Media at St. Vincent College. 26 February 2007. Video.
17. Ibid.
18. Newell, David. Personal Interview. 11 February 2012. Email.
19. Costa, Johnny. Press release for "Melodies in the Key of Childhood: The Music of Fred Rogers." Family Communications, Inc. July 1992. Print.
20. Negri, Joe. Personal Interview. 8 July 2017. Audio.
21. Marsalis, Wynton. Personal Interview. 23 August 2017. Audio.
22. Lynch, Elaine. Interview by Jessica Wiederhorn. The Narrative Trust. Fred Rogers Oral History Collection. Fred Rogers Center for Early Learning and Children's Media at St. Vincent College. 6 April 2006. Video.
23. Ibid.
24. Rogers, Fred. Interview by Karen Herman. Academy of Television Arts & Sciences Archive of American Television. 22 July 2000. Video.
25. Taff, Paul. Interview by Melanie Shorin. The Narrative Trust. Fred Rogers Oral History Collection. Fred Rogers Center for Early Learning and Children's Media at St. Vincent College. 28 June 2007. Video.
26. Isler, William. Personal Interview. 30 June 2012. Email.
27. Daley, Eliot. Personal Interview. 15 August 2011. Audio.

CHAPTER 11

1. Author's experience as a reporter at *The Providence Journal & Evening Bulletin*. Providence, RI. 1960s.
2. Lynch, Elaine. Personal Interview. 5 September 2011.
3. Rogers, Joanne. Interview by Jessica Wiederhorn. The Narrative Trust. Fred Rogers Oral History Collection. Fred Rogers Center for Early Learning and Children's Media at St. Vincent College. 14 June 2007. Video.
4. Creshkoff, Larry. *WGBH Alumni*. Boston, MA. 20 March 2000. Print.
5. Ambrosino, Michael. Interview by Jessica Wiederhorn. The Narrative Trust. Fred Rogers Oral History Collection. Fred Rogers Center for Early Learning and Children's Media at St. Vincent College. 31 July 2007. Video.
6. Hill, George. Interview by Jessica Wiederhorn. The Narrative Trust. Fred Rogers Oral History Collection. Fred Rogers Center for Early Learning and Children's Media at St. Vincent College. 26 February 2007. Video.
7. Mallinger, Pepper. Personal Interview. 8 February 2012.
8. Bianculli, David. *Dangerously Funny: The Uncensored Story of the Smothers Brothers Comedy Hour*. New York: Simon and Schuster, 2010. Pages 279–280, 294–298, 321. Print.
9. Goldstein, Richard. "John Pastore, Prominent Figure in Rhode Island Politics, Dies at 93." *New York Times*. New York, NY. July 2000. Print.
10. Lynch, Elaine. Interview by Jessica Wiederhorn. The Narrative Trust. Fred Rogers Oral History Collection. Fred Rogers Center for Early Learning and Children's Media at St. Vincent College. 6 April 2006. Video.
11. Mallinger, Pepper. Personal Interview. 8 February 2012.
12. Ibid.
13. Pastore, John O. and Fred Rogers. Correspondence. Fred Rogers Archive. Fred Rogers Center for Early Learning and Children's Media. 1969–1978. Print.
14. Daley, Eliot. "QED Renaissance." Pittsburgh, PA. November 1970. Print.
15. Rogers, Joanne. Personal Interview. 15 September 2011.

CHAPTER 12

1. Greenwald, Arthur. Interview by Elizabeth Deane. 2 January 2016. Telephone.
2. Fred Rogers Interview, by Karen Herman on July 22, 1999 for *The Interviews: An Oral History of Television*. Visit TelevisionAcademy .com/Interviews for more information.
3. Gruner, Nancy. Interview by Jessica Wiederhorn. The Narrative Trust. Fred Rogers Oral History Collection. Fred Rogers Center for Early Learning and Children's Media at St. Vincent College. 14 June 2007. Video.
4. Daley, Eliot. Personal Interview. 15 August 2011. Audio.
5. Ibid.
6. Lynch, Elaine. Interview by Jessica Wiederhorn. The Narrative Trust. Fred Rogers Oral History Collection. Fred Rogers Center for Early Learning and Children's Media at St. Vincent College. 6 April 2006. Video.
7. Anderson, Daniel. Interview by Jessica Wiederhorn. The Narrative Trust. Fred Rogers Oral History Collection. Fred Rogers Center for Early Learning and Children's Media at St. Vincent College. 6 April 2009. Video.
8. Newell, David. Interview by Melanie Shorin. The Narrative Trust. Fred Rogers Oral History Collection. Fred Rogers Center for Early Learning and Children's Media at St. Vincent College. 28 February 2007. Video.
9. Sharapan, Hedda. Interview by Jessica Wiederhorn. The Narrative Trust. Fred Rogers Oral History Collection. Fred Rogers Center for Early Learning and Children's Media at St. Vincent College. 27 February 2007. Video.
10. Mallinger, Pepper. Personal Interview. 8 February 2012. Audio.
11. Ibid.
12. Greenwald, Arthur. Interview by Elizabeth Deane. 2 January 2016. Telephone.
13. Ibid.
14. Ibid.
15. Ibid.
16. Seamans, Elizabeth. Personal Interview. 12 April 2011. Audio.
17. Ibid.
18. Ibid.
19. Whitmer, Margy. Interview by Melanie Shorin. The Narrative Trust. Fred Rogers Oral History Collection. Fred Rogers Center for Early Learning and Children's Media at St. Vincent College. 2 March 2007. Video.
20. Rogers, Fred. *Dear Mister Rogers, Does It Ever Rain in Your Neighborhood?* New York: Penguin Books, 1996. Page 68. Print.
21. Seamans, Elizabeth. Personal Interview. 12 April 2011. Audio.
22. Ibid.
23. Ibid.
24. Ibid.
25. Seamans, Joe. Personal Interview. 17 May 2011. Audio.
26. Ibid.
27. Ibid.
28. Cox, Basil. Interview by Jessica Wiederhorn. The Narrative Trust. Fred Rogers Oral History Collection. Fred Rogers Center for Early Learning and Children's Media at St. Vincent College. 1 March 2007. Video.
29. Daley, Eliot. Personal Interview. 15 August 2011. Audio
30. Rogers, Fred. Speech. National Symposium on Children and Television. Chicago, IL. October 1971.
31. Sharapan, Hedda. Interview by Jessica Wiederhorn. The Narrative Trust. Fred Rogers Oral History Collection. Fred Rogers Center for Early Learning and Children's Media at St. Vincent College. 27 February 2007. Video.
32. Ibid.
33. Seamans, Elizabeth. Personal Interview. 12 April 2011. Audio.
34. Singer, Dorothy. Interview by Jessica Wiederhorn. The Narrative Trust. Fred Rogers Oral History Collection. Fred Rogers Center for Early Learning and Children's Media at St. Vincent College. 27 June 2007. Video.
35. Ibid.
36. Whitmer, Margy. Interview by Melanie Shorin. The Narrative Trust. Fred Rogers Oral History Collection. Fred Rogers Center for Early Learning and Children's Media at St. Vincent College. 2 March 2007. Video.
37. Newell, David. Interview by Melanie Shorin. The Narrative Trust. Fred Rogers Oral History Collection. Fred Rogers Center for Early Learning and Children's Media at St. Vincent College. 28 February 2007. Video.
38. Marsalis, Wynton. Personal Interview. 23 August 2017. Audio.

CHAPTER 13

1. Sedgwick, John. "Who the Devil Is Fred Rogers?" *Wigwag*. November 1989. Print.

2. Ibid.
3. Negri, Joe. Personal Interview. 8 July 2017. Audio.
4. Ibid.
5. Crozier, Elaine Rogers. Personal Interview. 27 September 2010. Audio.
6. Ibid.
7. Horton, Michael. Personal Interview. 31 August 2017. Audio.
8. Ibid.
9. Ibid.
10. Aber, Charlies R. Interview by Jessica Wiederhorn. The Narrative Trust. Fred Rogers Oral History Collection. Fred Rogers Center for Early Learning and Children's Media at St. Vincent College. 30 November 2007. Video.
11. Whitmer, Margy. Interview by Melanie Shorin. The Narrative Trust. Fred Rogers Oral History Collection. Fred Rogers Center for Early Learning and Children's Media at St. Vincent College. 2 March 2007. Video.
12. Seamans, Elizabeth. Personal Interview. 12 April 2011. Audio.
13. Whitmer, Margy. Interview by Melanie Shorin. The Narrative Trust. Fred Rogers Oral History Collection. Fred Rogers Center for Early Learning and Children's Media at St. Vincent College. 2 March 2007. Video.
14. Seamans, Elizabeth. Personal Interview. 12 April 2011. Audio.
15. Newell, David. Interview by Melanie Shorin. The Narrative Trust. Fred Rogers Oral History Collection. Fred Rogers Center for Early Learning and Children's Media at St. Vincent College. 28 February 2007. Video.
16. Whitmer, Margy. Interview by Melanie Shorin. The Narrative Trust. Fred Rogers Oral History Collection. Fred Rogers Center for Early Learning and Children's Media at St. Vincent College. 2 March 2007. Video.
17. Sharapan, Hedda. Interview by Jessica Wiederhorn. The Narrative Trust. Fred Rogers Oral History Collection. Fred Rogers Center for Early Learning and Children's Media at St. Vincent College. 27 February 2007. Video.
18. Whitmer, Margy. Interview by Melanie Shorin. The Narrative Trust. Fred Rogers Oral History Collection. Fred Rogers Center for Early Learning and Children's Media at St. Vincent College. 2 March 2007. Video.
19. Ibid.
20. Long, Michael. "Was Mister Rogers Racist? Twelve Facts About Our Favorite Neighbor." *Huffpost.* 7 August 2015. https://www.huffingtonpost.com/michael-g-long/was-mister-rogers-racist-_b_7939498.html.
21. Clemons, François. "Walking the Beat in Mr. Rogers' Neighborhood, Where a New Day Began Together." Interview by Karl Lindholm. *StoryCorps.* March 2016. Podcast.
22. Ibid.
23. Ibid.
24. Ibid.
25. Ibid.
26. Ibid.
27. Long, Michael. *Peaceful Neighbor: Discovering the Countercultural Mister Rogers.* Louisville: Westminster John Knox Press, 2015. Print.
28. Clemons, François. "Walking the Beat in Mr. Rogers' Neighborhood, Where a New Day Began Together." Interview by Karl Lindholm. *StoryCorps.* March 2016. Podcast.
29. Daley, Eliot. Personal Interview. 15 August 2011. Audio.
30. Briggs, Kenneth. "Mr. Rogers Decides It's Time to Head for New Neighborhoods." *New York Times.* 8 May 1975. Print.
31. Hirsch, William. Personal Interview. 7 November 2011. Audio.
32. Horton, Michael. Personal Interview. 31 August 2017. Audio.
33. Wartella, Ellen. Interview by Jessica Wiederhorn. The Narrative Trust. Fred Rogers Oral History Collection. Fred Rogers Center for Early Learning and Children's Media at St. Vincent College. 13 April 2009. Video.
34. Ibid.
35. Ibid.
36. Galinksy, Ellen. Interview by Melanie Shorin. The Narrative Trust. Fred Rogers Oral History Collection. Fred Rogers Center for Early Learning and Children's Media at St. Vincent College. 21 September 2007. Video.
37. Briggs, Kenneth A. "Mr. Rogers Decides It's Time to Head for New Neighborhoods." *New York Times,* 8 May 1975. Online. www.nytimes.com/1975/05/08/archives/mr-rogers-decides-its-time-to-head-for-new-neighborhoods.html.
38. Seamans, Elizabeth. Personal Interview. 12 April 2011. Audio.
39. Whitmer, Margy. Interview by Melanie Shorin. The Narrative Trust. Fred Rogers Oral History Collection. Fred Rogers Center for

Early Learning and Children's Media at St. Vincent College. 2 March 2007. Video.

40. Aber, Charles R. Interview by Jessica Wiederhorn. The Narrative Trust. Fred Rogers Oral History Collection. Fred Rogers Center for Early Learning and Children's Media at St. Vincent College. 30 November 2007. Video.

CHAPTER 14

1. Stamberg, Susan. Interview by Jessica Wiederhorn. The Narrative Trust. Fred Rogers Oral History Collection. Fred Rogers Center for Early Learning and Children's Media at St. Vincent College. 2 September 2009. Video.
2. Ibid.
3. Ibid.
4. Ibid.
5. Ibid.
6. Rogers, James. Interview by Melanie Shorin. The Narrative Trust. Fred Rogers Oral History Collection. Fred Rogers Center for Early Learning and Children's Media at St. Vincent College. 15 October 2007. Video.
7. Ibid.
8. Ibid.
9. Isler, William. Personal Interview. 30 June 2012. Email.
10. McFeaters, Peggy Moberg. Interview by Jessica Wiederhorn. The Narrative Trust. Fred Rogers Oral History Collection. Fred Rogers Center for Early Learning and Children's Media at St. Vincent College. 21 July 2009. Video.
11. Fred Rogers Interview, by Karen Herman on July 22, 1999 for The Interviews: An Oral History of Television. Visit TelevisionAcademy .com/Interviews for more information.
12. Ibid.
13. Ibid.
14. Sharapan, Hedda. Interview by Jessica Wiederhorn. The Narrative Trust. Fred Rogers Center for Early Learning and Children's Media at St. Vincent College. 27 February 2007. Video.
15. Ibid.
16. Linn, Susan. Interview by Jessica Wiederhorn. The Narrative Trust. Fred Rogers Oral History Collection. Fred Rogers Center for Early Learning and Children's Media at St. Vincent College. 31 July 2007. Video.

17. Linn, Susan. "With an Open Hand: Puppetry on Mister Rogers' Neighborhood." In Mister Rogers' Neighborhood: Children, Television and Fred Rogers, edited by Mark Collins and Margaret Mary Kimmel. Pittsburgh: University of Pittsburgh Press, 1996. Pages 93–94. Print.
18. Ibid.
19. Charron, Peggy. Changing Channels: Living Sensibly with Television. Boston: Addison-Wesley, 1982. Print.
20. The Punch and Judy Show 1832. Illustrated by Collier and Cruikshank. Prepared by Christopher van Der Craats. Website. www .punchandjudy.com/scriptsframeset.htm.
21. Edgerton, Gary R. The Columbia History of American Television. New York: Columbia University Press, 2007. Pages 159–169. Print.
22. Nix, Crystal. "Burr Tillstrom, Puppeteer, Dies." New York Times. 8 December 1985. Print.
23. Blau, Eleanor. "Jim Henson, Puppeteer, Dies; The Muppets' Creator was 53." New York Times. 17 May 1990. Print.
24. Meier, Barry. "Kermit and Miss Piggy Join Disney Stable." New York Times. 18 February 2004. Print.
25. Blau, Eleanor. "Jim Henson, Puppeteer, Dies; The Muppets' Creator was 53." New York Times. 17 May 1990. Print.
26. Charron, Peggy. Changing Channels: Living Sensibly with Television. Boston: Addison-Wesley, 1982. Print.
27. Lynch, Elaine. Interview by Jessica Wiederhorn. The Narrative Trust. Fred Rogers Oral History Collection. Fred Rogers Center for Early Learning and Children's Media at St. Vincent College. 6 April 2006. Video.
28. Ibid.

CHAPTER 15

1. Old Friends, New Friends. Program 105, "Memories." The Fred Rogers Company. 13 April 1978. Video.
2. Ibid.
3. Newell, David. Personal Interview. 22 September 2011. Audio.
4. Cox, Basil. Personal Interview. 11 November 2010. Audio.
5. Newell, David. Personal Interview. 22 September 2011. Audio.

6. Whitmer, Margy. Interview by Melanie Shorin. The Narrative Trust. Fred Rogers Oral History Collection. Fred Rogers Center for Early Learning and Children's Media at St. Vincent College. 2 March 2007. Video.

7. Briggs, Kenneth. "Mr. Rogers Decides It's Time to Head for New Neighborhoods." *New York Times.* 8 May 1975. Print.

8. Ibid.

9. Cox, Basil. Interview by Jessica Wiederhorn. The Narrative Trust. Fred Rogers Oral History Collection. Fred Rogers Center for Early Learning and Children's Media at St. Vincent College. 1 March 2007. Video.

10. Ibid.

11. Whitmer, Margy. Interview by Melanie Shorin. The Narrative Trust. Fred Rogers Oral History Collection. Fred Rogers Center for Early Learning and Children's Media at St. Vincent College. 2 March 2007. Video.

12. Seamans, Elizabeth. Interview by Melanie Shorin. The Narrative Trust. Fred Rogers Oral History Collection. Fred Rogers Center for Early Learning and Children's Media at St. Vincent College. 26 February 2007. Video.

13. *Old Friends, New Friends.* Program 208, "Senator John Heinz." The Fred Rogers Company. Aired 29 August 1980. Video.

14. Ibid.

15. *Old Friends, New Friends.* Program 201, "Lee Strasberg." The Fred Rogers Company. Aired 11 July 1980. Video.

16. Cox, Basil. Interview by Jessica Wiederhorn. The Narrative Trust. Fred Rogers Oral History Collection. Fred Rogers Center for Early Learning and Children's Media at St. Vincent College. 1 March 2007. Video.

17. Seamans, Elizabeth. Interview by Melanie Shorin. The Narrative Trust. Fred Rogers Oral History Collection. Fred Rogers Center for Early Learning and Children's Media at St. Vincent College. 26 February 2007. Video.

18. Ibid.

19. Rogers, Fred. Speech. Thiel College. Greenville, PA. 13 November 1969. Print.

20. Edgerton, Gary R. *The Columbia History of American Television.* New York: Columbia University Press, 2007. Pages 191–192, 244–250. Print.

21. Stamberg, Susan. Interview by Jessica Wiederhorn. The Narrative Trust. Fred Rogers Oral History Collection. Fred Rogers Center for Early Learning and Children's Media at St. Vincent College. 2 September 2009. Video.

22. Palmer, Chris. "Mister Rogers' Christmas Message." *Bangor Daily News.* Bangor, ME. 16 December 1977. Print.

23. Daley, Eliot. Personal Interview. 15 August 2011. Audio.

24. Ibid.

25. Cox, Basil. Interview by Jessica Wiederhorn. The Narrative Trust. Fred Rogers Oral History Collection. Fred Rogers Center for Early Learning and Children's Media at St. Vincent College. 1 March 2007. Video.

26. Galinksy, Ellen. Interview by Melanie Shorin. The Narrative Trust. Fred Rogers Oral History Collection. Fred Rogers Center for Early Learning and Children's Media at St. Vincent College. 21 September 2007. Video.

27. Lynch, Elaine. Interview by Jessica Wiederhorn. The Narrative Trust. Fred Rogers Oral History Collection. Fred Rogers Center for Early Learning and Children's Media at St. Vincent College. 6 April 2006. Video.

28. Cox, Basil. Personal Interview. 11 November 2010. Audio.

CHAPTER 16

1. Newell, David. Personal Interview. 22 September 2011. Audio.

2. Ibid.

3. Rogers, Fred. Speech. Academic Conference at Yale University. New Haven, CT. 1 January 1972. Print.

4. Rogers, Fred. Speech. Indiana University of Pennsylvania Commencement. Indiana, PA. Spring 1992. Print.

5. Newell, David. Personal Interview. 22 September 2011. Audio.

6. Transcript of Conversation between Margaret McFarland and Fred Rogers. Fred Rogers Center Archives. 30 July 1980. Print.

7. Newell, David. Personal Interview. 2 December 2010. Audio.

8. Ibid.

9. Pasquale, Buba. Personal Interview. 23 May 2012. Audio.

10. Paley, Vivian Gussin. *A Child's Work: The Importance of Fantasy Play.* Chicago: University of Chicago Press, 2005. Print.

11. Singer, Dorothy. Interview by Jessica Wiederhorn. The Narrative Trust. Fred Rogers

Oral History Collection. Fred Rogers Center for Early Learning and Children's Media at St. Vincent College. 27 June 2007. Video.

12. Ibid.

13. Rogers, Fred. Speech. American Academy of Child Psychiatry. 7 October 1971. Print.

14. Hart, Betty, and Todd Risley. *Meaningful Differences in the Everyday Experience of Young American Children.* Baltimore: Paul H. Brookes Publishing Co, 1995. Print.

15. Ganz, Joan. Interview by Jessica Wiederhorn. The Narrative Trust. Fred Rogers Oral History Collection. Fred Rogers Center for Early Learning and Children's Media at St. Vincent College. 20 April 2009. Video.

16. Whitmer, Margy. Interview by Melanie Shorin. The Narrative Trust. Fred Rogers Oral History Collection. Fred Rogers Center for Early Learning and Children's Media at St. Vincent College. 2 March 2007. Video.

17. Ibid.

18. Rogers, Fred. *Dear Mister Rogers, Does It Ever Rain in Your Neighborhood?* New York: Penguin Books, 1996. Print.

19. Ibid.

20. Gardiner, Harris. "Out-of-Wedlock Birthrates are Soaring, U.S. Reports." *New York Times.* 13 May 2009. Print.

21. *Mister Rogers' Neighborhood.* Episode 1476. The Fred Rogers Company. Aired 16 February 1981. Television.

22. Gerbner, George. "Fred Rogers and the Significance of Story." *Mister Rogers' Neighborhood: Children, Television, and Fred Rogers,* edited by Mark Collins and Margaret Mary Kimmel. Pittsburgh: University of Pittsburgh Press, 1996. Print.

CHAPTER 17

1. Erlanger, Howard, and Pam Erlanger. Interview by Jessica Wiederhorn. The Narrative Trust. Fred Rogers Oral History Collection. Fred Rogers Center for Early Learning and Children's Media at St. Vincent College. 26 August 2009. Video.

2. Ibid.

3. Rogers, Fred. "I'd Like to Be Just Like Mom and Dad." *Mister Rogers' Neighborhood.* Episode 3. Aired 21 February 1968. Television.

4. Erlanger, Howard, and Pam Erlanger. Interview by Jessica Wiederhorn. The Narrative Trust. Fred Rogers Oral History Collection.

Fred Rogers Center for Early Learning and Children's Media at St. Vincent College. 26 August 2009. Video.

5. Ibid.

6. Whitmer, Margy. Interview by Melanie Shorin. The Narrative Trust. Fred Rogers Oral History Collection. Fred Rogers Center for Early Learning and Children's Media at St. Vincent College. 2 March 2007. Video.

7. Erlanger, Howard, and Pam Erlanger. Interview by Jessica Wiederhorn. The Narrative Trust. Fred Rogers Oral History Collection. Fred Rogers Center for Early Learning and Children's Media at St. Vincent College. 26 August 2009. Video.

8. Erlanger, Jeffery. Academy of Television Arts and Sciences' 14th Annual Hall of Fame. Leonard H. Goldenson Theatre. Los Angeles. 27 February 1999. Video.

9. Aber, Charles R. Interview by Jessica Wiederhorn. The Narrative Trust. Fred Rogers Oral History Collection. Fred Rogers Center for Early Learning and Children's Media at St. Vincent College. 30 November 2007. Video.

10. Lynch, Elaine. Interview by Jessica Wiederhorn. The Narrative Trust. Fred Rogers Oral History Collection. Fred Rogers Center for Early Learning and Children's Media at St. Vincent College. 6 April 2006. Video.

11. Aberlin, Betty. Interview by William Madison. *Billevesées: Fiction, Nonfiction, and Nonsense from an American in Paris (Sometimes).* 22 March 2009. Blog post. www.billmadison.blogspot.com/2009/03/interview-betty-aberlin.html.

12. Whitmer, Margy. Interview by Melanie Shorin. The Narrative Trust. Fred Rogers Oral History Collection. Fred Rogers Center for Early Learning and Children's Media at St. Vincent College. 2 March 2007. Video.

13. Ibid.

14. Ibid.

15. Ibid.

16. Aber, Charles R. Interview by Jessica Wiederhorn. The Narrative Trust. Fred Rogers Oral History Collection. Fred Rogers Center for Early Learning and Children's Media at St. Vincent College. 30 November 2007. Video.

17. Ibid.

18. Rogers, James. Interview by Melanie Shorin. The Narrative Trust. Fred Rogers Oral

History Collection. Fred Rogers Center for Early Learning and Children's Media at St. Vincent College. 15 October 2007. Video.

19. Kellison, Daniel. "Dinner with Daniel: Michael Keaton." Grantland.com. 13 July 2012. Online. www.grantland.com/features/qa-batman-beetlejuice-star-michael-keaton-mister-rogers-fly-fishing-roles-turned-more/.

20. Whitmer, Margy. Interview by Melanie Shorin. The Narrative Trust. Fred Rogers Oral History Collection. Fred Rogers Center for Early Learning and Children's Media at St. Vincent College. 2 March 2007. Video.

21. Ibid.

22. Aber, Charles R. Interview by Jessica Wiederhorn. The Narrative Trust. Fred Rogers Oral History Collection. Fred Rogers Center for Early Learning and Children's Media at St. Vincent College. 30 November 2007. Video.

23. Ibid.

24. Whitmer, Margy. Interview by Melanie Shorin. The Narrative Trust. Fred Rogers Oral History Collection. Fred Rogers Center for Early Learning and Children's Media at St. Vincent College. 2 March 2007. Video.

25. Ibid.

26. Newell, David. Interview by Melanie Shorin. The Narrative Trust. Fred Rogers Oral History Collection. Fred Rogers Center for Early Learning and Children's Media at St. Vincent College. 28 February 2007. Video.

27. Sharapan, Hedda. Interview by Jessica Wiederhorn. The Narrative Trust. Fred Rogers Oral History Collection. Fred Rogers Center for Early Learning and Children's Media at St. Vincent College. 27 February 2007. Video.

28. Newell, David. Interview by Melanie Shorin. The Narrative Trust. Fred Rogers Oral History Collection. Fred Rogers Center for Early Learning and Children's Media at St. Vincent College. 28 February 2007. Video.

29. Newell, David. Interview by Melanie Shorin. The Narrative Trust. Fred Rogers Oral History Collection. Fred Rogers Center for Early Learning and Children's Media at St. Vincent College. 28 February 2007. Video.

30. Ibid.

31. Rogers, Fred. Interview by David Letterman. Late Night with David Letterman. New York. 17 February 1982. Video.

32. Whitmer, Margy. Interview by Melanie Shorin. The Narrative Trust. Fred Rogers Oral History Collection. Fred Rogers Center for Early Learning and Children's Media at St. Vincent College. 2 March 2007. Video.

33. Ibid.

34. Ibid.

35. Ibid.

36. Sharapan, Hedda. Interview by Jessica Wiederhorn. The Narrative Trust. Fred Rogers Oral History Collection. Fred Rogers Center for Early Learning and Children's Media at St. Vincent College. 27 February 2007. Video.

37. Greenwald, Arthur. Interview by Elizabeth Deane. 2 January 2016. Telephone.

38. Rogers, Fred. Interview by Katie Couric. Today. Pittsburgh, PA. 18 December 2001. Video.

CHAPTER 18

1. Rogers, Fred. Dear Mister Rogers, Does It Ever Rain in Your Neighborhood? New York: Penguin Books, 1996. Print.

2. Lynch, Elaine. Interview by Jessica Wiederhorn. The Narrative Trust. Fred Rogers Oral History Collection. Fred Rogers Center for Early Learning and Children's Media at St. Vincent College. 6 April 2006. Video.

3. Rogers, Fred. Dear Mister Rogers, Does It Ever Rain in Your Neighborhood? New York: Penguin Books, 1996. Print.

4. Fred Rogers Interview, by Karen Herman on July 22, 1999 for The Interviews: An Oral History of Television. Visit TelevisionAcademy.com/Interviews for more information.

5. Rogers, Fred. Dear Mister Rogers, Does It Ever Rain in Your Neighborhood? New York: Penguin Books, 1996. Print.

6. Whitmer, Margaret, Joseph J. Kennedy IV, and Rick Sebak. Fred Rogers: America's Favorite Neighbor. Pittsburgh: Family Communications: WQED Multimedia. 2003. Video.

7. Rogers, Fred. Speech. Opening Ceremonies Sesquicentennial. St. Vincent Archabbey and College. Latrobe, PA. Fred Rogers Archive. Fred Rogers Center for Early Learning and Children's Media at St. Vincent College. 25 April 1995. Print.

8. Ibid.

9. Mister Rogers' Neighborhood. Episode 1446. The Fred Rogers Company. 5 May 1975. Video.

10. Negri, Joe. Personal Interview. 8 July 2017. Audio.
11. Marsalis, Wynton. Personal Interview. 23 August 2017. Audio.
12. Negri, Joe. Personal Interview. 8 July 2017. Audio.
13. Ibid.
14. Marsalis, Wynton. Personal Interview. 23 August 2017. Audio.
15. Ibid.
16. Aber, Charles R. Interview by Jessica Wiederhorn. The Narrative Trust. Fred Rogers Oral History Collection. Fred Rogers Center for Early Learning and Children's Media at St. Vincent College. 30 November 2007. Video.
17. Aberlin, Betty. Interview by William Madison. *Billevesées: Fiction, Nonfiction, and Nonsense from an American in Paris (Sometimes)*. 22 March 2009. Blog post. www.billmadison.blogspot.com/2009/03/interview-betty-aberlin.html.
18. Horton, Michael. Personal Interview. 31 August 2017. Audio.
19. Ibid.
20. Ibid.
21. Negri, Joe. Personal Interview. 8 July 2017. Audio.
22. Aber, Charles R. Interview by Jessica Wiederhorn. The Narrative Trust. Fred Rogers Oral History Collection. Fred Rogers Center for Early Learning and Children's Media at St. Vincent College. 30 November 2007. Video.
23. Aberlin, Betty. Interview by William Madison. *Billevesées: Fiction, Nonfiction, and Nonsense from an American in Paris (Sometimes)*. 22 March 2009. Blog post. www.billmadison.blogspot.com/2009/03/interview-betty-aberlin.html.
24. Millman, Joyce. "Fred Rogers." Salon.com. 10 August 1999. Online. www.salon.com/1999/08/10/rogers_2/.
25. Rogers, Fred. Letter to Bill Baird. "Josephine the Giraffe." Handwritten.
26. Aber, Charles R. Interview by Jessica Wiederhorn. The Narrative Trust. Fred Rogers Oral History Collection. Fred Rogers Center for Early Learning and Children's Media at St. Vincent College. 30 November 2007. Video.
27. Ma, Yo-Yo. Interview by Jessica Wiederhorn. The Narrative Trust. Fred Rogers Oral History Collection. Fred Rogers Center for Early Learning and Children's Media at St. Vincent College. 17 August 2009. Video.
28. Ibid.
29. Ibid.
30. Ibid.
31. Ibid.
32. Marsalis, Wynton. Personal Interview. 23 August 2017. Audio.
33. Ibid.

CHAPTER 19

1. Cox, Basil. Interview by Jessica Wiederhorn. The Narrative Trust. Fred Rogers Oral History Collection. Fred Rogers Center for Early Learning and Children's Media at St. Vincent College. 1 March 2007. Video.
2. Ibid.
3. Barry, Dave. *Dave Barry Turns 50*. New York: Random House. 1998. Page 44. Print.
4. Cox, Basil. Interview by Jessica Wiederhorn. The Narrative Trust. Fred Rogers Oral History Collection. Fred Rogers Center for Early Learning and Children's Media at St. Vincent College. 1 March 2007. Video.
5. Daley, Eliot. Personal Interview. 15 August 2011. Audio.
6. Isler, William. Personal Interview. 30 June 2012. Email.
7. Newell, David. Interview by Melanie Shorin. The Narrative Trust. Fred Rogers Oral History Collection. Fred Rogers Center for Early Learning and Children's Media at St. Vincent College. 28 February 2007. Video.
8. Isler, William. Personal Interview. 30 June 2012. Email.
9. Rogers, Joanne. Interview by Jessica Wiederhorn. The Narrative Trust. Fred Rogers Oral History Collection. Fred Rogers Center for Early Learning and Children's Media at St. Vincent College. 14 June 2007. Video.
10. Newell, David. Interview by Melanie Shorin. The Narrative Trust. Fred Rogers Oral History Collection. Fred Rogers Center for Early Learning and Children's Media at St. Vincent College. 28 February 2007. Video.
11. Daley, Eliot. Personal Interview. 15 August 2011. Audio.
12. Ibid.
13. Ibid.
14. "Klan Is Told to Stop Imitating 'Mister Rogers' on the Phone." *New York Times*. 12 October 1990. Print.

15. Feder, Don. *Who's Afraid of the Religious Right*. Washington, D.C.: Regnery Publishing, 2006. Page 126. Print.

16. Rogers, Fred. *You Are Special*. New York: Viking Penguin, 1994. Print.

17. Rogers, Joanne. Personal Interview. 2 November 2010. Audio.

18. Rogers, John. Interview by Jessica Wiederhorn. The Narrative Trust. Fred Rogers Oral History Collection. Fred Rogers Center for Early Learning and Children's Media at St. Vincent College. 24 April 2008. Video.

19. Ibid.

20. Ibid.

21. Rogers, Joanne. Personal Interview. 2 November 2010. Audio.

22. Ibid.

23. "Fred Rogers Moves into a New Neighborhood—and So Does His Rebellious Son." *People Magazine*. May 1978. Print.

24. Ibid.

25. Ibid.

26. Rogers, Joanne. Interview by Jessica Wiederhorn. The Narrative Trust. Fred Rogers Oral History Collection. Fred Rogers Center for Early Learning and Children's Media at St. Vincent College. 14 June 2007. Video.

27. Hirsch, William. Personal Interview. 7 November 2011. Audio.

28. Rogers, Joanne. Interview by Jessica Wiederhorn. The Narrative Trust. Fred Rogers Oral History Collection. Fred Rogers Center for Early Learning and Children's Media at St. Vincent College. 14 June 2007. Video.

29. Rogers, James. Interview by Melanie Shorin. The Narrative Trust. Fred Rogers Oral History Collection. Fred Rogers Center for Early Learning and Children's Media at St. Vincent College. 15 October 2007. Video.

30. Rogers, Joanne. Personal Interview. 2 November 2010. Audio.

31. Rogers, James. Interview by Melanie Shorin. The Narrative Trust. Fred Rogers Oral History Collection. Fred Rogers Center for Early Learning and Children's Media at St. Vincent College. 15 October 2007. Video.

32. Rogers, Joanne. Personal Interview. 2 November 2010. Audio.

33. Rogers, James. Interview by Melanie Shorin. The Narrative Trust. Fred Rogers Oral History Collection. Fred Rogers Center for Early Learning and Children's Media at St. Vincent College. 15 October 2007. Video.

34. Rogers, John. Interview by Jessica Wiederhorn. The Narrative Trust. Fred Rogers Oral History Collection. Fred Rogers Center for Early Learning and Children's Media at St. Vincent College. 24 April 2008. Video.

35. Rogers, Joanne. Personal Interview. 2 November 2010. Audio.

36. Rogers, John. Interview by Jessica Wiederhorn. The Narrative Trust. Fred Rogers Oral History Collection. Fred Rogers Center for Early Learning and Children's Media at St. Vincent College. 24 April 2008. Video.

37. Rogers, James. Interview by Melanie Shorin. The Narrative Trust. Fred Rogers Oral History Collection. Fred Rogers Center for Early Learning and Children's Media at St. Vincent College. 15 October 2007. Video.

38. Ibid.

39. Ibid.

40. Ibid.

41. Ibid.

42. Rogers, John. Interview by Jessica Wiederhorn. The Narrative Trust. Fred Rogers Oral History Collection. Fred Rogers Center for Early Learning and Children's Media at St. Vincent College. 24 April 2008. Video.

43. Rogers, James. Interview by Melanie Shorin. The Narrative Trust. Fred Rogers Oral History Collection. Fred Rogers Center for Early Learning and Children's Media at St. Vincent College. 15 October 2007. Video.

44. Rogers, John. Interview by Jessica Wiederhorn. The Narrative Trust. Fred Rogers Oral History Collection. Fred Rogers Center for Early Learning and Children's Media at St. Vincent College. 24 April 2008. Video.

45. Rogers, James. Interview by Melanie Shorin. The Narrative Trust. Fred Rogers Oral History Collection. Fred Rogers Center for Early Learning and Children's Media at St. Vincent College. 15 October 2007. Video.

46. Rogers, John. Interview by Jessica Wiederhorn. The Narrative Trust. Fred Rogers Oral History Collection. Fred Rogers Center for Early Learning and Children's Media at St. Vincent College. 24 April 2008. Video.

47. Rogers, Joanne. Personal Interview. 2 November 2010. Audio.

48. Rogers, James. Interview by Melanie Shorin. The Narrative Trust. Fred Rogers Oral History Collection. Fred Rogers Center for Early Learning and Children's Media at St. Vincent College. 15 October 2007. Video.

49. Rogers, Joanne. Interview by Jessica Wiederhorn. The Narrative Trust. Fred Rogers

Oral History Collection. Fred Rogers Center for Early Learning and Children's Media at St. Vincent College. 14 June 2007. Video.

50. Rogers, John. Interview by Jessica Wiederhorn. The Narrative Trust. Fred Rogers Oral History Collection. Fred Rogers Center for Early Learning and Children's Media at St. Vincent College. 24 April 2008. Video.

51. Ibid.

52. Ibid.

53. Rogers, James. Interview by Melanie Shorin. The Narrative Trust. Fred Rogers Oral History Collection. Fred Rogers Center for Early Learning and Children's Media at St. Vincent College. 15 October 2007. Video.

54. Ibid.

CHAPTER 20

1. Junod, Tom. Interview by Jessica Wiederhorn. The Narrative Trust. Fred Rogers Oral History Collection. Fred Rogers Center for Early Learning and Children's Media at St. Vincent College. 29 July 2008. Video.

2. Ibid

3. Ibid.

4. Ibid.

5. Negri, Joe. Personal Interview. 8 July 2017. Audio.

6. Junod, Tom. Interview by Jessica Wiederhorn. The Narrative Trust. Fred Rogers Oral History Collection. Fred Rogers Center for Early Learning and Children's Media at St. Vincent College. 29 July 2008. Video

7. Ibid.

8. Whitmer, Margy. Interview by Melanie Shorin. The Narrative Trust. Fred Rogers Oral History Collection. Fred Rogers Center for Early Learning and Children's Media at St. Vincent College. 2 March 2007. Video.

9. Rogers, Fred. Interview by Arsenio Hall. Arsenio Hall Show. 1993. Video.

10. Ibid.

11. Rogers, Fred. Interview by Joan Rivers. Tonight Show. 7 July 1983. Video.

12. Ibid.

13. Rogers, Fred. Interview by Joan Rivers. Tonight Show. 29 April 1986. Video.

14. Carson, Johnny. Tonight Show. 1978. Video.

15. Hendrickson, Paul. "In the Land of Make Believe, the Real Mister Rogers." Washington Post. 18 November 1982. Print.

16. Rogers, Fred. Interview by Johnny Carson. Tonight Show. 1978. Video.

17. Aber, Charles R. Interview by Jessica Wiederhorn. The Narrative Trust. Fred Rogers Oral History Collection. Fred Rogers Center for Early Learning and Children's Media at St. Vincent College. 30 November 2007. Video.

18. Junod, Tom. Interview by Jessica Wiederhorn. The Narrative Trust. Fred Rogers Oral History Collection. Fred Rogers Center for Early Learning and Children's Media at St. Vincent College. 29 July 2008. Video.

19. Fales, Dale. Personal Interview. 8 August 2013. Email.

20. Junod, Tom. Interview by Jessica Wiederhorn. The Narrative Trust. Fred Rogers Oral History Collection. Fred Rogers Center for Early Learning and Children's Media at St. Vincent College. 29 July 2008. Video.

21. Ibid.

22. Seamans, Elizabeth. Personal Interview. 12 April 2011. Audio.

23. Rogers, Fred. Interview with Charlie Rose. Charlie Rose. 20 September 1994. Television.

24. Kerr, The Rev. Clark. Personal Interview. 15 March 2011. Audio.

25. Rogers, Fred. Note to Self. Folder FMR Thoughts and Prayers. Fred Rogers Center for Early Learning and Children's Media at St. Vincent College. 1979. Letter.

26. Whitmer, Margy. Interview by Melanie Shorin. The Narrative Trust. Fred Rogers Oral History Collection. Fred Rogers Center for Early Learning and Children's Media at St. Vincent College. 2 March 2007. Video.

CHAPTER 21

1. Mister Rogers' Neighborhood. Episode 1493. Aired 2 March 1982. Video.

2. Mister Rogers' Neighborhood. Episode 1711. Aired 17 February 1997. Video.

3. Crozier, Elaine Rogers. Interview by Jessica Wiederhorn. The Narrative Trust. Fred Rogers Oral History Collection. Fred Rogers Center for Early Learning and Children's Media at St. Vincent College. 18 October 2007. Video.

4. Ibid.

5. Varion, Jeff. Personal Interview. 9 February 2012. Audio.

6. Ibid.
7. Ibid.
8. Isler, William. Personal Interview. 30 June 2012. Email.
9. Rogers, Fred. Speech. Marquette University. Milwaukee, WI. 20 May 2001. Print.
10. "Trouble in Mr. Rogers' Neighborhood." *Boston Globe.* 22 June 1996. Print.
11. Gardner, William E. Proceedings, Nantucket Historical Association. 1947. Print.

CHAPTER 22

1. Cox, Basil. Interview by Jessica Wiederhorn. The Narrative Trust. Fred Rogers Oral History Collection. Fred Rogers Center for Early Learning and Children's Media at St. Vincent College. 1 March 2007. Video.
2. Newell, David. Interview by Melanie Shorin. The Narrative Trust. Fred Rogers Oral History Collection. Fred Rogers Center for Early Learning and Children's Media at St. Vincent College. 28 February 2007. Video.
3. Seamans, Elizabeth. Personal Interview. 12 April 2011. Audio.
4. Rogers, Fred. Speech to Public Broadcasting Service. 17 June 1989. Washington, D.C.: Speech.
5. Rogers, Fred. Commencement speech. Eastern Michigan University. Ypsilanti, MI. 15 April 1973. Print.
6. Rogers, Fred. Commencement speech. Dartmouth University. Hanover, NH. 9 June 2002. Print.
7. Rogers, Fred. Speech. Thiel College. Greenville, PA. 13 November 1969. Print.
8. Ibid.
9. Sharapan, Hedda. Interview by Jessica Wiederhorn. The Narrative Trust. Fred Rogers Center for Early Learning and Children's Media at St. Vincent College. 27 February 2007. Video.
10. Ibid.
11. Rogers, Fred. *Dear Mr. Rogers, Does It Ever Rain in Your Neighborhood?* New York: Penguin Books, 1996. Print.
12. Ibid.
13. Ibid.
14. Ibid.
15. Rogers, Fred. Speech. Thiel College. Greenville, PA. 13 November 1969. Print.
16. Green, John. Speech. Kenyon College. Gambier, OH. 21 May 2016. Print.

17. Dark, David. "In the Age of Trump, Can Mr. Rogers Help Us Manage Our Anger?" *America Magazine.* 1 May 2017. Print.
18. Junod, Tom. "Can You Say . . . Hero?: Fred Rogers Has Been Doing the Same Small Good Thing for a Very Long Time." *Esquire.* November 1998.
19. Ibid.
20. "Koko Meets Mr. Rogers, Her Favorite Celebrity." YouTube. 28 May 1999. Video. www.youtube.com/watch?v=cn79Lgfh1hw.
21. Mikkelson, David. "Mr. Rogers' Rumor Neighborhood." Snopes.com. 19 June 2007. Online. www.snopes.com/fact-check/fred-rogers-rumors/.
22. Cox, Basil. Interview by Jessica Wiederhorn. The Narrative Trust. Fred Rogers Oral History Collection. Fred Rogers Center for Early Learning and Children's Media at St. Vincent College. 1 March 2007. Video.
23. Mikkelson, David. "Mr. Rogers' Rumor Neighborhood." Snopes.com. 19 June 2007. Online. www.snopes.com/fact-check/fred-rogers-rumors/.
24. Mikkelson, Barbara. "Mr. Rogers' Returned Car." Snopes.com. 18 September 2008. Online. www.snopes.com/fact-check/remorseful-car-thieves/.
25. Pae, Peter. "This Neighborhood Hasn't Changed a Bit Over the Decades." *The Wall Street Journal.* 2 March 1990. Print.

CHAPTER 23

1. Whitmer, Margy. Interview by Melanie Shorin. The Narrative Trust. Fred Rogers Oral History Collection. Fred Rogers Center for Early Learning and Children's Media at St. Vincent College. 2 March 2007. Video.
2. Newell, David. Interview by Melanie Shorin. The Narrative Trust. Fred Rogers Oral History Collection. Fred Rogers Center for Early Learning and Children's Media at St. Vincent College. 28 February 2007. Video.
3. Cox, Basil. Interview by Jessica Wiederhorn. The Narrative Trust. Fred Rogers Oral History Collection. Fred Rogers Center for Early Learning and Children's Media at St. Vincent College. 1 March 2007. Video.
4. Fred Rogers Interview, by Karen Herman on July 22, 1999 for *The Interviews: An Oral History of Television.* Visit TelevisionAcademy.com/Interviews for more information.

5. Rogers, Fred. Interview by Charlie Rose. *Charlie Rose.* 20 September 1994. Video.
6. Whitmer, Margy. Interview by Melanie Shorin. The Narrative Trust. Fred Rogers Oral History Collection. Fred Rogers Center for Early Learning and Children's Media at St. Vincent College. 2 March 2007. Video.
7. Isler, William. Personal Interview. 30 June 2012. Email.
8. Rogers, Joanne. Interview by Jessica Wiederhorn. The Narrative Trust. Fred Rogers Oral History Collection. Fred Rogers Center for Early Learning and Children's Media at St. Vincent College. 14 June 2007. Video.
9. Isler, William. Personal Interview. 30 June 2012. Email.
10. Fred Rogers Interview, by Karen Herman on July 22, 1999 for *The Interviews: An Oral History of Television.* Visit TelevisionAcademy.com/Interviews for more information.
11. Newell, David. Interview by Melanie Shorin. The Narrative Trust. Fred Rogers Oral History Collection. Fred Rogers Center for Early Learning and Children's Media at St. Vincent College. 28 February 2007. Video.
12. Owen, Rob. "There Goes the Neighborhood: Mr. Rogers Will Make Last Episodes of Show in December." *Pittsburgh Post-Gazette.* 12 November 2000. Print.
13. Ibid.
14. Carvajal, Doreen. "Still Around the Neighborhood: 'Mister Rogers' Ends Production, but Mr. Rogers Keeps Busy." *New York Times.* 10 April 2001. Print.
15. Ibid.
16. Ibid.
17. Rogers, Fred. Speech. Thiel College. Greenville, PA. 13 November 1969. Print.

CHAPTER 24

1. Daley, Eliot. Personal Interview. 15 August 2011. Audio.
2. Cox, Basil. Interview by Jessica Wiederhorn. The Narrative Trust. Fred Rogers Oral History Collection. Fred Rogers Center for Early Learning and Children's Media at St. Vincent College. 1 March 2007. Video.
3. Lynch, Elaine. Interview by Jessica Wiederhorn. The Narrative Trust. Fred Rogers Oral History Collection. Fred Rogers Center for Early Learning and Children's Media at St. Vincent College. 6 April 2006. Video.

4. Rogers, Joanne. Interview by Jessica Wiederhorn. The Narrative Trust. Fred Rogers Oral History Collection. Fred Rogers Center for Early Learning and Children's Media at St. Vincent College. 14 June 2007. Video.
5. Hirsch, William. Personal Interview. 7 November 2011. Audio.
6. Ibid.
7. Horton, Michael. Personal Interview. 31 August 2017. Audio.
8. Hirsch, William. Personal Interview. 7 November 2011. Audio.
9. Rogers, Joanne. Personal Interview. 28 September 2011. Audio.
10. Rogers, John. Interview by Jessica Wiederhorn. The Narrative Trust. Fred Rogers Oral History Collection. Fred Rogers Center for Early Learning and Children's Media at St. Vincent College. April 24, 2008. Video.
11. Daley, Eliot. Personal Interview. 15 August 2011. Audio.
12. Rogers, Joanne. Interview by Jessica Wiederhorn. The Narrative Trust. Fred Rogers Oral History Collection. Fred Rogers Center for Early Learning and Children's Media at St. Vincent College. 14 June 2007. Video.
13. Horton, Michael. Personal Interview. 31 August 2017. Audio.
14. Heinz Kerry, Teresa. Remarks. Fred Rogers Memorial Service. Heinz Hall. Pittsburgh, PA. 3 May 2003. Print.
15. "Fred Rogers." Wikipedia. 6 April 2018. Accessed 8 April 2018. en.wikipedia.org/wiki/Fred_Rogers.
16. Sharapan, Hedda. Interview by Jessica Wiederhorn. The Narrative Trust. Fred Rogers Oral History Collection. Fred Rogers Center for Early Learning and Children's Media at St. Vincent College. 27 February 2007. Video.
17. Rogers, Fred. "Adults PSA 1:30." Fred Rogers Center for Early Learning and Children's Media at St. Vincent College. Video.

CHAPTER 25

1. Santomero, Angela. Interview by Jessica Wiederhorn. The Narrative Trust. Fred Rogers Oral History Collection. Fred Rogers Center for Early Learning and Children's Media at St. Vincent College. 29 July 2008. Video.
2. Ibid.

3. Sileg, Josh. Interview by Jessica Wieder-horn. The Narrative Trust. Fred Rogers Oral History Collection. Fred Rogers Center for Early Learning and Children's Media at St. Vincent College. 6 March 2009. Video.

4. Ibid.

5. Cofer, Lynette Friedrich. "Make-Believe, Truth and Freedom." *Mister Rogers' Neighborhood: Children, Television and Fred Rogers*, edited by Mark Collins and Margaret Mary Kimmel. Pittsburgh: University of Pittsburgh Press, 1996. Print.

6. Ibid.

7. McCullough, David. "An Evening with David McCullough." Senator John Heinz History Center. Pittsburgh, PA. 28 November 2017. Audio.

8. Demain, Bill. "How Mister Rogers Saved the VCR." *Mental Floss*. 9 January 2012. Print.

9. Breznican, Anthony. "Remembering Mr. Rogers, a True Life Helper when the World Still Needs One." *Entertainment Weekly*. 23 May 2017. Print.

10. Zaslow, Jeffrey. "Blame It on Mr. Rogers: Why Young Adults Feel So Entitled." *Wall Street Journal*. 5 July 2007. Print.

11. Fox News. 29 April 2010. Television.

12. Chua, Amy. *Battle Hymn of the Tiger Mother*. New York: Penguin Press, 2011. Print.

13. Rogers, Fred. Address at the Public Broadcasting Service (PBS) Development Conference. Tucson, AZ. 1991.

INDEX